OXFORD STUDIES IN

OXFORD STUDIES IN METAPHYSICS

Editorial Advisory Board
David Chalmers (Australasian National University)
Tamar Gendler (Yale University)
Sally Haslanger (MIT)
John Hawthorne (Oxford University)
Hud Hudson (Western Washington University)
Kathrin Koslicki (Tufts University)
E. J. Lowe (University of Durham)
Brian McLaughlin (Rutgers University)
Trenton Merricks (University of Virginia)
Kevin Mulligan (University of Geneva)
Theodore Sider (NYU)
Timothy Williamson (Oxford University)

Managing Editor
Jason Turner (Rutgers University)

OXFORD STUDIES IN METAPHYSICS

Volume 4

Edited by
Dean W. Zimmerman

UNIVERSITY PRESS

OXFORD
UNIVERSITY PRESS

Great Clarendon Street, Oxford OX2 6DP

Oxford University Press is a department of the University of Oxford.
It furthers the University's objective of excellence in research, scholarship,
and education by publishing worldwide in

Oxford New York

Auckland Cape Town Dar es Salaam Hong Kong Karachi
Kuala Lumpur Madrid Melbourne Mexico City Nairobi
New Delhi Shanghai Taipei Toronto

With offices in

Argentina Austria Brazil Chile Czech Republic France Greece
Guatemala Hungary Italy Japan Poland Portugal Singapore
South Korea Switzerland Thailand Turkey Ukraine Vietnam

Oxford is a registered trade mark of Oxford University Press
in the UK and in certain other countries

Published in the United States
by Oxford University Press Inc., New York

© the several contributors 2008

The moral rights of the authors have been asserted
Database right Oxford University Press (maker)

First published 2008

All rights reserved. No part of this publication may be reproduced,
stored in a retrieval system, or transmitted, in any form or by any means,
without the prior permission in writing of Oxford University Press,
or as expressly permitted by law, or under terms agreed with the appropriate
reprographics rights organization. Enquiries concerning reproduction
outside the scope of the above should be sent to the Rights Department,
Oxford University Press, at the address above

You must not circulate this book in any other binding or cover
and you must impose the same condition on any acquirer

British Library Cataloguing in Publication Data

Data available

Library of Congress Cataloging in Publication Data

Data available

Typeset by Laserwords Private Limited, Chennai, India
Printed in Great Britain
on acid-free paper by
CPI Antony Rowe, Chippenham, Wiltshire

ISBN 978-0-19-954298-7
ISBN 978-0-19-954299-4 (Pbk.)

1 3 5 7 9 10 8 6 4 2

PREFACE

Oxford Studies in Metaphysics is dedicated to the timely publication of new work in metaphysics, broadly construed. The subject is taken to include not only perennially central topics (e.g. modality, ontology, and mereology) but also metaphysical questions that emerge within other subfields (e.g. philosophy of mind, philosophy of science, and philosophy of religion). Each volume also contains an essay by the winner of the *Oxford Studies in Metaphysics* Younger Scholar Prize, an annual award described within.

D.W.Z.

New Brunswick, NJ

CONTENTS

Oxford Studies in Metaphysics: Younger Scholar Prize
    Announcement   ix

I. QUINE'S 1946 LECTURE ON NOMINALISM: A SYMPOSIUM

1. Nominalism   3
   Willard Van Orman Quine
2. Quine and Tarski on Nominalism   22
   Paolo Mancosu
3. Cats, Dogs, and so on   56
   John P. Burgess
4. Quine's Lecture on Nominalism from the Perspective of a Nominalist   79
   Charles Chihara
5. A World of Concrete Particulars   99
   Joseph Melia
6. Quine's 1946 Lecture on Nominalism   125
   Peter van Inwagen

II. SOME PRINCIPLES CONCERNING DEPENDENCE AND NECESSITY

7. *Ceteris Absentibus* Physicalism   145
   Stephan Leuenberger
8. Truthmakers and Predication   171
   Daniel Nolan
9. On Locating Composite Objects   193
   Jacek Brzozowski

III. GUNK AND BLOBS

10. Gunk, Topology, and Measure 225
    Frank Arntzenius
11. The Structure of Gunk: Adventures in the Ontology of Space 248
    Jeffrey Sanford Russell
12. Beware of the Blob: Cautions for Would-Be Metaphysicians 275
    Mark Wilson

Index 321

THE *OXFORD STUDIES IN METAPHYSICS* YOUNGER SCHOLAR PRIZE

Sponsored by the A. M. Monius Institute[1] and administered by the editorial board of *Oxford Studies in Metaphysics*, the essay competition is open to scholars who are within ten years of receiving a Ph.D. or students who are currently enrolled in a graduate programme. (Independent scholars should enquire of the editor to determine eligibility.) The award is $2,500. Winning essays will appear in *Oxford Studies in Metaphysics*, so submissions must not be under review elsewhere.

Essays should generally be no longer than 10,000 words; longer essays may be considered, but authors must seek prior approval by providing the editor with an abstract and word count by 1 November 2008. To be eligible for next year's prize, submissions must be electronically submitted by 15 January 2009 (paper submissions are no longer accepted). Refereeing will be blind; authors should omit remarks and references that might disclose their identities. Receipt of submissions will be acknowledged by e-mail. The winner is determined by a committee of members of the editorial board of *Oxford Studies in Metaphysics*, and will be announced in late February 2009. At the author's request, the board will simultaneously consider entries in the prize competition as submissions for *Oxford Studies in Metaphysics*, independently of the prize.

Previous winners of the Younger Scholar Prize are:

Thomas Hofweber, "Inexpressible Properties and Propositions", Vol. 2;

Matthew McGrath, "Four-Dimensionalism and the Puzzles of Coincidence", Vol. 3;

---

[1] The A. M. Monius Institute is a non-profit organization dedicated to the revival of traditional metaphysics. Information about other activities of the A. M. Monius Institute may be found at <http://www.ammonius.org>.

Cody Gilmore, "Time Travel, Coinciding Objects, and Persistence", Vol. 3;

Stephan Leuenberger, "*Ceteris Absentibus* Physicalism", Vol. 4;

Jeffrey Sanford Russell, "The Structure of Gunk: Adventures in the Ontology of Space", Vol. 4.

Brad Skow, "Extrinsic Temporal Metrics", forthcoming in Vol. 5.

Enquiries should be addressed to the Editor: dwzimmer@rci.rutgers.edu

Part I

QUINE'S 1946 LECTURE ON NOMINALISM: A SYMPOSIUM

1. Nominalism

Willard Van Orman Quine

INTRODUCTION: THE ORIGIN OF THE MANUSCRIPT AND OF THE PUBLICATION PROJECT

Quine's lecture "Nominalism", transcribed below, was made available by his son, Dr Douglas Boynton Quine. The manuscript was listed as one of a series of lectures in Dr Quine's website dedicated to his father (<www.wvquine.org>). I happened to peruse the site at some point in 2006 while doing work on Quine's nominalism. The title of the lecture obviously piqued my curiosity and I then got in touch with Dr Quine. Once in possession of a pdf of the original lecture, I quickly convinced myself that the lecture contained the most systematic exposition of Quine's views on nominalism I had ever seen and asked for permission to publish a transcription of the lecture, which Dr Quine generously granted. The lecture greatly improves our understanding of Quine's engagement with nominalism (see my chapter in this volume for details).

But how did the manuscript of the lecture reach us? In answer to this question, Dr Quine wrote the following:

After my father died, I found in his office a small two drawer (14 inch deep) metal filing cabinet for 3 inch by 5 inch note cards. He typically lectured from verbatim lecture notes since the nature of his work made carefully formed phrases an essential element of his art. The drawers were filled with his note cards ranging from brief remarks presented at memorials and retirement celebrations to complete lectures (such as this set ["Nominalism"]) and even an entire course (613 note cards): his Harvard University Summer School course on Hume from 1946. I posted details of

© 2006 by Douglas Boynton Quine; Introduction, Transcription, Notes, and Bibliography by Paolo Mancosu.

each of these sets of cards under the heading 'unpublished manuscripts and verbatim lectures' at the wvquine.org web site that I had first created for him in 1996. Over the years, a number of scholars have expressed interest in various items. When Prof. James Buickerood expressed interest in the Hume lectures, I scanned them for him and he subsequently transcribed and published them as:

W. V. Quine, "Lectures on David Hume's Philosophy" ed. James G. Buickerood in *Eighteenth-Century Thought* 1 (2003): 171–254.

More recently, you expressed interest in the "Nominalism" lecture so I scanned the cards and provided them to you for transcription and publication. I've also tried to help decode the handwriting when my years of experience with his script and familiarity with his "voice" provided clues despite a lack of deep philosophical training." (E-mail communication dated April 7, 2007.)

I would like to thank Dr Quine for scanning the lecture, for helping decode some difficult passages, for granting permission to publish, and for his kindness and generosity throughout the process. Meanwhile, Professor Zimmerman had got wind of the existence of the lecture and suggested publishing it as the opening essay in a symposium dedicated to "Nominalism". I would like to thank him for providing such an ideal venue for publishing Quine's original essay and for his advice throughout the process.

Editorial remarks. The text is written on 87 cards (3 inch by 5 inch) numbered C0 to C85 with a card numbered C82a spliced between C82 and C83. I have not transcribed the passages that have strikethroughs for they do not add any important modifications to the content of the text. Quine also timed the talk and some cards report the time elapsed in lecturing. These I have reported by notation such as ≪60 min.≫. My tentative readings for unclear passages are in bold characters and in between bold double angular brackets. Other abbreviations are also spelled out, upon their first occurrence, within bold single angular brackets. In addition, articles and books mentioned by Quine are also given a bibliographical entry in bold single angular brackets. The entry refers to the bibliography that follows the notes at the end of the transcription. Finally, all notes to the text are mine.

"Nominalism".

Presented at Harvard Philosophical Colloquium, Emerson B, 3:00 p.m., March 11, 1946.

[ii. Particulars.]

What I mean by nominalism — to give it a rough formulation preparatory to further analysis — is the view that there are only particulars. Just this simple doctrine. There are no universals, as opposed to particulars. This, has a good historical claim, I think, to the name of nominalism, but I'm not interested today in pressing that claim. What I am talking about today

---

because of limitations of time. We have become somewhat clearer, in ways which it wouldn't be convenient to set forth here, on the nature of the technical problem of making a go of nominalism. But we can't claim much; the issue of nominalism is still an open problem, though a clearer problem than it used to be to me. I feel sure that nominalism can be executed, but I don't know in which sense. 60 min.

NOMINALISM

Presented at Harvard Philosophical Colloquium, Emerson B, 3:00 p.m., March 11, 1946.

[i. *Introduction*]

This isn't going to be a defense of nominalism. Nor is it going to be a refutation of nominalism. Nor is it going to be a positivistic argument that the whole problem of universals—the issue of nominalism—is meaningless because metaphysical.

On this latter point, at least, I'm going to adopt and defend a positive—if non-positivistic—position: that the problem of universals has, or can be given, an important meaning, and that the nominalistic issue is a real one. If, after I have tried to formulate the issue, I seem to be on the fence with regard to it, it will not be because of indifference. It will be, rather, for the same sort of reason that has prevented doctors from producing a specific for colds: difficulties of the problem. Difficulties, in the case of the nominalistic issue, which become clearly visible only after progress has been made in sharpening the issue and analyzing some of the problems that prove subsidiary to it. My purpose in this talk is to report some progress in this regard. But, as a token of good faith, and in compensation for not coming to a conclusion, I'll put my cards on the table now and avow my prejudices: I should like to be able to accept nominalism.

[ii. *Particulars*]

What I mean by nominalism—to give it a rough formulation preparatory to further analysis—is the view that there are only particulars. Just this simple doctrine. There are no universals, as opposed to particulars. This doctrine has a good historical claim, I think, to the name of nominalism, but I'm not interested today in pressing that claim. What I am talking about today is, in any case, this doctrine. And clearly it depends on the meaning of 'particular'.

The likely ways of construing particulars are of two sorts, corresponding to the opposition between idealism and realism. This term 'realism' is confusing, of course, in that it has two senses both of which are relevant to present discussion: realism as opposed to nominalism and realism as opposed to idealism. I may speak of the two ways of construing particulars simply as the *mental* and the *physical*.

Mental version: particulars are simple experiences: concrete, specific mental events.

Physical version: particulars are concrete spatial objects, or better physical events, i.e., stretches of varying lengths in the histories of physical objects.

So we may have nominalism (rejection of universals) with either an idealism of particulars or a realism of particulars. The general problems raised by nominalism are much the same in either case; but, in order to be as specific as possible, I'll make an arbitrary choice regarding particulars—choosing the physical. The doctrine to be considered, then, is a nominalism of universals combined with a realism (as opposed to idealism) of particulars.

It is the doctrine that the only things there are are spatio-temporally extended physical objects. What these objects are like, in detail, it is the business of physics to say; the philosophical content of the doctrine is merely (a) that it *is* the business of physics to say, and (b) that there is nothing other than these things.

According to current physics, these things are made up of quanta of energy, each of which is an approximation to a point-event. We may for convenience regard every aggregate of such quanta as a physical object—a *particular*, in the present sense—no matter how scattered its parts may be, no matter how intermingled with extraneous quanta. But an aggregate in the sense not of a class but of a heap of stones: a total concrete object of which the constituent quanta and all aggregates of them are *parts*—spatial parts, really spatio-temporal parts.

This gives us a lot of things, but, according to current physics, only finitely many. Eddington has computed the total number of quanta in the entire extent and duration of the universe: if we call this number k, then the total number of things in the universe—the total number of particulars, in the adopted sense—can be shown by a familiar mathematical principle to be 2^k.
≪9 min.≫

[iii. *Nominalism is not extensionalism, nor conceptualism*]

So nominalism is distinct from the doctrine known in modern logic as extensionalism. The main point of the latter doctrine is rejection of properties, or attributes, in favor of classes. But classes are universals equally with attributes, and nominalism in the defined sense rejects both. The fact that classes are universals is something obscured by calling them "mere aggregates", and feeling that this likens them to heaps, which are indeed particular. A *heap* of stones *is* a particular, bigger than but no less particular and concrete than any single stone which occurs in it as a part. But the class of stones in the heap cannot be identified with the heap.

For, if it could, then by the same token the class of molecules of stones in the heap could be identified with the heap; and then there would be no distinguishing between the two classes. This would be unacceptable, since we want to say that the one class has some 150 members while the other has some trillions.

Classes are as universal and as abstract as attributes. Indeed their only difference—and one which does not concern us here, is that classes having exactly the same members are the same class, while attributes which are true of exactly the same things are sometimes distinguished.

Equally, nominalism is not the same as the doctrine that universals are mental entities rather than Platonic ideas subsisting independent of man.

This doctrine—conceptualism—has a certain kinship to nominalism, notably in the fact that both doctrines are incompatible with classical mathematics; for it can be proved from the assumptions of classical mathematics not merely that there are universals, namely classes, but that there are classes doomed never to be apprehended by the mind of man. But the nominalist is not pacified by conceptualism. If the attribute of *roundness* is taken to be a mental pattern, or pattern of behavior, or type of mental event, so that different mental events are instances of the *same* roundness, then it is still universal rather than particular, and its subjectivity does not excuse it.
≪13 min.≫

[iv. *On the struthionism of certain positivists*]

There is a tendency among *logical positivists* to regard the whole issue over universals, and in particular the doctrine of nominalism, as meaningless.

This tendency is not universal among them; Hans Hahn, a mathematician of the Vienna Circle, came out in favor of nominalism in his pamphlet "Ueberfluessige Wesenheiten" <**Hahn 1930**>; though to my regret I can't find satisfaction in the arguments which he advances.

Other logical positivists such as Carnap have occasionally been misconstrued, notably by Prof. Urban in his *Language and Reality* <**Urban 1939**> under the head of 'neo-nominalism', as embracing not merely nominalism but an absurdly extreme form of it: repudiation of everything, concrete and abstract, except words.

Properly understood, however, the attitude of Carnap and his followers is rather that there is no such issue: that the affirmation or denial of nominalism, along with the rest of what the Vienna Circle refers to rather vaguely as metaphysics, is meaningless.

I object to this idea, however, as *struthionism*—by which I mean that it involves the *struthionic* fallacy: that of burying one's head in the sand. The derivation is from στρουθιῶν, *ostrich*.

There is no *a priori* ground for throwing out the statement "There are only particulars" as meaningless; for I have explained in intelligible terms what is to be meant by particulars (there are alternatives, indeed); and the other words of the sentence—'there are' and 'only'—are very decidedly parts of the positivist's own scientific vocabulary, and that of math. itself. Rejection of the compound would appear to be utterly *ad hoc*.

There is indeed room for clarifying the meaning and implications, still, of the nominalist thesis; and this I favor doing.

[v. *Use of universal terms no renunciation of nominalism*]

The most commonplace objections to nominalism clearly reflect the need of clarifying and analyzing the thesis. I suppose the objection most commonly felt is that we *do* have ideas of roundness, of populousness, of independence, etc., and that we entertain these ideas when we understand the words or translate them into another language.

Now in a sense the nominalist would agree that we "have an idea of roundness", "of independence", etc., but he would say that this whole phrase is merely a condensed or metaphysical way of saying that we understand the term 'round' or a synonym, or that we behave in such-and-such distinguishing ways on being presented with any round object, and so on; and he would claim that this description can be formulated finally in thus presupposing no universal objects. To maintain the opposite, and that the so-called "understanding of roundness" involves apprehension of a universal object, is—in the absence of some further argument—only a flat assertion, and a *petitio principii*.

The nominalist may protest equally against Russell's conclusion (Inquiry into Mng. and Truth, pp. 436 f) <**Russell 1940**>; he has just finished arguing that universals like 'yellow' can, at least, be eliminated in favor of similarity of particulars. "I conclude, ∴, though with hesitation, that there are universals, and not merely general words. Similarity, at least, will have to be admitted... It will be observed that the above argument only proves the necessity of the word 'similar', not of the word 'similarity'.... There are oc'ces <**occurrences**> which require for their verbal descrin <**description**> sentences of the form 'a is similar to b'... The word 'yellow' is necessary because there are yellow things; the word 'similar' is necessary because there are pairs of similar things. And the similarity of 2 things is as truly a non-linguistic fact as the yellowness of 1 thing."[1] Here the nominalist might object, the alleged

---

[1] The full, and correct, passage in Russell reads as follows:

I conclude, therefore, though with hesitation, that there are universals, and not merely general words. Similarity, at least, will have to be admitted; and in that case it seems hardly worth while to adopt elaborate devices for the exclusion of other universals.

It should be observed that the above argument only proves the necessity of the word "similar", not of the word "similarity." Some propositions containing the word "similarity" can be replaced by equivalent propositions containing the word "similar," while others cannot. Suppose, for example, I say "similarity exists." If "exists" means what it does when I say "the President of the United States exists,"

irreducibility of the word 'similar' is no ground for claiming a corresponding universal object. The nominalist may grant that *the similarity of 2 things* is a non-linguistic *fact*—by which he may mean merely that the statement to the effect that 2 things are similar does not follow from the rules of language. But this is not to say that there is a universal object "similarity".

[vi. *The plea of syncategorematicity*]

The nominalist's main point, in such a defense, is that we may use words, which are *meaningful* in the sense of figuring in true and false statements, without thereby implying that there are objects—universals, e.g.—which the words are names of. Words can, he urges, be syncategorematic: and this there is hardly an opponent of nominalism who will deny. Words like 'of': or 'which': etc. Even nouns: e.g. 'sake'. Who ever heard of a *sake*, even as an abstract object. Do people really have *sakes*? When I speak of my sake, asking you to do something for it, it is only a manner of speaking. And the same may be said of universals generally, according to the nominalist. Even when I use a universal term as if it named an object—saying e.g. 'I have an *idea of roundness*'—it can still be taken as a mere idiom or metaphysical manner of speaking, no more ontological than the idiom 'for my sake'. But this is surely *too* easy. It is as though one could talk about anything he likes and yet deny that he is talking about it, simply by pleading that the key words of his discourse are to be viewed as syncategorematic.

The nominalist would have altogether too easy a time of it. He could avail himself of any terminology and any conceptual scheme devised by the most ardent realist, and enjoy whatever conveniences

my statement is non-sense. What I can mean may, to begin with, be expressed in the statement: There are occurrences which require for their verbal description sentences of the form "a is similar to b." But this linguistic fact seems to imply a fact about the occurrences described, namely the sort of fact that is asserted when I say "a is similar to b." When I say "similarity exists," it is this fact about the world, not a fact about language, that I mean to assert. The word "yellow" is necessary because there are yellow things; the word "similar" is necessary because there are pairs of similar things. And the similarity of two things is as truly a non-linguistic fact as the yellowness of one thing.   (Russell 1904: 436–7)

it might have, and yet disavow all consequences having to do with presupposition of unwelcome entities. Clearly all content would vanish from questions of what there is and is not. ≪22 min≫

[vii. *To be is to be the value of a variable*]

But the notion of existence is too fundamental to be dismissed thus easily. The idiom 'there is' is so ubiquitous in science and everyday discourse that if we find "What is there?" turning out empty or meaningless we shall do well to suspect our analysis.

It is in fact *not* possible, I maintain, for one to make use of any and every terminology or conceptual scheme that he likes and still remain innocent of ontological commitments. He may declare various of his nouns syncategorematic, and indeed we *can't* convict him of ontological commitments on the score merely of the nouns he uses; but we can catch him on his *pronouns*.

This may seem a queer distinction to make but I think it is fundamental. What I have in mind here when I speak loosely of pronouns corresponds in the notation of modern logic to the so-called bound vbls. <**variables**> or apparent vbls.: the vbls. of quantification. The 'x' which we use when we say 'there is something x such that'. If someone says 'there is something x such that it is a prime no. <**number**> and exceeds 10 million'. No appeal to the syncategorematic status of any of his nouns will absolve him from implying that there are such things as numbers. It is no use to appeal that 'x' itself is syncategorematic: in a sense it *is* syncategorematic, but the point is that the idiom 'there is something x such that' is by its very meaning a flat assertion of existence, insofar as this idiom and the term 'existence' (or 'being') mean anything at all.

I won't dwell further on this now, for it is a view that I have set forth in 'Notes on existence and necessity' (J. of Ph., early '43) <**Quine 1943**> and in other places there cited. My conclusion is that in order to decide what entities are presumed to exist, by a given discourse, we are to examine the *vbls.* used in that discourse, and consider what *values* they are presumed to take on. The vbl., not the constant name, is the decisive thing. In fact, as I have shown in §27 of *Math. Logic* <**Quine 1940**>, there is an artificial but quite straightforward procedure whereby all use of names, or nouns, can be eliminated from use, so that the whole burden of reference to reality, reference to objects, comes to be carried quite adequately by variables of quantification. To be, then, from the point of view of any given written or spoken doctrine, is to be the value of a vbl. The thesis of nominalism becomes this: Discourse adequate to the whole of science can be so framed that nothing but particulars need be admitted as values of the variables. Occam's Razor does the rest.

If Russell wants to show that the assumption of a universal object *similarity* is necessary, he must, according to the formulation now arrived at, show that similarity has to be admitted as a value of a vbl. This he has not shown. ≪28 min.≫

[viii. *Commitments of mathematics*]

Let it not be felt, however, that I have fortified nominalism against Russell and others by redefining it as an unassailable doctrine. The version which I have given to nominalism is, I think, a distillation of the essential content of what has vaguely been intended as nominalism all along. Certainly it does justice to my own nominalistic impulses, and I think more can be claimed for it than that. And it is *not* an unassailable doctrine; on the contrary, it proves to stand in opposition to the whole force of classical mathematics.

For, it is impossible to get classical math. without admitting universals—classes—as values of bound variables.

It is impossible even to express certain principles of elementary arith. without admitting certain universals—viz. whole nos. <**numbers**>—as values of bd. <**bound**> vbls.

El. <**Elementary**> logic is compatible with nominalism: truth fncn. thy <**truth functional theory**> and entire thy of qfn. <**quantification**>. Can also throw in the whole theory of identity.

Portions even of the theory of classes. This seems a contradiction in terms—that part of the theory of classes should be compatible with nominalism—but it is a fact. The point is that portions of the so-called theory of classes can be constructed on the basis of logic of truth functions and qfn. and identity, through notational conventions, so that we seem to be talking about classes, but it is only a manner of speaking. This is what I call the *virtual* theory of classes, as opposed to the real. It can be made to include the Boolean algebra of classes and part of the theory of unit classes. But the rest of class theory can't be reconstructed on such a virtual basis;

it needs assumptions of universals as genuine entities—values of bd. vbls.

The situation is similar with relations. Much of the theory of rel'ns <**relations**> can be developed as a virtual theory, in which we seem to talk of rel'ns, but can explain our notation in terms ≪**finally**≫ of just the logic of truth-functions, quantification and identity. This portion of relation theory includes the bulk of the rel'n theory of P.M. <**Principia Mathematica**>, but not all; an example of what cannot be got on this basis is the theory of the ancestral, which some of you know about. This and other parts of rel'n theory must await a basis where universals are admitted as genuine values of b'd vbls. Most of this on virtual theory is set forth in my Pg. <**Portuguese**> book <**Quine 1944**>, pp. 218–223. ≪33 min.≫

[ix. *Consequences for nominalism*]

A formulation of nominalism that I reached earlier was this: Discourse adequate to the whole of science can be so framed that nothing but particulars need be admitted as value of the vbls.

Now surely classical math. is part of science; and I have said that universals have to be admitted as values of its vbls.; so it follows that the thesis of nominalism is false. What has the nominalist to say to this?

He need not give up yet; not if he loves his nominalism more than his math. He can make his adjustment by repudiating as philosophically unsound those parts of science which resist his tenets; and his position remains strong so long as he can persuade us that these rejected parts of science are neither intrinsically desirable as ends nor necessary as means to other parts which *are* intrinsically desirable.

One reasonable touchstone of intrinsic desirability of a part of science, as an end rather than merely as a means to other parts, is its efficacy in predicting experience. By this standard, math. has no intrinsic desirability; so that the defense of nominalism, so far as its incompatibility with math. is concerned, must consist in showing that the portions of math. which go by the board are *dispensable* as a *means* to those parts of science which *are* effective in prediction. It must consist in showing how the service of classical math. as an auxiliary to the natural sciences could be performed, adequately though more clumsily, by those fragments of math. or logic which are still constructible from a nominalistic point of view. The added clumsiness needn't matter; for, once the possibility is established, the nominalist can wink at the use of short-cuts which draw on the less clumsy resources of classical math. He can wink at this because the short-cuts will have been justified as mere abbreviations of procedures which could be expected within what he calls a philosophically sound methodology. This is how he might try to square himself with mathematics; but I don't know that he can do it.

[x. *Motives for nominalism*]

Now, why should the nominalist want to go through all this trouble? Why does he prefer particulars to universals in the first place?

I think the motives must be distinguished according as our nominalist adopts a mental or physical version of particulars; though there is a sameness of general spirit regardless. In the mental case (!), his motive may be an extreme sensationalism: what we are presented with are sensory events, and it is unphilosophical to assume entities beyond them, *in particular universals*.

In the physical case, his mentality is likely to be that of Lord Kelvin, who insisted that he did not understand a process until it was reduced to terms of impact of bodies like billiard balls. The nominalist would out-Kelvin Kelvin in avoiding also the universals which Kelvin no doubt accepted without giving them a thought; for the nominalist feels that these are even more unaccountable than the principles of entelechy or gravitation which Kelvin himself found unsatisfactory.

Modern physics may seem to have cut the ground from under this physical type of nominalist, in abandoning even Kelvin's billiard balls. Tangibility is abandoned as a standard of reality even of particulars. Physical ontology itself takes on a nebulousness which might well discourage the nominalist in his efforts to tidy up reality.

But the nominalist spirit is capable of surviving this. He can defer to the physicist regarding the question what is real by physical standards, and insist nevertheless that there is to be nothing else. The physicist in his verbal expositions of his theory borrows from the general as well as from his own field, and in so doing he may very well seem even to countenance universals; but the nominalist reserves the right to refurbish this conceptual scheme of commonsense, which is not the physicist's responsibility—and to produce a substitute conceptual scheme which, while still theoretically adequate to the physicist's purposes, will not countenance any entities beyond those whose existence it is within the *physicist*'s professional competence to assert.

Besides this initial impetus to nominalism, there are *a posteriori* considerations which confirm the nominalist in his prejudices. For one thing there are the logical paradoxes, the simplest of which is Russell's of the class of all classes not members of themselves. These paradoxes are attributable to admitting universals. They do not arise in that part of logic that can be developed in a *virtual* theory of classes and relations, by not taking classes and relations as values of bound variables. And though the paradoxes *can* be avoided by *ad hoc* restrictions, wholly lacking in intuitive justification, they can be avoided *only* thus; and the nominalist says "I told you so".

Another *a posteriori* impetus to the nominalist comes from Gödel's theorem of the incompletability of elementary arithmetic. Since arithmetic is *a priori*, rather than empirical, truth in arithmetic would seem, by normal epistemological standards, to consist in demonstrability; and accordingly the proof by Gödel that there is no possible consistent system of axioms for elementary arithmetic which will not leave some truths of elementary arithmetic indemonstrable, is a blow. But Gödel's theorem presumably does not hold for that portion of elementary arithmetic, or reasonable facsimile thereof, which can be achieved within the bounds of nominalism. ≪43 min.≫

[xi. *Fusions as surrogates for universals*]

In executing nominalism (executing in the sense of the executive, not the executioner), the constantly recurring problem is of course that of finding particulars such that reference to them can be made to serve various of the purposes for which we ordinarily resort to reference to universals. In the case of many universals, such proxy particulars come readily to hand; namely, those particulars which, in the terminology of Dr. Goodman's thesis <**Goodman 1941**>, are called the *fusions* of the universals in question. The fusion of a class of particulars is the smallest particular which has all the original particulars as parts. If our class has as members the slices of a sliced loaf of bread, the fusion of the class is the sliced loaf itself—which, unlike the class, is a particular. The fusion of the class of all gold objects is the scattered particular which is the spatiotemporal composite of all atoms of gold; it is still a particular, for all its scatteredness; scatteredness is merely a certain complexity of shape. The fusion of the class of stones in a heap, to recur to my earlier example, is the heap itself; and the fusion of the molecules of the heap is again the heap.

Now it happens that the purposes of many universals, notably *gold* and *red*, can be served quite adequately by their fusions. Where the realist (or let us say Platonist, meaning, for the present, realist as opposed to nominalist) would say: 'the *attribute gold* is a metal, and is an *attribute* of the coating of my watch', the nominalist can say: 'the *particular gold* (meaning the described fusion) is a metal and *contains* the coating of my watch as a part.' Where the Platonist would say 'The attribute *red* is a color and is an attribute of Emerson Hall', the nominalist can say 'The particular *red* (meaning the fusion) is a color and contains the coating of Emerson Hall as a part.'

What is more to the point technically, *gold* and *red* in these particular senses—the fusions—can, unlike classes, be admitted as values of bound variables without exceeding nominalism.

But this device enables us to supplant only certain favored universals by particulars. It will not work for the class of stones in the heap, for the reasons I indicated earlier when I argued that classes are universals. And it will not work for such universals as *man* or *round*. These limitations have been discussed by Dr. Goodman, though not specifically in connection with nominalism, in his thesis. But even where a fusion won't serve outright to supplant a universal, it is often helpful along with other devices in special contexts.

[xii. *Expressions as surrogates for universals*]

Another nominalistic surrogate for universals, and a more traditional one, is the sheer word or phrase—the *flatus vocis*. Instead of speaking platonically of *universals* which are *attributes* of this and that particular, the nominalist might speak, it would seem, of the corresponding *expressions,* and speak of them as *denoting* this and that particular; and in general much the same net purposes would be served. This device is, in fact, the etymology of the name 'nominalism'.

We could never hope by this method to get an equivalent of the rich world of universals entertained by classical mathematics; for it can be proved by the principles of classical mathematics that the realm of linguistic expressions even though infinite (supposing expressions can be longer and longer without limit), is yet of a lower order of infinity than the total realm of universals; the realm of classes; even the realm of real numbers. We might, however, hope to get an equivalent of a big enough slice of the world of universals to get by with.

But the predicament to be anticipated here is that names, or words generally, are themselves universals: for they are not particular inscriptions, mounds of ink or neon tubes, but general *forms* of inscriptions. So that words as a surrogate for universals are a reversion to universals. This argument against nominalism was advocated by Uuno Saarnio, the Finn, in his *Untersuchungen zur symbolische Logik* <**Saarnio 1935**>. Actually, however, this is one obstacle that nominalism can surmount. For it turns out on investigation that many at least of the important constructions involving reference to expressions, i.e. classes of inscriptions, can be carried out equally well by talking about inscriptions themselves, and bringing them into geometrical similarity with one another. The similarity itself does not (as Russell might suggest) survive as a universal, because all we use is a syncategorematic predicate 'is similar to', without admitting similarity as a value of bound variables; hence without assuming any such *entity* as similarity. ≪49 min.≫

[xiii. *Number in nominalism*]

Since classical elementary arithmetic is incompatible with nominalism, an important proving ground for nominalistic constructions is in the applications of number to commonplace situations. Dr. Goodman and I worked together over the example 'Dogs are more numerous than cats' at some length. But I can explain the outcome of that example better if I start with a simpler one: 'there are at least 9 planets.' This can be translated into nominalistic terms as follows: 'there are objects r, s, t, u, v, w, x, y, and z such that r is not s, nor t, nor u etc., and s is not t, nor u, nor v etc., and so on through the list, and r is a planet, and s is a planet, and so on.' The idiom 'is a planet' here does not imply a universal object, because it can be taken as a syncategorematic constant; and similarly for any other predicate of particulars, so long as it occurs only in predicative position. Universals are invoked only when they come in as values of variables and this does not happen here.

In the same way we can define 'there are at least 10 planets' or any other fixed number. And then we can define 'there are exactly 9 planets' to mean 'there are at least 9 planets and there are not at least 10 planets'.

This gives us a paradigm for the nominalist translation, in general, of 'there are at least n so-and-sos' and 'there are exactly n so-and-sos', where in place of 'n' we have any specified numeral, and in place of 'so-and-so' any specified general term denoting particulars.

In short, we are able nominalistically to define *any* specific Arabic numeral *in the context* of application to any specific predicate which applies to particulars; we are able to do thus without implying that there are numbers or other universals.

The case 'there are more dogs than cats' can now be handled, curiously enough, *if* we know Eddington's number k (the number of quanta in all space-time) and hence the number of particulars in the universe (which will be 2^k).

For, we can then explain 'there are more dogs than cats' as meaning 'there are at least 1 dog and not at least 1 cat or at least 2 dogs and not at least 2 cats or at least 3 dogs and not at least 3 cats or [and so on up to 2^k]'.

Of course a lower limit than 2^k could be used, so long as we knew it exceeded the number of cats; but the point of 2^k is that it would work for all examples of 'there are more so-and-so's than such and suches'.

Other related idioms, e.g. 'there are more than twice as many dogs as cats', 'one tenth the Frenchmen live in Paris', etc. can be handled in ways closely related to this example.

But now we encounter an odd problem, which may metaphorically be called that of the ink shortages.

I haven't written out the definition of 'there are more dogs than cats', I've only sketched it. It starts with the clause 'there is at least one dog and not at least one cat';[2] next there is 'or' and the clause 'there are at least 2 dogs and not at least 2 cats'; and so on for 2^k clauses. But 2^k is the number of particulars in all space-time, so there can't be 2^k clauses in the ≪**sense**≫ of inscriptions; there isn't room in the world throughout its past and future history. So *is* there a definition of 'there are more dogs than cats' after all?

This difficulty can be handled by means of a series of conventions of definitional abbreviations, whereby the whole expression can be compressed to manageable proportions. But it is necessary to recognize that definition takes on a new status in this connection: definitional abbreviation ceases to be a mere convenience, and becomes a theoretical necessity; and moreover the expansions are non-existent and impossible, because of the limits of the universe. We cannot say the expanded expression exists as a *form* without inscribed instances, because we have forsworn universals. If under these circumstances the admission of so-called definitional abbreviations seems a concession to nominalism, then the need of this concession is one of nominalism's weaknesses.

Going back to the example 'there are more dogs than cats' another point that has occurred to all of you is that it is ridiculous to make the statement depend on the number of quanta of energy in space-time. This I grant; and if another translation cannot be found which is free of this dependence, I weep for nominalism.

Certainly all such troubles can be avoided by admitting 'and so on' as an irreducible part of the language, and maybe this is the best course; though the same puristic or Spartan attitude which inspires nominalism might lead one to feel that 'and so on' is indefensible and meaningless in cases where it is impossible in principle to expand it.

Moving to more abstract matters, it is interesting to see how arithmetic itself fares, as distinct from its applications. We have seen how to define each of the specific numerals, in context. It proves possible also to define, for the same contexts, the notations of arithmetical equality, sum, product and power—but only as applied to specific numbers. It turns out that the identities of arithmetic, e.g. '$7^2 + 1 = 5^2 \times 2$', all turn out on expansion of definitions to boil down to self-identities of the form '$x = x$'; so that the arithmetic

---

[2] Reading 'dog' in original for 'cat'.

of constants becomes *analytic* in a very extreme sense. How about algebra or arithmetic using numerical *variables*? Something closely resembling it can be got in the *syntax of* the arithmetic of constants; the extent of its formal divergence from classical patterns has yet to be explored, but it is bound to diverge appreciably.

I have had to omit mention of some of the less easily conveyed results that have come of my discussions with Dr. Goodman on these problems, because of limitations of time. We have become somewhat clearer, in ways which it wouldn't be convenient to set forth here, on the nature of the technical problem of making a go for nominalism. But we can't claim much; the issue of nominalism is still an open problem, though a clearer problem than it used to be to me.

I feel sure that nominalism can be executed, but I don't know in which sense. ≪60 min.≫

REFERENCES

Goodman, N. (1941). *A Study of Qualities*. Dissertation, Harvard University. Reprinted in 1990 by Garland (New York), as part of its Harvard dissertations in Philosophy Series.

Hahn, H. (1930). 'Überflüssige Wesenheiten (Occams Rasiermesser)'. *Veröffentlichungen des Vereines Ernst Mach*. Vienna: Verlag Artur Wolf. Reprinted in H. Hahn, *Empirismus, Logik, Mathematik* (Frankfurt: Suhrkamp, 1988), 21–37.

Quine, W. (1940). *Mathematical Logic*. New York: Norton.

―― (1943). 'Notes on Existence and Necessity'. *Journal of Philosophy* 40/5: 113–27.

―― (1944). *O sentido da nova logica*. Sao Paulo: Martins.

Russell, B. (1940). *An Inquiry into Meaning and Truth*. London: Allen & Unwin.

Saarnio, U. (1935). *Untersuchungen zur symbolischen Logik. I. Kritik des Nominalismus und Grundlegung der logistischen Zeichentheorie (Symbologie)*, Acta Philosophica Fennica, Helsinki, Fasc. I, 154 pp.

Urban, W. M. (1939). *Language & Reality: The Philosophy of Language & the Principles of Symbolism*. London: Allen & Unwin.

2. Quine and Tarski on Nominalism

Paolo Mancosu

In this chapter I would like to trace the trajectory of two important nominalists in twentieth-century analytic philosophy, Quine and Tarski. Each one of them had his own trajectory with regard to nominalism but their paths intersected at two important points: the academic year 1940–1 when both were at Harvard (together with Carnap) and in 1953 at the conference in Amersfoort organized by Beth on "Platonism and Nominalism in Contemporary Logic". These two points of intersection will be important in the exposition but I will also be interested in their individual development with respect to the topic at hand.

The association of Quine and Tarski is not arbitrary. Quine and Tarski were kindred philosophical spirits. Writing to Marja Tarski after Tarski's death, Quine wrote:

Besides being so much my mentor in logic, Alfred was a kindred spirit philosophically. Invariably when issues arose in the philosophy of logic, whether privately or in a group or at a logic convention, we found ourselves in full agreement. One notable case was our joint effort against Carnap on analytic and synthetic judgments, when we were all three together at Harvard in 1941.   (Quine to Marja Tarski, January 7, 1984; Quine archive, MS Storage 299, Box 8; By permission of the Houghton Library, Harvard University [henceforth abbreviated as BPH-LHU])

He could just as well have mentioned their engagement with nominalism as another example of intellectual kinship.

However, there are also important disanalogies. While in Quine's case we have extensive evidence of his nominalist sympathies in the published output, Tarski never published on nominalism and everything about his nominalist commitment needs to be gathered from archival sources.

The archival situation differs drastically for Quine and Tarski. Tarski reached the United States in 1939. The invasion of Poland by the Nazis led to the eventual loss of his Warsaw belongings and thus the notes taken by Carnap on the 1940–1 meetings represent the first useful source for Tarski's nominalism.[1] The Tarski archive at the Bancroft Library in Berkeley contains very little from the pre-war period. Since Tarski did not leave a single paper or lecture discussing his nominalist tendencies the reconstruction of his thought on this matter needs to be carried out with the help of sources other than those kept at the Bancroft Library. By contrast, Quine's archive at the Houghton Library in Harvard contains a rich record of Quine's intellectual engagement with nominalism dating back at least to 1935. The archive is still uncatalogued and thus it is not accessible in its entirety. However, what I was able to consult is enough, I believe, to give a rich picture of Quine's reflections on nominalism from 1935 to its eventual abandonment after the Goodman–Quine 1947 paper. It also contains his lecture at the Amersfoort conference organized by Beth in 1953 (Quine 1953a).

Section 1 describes Quine's engagement with nominalism up to 1940. Then in section 2 I will summarize the impact of the 1940–1 discussions on nominalism between Carnap, Quine, and Tarski and mention their influence on Goodman. Section 3 will be on Quine's allegiance to nominalism and his subsequent reluctant acceptance of Platonism. The last section will then focus on the Amersfoort meeting and will exploit Beth's reports on the meeting to draw some welcome information about Tarski's defense of nominalism in Amersfoort. This story is too long to be recounted in one chapter and thus my strategy will be to emphasize points that go beyond what is already known in the literature.

1. QUINE ON NOMINALISM: 1932–1940

In his autobiography, Quine claims: "Already in 1932 and 1933 in Vienna and Prague ... I felt a nominalist's discontent with classes" (1988a: 14). If this is correct, Quine's discontent antedates his meeting with Lesniewski. His early correspondence with Lesniewski (1934) does not contain any discussion of nominalism and Quine's first recorded reflections on nominalism do not seem to be directly influenced by Lesniewski. Moreover, Quine in his autobiography points out that in Warsaw, in 1933, he was trying to convince

[1] The notes will be published in their entirety in G. Frost-Arnold, *Carnap, Tarski, and Quine in Conversation: Logic, Science, and Mathematics*, Open Court Press, La Salle.

Lesniewski that quantifying over semantical categories carried ontological commitment (1988a: 13; see also 26) This raises the question of the sources of Quine's nominalist discontent. One might think that perhaps Whitehead's mereological investigations and Leonard's thesis on the calculus of individuals might have provided the grounds of the discontent. But, as Marcus Rossberg has pointed out to me, Leonard's work was not developed with nominalist goals in mind and I think the same can be said of Whitehead's mereology. In any case, the texts I was able to consult do not seem to reflect the influence of Lesniewski, Leonard, or Whitehead. My sense is that Quine takes his start more mundanely from the classical debates on the foundations of mathematics (Russell's no class theory, Poincaré and Weyl on predicativity, etc.)

The first written source I was able to locate of Quine's reflection on nominalism is a three-page entry in a notebook of c.300 pages entitled: *Logic Notes. Mostly 1934–1938*. (This notebook, Quine 1934, is mentioned in Quine's autobiography (1988a: 44).) On p.134 we find an entry entitled "Philosophical Background of the conceptual calculus" dated 1935. The problem discussed is denotation of the expressions of the calculus of concepts, that is sentences and nouns. First, Quine presents an interpretation of such denotation and then contrasts it with a nominalist interpretation. Whereas "nouns are frequently regarded as denoting some manner of subsistent entities—classes and relations; ... sentences are not ordinarily regarded as denoting at all". Quine goes on to suggest that for unification's sake, it is convenient to consider sentences as denoting truth values, i.e. truth and falsity. However, one should not believe that classes, relations, and truth values are real:

> But all these elements are obviously hypostatized and gratuitous entities—the relations, classes and truth-values alike. The sound way of approaching the calculus is singly to view it as a calculus whose expressions figure as nouns and sentences; not to look for elements. All the traditional abstract-algebraic reference to elements, e.g. discussions of the multiplicity of elements is reducible to such discussion of the behavior of expressions themselves. (1934: 135, BPHLHU)

Quine continues discussing another way in which nouns can denote. This time the discussion is about general nouns, such as 'cat'. According to Quine, 'cat' denotes not the class of all cats, but each cat, just as 'Socrates' denotes Socrates and not the unit class containing Socrates. Similarly, relational nouns denote sequences of individuals.

In the present sense of denotation, the expressions of the conceptual calculus denote nothing but individuals and sequences of such; no entities of the sort which they might be said to denote in the previous sense of denotation. This is what is described in ordinary terms as the confinement of the elements of the calculus and concepts of first type. Now the erection of concepts of higher type upon this basis amounts to showing that objects higher in type than individuals never need to be assumed to exist at all; it is therefore nothing more nor less than a logical validation of nominalism, a solution of the problem of universals. The ontology on which the conceptual calculus may be regarded as ultimately based comprises concrete individuals; better, simply concrete objects, which is all I envisage for an individual. Actual entities, if one likes. These may be parts spatially or temporally one of another, and various of them may be discontinuous in space or in time; neat balls of substance are not essential, heaps are eligible as well. But they are concrete existents.   (1934: 135–6, BPHLHU)

Having shown how to give a nominalist interpretation of the calculus of concepts (predicates refer to single objects; relatives to "objects several at a time in serial fashion" and sentences refer to nothing), Quine points out that for simplicity one might introduce the fictional notion of sequence of concrete objects and regard relations as referring to such sequences and predicates as referring to sequences of length one (i.e. the objects themselves). Finally, true sentences can be seen as referring to a sequence of length zero.

The above interpretation of the calculus of concepts contains already many elements of the later Quinian views on nominalism. The universals are identified with objects of higher type in the classical account and the nominalist solution to the problem of universals consists in showing that nothing need be assumed in addition to concrete objects and their 'sums'. The mereological inspiration of the passage is evident but it is not clear whether any or which of the mereologists mentioned earlier—Lesniewski, Whitehead, and Leonard—might have played a role here.

The mentioned passage also spells out how denotation is to be interpreted when one does not hypostatize that common nouns denote classes (or relations). This is a theme that recurs often in the successive lectures on nominalism. Consider for instance the first lecture Quine gave on nominalism and to which we now turn. The lecture is entitled "Nominalism" and was delivered at the Philosophy Club in Harvard on October 25, 1937 (Quine 1937a).

The lecture, like later ones on nominalism given by Quine, begins with the opposition between realists, who affirm the reality of universals, and nominalists, who deny their reality. Here universals are "thought of as comprising properties, attributes, qualities, classes, relations" (1937a: 1). Through a series of quick reductions, Quine claims qualities are not to be distinguished from properties and the same for attributes. Furthermore, there is no need to distinguish between properties and classes: "for any property can be construed as the class of all objects having that property and conversely any class can be construed as the property of belonging to that class". Finally, since relations can be reduced to classes (using a trick due to Wiener) the problem of nominalism can be addressed by simply discussing classes.

So we can think of universals from now on simply as classes. Now the claim of nominalism is that there is no such thing. No abstract objects corresponding to abstract words. (1937a: 3, BPHLHU)

It would be a mistake, however, to think that Quine is simplifying the ground for a defense of nominalism. On the contrary, he claims that he will be concerned to object to nominalism.

Quine wants to convey "the *feeling* of the nominalist" by recounting "a fictitious history of the class-concept". One begins with concrete objects and nouns to denote such:

Suppose we have settled what things are to be regarded as concrete objects. *These are all there are.* Men use words and phrases to *denote* concrete objects. A noun (substantive or adjective, word or phrase) may denote many concrete objects: M-a-n denotes Jones, also Smith, etc.; each man. (1937a: 3, BPHLHU)

Proper nouns denote only one object and this is a very convenient feature, for "manipulating them is almost like manipulating their denotations" (1937a: 4). It is this feature of proper nouns that leads us unconsciously, the story continues, "to force all nouns into the pattern of proper nouns". This is done by postulating for each common noun a single entity, i.e. by inventing the class of cats or the property feline to serve as denotation for c-a-t. Men then come to believe in the class (or the property) just as much as in the concrete cats and thus

these creations have proved to be Frankenstein monsters—have taken subsequent developments into their own hands. (1937a: 6, BPHLHU)

In fact, having postulated the class of cats and having come to believe in them, one can now let a new noun, such as

s-p-e-c-i-e-s denote this, that, and the other *class*. Then just as propriefication of c-a-t creates a class of objects as a new alleged object, so propriefication of c-l-u-b or s-p-e-c-i-e-s will create a class of classes of objects as a new object. (1937a: 6, BPHLHU)

And Quine here points out that this passage is decisive. For, with first level nouns such as c-a-t we can treat the notion of class as a mere manner of speaking; but "once classes of classes have come in, we can't eliminate reference to classes by any obvious rephrasing of our statements" (1937a: 8). Whereas first level nouns can be read as always involving distributive predication ("Men are mortal" can be paraphrased as "Every man is mortal") with second level nouns we have collective predication ("Men are a species" cannot be rephrased with distributive quantification over the individual man) and thus "involve an apparently irreducible reference to the class of all men":

And such second or higher level nouns occur constantly in discourse; in particular all numerical words are of at least 2nd level; and the noun n-u-m-b-e-r itself is at least 3rd level. (1937a: 8, BPHLHU)

It thus appears that the nominalist is in trouble for he cannot reject these new objects without giving up most ordinary discourse.

In an attempt to pursue the nominalist line, Quine argues that perhaps the nominalist can find a way to identify such objects with concrete objects. If this could be done the relationship of belonging would turn out to be a relationship between a concrete object and another concrete object. And classes of concrete objects could now be identified with another concrete object and thus classes of classes could also be identified with concrete objects and so on. The natural strategy to pursue is to use the noun itself as the assigned concrete object for the class. Then *"belonging to* would coincide with *denoted by"*. Since there are several nouns that denote the same class of objects, Quine goes on to suggest that to make the class unique we pick a specific noun (the shortest noun of the kind and among the shortest the first in the lexicographic ordering). Thus, we now have the doctrine that universals are 'mere names'. However, there are two difficulties raised against the suggestion. The first is related to Grelling's paradox. A noun is said to be *heterological* if it doesn't denote itself. Is 'heterological' heterological or not? If it is, it is not and if it is not, it is. What the objection shows is that there is no systematic way of assigning to each class of concrete objects a concrete object (using its name). In fact, Quine goes on to generalize the point by claiming that there is no way to associate to each class of concrete objects a concrete object (not necessarily a name). This is done by appealing to Cantor's theorem according to which the cardinality of the class consisting of the classes of concrete objects is strictly greater than the cardinality of all concrete objects. Quine points out that if one is willing to weaken the logic, say to intuitionistic logic, than there are ways to effect such a nominalization. It is not clear from the context whether Quine is referring here to the intuitionism of Brouwer or the intuitionism (more precisely, predicativism) of Poincaré and Weyl. In any case, the conclusion he draws would apply to both:

Nominalism, then, in any sense such as has here been considered, is incompatible with ordinary logic and mathematics; possible only if we are prepared for the intuitionist sacrifices. (1937a: 13, BPHLHU)

In the last two pages of the lecture, Quine concludes by remarking that Carnap, although often considered a nominalist, simply nominalizes the problem of universals and thus rejects the meaningfulness of the general question what universals are. Thus, Quine concludes, Carnap has very little to say about the problem of reduction of all statements to statements about concrete things. In arguing against the Carnapian take on universals, Quine remarks on what he takes to be the purposes of nominalism:

1) To avoid metaphysical questions as to the connection between the realm of universals and the realm of particulars; how universals enter into particulars, or particulars into universals.

2) To provide for reduction to statements ultimately about tangible things, matters of fact. This by way of keeping our feet on the ground—avoiding empty theorizing. (1937a: 14, BPHLHU)

Thus, whereas Carnap has achieved something with respect to goal (1) he has not achieved anything concerning goal (2). But Quine concludes that "a nominalism which will gain this end [goal (2)] must pay for it with a good slice of classical logic and mathematics" (p.14, BPHLHU)

It is important to point out that there is a certain ambiguity as to what the thesis of nominalism is supposed to be. Sometimes the abstract/concrete distinction seems fundamental; at times the universal/particular. These are obviously not the same (see Cohnitz and Rossberg 2006).

Thus, as of October 25, 1937, Quine seems unwilling to espouse a nominalistic philosophy of logic and mathematics. The argument does not rely on natural science but rather on the sacrifices to classical logic and mathematics that the nominalist program would require.

On May 5, 1938 we find Quine rethinking the whole issue by reflecting on the fact that Cantor's theorem fails in his *New Foundations for Mathematical Logic*. And since it was appeal to Cantor's theorem that seemed to block the possibility of a nominalist reconstruction of classical logic and mathematics, this leads Quine to reconsider the issue of nominalism:

> In view of the ambiguous position assumed by Cantor's theorem in the light of my liberalization of the theory of types (see "On Cantor's Theorem", Journal of Symbolic Logic, 1937) we are perhaps justified in reopening the question of the nominalistic identifiability of classes with terms (expressions). From the classical point of view, this course is blocked by the fact expressions can be correlated with the natural numbers (lexicographically) whereas classes cannot. But perhaps the alleged class which would be cited as violating any given correlation of terms and classes is actually a spurious class; perhaps the term purporting to express it is unstratified (see "On the theory of types", Journal of Symbolic Logic, 1938)   (1934: 209, BPHLHU)

The remaining account of what terms denote is given along the lines of the 1937 lecture. Proper nouns denote single objects; common nouns denote many objects. Classes are then identified with the earliest term in the lexicographic ordering denoting the objects in the class. He concludes:

> Just as, under my previous procedure, all objects were construed as classes, so now all objects are to be constructed as terms; and terms of the class

kind, i.e. terms which are lexicographically earlier than all coextensive terms. (1934: 211, BPHLHU)

We see then in these notes from 1938 a revamped interest in the possibilities of nominalism.

We now need to mention two articles and an unpublished lecture from 1939. The unpublished lecture is the original lecture Quine wrote for the Congress of the Unity of Science in Harvard: "A Logistical Approach to the Ontological Problem". This original version (Quine 1939a) is much longer than the short article which had been pre-circulated in 1939 (Quine 1939b/1966) and which was eventually published in *The Ways of Paradox*. The first part of the lecture found its way as "Designation and Existence" (Quine 1939c). Still, some interesting passages occurring in the unpublished long version did not find their way into the two published articles and are of interest. In 'Designation and Existence', Quine arrives at his famous slogan "to be is to be the value of a variable". On the basis of the analysis carried out in the article the following five claims are taken by Quine to be identical except for wording:

(a) "there is such a thing as appendicitis"
(b) "the word 'appendicitis' designates"
(c) "the word 'appendicitis' is a name"
(d) "the word 'appendicitis' is a substituend for a variable"
(e) "the disease appendicitis is a value of a variable"

For the nominalist, Quine says, 'appendicitis' "is meaningful and useful in context; yet the nominalist can maintain that the word is not a *name* of any *entity* in its own right." The difference between a nominalist and a realist language consists in whether abstract words such as "appendicitis" can be substituted for the variables:

> Words of the abstract or general sort, say "appendicitis" or "horse" can turn up in nominalistic as well as realistic languages; but the difference is that in realistic languages such words are substituends for variables... whereas in nominalistic languages this is not the case   (1939a: 20; 1939c: 708, BPHLHU)

Nominalism is then characterized as follows:

> As a thesis in philosophy of science, nominalism can be formulated thus: it is possible to set up a nominalistic language in which all of natural science can be expressed. The nominalist, so interpreted, claims that a language adequate to all scientific purposes can be framed in such a way that its

variables admit only concrete entities, individuals, as values—hence only proper names of concrete objects as substituends. Abstract terms will retain the status of syncategorematic expressions, designating nothing, so long as no corresponding variables are used. (1939a: 21; 1939c: 708, BPHLHU)

Now various types of contextual definitions will allow the introduction of fictitious entities; the nominalist might even speak as if there were such entities but in doing so he will not renounce his nominalism for quantification over such entities can be shown to be dispensable. However, the contextual definitions must be shown to be eliminable.[2]

An important clarification, which is somehow obfuscated in the short published version, concerns the boundaries between the concrete and the abstract. This is where the unpublished version of the lecture gives something additional to the published version of 1939:

The essential point in the controversy between nominalism and realism can be made independent of any one view as to the boundary between the concrete and the abstract. All ways of specifying the realm of concrete or individual objects will, I suggest, share this common feature: the totality of individuals will be a I[Ein]-Ding rather than a II[Zwei]-Ding, in von Neumann's terminology; it will be *immanent* rather than *transcendent* in the terminology of my abstract. That is to say, the totality of individuals will be small enough to have a cardinal number; perhaps an infinite cardinal number, but still a cardinal number. Nominalism then becomes the doctrine that all science can be expressed in a language the total range of whose variables is immanent rather than transcendent. The nominalist has not yet provided such a language and shown it to be adequate to science, but he thinks he can. (1939a: 24–5, BPHLHU)

The set-up described in the above passage will recur in Quine's and Tarski's presentation at the Amersfoort conference. In addition to declaring that alternative positions as to the boundary between the concrete and the abstract are possible, Quine's point of view is extremely liberal concerning how many concrete objects might be available to the nominalist. He seems worried to exclude the possibility of entertaining proper classes of concrete objects. This

---

[2] The theory of virtual classes offered first in Quine 1944 was also a tool that the nominalist could exploit. On the philosophical import of such a theory see Martin 1964.

is in tension with one of the theses that Quine will defend at least until 1947, i.e. that the concrete objects are finite. This is also the first time that the issue of the adequacy of nominalism to natural science is raised. It might not sound like Quine is committing himself to the nominalist position but I think this lecture marks the debut of Quine's hopeful engagement with nominalism. The day before delivering his lecture he commented on a paper by Tarski and concluded his remarks by saying:

> [Tomorrow: my paper] Strong argument for nominalism. Probably can't get classical mathematics. But enough mathematics for physical science? If this could be established, good reason then to consider the problem solved. (Sept. 8, 1939, Occasional lectures, 1939, MS Storage 299, vol. 11; Quine Archive, Houghton Library, BPHLHU)

At this point science becomes the benchmark for the possible success of nominalism. Classical mathematics is hardly recoverable nominalistically but if we recover enough mathematics to do science then the nominalist reconstruction of science can be said to be successful. The short version of the paper (Quine 1939b/1966) gives a similar but completely uncommitted analysis. After raising the issue in the form of "How economical an ontology can we achieve and still have a language adequate to all purposes of science?" Quine concludes the published essay as follows:

> If, as is likely, it turns out that fragments of classical mathematics must be sacrificed under all such [nominalistic] constructions, still one resort remains to the nominalist: he might undertake to show that those recalcitrant fragments are inessential to science. (1939b/1966: 69)

With this lecture the topic of nominalism moves from the domain of the semantics for abstract terms to concerns more directly related to the problem of whether a nominalist language for science can be successfully constructed. This topic is central in the discussions on nominalism that Quine, Carnap, and Tarski carried out while together at Harvard in 1940–1.

2. HARVARD 1940–1941

In a previous paper (Mancosu 2005), I have described the context and content of the Harvard conversations exploiting the notes taken by Carnap during the discussions. Many topics were touched upon but two stand out: the criticism of the analytic-synthetic distinction which saw Tarski and Quine together opposed to Carnap; and the project for a nominalistic/finitistic construction of mathematics and science. In 1942, Quine wrote to Woodger summarizing the main topics of discussion:

> Last year logic throve. Carnap, Tarski and I had many vigorous sessions together, joined also, in the first semester, by Russell. Mostly it was a matter of Tarski and me against Carnap, to this effect. (a) C[arnap]'s professedly fundamental cleavage between the analytic and the synthetic is an empty phrase (cf. my "Truth by convention"), and (b) consequently the concepts of logic and mathematics are as deserving of an empiricist or positivistic critique as are those of physics. In particular, one cannot admit predicate variables (or class variables) primitively without committing oneself, insofar to the "reality of universals", for better or worse; and meanwhile C.'s disavowal of "Platonism" is an empty phrase (cf. my "Description and Existence"). Other points on which we took C. to task are (c) his attempt to make a general semantics rather than sticking to a convenient canonical form for object languages and studying the semantics thereof more simply and briefly and yet more in detail; (d) his resuscitation of intensional functions. C. argued reasonably and well, as always, and the discussions were good fun. (Quine to Woodger, May 2, 1942, Woodger papers, University College London, Special Collection, GB 0103 WOODGER)

Here I will only give a brief survey of the second topic discussed in the meetings and refer to Mancosu 2005 and Frost-Arnold forthcoming (a and b) for more details and further references.

The topic of eliminating abstract ('unthingly') objects is discussed in a lecture "Logic, Mathematics and Science" read by Quine at Harvard on December 20, 1940 (Quine 1940). Discussing concrete objects (such as electrons, atoms, bacteria, tables, chairs, sense qualities) versus universals ('unthingly' objects such as centimeters, distances, temperatures, electric charges, energy, lines, points, classes (or properties)) Quine says:

> I don't insist on eliminating classes or other unthingly objects. It is not clear that the unthingly can be eliminated without losing science. (1940: 6, BPHLHU)

The conversations between Quine, Carnap, and Tarski in 1941 had exactly the aim of seeing how far one could pursue the program of elimination of the "unthingly" without sacrificing science. This was structured in two stages. The first consisted in identifying a nominalistic system of mathematics; the second stage was to provide a reconstruction of science on that basis. The discussion for the first part takes its start from Tarski's proposal for what should be taken to be a nominalistic language. For instance, on January 10, 1941, Tarski describes as follows his nominalistic commitments:

I understand basically only languages which satisfy the following conditions:
1. Finite number of individuals
2. Realistic [reistic?, PM] (Kotarbinski): the individuals are physical things;
3. Non-platonic: there are only variables for individuals (things) not for universals (classes and so on)
Other languages I "understand" only the way I "understand" [classical] mathematics, namely as a calculus; I know what I can infer from other [sentences] (or have inferred; "derivability" in general is already problematic). In the case of any higher "platonic" sentences [Aussagen] in a discussion I always interpret them as sentences that a determined proposition can be inferred (has been inferred, resp.) from certain other propositions (he means it probably thus: the assertion of a certain proposition is interpreted as saying: this proposition holds in the determined given system; and this means: it is derivable from certain basic assumptions).   (RC 090-16-28)

The requirement on a finite number of individuals was later relaxed by Tarski by leaving open the possibility that the individuals could be infinite. This was a step in the directions of distinguishing the finitism expressed in condition 1 from the properly nominalistic requirements of conditions 2 and 3. Throughout the 1940–1 discussion the distinction is however never made systematically. In addition, the notion of understanding, which conditions 1, 2, and 3 are supposed to ground, is never discussed in detail despite the repeated discussions as to which systems of classical mathematics could be properly said to be understood.

These discussions led to quite a tension between Tarski and Quine on the one side and Carnap on the other side. Carnap was in fact reluctant to ground arithmetic on factual matters (such as the cardinality of the existing concrete objects), whereas Tarski and Quine shared a strong commitment to finitism or at least non-infinitism. Moreover, Carnap was sympathetic to uses of modality (possible sequences etc.) whereas Quine and Tarski rejected any appeal to modality as begging the issue.

Nominalism was certainly important to Tarski. In a letter to Woodger, written in 1948, he wrote:

The problem of constructing nominalistic logic and mathematics has intensively interested me for many-many years. Mathematics—at least the so-called classical mathematics—is at present an indispensable tool for scientific research in empirical science. The main problem for me is whether this tool can be interpreted or constructed nominalistically or replaced by another nominalistic tool which should be adequate for the same purposes. (Tarski to Woodger, November 21, 1948, Woodger Papers, University College London, Special Collection, GB 0103 WOODGER)

The Carnap transcripts of the 1940–1 meetings are the best source for giving us a more detailed picture of Tarski's position on nominalism. A number of nominalistic tenets appear already in the report of discussions concerning the nature of typed vs untyped languages. Consider the following conversation:

I [Carnap]: Should we construct the language of science with or without types?

He [Tarski]: Perhaps something else will emerge. One would hope and perhaps conjecture that the whole general set theory, however beautiful it is, will in the future disappear. With the higher types Platonism begins. The tendencies of Chwistek and others ("Nominalism") of speaking only of what can be named are healthy. The problem is only how to find a good implementation. (RC 090-16-09)

Tarski comes back to the same claim about the Platonist commitment involved in higher order quantifications several times during the 1940–1 meetings. For instance:

Tarski: A Platonism underlies the higher functional calculus (thus the use of a predicate variable, especially of higher type). (RC 102-63-09)

Since I cannot summarize here the 80 pages of notes taken by Carnap of these discussions let me simply state what the upshot of the discussion was. The starting point was trying to find a part of classical mathematics that could be rendered intelligible according to the finitist/nominalistic criteria enunciated by Tarski. There was disagreement as to which fragments of classical mathematics could be considered intelligible and common agreement was only found for a quantification-free system of elementary arithmetic (formulated with relations as opposed to functions to avoid commitment to infinitely many entities). An interpretation for the system was then sought by ordering the concrete individuals in the world. Since the individuals in the world might be finite a number of complications ensued. But then the discussion turned to the delineation of a nucleus language that would satisfy the nominalistic requirements and be strong enough to formulate the *metatheory* necessary for the mathematics needed in science. The idea was that even a piece of Platonistic mathematics might be rendered (partially) intelligible by a nominalist metatheory. In one of the last meetings, Carnap summarized the upshot of the discussions. On June 18, 1941 we have the last meeting on the nucleus language. Present are Carnap, Tarski, Quine, Goodman, and Hempel. Carnap in his notes gives a final evaluation of where the discussion stands:

Summary of what has been discussed so far. The nucleus language must serve as syntax language for the construction of the universal language of science (including classical mathematics, physics etc.) The language of science receives a partial interpretation through the fact that the nucleus language is assumed to be understood...

Concerning the logico-arithmetical part of the nucleus language. Unbounded quantifiers...No objections from [the] finitist [point of view] since the values of the variables are physical things. It remains undecided whether their number is finite or infinite. As numbers one takes the things themselves for which we presuppose an ordering on the basis of a successor relation...

The descriptive part. We have not managed to find agreement on whether it is better to start with thing-predicates or sense data predicates. I [Carnap], and probably Tarski, favor the first solution. Hempel adds Popper. For the second solution: Goodman and Quine.

Finally: the language must be as intelligible as possible. It is however unclear what we mean by this. Should we perhaps ask children (psychologically) what they learn first or most easily?   (RC 090-16-05)

Several issues would require elaboration at this point such as the importance of 'understanding' in these discussions, the systematic confusion between nominalism and finitism and other topics. These are treated in detail in Mancosu 2005 and Frost-Arnold forthcoming (a). In addition, the issue of finitude of the world divided Quine from Carnap and Tarski; finally, what kinds of entities could truly be conceived as concrete? I will come back to some of these issues later. We now go back to Quine and we will not hear about Tarski's nominalism until the description of the Amersfoort meeting.

3. CAUTION, COMMITMENT, AND ABANDONMENT (QUINE 1941–1948)

3.1 Caution

The 1940–1 meetings spurred Goodman and Quine into pursuing a nominalist program. Goodman was in charge of writing a report on the discussions that took place in 1941 at Harvard (and which he witnessed in first person) although he found it hard to say what had really been achieved:

> Another confession is that I didn't do much more on the outline of the 4-cornered conversations of last semester. Your letter confirmed my suspicion that all we achieved was a somewhat bare skeleton of a program, and so many difficulties and questions occurred to me that I lost interest in trying to set anything down until there is something more solid to set on. I hope that you and I will be able to work together towards tightening and realizing the program, as we had begun to. Perhaps this season, with all the Tarski and Carnap meetings out, you will have time for it again. (Goodman to Quine, September 12, 1941; MS Storage 299, box 4, folder Goodman, BPHLHU)

This 'program' eventually led to the Goodman–Quine article of 1947. But Quine's position on nominalism, even one year before the Goodman–Quine article, was one of caution. We have a lecture from March 11, 1946, which in my opinion is the clearest statement of Quine's conception of nominalism. The lecture (which is published in this special issue of Oxford Studies in Metaphysics) presents nominalism as the thesis that there are only particulars and that there are no universals. From the outset Quine says that the paper will not be either a defense or a refutation of nominalism. But he adds: "I will put my cards on the table now and avow my prejudices: I should like to be able to accept nominalism." But the sympathy for nominalism does not blind Quine to the problems that the program faces and playing on the double meaning of 'executing' (as pertaining either to the executive or the executioner) he concludes the lecture by saying: "I feel sure that nominalism can be executed, but I don't know in which sense". But that in itself could be seen as a positive gain. In comparison to the Carnapian rejection of the problem of universals, Quine argued that 'nominalism' is a meaningful philosophical position. Much of the lecture itself goes over a number of topics with which we are by now familiar. In particular, following the doctrine that 'to be is to be the value of a variable', Quine recasts the nominalistic thesis as: "Discourse adequate to the whole of science can be so framed that nothing but particulars need be admitted as values of the variables." Faced with the objection that mathematics quantifies over abstract objects, Quine proposes a way out for the nominalist:

Now surely classical math. is part of science; and I have said that universals have to be admitted as values of its vbls.; so it follows that the thesis of nominalism is false. What has the nominalist to say to this?

He need not give up yet; not if he loves his nominalism more than his math. He can make his adjustment by repudiating as philosophically unsound those parts of science which resist his tenets; and his position remains strong so long as he can persuade us that these rejected parts of science are neither intrinsically desirable as ends nor necessary as means to other parts which are intrinsically desirable. (1946)

If the goal of science is efficacy in predicting experience then one could try to argue that some parts of mathematics "are *dispensable* as a *means* to those parts of science which are effective in prediction".

I will only emphasize a few points of interest. While discussing whether Quine's thought is undergoing a shift here is complicated by Quine's attempt to provide a viable argument on behalf of the nominalist, the general question to be kept in mind is: once science is taken to be authoritative for metaphysics, exactly which aspects of science are relevant to metaphysics? The focus on those parts of science which are "effective in prediction" (1946) seems to stand in contrast to passages mentioned previously where the focus was on "all scientific purposes" (1939) or "all purposes" of science (1939). But already in 1940 the goal of science is characterized as "prediction with regard to ordinary things" (Quine 1940: 7). Concerning the relation between science and ontology, it might also be useful to point out that whereas Tarski focuses on languages that can be understood, Quine tries to focus on scientific goals and criteria. And this links Quine's position to that of Russell. Quine seems to agree with Russell, as against Carnap, that philosophy requires metaphysics and that metaphysical questions are genuine questions because they can be answered by appeal to our best science.

Another issue concerns Quine's choice of particulars. Nominalism, Quine says, can be constructed in two versions, mental or physical. The first version starts from mental entities. In this case the particulars are simple experiences: concrete, specific mental events. The physical version starts from physical events, i.e. the particulars are spatio-temporally extended physical objects. One important point is Quine's conviction that modern physics warrants the claim that the universe is finite:

> According to current physics, these things are made up of quanta of energy, each of which is an approximation to a point-event. We may for convenience regard every aggregate of such quanta as a physical object—a *particular*, in the present sense—no matter how scattered its parts may be, no matter how intermingled with extraneous quanta. But an aggregate in the sense not of a class but of a heap of stones: a total concrete object of which the constituent quanta and all aggregates of them are *parts*—spatial parts, really spatio-temporal parts.
>
> This gives us a lot of things, but, according to current physics, only finitely many. Eddington has computed the total number of quanta in the <C12> entire extent and duration of the universe: if we call this number k, then the total number of things in the universe—the total number of particulars, in the adopted sense—can be shown by a familiar mathematical principle to be 2^k. (1946)

This is a position Quine defended also in the conversations with Tarski and Carnap. Moreover, the first version, but not the published version, of the Goodman–Quine article sent for publication also contained the same finitistic commitment. The reason for the change will be described in the next section.

3.2 Commitment: Goodman–Quine 1947

This is of course not the place to give an account of the Goodman–Quine paper from 1947, which has been described in detail elsewhere (see Decock 2002, Cohnitz and Rossberg 2006, Gosselin 1990). In it, Goodman and Quine managed to provide a nominalist analysis of the predicates 'proof' and 'theorem' and the latter was an impressive result. I would like to point out only two facts related to this paper that emerge from the study of the correspondence between Goodman and Quine. The first concerns infinity. We have seen that in previous talks and articles, Quine defended the idea that the world contains finitely many individuals and appealed to physics for support. This was also the thesis contained in the first version of the Goodman–Quine article. However, some objections by Church led Quine to send a revision of the paper weakening his finitism to a non-infinitism. In two successive letters, Church had pointed out to Quine to be careful in his claims about modern cosmological theories. On August 13, 1947, Church wrote:

> I am not familiar with all the latest cosmologies of the physicists. In fact I do not take them seriously because it seems to me obvious that from observation of the visible portion of the universe, which *may* be relatively very small, the step to extrapolation to the nature of the whole universe is too great to be in the least trustworthy. However, I have not heard of any cosmological theory which makes space-time finite in all four dimensions. I do know of theories which make three dimensions finite and the fourth or time-like dimension infinite; but on the basis of these, your remarks about finiteness of the number of inscriptions seems to me doubtful. At least in a spoken language an inscription or an utterance may be extended in time as well as in space and this quite apart from difficulties about determining simultaneity over long distances. (MS Storage 325, Letters with editors, box 1, BPHLHU)

This was enough to make Quine change his mind. He wrote to the editor of the *Journal of Symbolic Logic*, Max Black, on August 26, 1947:

> I am glad Goodman and my paper is accepted. But now, thanks to some correspondence with Church, I've become uneasy over remarks relating to the finitude of the physical world. Accordingly I'd like to ask you to supplant pages 2 and 3 by the revised pages 2 and 3 here enclosed, and to paste the new footnote 4, herewith enclosed, over the old footnote 4. (MS Storage 325, Letters with editors, box 1, BPHLHU)

The new footnote reads:

> According to quantum physics, each physical object consists of a finite number of spatio-temporally scattered quanta of action. For there to be infinitely many physical objects, then, the world would have to have infinite extent along at least one of its spatio-temporal dimensions. Whether it has is a question upon which the current speculation of physicists seems to be divided. (Goodman–Quine 1947: 106)

In the Amersfoort talk in 1953, Quine summarizes the issue of the size of the universe as follows:

Nominalism in itself guarantees *no* infinite. For, if the only entities, are the concrete (in some sense), then surely they are finite or, at best, not to be *presumed* infinite except by evidence of natural science. It is not for the nominalistic mathematician to declare the size of the universe; his constructions must be compatible with any finite size, but not require finitude. Here, then, seemingly a clear mathematical, even quantitative, reflection of the difference between nominalism, conceptualism and strict Platonism: noninfinitism, denumerable infinitism, and indenumerable infinitism.   (1953a: 4, BPHLHU)

Thus we need to correct what Decock 2002 writes on this matter when he claims that "According to Quine nominalists decline the use of infinities. The reason is that we cannot know whether there are infinitely many objects in the universe or not. Nominalists can only accept a finite universe of objects." (Decock 2002: 40). While the first two sentences are correct the textual support given for the third (Quine 1953b: 129) does not warrant the claim. What the text referred to by Decock explicitly states is: "the nominalist ... is not going to impute infinitude to his universe of particulars unless it happens to be infinite as a matter of objective fact" (p. 129). As is evident from the passages I mentioned previously, the nominalist must carry out his work without presupposing either finiteness or infinity of the world. In that sense he is non-infinitist because his constructions must be compatible with the possibility that the universe is finite. Cohnitz and Rossberg 2006 (p. 84) also make the same erroneous claim as Decock arguing from the premise that "Since inscriptions are physical marks, the number of variables will be constrained by the size of the universe, which is very big, yet finite as current science tells us."

A longer discussion would be required to clarify the loose talk of what characterizes the entities that the nominalist can allow: concrete, particulars, individuals. The three are not the same (just as much as abstract and universal entities need not be the same); but Quine, in his articles and lectures, does not seem to distinguish between them and proceeds as if the concrete/abstract and particular/universal are equivalent ways of capturing the opposition between nominalism and realism. In particular, Goodman was pushing for a version of nominalism in which the notion of a particular had center stage. This led to some discussions about what terminology to use in the Goodman–Quine paper. Just a few months before the publication Quine wrote to Goodman:

> Search your heart regarding the word 'particularism'. I am feeling renewed misgivings. Seems a shame to disavow a noble tradition when we are squarely in line with it. Nominalism is negative and so are we. If we cared here to emphasize a positive stand in favor e.g. of physical objects as against phenomena, or vice versa, then indeed I'd favor dropping 'nominalism' in favor of the appropriate more special term. (Quine to Goodman, June 12, 1947, MS Storage 299, box 4, folder Goodman, BPHLHU)[3]

Since this chapter is not about Goodman's nominalism, I will simply refer the reader to chapter 4 of Cohnitz and Rossberg 2006 and to Goodman 1988 and Quine 1988b for a retrospective evaluation of their differences.

3.3 Quine's abandonment of nominalism

In his autobiography for the Schilpp volume Quine rejects what he perceives as a misunderstanding of his position:

> Renewed sections with Goodman led to "Steps towards a constructive nominalism", an effort to get mathematics into an ontology strictly of physical objects. We settled for a formalistic account of mathematics, but still had the problem of making do with an inscriptional proof theory in a presumably finite universe. Our project was good, I think, and well begun. But our paper created a stubborn misconception that I am an ongoing nominalist. Readers try in the friendliest ways to reconcile my writings with nominalism. They try to read nominalism into "On what there is" and find, or should find, incoherence. (1988a: 26)

---

[3] On the same topic it is interesting to read what Goodman writes to Quine on June 28, 1948: "I have finally been forced to give up the term 'nominalism' for the purpose for which it had been used in the thesis because the difficulty of keeping this use distinct from the other was too great. As a result, I use 'particularism' for what I earlier called nominalism. Had it not been that your articles and our joint one used 'nominalism' as they did, I probably would have kept the term for the use made of it in the thesis and used 'particularism' for the other purpose; as I think a fairly good case could be made out for the thesis that what I now call 'Particularism'—the refusal to countenance any other individuals than concrete ones—is closer to the rather amorphous traditional nominalism than is what you and we have called nominalism—the refusal to countenance any other entities than individuals." (MS Storage 299, box 4, folder Goodman, BPHLHU)

That a gap exists between "On what there is" (1948) and the 1947 paper with Goodman was obvious to Quine already at the time of publication of "On what there is". This shift can be captured in the remarks made by Quine to Woodger in two successive letters. In the first one, dated January 26, 1948, Quine is discussing an analysis of lexicographic ordering put forth by Woodger and tells Woodger: "your approach suggests that you share our [Quine and Goodman's] nominalistic prejudices." But in the following letter dated March 22, 1948, Quine tells Woodger that his thinking in ontology is undergoing rapid transformations:

> A brief reflection now on ontology. I suppose the question what ontology to accept is in principle similar to the question what system of physics or biology to accept: it turns finally on the relative elegance and simplicity with which the theory serves to group and correlate our sense data. We accept a theory of physical objects, ranging from subatomic particles to island universes, because this gives us the neatest and most convenient filing cabinet yet known in which to file away our experiences. Now the positing of abstract entities (as values of variables) is the same kind of thing. As an adjunct to natural science, classical mathematics is probably unnecessary; still it is simpler and more convenient than any fragmentary substitute that could be given meaning in nominalistic terms. Hence the motive—and a good one—for positing abstract entities (which classical mathematics) needs. The platonistic acceptance of classes leads to Russell's paradox et al., and so has to be modified with artificial restrictions. But so does the acceptance of a physical ontology, in latter days, lead to strange results: the wave-corpuscle paradox and the indeterminacy. It seems, more than ever, that the assumption of abstract entities and the assumptions of the external world are assumptions of the same sort. It remains important to study the boundary between that part of discourse which makes the assumption of abstract entities and that part which does not. I have worked on both sides of the boundary myself, and propose to continue to do so; but I tend nowadays to stress the distinction. These very relativistic and tolerant remarks differ in tone from passages in my paper with Goodman and even in my last letter, I expect. My ontological attitude seems to be evolving rather rapidly at the moment.   (MS Storage 299, box 9, folder Woodger, BPHLHU)

This is in fact the ontological attitude that will be displayed in "On what there is", which marks the passage from the "nominalistic predjudice" of the Goodman–Quine paper to the reluctant Platonism of later years. Finally, let me point out that the argument presented to Woodger is not quite the classical 'indispensability' argument. Quine says to Woodger that perhaps classical mathematics might turn out to be unnecessary for natural science but it is on account of the theoretical virtues yielded by a systematization using classical mathematics that we should accept it with its Platonistic commitments. Recent developments of indispensability arguments (Colyvan 2001, Baker 2005) are more in line with this version of the argument than with the classical Putnam–Quine version of it.

4. TARSKI AGAIN

In this section we come back to Tarski's nominalism. I will exploit Willem Beth's reports of a meeting in Amersfoort in 1953 to complete the picture of Tarski's engagement with nominalism.

4.1 Beth on nominalism (Brussels 1953)

The analysis of Beth's writings on nominalism reveals an interesting shift. Thanks to the documents contained in the Beth archive we are well informed about this shift. On January 24, 1953, Beth gave a lecture in French in Brussels. The title of the lecture was "La Reconstruction nominaliste de la logique" (Beth 1953a). In this lecture Beth surveys the developments in set theory and logic that saw as protagonists Cantor, Zermelo, Frege, and Russell. He points out that both Zermelo's system and Russell's type theory emerged as a way to give a solution to the paradoxes. He then emphasizes that both systems contain elements that derive from a "Platonist" conception. In Zermelo's case this is revealed first of all by the fact that each individual results from the compression of a multitude into a unity, "which reminds one of the methods of the theory of forms". Moreover, Beth adds, in Zermelo's theory this Platonism is even more evident on account of the fact that each individual is the result of such a compression. By contrast, Russell's system allows for true individuals that are not the result of a compression. When we compress a multitude we end up with an entity of higher order. But Beth points out that Quine has insisted on the presence of Platonist elements also in the theory of types. The reason given is that the higher order entities are treated just like the individuals. This is especially evident by the fact that one can quantify not only over individuals but we can quantify also over higher order entities. In this way the higher order entities take on a concrete or substantial character so that the "universals solidify themselves". This leads Beth to reflect on whether one could give an alternative, "nominalist", interpretation of the systems in question so as to avoid the Platonist commitments. What seemed clear to him is that the analysis of the paradoxes has shown that one cannot have at the same time a uniform quantification and an unlimited compression. A requirement for nominalism, given without argument, is that nominalism must require a uniform quantification. He grants that one can construct systems of logic that satisfies nominalist requirements; first order logic is a prominent example, but the problem is that first order logic is not sufficient to reconstruct mathematics. And even allowing a certain amount of compressibility (I think Beth is here thinking of "predicative theories") one ends up with non-standard models and thus with an unsatisfactory reconstruction of mathematics. One thing that is common to both Zermelo's system and Russell's system is the notion of "membership" (either in the form of "a universal inheres in an individual" or "an individual is a member of a class"). Perhaps this is the notion at the root of both systems that one should try to eliminate. Beth mentions that such an attempt could be made replacing "membership" by the relation of inclusion (i.e. part and whole). However this solution also presents various problems and Beth concludes his talk by stating that the nominalist reconstruction of logic and mathematics faces considerable difficulties and that the nominalist requirements are not in harmony with the needs of classical logic and mathematics. However, he sees more of a future for nominalism at the level of metalogic. Although he does not mention here explicitly the work by Goodman and Quine, it is clear that he was aware of it as he mentioned it in the article published on February 14, 1953 in *Folia Universalis* (Beth 1953b).

Summarizing, in Beth's first contribution on nominalism we find:

(a) a sympathetic description of the program while not renouncing a Platonist attitude;

(b) a critical attitude with respect to the prospects of success for a nominalist reconstruction of mathematics (see also the letter to Scholz quoted in van Ulsen 2000: 62);

(c) only mention of Quine and Goodman as prominent nominalists.

4.2 The Amersfoort summer conference of 1953

An important development in Beth's account of nominalism takes place as a consequence of a summer meeting he organized in Amersfoort on the topic of "Nominalism and Platonism in Contemporary Logic". The change can be traced most clearly in a series of publications. First of all, the report "Summer Conference 1953" and the article "Reason and Intuition" also published in 1953 (both in Dutch). More elaborate accounts are then to be found in the volumes *L'Existence en mathématiques* (1955) and *The Foundations of Mathematics* (1959). The two prominent speakers at the conference were Quine and Tarski. I have already mentioned that Quine's lecture for the summer meeting is still extant in the Houghton Library and I have already quoted a passage from it.[4] However, most of Quine's lecture is centered on the opposition between ontology and ideology, and this does not add much to the published Quine 1951. My interest in this material rests especially in the amount of information we can extract from these articles concerning Tarski's nominalism. This provides a welcome complement to the information we were able to extract from the Carnap notes of the Harvard meetings in 1940-1.

Let's begin with the report on the summer conference (Beth 1953/4a). Beth presented Quine and Tarski as "the most authoritative spokesmen" of the nominalist efforts in logic. After describing the Quinian distinction between ontology and ideology, and the

---

[4] It is quite likely that Tarski never wrote a finished text for the lecture. Before the conference, on June 20, 1953, he wrote to Quine: "Dear Van, Some time ago Beth asked me whether I would be willing to take part in the conference on nominalism and Platonism and to give a talk there. I told him that I was interested in the topic and would be glad to attend the conference (should my plans of going this summer to Europe eventually materialize), but I also pointed out to him that it would be too late for me to prepare any formal talk and that I could only promise to make some contribution to the discussion. Now I have received a formal invitation and I am planning to answer in the same style. On the other hand it occurs to me that, if we are both to spend in Belgium a part of August and find time to refresh Washington talks in our memory, we might be able to concoct something by joining our forces. There are some points which interest me very much—e.g. the possibility of a semantic interpretation of quantifiers with variables of higher orders." (MS Storage 299, box 8, folder Tarski)

nominalist rejection of a gap between the two, he mentioned Quine's taxonomy (this is not in Quine's written notes for the lecture) as to the possible views that a nominalist can take vis-à-vis platonistic mathematics:

(1) he may try to build a new, nominalist mathematics;
(2) he may, after the example of Hilbert's formalism, conceive of classical mathematics as a formal system, the structure of which can be described nominalistically, but which does not require a nominalist interpretation;
(3) he may try to find a nominalist interpretation of classical mathematics.

Quine's sympathies lie with the third option. As an aside, let me point out here that the 1940–1 discussions contain elements of all three strategies and that Goodman–Quine 1947 carries out a version of the second strategy. The difficulties of the enterprise are well known. In what sense could Principia Mathematica be given, despite its Platonist commitments, a nominalist interpretation? Already when quantifying over the natural numbers, construed as classes in Principia, we can find no obvious nominalist interpretation. There is the alternative possibility of identifying the natural numbers with concrete objects "but then one has to assume that there are infinitely many concrete objects, and such an assumption a nominalist will hardly be prepared to make".

The difficulties become even worse when we move to analysis, given the ubiquitous use of impredicative definitions: they not only give rise to universals but also quantify over universals. Impredicative definitions are objected to also by non-nominalists. Thus, in addition to nominalism and Platonism there is a third option: conceptualism. This position accepts quantification over universals but rejects impredicative definitions. However, on account of Löwenheim–Skolem's theorem and Gödel's results on the construction of an inner model for ZF, through the constructible sets L, the opposition between Platonism and conceptualism is not as stark ("this contrast begins to wane", says Quine in the lecture) as it may appear at first sight.

Then Beth proceeds to summarize Tarski's lecture:

Prof. Tarski agreed with Quine's exposition of the nominalist view, and elaborated on various points. He distinguished a 'basic ontology' B and an 'extended ontology' E. The sciences may serve as an illustration: there, B consists of the objects accessible to macroscopic observation, while atoms, electrons and so on belong to E. The line between B and E cannot be drawn sharply, and transferring certain elements from B to E or vice versa does not, from the nominalist view, yield any gain. We may however try to reduce B and E simultaneously by assuming an empiricist stance with respect to B and a nominalist stance with respect to E. B then provides us with a minimal supply of concrete objects, and E should provide an ontology of universals acceptable to the nominalist. The problem here lies, as we have seen, in finding a nominalist interpretation of the quantifiers whose range consists in universals (classes).   (Beth 1953/4a: 43)

Thus, we see that Tarski agrees with Quine on the third strategy for nominalism, i.e. a reinterpretation of formal systems acceptable by nominalistic standards. It is at this point that we find an important and rare reference to Lesniewski, which shows that Lesniewski's point of view had left a mark on Tarski's approach to nominalism:

Tarski reminded the audience that the nominalistically acceptable universals are those for which a specific expression is available. Lesniewski has pointed to the possibility of restricting the range of the quantifiers in question to universals that are acceptable in this sense. The question arises whether on accepting such an ontology the usual laws of logic remain valid, as these laws are taken over from a system that is founded on platonist assumptions. According to Tarski, the results of Gödel's mentioned suggest that there will be no difficulties at this point. But at other points there are difficulties.   (Beth 1953/4a: 43)

The idea would thus be that of using substitutional quantification instead of objectual quantification. Tarski saw the work by Gödel as providing an ontology of abstract universals (classes) that could be named. Perhaps he saw in this result the vindication of the hope he had expressed in 1941:

The tendencies of Chwistek and others ("Nominalism") of speaking only of what can be named are healthy. The problem is only how to find a good implementation.   (RC 090-16-09)

But other difficulties for the nominalist project were pointed out by Tarski. First of all, the domain B must yield infinitely many objects:

(i). E has to supply an infinite number of objects. But this is only justified if B covers an infinite number of objects, and this is an assumption that sits ill with an empiricist stance toward B.   (Beth 1953/4a: 43)

We have discussed at length the issue of the cardinality of the concrete objects and I will not insist more on it (but see below for how the connection between B's infinity and E's infinity was likely established by Tarski). A second issue concerns the kind of predicates that can be applied in B. For instance, a use internal to B of the truth predicate seems to be unavailable:

(ii) The empiricist stance toward B leads to more problems. What kind of logic can be applied in B? Predicates like 'red' are admissible here; the introduction of the predicate 'true' presupposes a transition to a higher-order logic, but that becomes possible only in E.   (Beth 1953/4a: 43)

But E should at least contain the natural numbers. But how can this be justified?

(iii) The problems mentioned under (i) and (ii) entail that even in E the construction of elementary arithmetic gives rise to objections. Namely, one of Peano's axioms implies the existence of an infinite number of objects and thus crosses the limits of E.   (Beth 1953/4a: 43–4)

Tarski's proposed solution clarifies the passage in the 1940–1 notes by Carnap when he said:

Other languages I "understand" only the way I "understand" [classical] mathematics, namely as a calculus; I know what I can infer from other [sentences] (or have inferred; "derivability" in general is already problematic). In the case of any higher "platonic" sentences [Aussagen] in a discussion I always interpret them as sentences that a determined proposition can be inferred (has been inferred, resp.) from certain other propositions (he means it probably thus: the assertion of a certain proposition is interpreted as saying: this proposition holds in the determined given system; and this means: it is derivable from certain basic assumptions).   (RC 090-16-28)

The if-thenism suggested by the previous quotation is stated quite explicitly in Amersfoort:

That this objection is not insurmountable was shown by Tarski in the following way. Let X be the axiom in question and let A be an arithmetical theorem whose proof involves axiom X. We now consider the statement: if X then A. This statement too is an arithmetical theorem, and to prove it we do not have to make an appeal to axiom X; by now casting all arithmetical theorems in the hypothetical form meant here, we evade any appeal to axiom X and thereby the necessity to cross the limits of E. In the application of arithmetical theorems to concrete numerical examples however, the hypothetical form: if X then A, is just as useful as the original theorem A.   (Beth 1953/4a: 44)

This concludes Beth's report. What is contained in section 13 of "Reason and Intuition" (Beth 1953/4b) only confirms the if-thenism attributed to Tarski.

There are also elements in Beth 1953/4b to think that Tarski went into more details on how to construct out of B the nominalistically acceptable universals contained in E. In 1953/4b Beth presents the construction by stages for both the Russell's type system and Zermelo's set theory and claims in note 16 to be following Tarski's exposition in Amersfoort. The idea is simple: one starts with a countable domain of individuals S1. Then one constructs out of those only classes which are definable. The union of the two sorts is the species S. The material bodies are those obtained in this way. Beth names this the 'cosmological hypothesis':

> The objects of the species S we can now identify with the material bodies, appealing to a 'cosmological hypothesis', according to which the universe contains countably many material bodies. (Beth 1953/4b, Eng. Trans. p. 95)

The latter assumption relies on the fact that B (called S1 in 1953b), the starting point of the construction, already gives us countably many objects. This leads us back to the difficulties already mentioned in 1953a. But Beth goes on to indicate that now the solution to the difficulties for set theory and type theory is to be found in the same if-thenism proposed for arithmetic:

> Naturally one can object to the appeal to a cosmological hypothesis as mentioned above; its necessity resulted from the acceptance of the axiom of infinity. A similar difficulty already arises with regard to elementary arithmetic, and we can adopt the solution given for this case. Let X be the axiom of infinity and A a theorem of Zermelo's theory (respectively Russell's) in the proof of which X plays a role. According to the deduction theorem, the theorem 'if X then A' can then be proved in the theory in question without having to make an appeal to axiom X. We can therefore leave the axiom of infinity out provided we give all the theorems in the proof of which it plays a role the hypothetical form just indicated. For all practical purposes 'if X then A' is just as useful to us as A. The interpretation given above remains tenable now, but we can leave open the question of how many material objects the universe contains. (Beth 1953/4b, Eng. Trans. p. 96)

Thus, it seems that Tarski was more sanguine than Quine in holding on to the nominalist project. He thought that if-thenism could provide acceptable nominalistic interpretations of classical calculi whereas Quine seems to have opted for conceptualism, a position he did not identify with nominalism.

CONCLUSION

I have attempted to provide new elements for a better understanding of Quine's and Tarski's nominalist engagement. Before concluding I would like to compare, very briefly, the nominalist strategies followed by Quine and Tarski (reinterpretation of classical axiomatic systems) with those present in the contemporary literature on nominalism.

In *A Subject with no Object*, Burgess and Rosen distinguish between revolutionary and hermeneutic nominalism. In the first approach, the revolutionary conception, the goal is reconstruction or revision: "the production of novel mathematical and scientific theories to replace current theories" (1997, p.6). Most of the reconstructed theories sound exactly like the classical theories but they are reconstructed or reinterpreted according to nominalist standards. In the case of hermeneutic nominalism, the nominalist claims that his preferred reconstruction or reinterpretation is what the classical theories have meant all along. I see no trace of hermeneutic nominalism in Quine and Tarski; their approach lies squarely in the revolutionary tradition. This is especially evident if we think of the position they defended in Amersfoort using Gödel's results on L as the reinterpretation of classical set theory and type theory. No claim is made there as to the fact that that's what set theory meant all along; rather they propose a reinterpretation according to which the nominalist standards are satisfied.

In itself, this does not mark a major difference with contemporary nominalist programs, which are usually revolutionary rather than hermeneutic. But nominalist programs differ greatly among each other. Some, following Goodman and Quine 1947, rely on mereological ideas. Tarski himself does not seem to emphasize mereology in his nominalist reconstruction; as for Quine, mereology shows up in some of the lectures from the 1930s and 1940s and in the article with Goodman. But in Amersfoort his approach does not rely on mereology.

Other contemporary programs rely on modality. Here Tarski and Quine reject appeal to modality explicitly; this is especially clear in the discussions with Carnap. However, it is interesting to point out that Tarski's (partial) if-thenism corresponds to the first step in Hellman's modal approach to nominalism. Tarski's if-thenism is partial as it seems limited to the axiom of infinity (or the successor axiom in arithmetic). Hellman's favorite reconstruction of classical mathematics begins by constructing for each theorem of, say, classical arithmetic an 'if-then' version and then by prefixing the 'if-then' statement with a possibility operator.

Finally, Field's version of nominalism appeals to points and regions of physical space. While Tarski and Quine would not be unsympathetic, I am not sure how they would have reacted to the proposal but certainly the infinity of such points and regions would have been an issue. In any case, they would have found Field's proposal of interest in addressing an issue that had been central to their concern: can nominalism be sufficient to account for the mathematics used in the natural sciences?

What is striking about Tarski and Quine in comparison to contemporary nominalism is the fact that the motivation for nominalism is not argued on epistemological grounds. Contemporary nominalism has been, by and large, an attempt to reply to Benacerraf's dilemma on how we can have access to abstract entities. Tarski and Quine seem to proceed to nominalism without the mediation of the epistemological problems. This might not be surprising as causal theories of knowledge were not dominant in the thirties and forties as they became after the sixties. Their anti-Platonism originates from metaphysical qualms and from methodological commitments favoring paucity of postulated entities. Perhaps this should be qualified by recalling that the issue of "understanding", obviously an epistemic notion, was central to Tarski's characterization of nominalism; nonetheless, this concern is different from those explicitly related to causal theories of knowledge.

ACKNOWLEDGMENTS

I would like to thank Arianna Betti, Wim de Jong, Paul van Ulsen, and Henk Visser for their help in tracking down some of the Beth articles and manuscripts. Special thanks to Mark van Atten who generously translated Beth 1953/4a into English for me. For comments and useful information on mereology I am also grateful to Marcus Rossberg. For specific comments on the chapter, I am grateful to Lieven Decock, Marcus Giaquinto, Sol Feferman, Chris Pincock, and Mark van Atten. I am also happy to acknowledge the help I received from the librarians at Houghton Library (Harvard) during my stay there and I want to express my gratitude for permission to reproduce the materials from the Quine archive. All quotations from the Quine Archive are by permission of the Houghton Library, Harvard University. Last but not least, many thanks to Douglas B. Quine and Dean Zimmerman for making this special issue of Oxford Studies in Metaphysics possible.

REFERENCES

Unpublished sources: references to unpublished sources are given explicitly in the bibliography. The only exception are the excerpts from the Carnap notes of the meetings with Quine and Tarski which are always given by reference to the signature in the Carnap archive, e.g. RC 090-16-28. For the original German see Mancosu 2005.

Baker, A. (2005). "Are there Genuine Mathematical Explanations of Physical Phenomena?" *Mind* 114: 223–38.

Beth, E. (1953a). *La Reconstruction nominaliste de la logique*, lecture delivered in Bruxelles on January 24, 1953, Archief E. W. Beth, Amsterdam.

____ (1953b). "Nominalisme in de hedendaagse logica". *Folia Civitatis*, 14 Feb.

____ (1953/4a). "Zomer Conferentie" *Algemeen Nederlands Tijdschrift voor Wijsbegeerte en Psychologie* 46: 41–5. English translation by Mark van Atten, unpublished.

____ (1953/4b). "Verstand en Intuïtie" *Algemeen Nederlands Tijdschrift voor Wijsbegeerte en Psychologie* 46: 213–24. English translation in E. Beth, *Aspects of Modern Logic*, Reidel, Dordrecht, pp. 86–101.

____ (1955). *L'Existence en mathématiques*. Paris: Gauthier-Villars.

____ (1959). *The Foundations of Mathematics*. Amsterdam: North Holland.

Burgess, J., and Rosen G. (1997). *A Subject with no Object*. Oxford: Oxford University Press.

Cohnitz, D., and Rossberg, M. (2006). *Nelson Goodman*. Montreal: McGill-Queen's University Press.

Colyvan, M. (2001). *The Indispensability of Mathematics*. Oxford: Oxford University Press.

Decock, L. (2002). *Trading Ontology for Ideology*. Dordrecht: Kluwer.

Frost-Arnold, G. (forthcoming (a)). "Tarski's Nominalism". In D. Patterson (ed.), *New Essays on Tarski and Philosophy*. Oxford: Oxford University Press.

——— (forthcoming (b)). *Carnap, Tarski, and Quine in Conversation: Logic, Science, and Mathematics*. La Salle, Ill.: Open Court Press.

Goodman, N. (1941). *A Study of Qualities*, Diss. Harvard University. Reprinted 1990, by Garland (New York), as part of its Harvard dissertations in Philosophy Series.

——— (1963). "A World of Individuals". In P. Benacerraf and H. Putnam, *Philosophy of Mathematics*, first edition, Englewood Cliffs: Prentice-Hall, 197–210. This article was originally published in 1956 and the appendix in 1958.

——— (1988). "Nominalisms". In Hahn and Schilpp 1988: 159–61.

——— and Quine, W. (1947). "Steps towards a Constructive Nominalism". *Journal of Symbolic Logic*, 12: 105–22.

Gosselin, M. (1990). *Nominalism and Contemporary Nominalism*. Dordrecht: Kluwer.

Hahn, H. (1930). "Überflüssige Wesenheiten (Occams Rasiermesser)". *Veröffentlichungen des Vereines Ernst Mach*. Vienna: Verlag Artur Wolf, 1930. Reprinted in H. Hahn, *Empirismus, Logik, Mathematik* (Frankfurt: Suhrkamp, 1988), 21–37.

Hahn, L. E., and P. A. Schilpp (eds.) (1988). *The Philosophy of W.V. Quine*. La Salle, Ill.: Open Court. (First edition 1986)

Mancosu, P. (2005). "Harvard 1940–41: Tarski, Carnap and Quine on a Finitistic Language of Mathematics for Science". *History and Philosophy of Logic* 26: 327–57.

Martin, R. (1964). "The Philosophical Import of Virtual Classes". *Journal of Philosophy* 61: 377–87.

Quine, W. V. O. (1934). *Logic Notes. Mostly 1934–38*, Notebook of 300 pp.; Quine archive, Houghton Library, *2002M-5, Box 02, Compositions 2UDC

——— (1936). "Towards a Calculus of Concepts". *Journal of Symbolic Logic* 1: 2–25.

——— (1937a). "Nominalism". Lecture delivered at the Philosophy Club, Harvard, October 25, 1937. Quine archive, Houghton Library, Occasional Lectures, 1935–8, MS Storage 299, box 11.

——— (1937b). "On Cantor's Theorem". *Journal of Symbolic Logic* 2: 113–19.

——— (1939a). "A Logistical Approach to the Ontological Problem". Sept. 8, 1939 (Unity of Science Congress). Quine archive, Houghton Library, Occasional Lectures, 1939, MS Storage 299, box 11.

——— (1939b/1966). "A Logistical Approach to the Ontological Problem", preprint. Published in Quine 1966.

——— (1939c). "Designation and Existence". *Journal of Philosophy* 36: 701–9.

_____ (1940). *Logic, Mathematics and Science*, read by Quine at Harvard on Dec. 20, 1940. Quine archive, Houghton Library, Occasional Lectures, 1940-7, MS Storage 299, box 11.

_____ (1941). *Elementary Logic*. Boston: Ginn. Rev. edn. Harvard University Press, 1966.

_____ (1944). *O sentido da nova logica*. Sao Paulo: Martins.

_____ (1946). *Nominalism*. Presented at Harvard Philosophical Colloquium on March 11, 1946, Original in possession of Douglas Quine. Transcription published in this volume.

_____ (1947a). "On the Problem of Universals". Lecture delivered at the Association of Symbolic Logic meeting in New York City on February 8, 1947, 27 pages. Quine archive, Houghton Library, Occasional Lectures, 1940-7, MS Storage 299, box 11.

_____ (1947b). "On Universals". *Journal of Symbolic Logic* 12: 74-84.

_____ (1948). "On What There Is". *Review of Metaphysics*. 2: 21-38.

_____ (1951). "Ontology and Ideology". *Philosophical Studies* 2: 11-15.

_____ (1953a). "Nominalism and Platonism in Modern Logic". Lecture delivered in Amersfoort in September 1953. Quine archive, Houghton Library, Occasional Lectures, 1951-5, MS Storage 299, box 11.

_____ (1953b). "Logic and the Reification of universals". In W. Quine, *From a Logical Point of View*. Cambridge, Mass: Harvard University Press.

_____ (1966). *The Ways of Paradox and Other Essays*. New York: Random House.

_____ (1985). *The Time of my Life: An Autobiography*. Cambridge, Mass.: MIT Press.

_____ (1988a). "Autobiography". In Hahn and Schilpp 1988: 2-46. (First edition 1986.)

_____ (1988b). "Reply to Nelson Goodman". In Hahn and Schilpp 1988: 162-3. (First edition 1986.)

Tarski, A. (1983). *Logic, Semantics, Metamathematics*. Oxford: Oxford University Press, Second edition. (First edition, 1956.)

_____ (1986). *Collected Papers*, ed. S. Givant and R. McKenzie vols. i-iv. Basel: Birkhäuser.

Van Ulsen, P. (2000). *E. W. Beth als Logicus*, ILLC Dissertation Series, Amsterdam.

3. Cats, Dogs, and so on

John P. Burgess

The discovery of the note cards for Quine's previously unpublished 1946 lecture on nominalism provides an obvious occasion for commenting on the differences between the issue of nominalism as Quine first publicized it to a wide philosophical audience and the issue of nominalism as debated among Quine's successors today. Yet as I read and reread the text of Quine's lecture, I found myself struck less by the differences between Quine's position there and the positions of present-day writers than by differences between Quine's position there and the positions of Quine himself in later writings—and not his writings from many years later but his writings from the next few years, and especially one of his writings from the very next year, his notorious joint paper with Goodman.

In §1 below I examine a number of differences between the lecture and the joint paper. In §2 below I examine a couple of differences between the lecture and papers of Quine in the immediately following years. (Two limitations in my discussion should be acknowledged in advance: I do *not* examine Quine's earlier published and unpublished work, treated in such careful detail in Paolo Mancosu's contribution to this volume; and I also ignore other works of his co-author Goodman.) In §3 I return to the comparison of the lecture with the joint paper, and show how differences noted in the preceding sections lead to differences in the treatment of comparisons of number, as in "There are more cats than dogs." I also indicate how these latter differences point to a road not taken in the history of modern nominalism.

1. FORMULATION OF NOMINALISM IN THE LECTURE AND THE JOINT PAPER

1.1 First Statement

One striking difference from the joint paper with Goodman can be found already in the introductory section (i) of Quine's lecture.

Quine there says he *would like* to be a nominalist. Goodman and Quine (1947), by contrast, infamously begin by announcing that they *are* nominalists. Quine was soon enough to say, however, that this latter announcement should be regarded merely as "a hypothetical statement of conditions for the construction in hand" (Quine 1953a: 173–4), so this conspicuous difference may be less important than it seems. (See Mancosu's paper, however, for the case for believing that Quine's temporary conversion from sympathy with nominalism to outright adherence was more than just a pose.)

Another striking difference emerges as soon as Quine begins to say in his lecture what nominalism *is*. In his section (ii) he describes the nominalist thesis as saying that there are only particulars and no universals, having already in his section (i) stated that the issue of nominalism is a revival of the supposed medieval "problem of universals". The latter theme is elaborated in Quine (1948), where a trio of modern views in philosophy of mathematics (logicism, intuitionism, formalism) are aligned with a trio of supposed medieval views (realism, conceptualism, nominalism). By contrast, in Goodman and Quine (1947) the issue is described as concerning not *universal* and *particular* but *abstract* and *concrete*, as it is in most of the later literature inspired by Quine.

Again, however, this conspicuous difference may be less important than it seems. For while there are philosophers for whom a contrast between the universal/particular and abstract/concrete distinctions is of importance, Quine is not one of them. In the usage of some philosophers, properties are universals, but classes are particulars, though both are abstract rather than concrete; but Quine specifically indicates in section (iii) of his lecture that this is not *his* usage: for *him* classes are as much universals as properties, and *extensionalism*, which renounces intensional properties in favor of the extensional classes, is not *nominalism*, which renounces them both. (By contrast, in Armstrong (1978), to cite one example of the opposing usage, what Quine calls "extensionalism" is called "class nominalism".) Nominalism in *this* sense is the common concern of the 1946 lecture and the 1947 joint paper.

What may be a more significant, if less striking, difference eventually emerges from amid a host of similarities. To cite the similarities first, they are the following:

- Both works offer examples of nominalistically unacceptable items, "universals" or "abstract" entities.
- Both works offer properties and classes as the primary such examples.
- Neither work gives a general characterization of nominalistically unacceptable items, the lecture taking "universals" simply to be non-particulars, the joint paper taking "abstract" entities simply to be non-concrete entities, with "particular" or "concrete" being the positive term
- Both works allow that mental entities (supposing, as Quine does not, that such exist) count as nominalistically acceptable, "particulars" or "concrete" entities.
- Both works, this allowed, dismiss mental entities from further consideration.
- Both works allow that physical entities (supposing, as Quine does, that such exist) count as nominalistically acceptable, "particulars" or "concrete" entities.
- Both works assume that parts of physical entities count as physical entities.
- Both works assume that aggregates of physical entities, however physically scattered and physically heterogeneous, count as physical entities.
- Neither work elaborates on these assumptions.
- Both works in principle allow temporal as opposed to spatial parts of physical entities to count as physical entities.
- Neither work in practice makes any use of temporal as opposed to spatial parts.

In the lecture, Quine says a tiny bit more about mental entities: that only mental *tokens* count as particulars, mental *types* counting as universals. In the lecture, Quine also gives an excuse, so to speak, for not elaborating on assumptions about physical entities. For he professes to leave the characterization to physical entities to the physicists. The sincerity of this profession may be questioned, since the assumptions indicated about parts and aggregates are made regardless of what physicists do or don't say.

Cats, Dogs, and so on | 59

In the lecture, temporal parts seem to be forgotten as soon as they are mentioned. For immediately after having admitted temporal parts among the physical entities, Quine turns to counting the number of physical entities, and forgets to include temporal parts in the count. Specifically, Quine, unlike most physicists then or now, at least pretends to take seriously Eddington's claim to have calculated the number of elementary particles in the universe. Calling this number k, Quine concludes that there are exactly 2^k physical entities; whereas, if temporal stages count, then the number ought to be 2^{kt}, where t is the number of moments of time.[1]

This brings us at last to another difference between the two works: where Quine in the lecture speaks as if the finitude of the number of physical entities were an established fact, the second section of the joint paper with Goodman opens by saying merely that the authors "decline to assume" there are infinitely many concrete entities. The latter, more cautious, position seems to be in line with the position in Hilbert (1926) that science reveals no unquestionable example of the infinite in nature. The published documents do not tell the whole story of the retreat from finitism to agnosticism, and Mancosu's archival work, reported in his chapter, discloses what was going on in the background: a certain amount of genuine deference to the opinion of physicists seems to have been involved. As will be seen later, the retreat makes a difference in how comparisons of number are treated in the two works.

---

[1] Eddington (1924) maintained that there were exactly $136 \cdot 2^{257}$ fundamental particles, namely,15 747 724 136 275 002 577 605 653 961 181 555 468 044 717 914 527 116 709 366 231 425 076 185 631 031 296 protons and an equal number of electrons. (Note that neutrons, the first elementary particles other than protons and electrons, were not discovered until 1930.) There can, of course, be only a finite number t of moments of time if there are still supposed to be only finitely many physical entities while temporal stages of physical entities count as physical entities. Thus Quine is assuming *without comment* that time is not infinite in either extent or divisibility. My figure kt for the number of particle-stages is based on the assumption that fundamental particles are neither created nor annihilated, so that the same number will exist at all moments of time. (Note that the positron and matter-antimatter pair creation and annihilation were not posited until 1928 and not discovered until 1932.) Needless to say, if one took seriously the representation of time by real numbers in physics, the temporal stages even of a single elementary particle, and even of one with a lifetime measured in nanoseconds, would offer an uncountable infinity of physical objects available for use as surrogates for abstract entities.

1.2 Second Statement

In the lecture Quine is not done with the formulation of the nominalist thesis after his opening sections (i)–(iii), but returns to the issue later in the paper, after offering various clarifications in sections (v)–(viii). These sections consist mainly of material that is now thoroughly familiar, that Mancosu shows was by no means novel even back in 1946, that is treated in very summary fashion in the joint paper, and that I will treat in very summary fashion here.

Quine writes in section (v) that using general predicate adjectives (e.g. "yellow") does not commit one to the existence of corresponding universals (e.g. yellowness). He adds in section (vi) that even the use of nouns does not commit one to the existence of corresponding objects, since even what is syntactically a noun may be semantically syncategorematic, meaningful in context but *referring* to nothing (e.g. "lurch" in "to leave in the lurch"). To the question, "Well, if the use of nouns doesn't commit us, what *does*?" Quine replies in section (vii) that we commit ourselves to their being Fs when we say "There are Fs." The slogan "To be is to be the value of a variable" and the phrase "ontological commitment" both make appearances in this discussion. By his criterion of ontological commitment, Quine emphasizes in section (viii), classical mathematics, even including elementary arithmetic, is heavily committed to universals (though some very rudimentary parts are not).

Quine then takes up in his next section, numbered (ix), a reformulation of the nominalist thesis in the light of these clarificatory discussions. The original formulation from section (i) read thus:

(1) There are only particulars.

The revised formulation from section (ix) reads thus:

(2) Discourse adequate to the whole of science can be so framed that nothing but particulars need be admitted.

(Actually, Quine writes "admitted *as values of the variables*", emphasizing his criterion of ontological commitment. I have truncated the quotation because that is not the aspect of it that will be important here.)

These two formulations certainly *appear* to be very different, and there will be no lack of philosophers who hold that neither of

Cats, Dogs, and so on | 61

(1) or (2) implies the other: it is entirely conceivable that universals should exist even if science can manage to ignore their existence; it is equally conceivable that universals should fail to exist even if science cannot manage without the pretense of their existence.

By way of connecting the two formulations, Quine immediately follows the second with the remark, "Occam's razor does the rest." Actually, what Quine is taking as self-evident here includes not only the legendary razor of the legendary William of Occam, according to which entities are not to be multiplied beyond necessity, but also its inverse, according to which entities *are* to be multiplied as far as necessity—where for Quine "necessity" means "necessity for *science*". Only to one who takes these assumptions for granted can the two formulations appear to be equivalent, using the razor to get from (2) to (1), and its inverse to get from (1) to (2).

1.3 Third Statement: the issue of instrumentalism

Actually, Quine amends his amended formulation, so that it is not the *whole* of science—which taken in its largest sense would include pure mathematics—whose needs are to be taken into consideration, but only the parts of science that are intrinsically "desirable as ends" plus the further parts that are indispensably "necessary as means" to these parts. Any other parts may be dismissed as "philosophically unsound". (Here we find Quine light-years away from the principle professed later in Quine (1969b) that epistemology should be "naturalized", with the philosopher becoming a citizen of the scientific community. Quine's epistemology at this stage is thoroughly "alienated", with the philosopher remaining a foreigner, passing judgment from the outside on soundness of its work.)

Quine identifies the intrinsically desirable part of science with its predictions of experience, and this leads later in section (ix) to his third formulation:

[T]he defense of nominalism, so far as its incompatibility with math[ematics] is concerned, must consist in showing that the portions of math[ematics] which go by the board are *dispensable* as a *means* to those parts of science which *are* effective in prediction. It must consist in showing how the service of classical math[ematics] as an auxiliary to the natural sciences could be performed, adequately though more clumsily, by those fragments of math[ematics] or logic which are still constructible from a nominalistic point of view.

Recall that according to *instrumentalism*, a philosophy of science quite popular in the decades preceding Quine's lecture, not only is intrinsic value in science confined to its empirical predictions, but so is *truth*. Even the parts of theoretical science that are indispensably necessary for obtaining empirical predictions, and therefore of undeniable instrumental value or usefulness, are only acknowledged to be useful *fictions*. David Hilbert's *formalist* philosophy of mathematics, according to which mathematical theories are not bodies of truths, but bodies of fiction whose value lies solely in their having true computational consequences, was consciously modeled on such instrumentalist philosophies of physics. Instrumentalism, which is prepared to regard all unobservable theoretical entities, however indispensably necessary for empirical predictions, as no more than useful fictions, obviously involves rejection of the inverse of "Occam's razor".

Now abstract entities or "universals" being unobservable, surely the *empirical* predictions of science can be formulated nominalistically, one would suppose. Embracing an instrumentalist philosophy of science would therefore seem to absolve the nominalist of any obligation to seek a nominalistic reformulation of theoretical science. Or rather, it would do so *provided the notion of consequence itself can be explained nominalistically*. Without this last proviso, nominalists cannot even *state* the instrumentalist philosophical position they might wish to adopt. But as Tarski pointed out in conversation in 1940, this last proviso is by no means obvious fulfilled. Essentially the whole aim of Goodman and Quine (1947) (where the Tarski conversation is cited) is to give a nominalistic definition of consequence and related metatheoretic notions. (There is some discussion of the Tarski conversations in Mancosu's contribution to this volume, but for a thorough treatment see Mancosu (2005).)

An instrumentalist might well be satisfied with these results, and there are instrumentalistic overtones to some of Goodman's and Quine's closing remarks in their paper. But the fact that all the joint authors do is to treat metatheoretic notions should not be taken as a conclusive indication that they are outright instrumentalists and hold that treating metatheoretic notions is all that *needs* to be done. Rather, this is all they do because this is all they know how to do.

Setting Goodman aside, Quine at least is clearly *not* satisfied with the results obtained in the joint paper. He rejects instrumentalism and insists that a nominalist must not dismiss the theoretical parts of science that are indispensably necessary for obtaining empirical predictions as fiction, but must seek a reformulation of them under which they will be true. This understanding of what the nominalist's task must involve is evident not only *before* the joint paper, as in the passage quoted above, but also *after* it, as in Quine (1953b).

There, alluding to the results of the joint paper, Quine describes the situation thus:

The nominalist, or he who preserves an agnosticism about the infinitude of entities, can still accommodate in a certain indirect way the mathematics of the infinitist—the conceptualist or platonist. Though he cannot believe such mathematics, he *can* formulate the rules of its prosecution. But he would like to show also that whatever service classical mathematics performs for science can in theory be performed equally, if less simply, by really nominalistic methods—unaided by a meaningless mathematics whose syntax is nominalistically described. And here he has his work cut out for him.   (p. 129)

The rejection of instrumentalism, obviously presupposed by the "indispensability arguments" of Quine's later, anti-nominalist period, thus was present in his thought even during his earlier, nominalist phase. The deeper *grounds* of his rejection of instrumentalism, however, only begin to become clear after the end of that phase, as his *holism* emerges towards the close of Quine (1951a). As will be seen in the next section, though the central message of Quine (1951a), the rejection of the analytic/synthetic distinction, has antecedents going back to Quine's most famous early paper, Quine (1936), *there is no trace of it in the 1946 lecture.*

As a result, the 1946 lecture gives no real reason that I can see why a nominalist should not be satisfied with instrumentalism. For that matter, it also gives no real reason that I can see why a philosopher should not be satisfied with "platonism". But that is an issue that needs a section of its own.

2. DEFENSE OF NOMINALISM IN THE LECTURE AND LATER PAPERS

2.1 Meaningfulness

There are inevitably certain differences between the lecture and the joint paper that arise out of their very different purposes. The joint paper begins with an announcement of allegiance to nominalism, and proceeds at once to positive constructive work, only alluded to and not expounded in the lecture, on a problem that arises if and when the nominalist thesis is embraced. The lecture, by contrast, provides background on the issue, defending the nominalist thesis only in the sense of arguing that it is not unmeaningful and not unmotivated, something taken for granted without argument in the joint paper. The sections of the lecture devoted to the meaningfulness and motivation of the thesis, (iv) and (x) respectively, have no real counterparts in the joint paper, and invite comparison, rather, with some of Quine's subsequent solo papers from the years down to 1953.

Here is the main argument from section (iv) against the claim of Carnap and other positivists that the issue of nominalism is meaningless:

> There is no *a priori* ground for throwing out the statement "There are only particulars" as meaningless; for I have explained in intelligible terms what is to be meant by particulars (there are alternatives, indeed); and the other words of the sentence—'there are' and 'only'—are very decidedly parts of the positivist's own vocabulary...

The argument is not effective against its main intended target, at least not as his position was soon to be spelled out in Carnap (1950). Quine evidently recognized as much, since in replying to the just-cited paper in Quine (1951c) he argues along quite different lines.

To review ever so briefly the Carnap–Quine exchange, Carnap distinguishes the use of "there are" in assertions and questions internal to some linguistic framework, and the use of "there are" in assertions and questions external to all linguistic frameworks. Mathematics is the language of science: mathematical abstractions are part of the linguistic framework of modern science. As a question internal to the linguistic framework of modern science, the question "Are there abstract entities?" is not meaningless, but it *is* uninteresting, because it is trivial. It may be immediately and obviously answered: "Yes, *of course*, there are abstract entities, for instance, numbers and functions and sets."

When philosophers use this interrogative form of words, however, it seems they have something else in mind, a question about the status of the linguistic framework itself, and about whether the things that exist *according to the framework* exist *in ultimate reality. That* kind of question Carnap rejects as meaningless. It is linguistic frameworks that provide criteria for evaluating answers to theoretical questions, including existence questions; outside linguistic frameworks there are no criteria for evaluating answers, making debate over existence questions interminable and futile. The question "Should such-and-such a linguistic framework be adopted?" is meaningful only if understood pragmatically, as asking, "Is the framework convenient?" and not if understood metaphysically, as asking, "Does the framework faithfully correspond to ultimate reality?"

Even from this brief summary, Carnap's answer to the above-quoted argument of Quine should be clear. Quine (1951c) responds with a quite different argument, drawing on the rejection of the analytic/synthetic distinction in Quine (1951a): Carnap's principle of tolerance, according to which linguistic frameworks are evaluated simply for their convenience, is to be rejected because the very notion of linguistic framework is to be rejected. His distinction between internal and external questions reduces to or depends on the distinction between analytic and synthetic, and is equally untenable.

Where Carnap sees two questions, first the pragmatic question whether it is convenient to adopt the abstract mathematical linguistic framework of modern science, and then once that framework has been adopted the question its adoption renders trivial, whether there are abstract entities as presupposed by the results of elementary arithmetic, Quine sees only one question. Kemeny (1954) asks in a review:

Would Quine propose to consult a physicist as to whether there *really* are an infinite number of primes?   (p. 135) and the answer is that in an important sense *he would*. In the end, as a post- and anti-nominalist, Quine does accept elementary arithmetic, including Euclid's theorem, and its presuppositions, including the existence of numbers, but *only* because abstract mathematics is indispensably necessary for technical physics. The result is that for Quine the status of natural numbers is like that of quarks; if anything, numbers are posits still more speculative than those elusive subparticles.

This leaves Quine open to the charge in Parsons (1980) that he cannot account for the *obviousness* of elementary arithmetic, but the evaluation of Quine's later position is not my concern here. My brief summary of the Carnap–Quine exchange has already brought out what for present purposes is the main point: Quine's final defense of the meaningfulness of ontological issues rests on the views argued in his single most famous paper, Quine (1953a), and on connecting issues like that of nominalism to the issue of analyticity; *but this connection is not made in the lecture.*

2.2 Motivation

Turning from section (iv) on the meaningfulness of nominalism to section (x) on the motivation for nominalism, the first thing to note is that there is no trace of the epistemological argument for nominalism that predominates in the later literature. This argument has been borrowed by nominalists from Benacerraf (1973) and relies on causal theories of knowledge. By contrast, the notion of causality plays no role in Quine's philosophy—readers familiar with the more recent nominalist literature will have noticed in the last section that this notion was not invoked by Quine in distinguish universal from particular or abstract from concrete, nor were the "causal isolation" or "causal inertness" of universals or abstract entities cited and complained of—presumably because he considers it insufficiently clear. And even if this were not so, his holist approach to epistemology would leave him unsympathetic to causal theories.

More significantly, no *other* serious arguments are advanced for nominalism in the lecture, either. (In this there is no contrast with the joint paper, where nominalism is described at the end of the introduction as "a philosophical intuition that cannot be justified by appeal to anything more ultimate".) The primary motivation Quine cites for nominalism is simply Victorian materialism, and Quine does not even pretend to offer an argument for *that*.

Quine concedes that modern physics has called Victorian materialism into question,[2] but says that the nominalist can simply retreat to a vaguer physicalism, leaving it to the physicists to say what the physical consists in, while insisting that whatever that is, that's *all* there is. How sincere he really is about deference to the physicists I have already questioned. That issue aside, the fact remains that the materialism or physicalism Quine professes is left by him simply as an unargued dogma, and while there are also a couple of secondary motivating considerations cited for nominalism, these are not strenuously urged and have little force.

Unsurprisingly, even after further explanations in later works we find expressions of perplexity about the point of the nominalist project. Kemeny (1954), for one, writes as follows:

The reviewer is still puzzled by the "why" of nominalism.... It is some *a priori* skepticism that leads him to the "heroic position" of nominalism.... (p. 136)

Quine's own phrase later in the lecture is not "*a priori* skepticism" but "[a] puristic and Spartan attitude," but these come to pretty much the same thing.

One of the secondary motivating arguments calls for remark:

Since arithmetic is *a priori* rather than empirical, truth in arithmetic would seem, by normal epistemological standards, to consist in demonstrability; and accordingly the proof by Gödel that there is no possible consistent system of axioms of elementary arithmetic which will not leave some truths of elementary arithmetic indemonstrable, is a blow. But Gödel's theorem presumably does not hold for that portion of elementary arithmetic, or reasonable facsimile thereof, which can be achieved within the bounds of nominalism.

What this argument is remarkable for is not its force. (It is, in fact, feeble. Why should the fact, if it is one, that our method

---

[2] "Victorian materialism" is my label, not Quine's: he describes the view in question as the view of Lord Kelvin. Note that by "modern" in "modern physics" I mean not just twentieth-century but nineteenth-century physics: Kelvin's old-fashioned mechanistic worldview of causation-by-contact, illustrated by a remark Quine quotes, had difficulty accommodating either a gravitational or an electromagnetic field.

of *discovering* arithmetical truth is by *a priori* deduction, be taken to imply that arithmetical truth *consists* in *a priori* deducibility? Why, that is to say, should it be thought that every arithmetical truth must be discoverable?) What this argument is remarkable for is its bland acceptance of the distinction between *a priori* and empirical—or analytic and synthetic. Quine thus not only does not bring forward in the lecture arguments based on his critique of the analytic/synthetic distinction, *but even brings forward one argument that depends on that distinction.*

2.3 The Issue of Ideology

The lack of any serious argument for nominalism in the lecture is disappointing, both in itself and for a couple of subsidiary reasons. For such an argument, had one been provided, could have been expected to shed light on a couple of important but dark issues: on the issue of what motivates the rejection of instrumentalism, and on the issue of what Quine (1951b) calls "ideology" as opposed to "ontology". The former issue has been briefly discussed in the preceding section, and a brief discussion of the latter issue will be in order here.

In supplying an interpretation for a first-order language one must do two things: indicate the domain over which the variables range, and indicate the interpretation of the primitive predicates of the language. These two are, to a first approximation, what Quine calls the theory's "ontology" and its "ideology". Quine in the lecture identifies nominalism as a purely ontological issue. As a result, while in the lecture he tells us that only mental and/or physical entities are acceptable to a nominalist, he does *not* correspondingly say that only mental and/or physical predicates are acceptable (whatever *that* would mean).

That nominalism has no ideological component is more explicitly and emphatically indicated in the joint paper:

We are not as *nominalists* concerned with the motive behind the demand that a given predicate of concrete individuals be defined in terms of certain other such predicates. Naturally the demand may arise from a feeling that the latter predicates are in some sense clearer, and we may as persons often share this feeling; but purely as nominalists we know no differences of clarity among predicates of concrete individuals. (p. 107)

Indeed, this had already been Quine's stance before 1946 and would still remain his stance after 1947.

There is, however, one inconspicuous but significant difference over ideology between the lecture and Quine's later papers. Ideology, or the choice of predicates, may be viewed as having two components: the choice of *simple* predicates, and the choice of logical operators for compounding more out of less complex predicates. I have not mentioned the latter issue in my discussion so far, since I have heretofore been discussing only theories based on classical, first-order logic. While nominalism as such imposes no restrictions at all on the choice of simply predicates, in his later works it is a feature of Quine's conception, not just of nominalism in particular, but of ontology in general, that it demands a restriction to classical, first-order logic.

It is on account of this feature that Quine has no patience with proposals, popular among later nominalists, to achieve the aims of nominalism by appeal to modality. Thus in responding to Charles Parsons in Quine (1986), he reminisces about Goodman and Quine (1947) in the following terms:

Goodman and I got what we could in the way of mathematics, or more directly metamathematics, on the basis of a nominalist ontology and without assuming an infinite universe. We could not get enough to satisfy us. But we would not for a moment have considered enlisting the aid of modalities. The cure would in our view have been far worse than the disease.

Actually, I am not even clear on what to count as existence in a modal framework. When I construe the objects of a theory as the values of its bound variables, I am supposing the theory to be regimented in standard fashion as a first-order extensional predicate logic with interpreted predicates. Other devices, whether modal operators or ancestral functions or intuitionistic connectives or substitutional quantifiers, simply obstruct ontological comparisons... (p. 397)

While the insistence on what he elsewhere calls "regimentation" in classical, first-order logic is especially clear in the above quoted late passage, where four different kinds of departures from that logic are recalled and rejected, the insistence goes back much earlier. It can be found in embryo at least as early as Quine (1953b), where it is indicated (p. 104) that the ontological commitments of theories formulated in combinatory logic à la Schönfinkel and Curry can be assessed *only relative to a translation into first-order logic*. In the printed record this remark gives the appearance of being a response to a criticism in Fitch (1948), but the source notes, Quine (1953a: 170), indicate that Quine (1953b) derives, along with Quine (1947), mainly from a February 1947 lecture, and Mancosu confirms that a version of the remark about combinators appears already in that unpublished lecture.

Now the *practice* in Goodman and Quine (1947) is indeed to proceed without using any non-classical logical operators, but I find there no declaration of *principle*. In the 1946 lecture, not only is no general ban on non-classical logical operators enunciated, but the option of employing one specific non-classical logical operator (closely related to one of the items on the list of those condemned in the response to Parsons quoted above) is even briefly contemplated as "maybe...the best course". The exploitation of this option is the "road not taken" that I will be exploring in the third and last part of this commentary.

3. A ROAD NOT TAKEN

3.1 Comparison of number in the joint paper

The later parts of the lecture allude increasingly sketchily to the positive nominalist project and results soon to be published with Goodman. One more major difference between the earlier work and the later eventually emerges in this connection, and the remainder of this note will be devoted to examining it.

In his discussion in the lecture Quine turns first to considering the materials available to the nominalist as surrogates for nominalistically unacceptable entities when reconstruing or reconstructing assertions that appear to involve universals. Section (xi) discusses mereology, without using that name or giving many explicit details, and mainly citing the dissertation Goodman (1941) rather than the work of Lesniewski, Whitehead, or other earlier writers. Section (xii) discusses linguistic expressions, emphasizing that it is only expressions in the sense of *tokens*, concrete inscriptions made of chalk or ink, not *types*, abstract, repeatable patterns of inscription, that the nominalist has available.

This latter short section ends by remarking

Many of the important constructions involving reference to expressions, i.e. classes of inscription, can be carried out equally well by talking about inscriptions themselves, and bringing them into geometrical similarity with one another.

This remark cries out for some commentary and comparison with the complicated treatment of inscriptions in Goodman and Quine (1947).

The problem faced by the joint authors in executing their nominalistic project is that they need to consider something *more* than what Quine mentions in the above-quoted passage, the geometric relation of similarity (sameness of shape regardless of difference of size) between sequences of letters, as between the following pair:

ababa

ababa

They find they need to consider also the notion of alikeness of sequences of letters in a sense that allows spacing to be neglected, as between the following pair:

a   bab   a

ab   aba

The latter notion proves to be more troublesome than the former.[3]

---

[3] Actually, the notion of geometric similarity itself is problematic if one is serious about deferring to physics, including general relativity and its curved space-time. In the hyperbolic and elliptical non-Euclidean geometries of Lobachevsky and Riemann, geometrically similar figures of different sizes simply do not exist—with triangles, in particular, the defect or excess of the angle sum as compared with the Euclidean 180° is greater or less according as the triangle is larger or smaller—and though the situation is more complicated with the more complicated kind of Riemannian geometry Einstein invokes, where the curvature is not globally constant but varies from location to location, it is not more favorable. In any case, even in a Euclidean world two inscriptions of single letters both being exes or both being wyes or both being zees, a notion that Goodman and Quine (1947) accept without analysis, is not really so simple a matter as their being geometrically similar.

Now two sequences are alike if they have equally many letters, and if given any proper initial segments of each having equally many letters, the next letters in each are either both ays or both bees or both cees... or both exes or both wyes or both zees. (The "alphabet" in Goodman and Quine (1947) in fact contains only a half-dozen "letters".) The essential difficulty lies in comparison of number, in defining what it is for two sequences of letters to contain equally many letters.

As a toy illustration of this problem, the problem is first considered of how to express nominalistically comparison of how many cats there are with how many dogs there are, a problem that is also discussed in the lecture, where the related problem about comparing the number of letters in two sequences is not mentioned. (Curiously, dogs are taken to outnumber cats in the lecture, while cats are taken to outnumber dogs in the joint paper.)

It must be said that there is something odd in both the lecture and the joint paper in the emphasis on merely *translating* such examples into nominalistically acceptable language. One would think that Quine should be equally concerned with giving nominalistic justifications of *inferences* involving such examples, as in

> There are more cats than dogs.
> There are more mice than cats.
> Therefore, there are more mice than dogs.

or, writing "Most *A*s are *B*s" for "More *A*s are *B*s than not," such a "plurative syllogism" as the following:

> Most cats in the house are female.
> Most cats in the house are black.
> Therefore, some cat in the house is black and female.

Indeed, one might well think that the very notion of "translation" in the relevant sense—a sense not implying literal synonymy—might best be analyzed in terms of preservation of inferential relations. But perhaps the reason why questions of inference are ignored and only questions of translation addressed is simply that the question of finding adequate nominalistic reformulations of the premises and conclusions in such arguments as those just cited proves to be difficult enough.

In order to analyze the central notion, Goodman and Quine implicitly make a couple of fairly strong assumptions about physical entities. (Treatment of syllogisms of the type indicated would, to begin with, require making all Goodman's and Quine's assumptions about physical entities and their sizes and parts explicit.) Let me give more details about these assumptions than they themselves do.

On the one hand, the joint authors assume that there are notions of "bigger than" and "smaller than" (the converse of "bigger than") and "the same size as" (the joint denial of "bigger than" and "smaller than") applicable to physical entities, with the crucial feature that if x is bigger than y, then x has a part the same size as y. In case the universe contains physically indivisible particles of different sizes, this first assumption means that we would have to count as physical entities geometrical parts of entities that have no physical parts. Specifically, they assume that each cat or dog will have a part of the same size as the smallest animal among all the cats and dogs. Such parts are called "bits" in the paper.

On the other hand, the joint authors assume that if the As are non-overlapping and each has a part that is a B, then there is an x such that the overlap of x with each A is a B. This second assumption recognizably amounts to a mereological version of the notorious axiom of choice. Specifically they are interested in the case where the As are cats (or dogs) and the Bs are *bits* of cats (or dogs, as the case may be). They assume that there will be a physical entity x consisting of one such part for each cat, and a physical entity y consisting of one such part for each dog. Their unstated assumptions about "smaller" and "bigger" and "same size" presumably are such as to imply that any two such entities x will be of the same size and likewise any two such entities y.

Given all these assumptions, the cats will be fewer than, as many as, or more than the dogs according as any such x is smaller than, the same size as, or bigger than any such y. And given all these assumptions, such a construction will work when comparing the numbers of As and Bs for any As and Bs that are non-overlapping. (Notably this includes the letters in two sequences, the case of ultimate interest.)

Are Goodman's and Quine's physical assumptions really needed? Well, given that nominalism as such imposes no ideological restrictions, the notion of alikeness of sequences might simply, for all nominalism cares, have been taken as an unanalyzed primitive.

More interestingly, the lecture of the year before points towards the possibility of another and quite different analysis.

3.2 Comparison of Number in the Lecture

Looking for a nominalistic translation of something like

(1) There are more cats than dogs.

Quine in the final section (xiii) of the lecture supposes that numerically definite quantifiers such as $\exists_1$ and $\exists_2$ and $\exists_3$ ("there exists at least one" and "there exists at least two" and "there exists at least three") have been explained in terms of the apparatus of first-order logic in the usual way:

(2a) $\exists_1 x X(x) \leftrightarrow_{\text{def}} \exists x X(x)$
(2b) $\exists_2 x X(x) \leftrightarrow_{\text{def}} \exists x(X(x)\ \&$
$\exists x'(X(x')\ \&\ x' \neq x))$
(2c) $\exists_3 x X(x) \leftrightarrow_{\text{def}} \exists x(X(x)\ \&$
$\exists x'(X(x')\ \&\ x' \neq x\ \&$
$\exists x''(X(x'')\ \&\ x'' \neq x\ \&\ x'' \neq x')))$

Relying on his assumption of the finitude of the number of physical entities—an assumption dropped by the time we get to the joint paper—he considers the proposal to express (1) as a disjunction beginning

(3) $(\exists_1 x\ \text{Cat}(x)\ \&\ \sim\exists_1 x\ \text{Dog}(x))\ \vee$
$(\exists_2 x\ \text{Cat}(x)\ \&\ \sim\exists_2 x\ \text{Dog}(x))\ \vee$
$(\exists_3 x\ \text{Cat}(x)\ \&\ \sim\exists_3 x\ \text{Dog}(x))\ \vee$

and continuing through 2^k disjuncts (the number of physical entities). He eventually rejects the proposal on the excellent grounds that there is not enough ink to write down so long a disjunction, and that it is preposterous to make the formulation of something so simple as (1) depend on something so complicated as Eddington's calculation of the number of elementary particles in the universe.

On an interpolated note card (number 82a), however, he says as an apparent afterthought: "Certainly all such troubles can be avoided by admitting 'and so on' as an irreducible part of the language." The full analysis could then be expressed simply as

(3′) $(\exists_1 x\ \text{Cat}(x)\ \&\ \sim\exists_1 x\ \text{Dog}(x))\ \vee$
$(\exists_2 x\ \text{Cat}(x)\ \&\ \sim\exists_2 x\ \text{Dog}(x))\ \vee$

$(\exists_3 x\, \text{Cat}(x)\ \&\ \sim\!\exists_3 x\, \text{Dog}(x)) \vee$
and so on

without need for further ink, or for any estimate of the number of physical objects (or indeed for any assumption that the number physical objects is finite, though it is presupposed that there are only finitely many cats and dogs).

Quine neither commits himself to this option nor rejects it out of hand, though he moves on to other matters, and by the time we get to the joint paper it has disappeared from the discussion. It is an interesting proposal, however, because "and so on" seems to allow straightforwardly the introduction of so-called substitutional quantifiers, one of the kinds of non-classical logical operators condemned in the remarks to Parsons quoted earlier.

3.3 And so on

This would be an approach to substitutional quantification different from those taken in the literature surveyed in Burgess and Rosen (1997): §III.A.2.a). Usually substitutional quantifiers are introduced either with no explanation in more familiar terms, with an explanation in terms of the actual existence of abstract expression-types, or with an explanation in terms of the possible existence of concrete expression-types. The possibility to which Quine's interjected remark seems to point would be to introduce them with an explanation in terms of a common three-word English phrase. The substitutional quantifications $\Pi X \Phi(X)$ and $\Sigma X \Phi(X)$ would be explained, respectively, as "$\Phi(A)$ and $\Phi(B)$ and $\Phi(C)$ and so on" and as "$\Phi(A)$ or $\Phi(B)$ or $\Phi(C)$ and so on," where A and B and C are a few examples of expressions of the right grammatical type (say for definiteness the first three in some standard enumeration).

Now actually we can understand an "and so on" statement "P and/or Q and/or R and so on" only to the extent that we recognize the pattern or schema of which P and Q and R are offered as examples. A *rigorous* version of "and so on" would require indicating this pattern *explicitly* somehow; and once that is done furnishing a few initial examples becomes in principle superfluous. The Polish Π/Σ notation has the virtue of displaying the pertinent pattern explicitly, and also of dispensing with the examples.

But the power of "and so on" is not exhausted by the "substitutional quantifier" notation since there may be other patterns than those that can be displayed as a schema $\Phi(X)$ with a letter X for which substitutions of the appropriate grammatical kind can be made. For instance, there are patterns where the successive terms are generated recursively, each from the one before, as when the definitions of $\exists_1$ and $\exists_2$ and $\exists_3$ are spelled out.

A notation that would make the recursive pattern explicit, as the Π/Σ notation does for substitutional quantifications, could be devised. It may be most convenient to work with stroke numerals "|", "||", "|||" rather than decimal numerals "1", "2", "3". We can then indicate a pattern by the following kind of recursive specifications, wherein "n" is a schematic letter for which such numerals may be substituted, and "X" a schematic letter for which one-place predicates (such as "Dog" and "Cat") may be substituted:

(4a) $\exists_| x X(x) \leftrightarrow_{\text{def}} \exists x X(x)$
(4b) $\exists_{n|} x X(x) \leftrightarrow_{\text{def}} \exists x (X(x) \,\&\, \exists_n x'(X(x') \,\&\, x' \neq x))$

(To be completely rigorous here, "x" should be regarded as a schematic letter for variables, the actual variables consisting of, say, the letter "v" followed by a string of accents. But this is really not the place for pedantic details.)

These specifications enable us to expand "$\exists_n x \,\text{Cat}(x) \,\&\, \sim\!\exists_n x \,\text{Dog}(x)$" into a first-order formula for any specific stroke numeral subscript. In place of (3) or (3') of the preceding subsection we may then define a "more" quantifier M using the substitution operator Σ as follows:

(5) $\text{M}x(\text{Cat}(x), \text{Dog}(x)) \leftrightarrow_{\text{def}}$
    $\Sigma n (\exists_n x \,\text{Cat}(x) \,\&\, \sim\!\exists_n x \,\text{Dog}(x))$

A similar approach would work for the ancestral, an example to which Quine refers several times over the course of the lecture. Here the initial recursive stipulation would look something like this:

(6a) $X^|(x, y) \leftrightarrow_{\text{def}} X(x, y)$
(6b) $X^{n|}(x, y) \leftrightarrow_{\text{def}} \exists y'(X^n(x, y') \,\&\, X(y', y))$

and the final definition something like this:

(7) Ancestor $(x, y) \leftrightarrow_{\text{def}} \Sigma n \,\text{Parent}^n(x, y)$

Becoming like Quine more sketchy in my exposition now—and leaving aside like Quine the complicated question of *rules of inference* for expressions involving the operators I am contemplating—let me say something about the possibilities of nominalistic reconstruction these operators open up. Ferreira (1999) may be cited for one suggestion as to how, with no more apparatus than I have sketched so far, we can get first-order arithmetic. Substitutional quantification together with first-order arithmetic rather directly gives predicative analysis, and the availability of the ancestral gives still more. Decades of work by proof theorists suggests that this much mathematics may well be more than enough for known applications. A route to nominalistic reformulation not just of the metatheory of science but of scientific theory itself thus seems to lie open. At any rate, it lies open unless one closes it off by taking the line that "'and so on' is indefensible and meaningless in cases where it is impossible in principle to expand it."

But that, of course, is an *ideological*, not an *ontological* line. Once more we confront the difficulty, which runs through all the literature from Quine's earliest contributions on, that the question, "How much of science can be reconstrued or reconstructed nominalistically?" has no definite answer unless it is specified what kind of ideology is allowed to accompany a nominalist ontology. No reasonable answer to this question can be expected without a deeper examination of the supposed *grounds* for nominalism than Quine ever undertook.

REFERENCES

Armstrong, David (1978). *Universals and Scientific Realism*, 2 vols. Cambridge: Cambridge University Press.
Benacerraf, Paul (1973). "Mathematical Truth". *Journal of Philosophy* 70: 661–80.
Burgess, John P., and Rosen, Gideon (1997). *A Subject with No Object*. Oxford: Oxford University Press.
Carnap, Rudolf (1950). "Empiricism, Semantics and Ontology". *Revue Internationale de Philosophie* 4: 20–40.
Eddington, Arthur (1924). *The Mathematical Theory of Relativity*. Cambridge: Cambridge University Press.
Ferreira, Fernando (1999). "A Substitutional Framework for Arithmetical Validity". *Grazer Philosophische Studien* 56: 133–149.
Fitch, Frederic (1948). Review of Quine (1947). *Journal of Symbolic Logic* 13: 48–9.

Goodman, Nelson (1941). "A Study of Qualities". Ph.D. dissertation, Department of Philosophy, Harvard University.
—— and Quine, W. V. (1947). "Steps toward a Constructive Nominalism". *Journal of Symbolic Logic* 12: 105–22.
Hahn, Edwin, and Schilpp, Paul (1986). *The Philosophy of W. V. Quine*, Library of Living Philosophers, vol. 18, La Salle: Open Court.
Hilbert, David (1926). "Über das Unendlich". *Mathematische Annalen* 95: 161–90; English translation in van Heijenoort (1967: 367–92).
Kemeny, John (1954). Review of Quine (1953b). *Journal of Symbolic Logic* 19: 135–6.
Lee, O. H. (ed.) (1936). *Philosophical Essays for A. N. Whitehead*. New York: Longmans.
Mancosu, Paolo (2005). "Harvard 1940–41: Tarski, Carnap and Quine on a Finitistic Language of Mathematics for Science". *History and Philosophy of Logic* 26: 327–57.
Parsons, Charles (1980). "Mathematical Intuition". *Proceedings of the Aristotelian Society*, 80: 145–68.
Quine, W. V. (1936). "Truth by Convention". In Lee (1936: 90–124).
—— (1947). "On Universals". *Journal of Symbolic Logic* 12: 74–84.
—— (1948). "On What There Is". *Review of Metaphysics* 2: 21–38.
—— (1951a). "Two Dogmas of Empiricism". *Philosophical Review* 60: 20–43.
—— (1951b). "Ontology & Ideology". *Philosophical Studies* 2: 11–15.
—— (1951c). "On Carnap's Views on Ontology". *Philosophical Studies* 2: 65–72.
—— (1953a). *From a Logical Point of View*. Cambridge, Mass.: Harvard University Press. (The page numbers for all passages quoted or cited here are the same in the 1961 second edition.)
—— (1953b). "Logic and the Reification of Universals". In Quine (1953a): 102–29).
—— (1969a). *Ontological Relativity and Other Essays*. New York: Columbia University Press.
—— (1969b). "Epistemology Naturalized". In Quine (1969a): 69–90).
—— (1986). "Reply to Parsons". In Hahn and Schilpp (1986: 396–403).
Van Heijenoort, Jean (1967) *From Frege to Gödel: A Source Book in Mathematical Logic, 1897–1931*. Cambridge, Mass.: Harvard University Press.

4. Quine's Lecture on Nominalism from the Perspective of a Nominalist

Charles Chihara

1. HOW QUINE VIEWED THE DISPUTE BETWEEN NOMINALISTS AND PLATONISTS

Quine begins his lecture on nominalism by stating that he is going to defend the position that, in the long-standing philosophical debate between nominalists and realists (or Platonists), there is something real and meaningful at issue. This dispute is seen to arise from the fact that the nominalist maintains, whereas the realist denies, that the only things that exist are "particulars". Quine addresses in his lecture a central problem regarding this debate: is there a reasonably clear and precise question being debated by the opposing philosophers, or is it hopelessly vague? As Quine sees it, the Logical Positivist's position that the question being debated is simply meaningless amounts to "burying one's head in the sand" (p. 9).

What Quine tried to do in his lecture was to introduce several new ideas that would add clarity and precision to the metaphysical theses being defended by the opposing camps. One big problem with philosophical debates about existence is that, as Quine was to express it later, "at best there is no simple correlation between the outward forms of ordinary affirmations and the existences implied" (Quine 1960: 242). So he put forward the idea of *ontological commitment*—a concept that he had introduced earlier and that he would develop further in subsequent works.[1] In his lecture, the idea is expressed as follows:

[I]n order to decide what entities are presumed to exist by a given discourse, we are to examine the vbls. used in that discourse, and consider what values they are presumed to take on. (p. 6).

Dean Zimmerman made many helpful suggestions based upon his careful reading of an earlier version of this chapter, for which I am grateful.

[1] See my Chihara 1973: ch. 3, s. 3, for a detailed discussion of Quine's criterion of ontological commitment and many of the criticisms that have been raised to it.

Thus, a sort of criterion for determining *what entities a discourse presupposes* (or assumes to exist)—its ontological commitments—is introduced as follows: to decide what the ontological commitments of a given discourse are, determine what entities are presumed to be values of the bound variables of that discourse. As a result of this proposal, the bound variables became the means by which the ontological commitments of a "discourse" (in the sense of a serious and lengthy speech or piece of writing about a topic) are to be determined. A person (in particular, a philosopher) will be ontologically committed to a certain kind of entity in so far as she affirms or accepts a discourse that is ontologically committed to that sort of entity.

In his lecture, Quine does not make it clear if, when speaking of ontological commitments, he is concerned only with those discourses explicitly expressed using the quantificational devices of mathematical logic or is also willing to speak of the ontological commitments of discourses that are expressed in an ordinary natural language. By the time *Word and Object* is written, he is arguing that the ontological commitments of a theory are clear and definite only when the theory is expressed, formulated, or explainable using the conceptual devices of mathematical logic:

> To paraphrase a sentence into the canonical notation of quantification is, first and foremost, to make its ontic content explicit, quantification being a device for talking in general of objects. ... To decline to explain oneself in terms of quantification, or in terms of those special idioms of ordinary language by which quantification is directly explained, is simply to decline to disclose one's referential intent.   (Quine 1960: 242–3)

These views about ontological commitment are closely related to another aspect of Quine's conception of the nominalism-realism debate. We need to ask: what motivates the nominalist to restrict her ontology to only particulars? Consider the nominalist who believes only in *physical* particulars.[2] Such a nominalist, Quine suggests, has a mentality similar to that of Lord Kelvin, "who insisted that he did not understand a process until it was reduced to terms of impact of bodies like billiard balls" (p. 15). Quine sees the nominalist as attempting "to tidy up reality" and to refurbish the

---

[2] Quine held in his lecture that, in addition to physical particulars, there are (or could be) mental particulars.

conceptual scheme of common sense, so as to "produce a substitute conceptual scheme which, while still theoretically adequate to the physicist's purposes, will not countenance any entities beyond those whose existence it is within the *physicist*'s professional competence to assert" (p. 16).

Quine's discussion of the nominalism-realism dispute in *Word and Object* is much clearer, not only because the *criterion of ontological commitment* to be used in the discussion is more clearly stated, but also because the dispute is discussed in the context of considering what should be required in formulating a satisfactory overarching scientific theory encompassing all of the sciences, where the language of this grand theory (its "canonical grammar") is set out to be essentially an extensional first-order logical language.[3] Thus, this language of science will come equipped with the devices of quantification and bound variables required in straightforward applications of the criterion of ontological commitment, eliminating the need for paraphrasing sentences of a natural language into a formalized language of mathematical logic.

Returning to the contents of the lecture, we can see how, using the ideas underlying his concept of ontological commitment, Quine is able to come up with a formulation of nominalism ("the thesis of nominalism") that seems sufficiently clear and precise to satisfy him:

> Discourse adequate to the whole of science can be so framed that nothing but particulars need be admitted as values of the [bound] vbls.   (p. 14)

Quine then puts forward a problem with nominalism (as formulated above) that was to occupy his thoughts for some time:

> Now surely classical mathematics is part of science; and I have said that universals have to be admitted as values of its vbls.; so it follows that the thesis of nominalism is false.   (p. 14)

Despite the above problem, Quine felt, at the time of the lecture, that "the issue of nominalism" was "still an open problem". He felt that the nominalist could take the position that some parts of science are "philosophically unsound" and dispensable. In particular, Quine suggested, she could reject parts of classical mathematics

---

[3] The discussion takes place in the chapter entitled "Ontic Decision", which immediately follows the section, entitled "A Framework for Theory", in which Quine sets out the features of the language of the theory of science in terms of which the ontic decisions are to be made.

as not needed to have a perfectly adequate science—only some fragment of classical mathematics may be needed to preserve all the predictions and verifications of current science. Roughly, this is the sort of position I took in my Chihara 1973: I suggested that science could get by with a system of mathematics (predicative mathematics) weaker than the whole of classical mathematics and argued that a version of predicative mathematics could be accepted by a nominalist who was willing to use modal notions.[4]

However, by the time Quine wrote *Word and Object*, he had come to believe that Platonism was the only reasonable position to take in the dispute. The reasons why he came to adopt such a position are to be found in his researches on the problems facing the nominalist in attempting to produce a scientific theory that incorporates a mathematical theory adequate to the needs of contemporary science. These researches convinced him that the nominalist "is going to have to accommodate his natural sciences unaided by mathematics; for mathematics, except for some trivial portions such as very elementary arithmetic, is *irredeemably committed* to quantification over abstract objects" (p. 269, italics mine).

2. THE EXISTENCE OF NON-MATHEMATICAL UNIVERSALS

I shall re-examine later in this chapter the reasoning that led Quine to side (reluctantly) with the Platonists. But first, let us consider Quine's attitude towards the belief in *non-mathematical universals*, such as attributes (or properties). When he gave his lecture, Quine saw no reason why the nominalist should believe in attributes. He justified his position by analyzing arguments that had been given, or that he thought a reasonable philosopher might give, for believing in the existence of attributes and then refuting these arguments.

---

[4] See my Chihara 2004: 105–8, for a fuller discussion of my early response to the Quinian position, giving additional details of my position as well as references to some early related works. For an explanation of predicative mathematics provided by an expert in the field, see Feferman (2005). There is growing evidence, due primarily to Feferman, that much (if not all) of the mathematics of contemporary science can be reproduced within a predicative system. See, for example, Feferman, (1998a: sections 8 and 9), and Feferman (1998b). See also Hellman (1998: sections 1 and 2).

Rather than going over these arguments and Quine's refutations of them, I should like to consider a recently published argument for the existence of such non-mathematical universals which Quine did not consider in his lecture.

The argument in question was put forth by John Burgess in his review (Burgess 2005) of my book *A Structural Account of Mathematics*. The argument begins with the statement

[1] There are now four books authored by Charles Chihara.

Burgess argues that [1] cannot be understood to be the assertion

[2] There are now four book *tokens* authored by Charles Chihara

since there are "not just four but hundreds or thousands of such tokens, scattered through various institutions and personal libraries" (Burgess 2005: 89). So Burgess understands [1] to be the assertion

[1'] There are now four book *types* authored by Charles Chihara.

Since book types are not particulars but some kind of non-mathematical universal, Burgess believes that the nominalist is faced with a serious difficulty, because anyone denying that we have adequate grounds for believing in such things as book types would have to either deny that the usual grounds for asserting [1] are adequate, or else hold that [1] does not imply that there are book types. Thus, the nominalist is faced with maintaining one of the following alternatives:

(a) the usual grounds for asserting [1] are not adequate;

or

(b) [1] does not imply that there are book types.

Let us consider alternative (a). What would it be to deny that the usual grounds for asserting [1] are adequate? Well, what are considered adequate grounds for asserting [1] in ordinary everyday situations? Here's what Burgess writes:

If you asked me . . . for evidence to justify the belief that there are now four books (*not* in the sense of book *tokens*) by Charles Chihara, we could point to four book tokens, each with the name 'Charles S. Chihara' on the title page, and each, apart from that one common feature, quite unlike every other.   (Burgess 2005: 89)

In ordinary everyday situations, the sort of evidence cited above seems to constitute perfectly adequate grounds for affirming [1]. So to choose the first alternative is to reject what practically everyone in ordinary situations takes to be acceptable.

What about alternative (b)? To deny the implication in question is to deny that "There are now four books..." implies that there are books (in the relevant sense of 'book'). From the linguistic point of view, such an implication seems to be hard to resist indeed. Neither alternative seems at all plausible to Burgess, so he naturally favors the Platonic position that book types exist.[5]

[5] The above argument was presented in the course of responding to my claim in my book that the nominalists I defend "do not attempt to judge common sense and science from some higher, better, and further standpoint" (as Burgess and Rosen seem to think nominalists always or typically do). Rather, I asserted, these nominalists attempt to develop an account of mathematics that is "compatible with both what science teaches us about how we humans obtain knowledge and also what we already know about how humans learn and develop mathematical theories" (Chihara 2004: 159). After complaining that I do not say what teaching of science I have in mind, Burgess suggests: "Presumably the alleged teaching of science should be something like this: 'We humans cannot justifiably believe anything implying the existence of abstract objects'." He then proceeds to develop the above argument against the nominalist. He concludes that it is implausible to suppose that the meaning ordinary literate people attach to such statements as [1] is some "complicated nominalistic version mentioning only concrete objects". He adds that he finds even more implausible the view that *unless* that is what ordinary people mean, the beliefs ordinary people express in asserting such things as [1] are unjustifiable. And he ends his attack with the rhetorical flourish: "But I find the claim that science teaches that those beliefs are unjustifiable least plausible of all" (p. 90).

I should note that Burgess's "refutation" of my view about the teachings of science is directed at a straw man. The quasi-philosophical view being attributed to me is not anything I ever espoused or put forward. What in fact I had in mind can be expressed roughly as follows: *science teaches us that humans are part of the animal kingdom and that, as such,* Homo sapiens, *like the other primates, obtain their knowledge of the world through their sense organs.*

Now Mathematical Platonists believe that the theorems of set theory are assertions (about sets) that set theorists have somehow discovered to be true. But sets are held by practically all Platonists to be entities that cannot be observed, sensed, or even detected by our most advanced scientific instruments. Indeed, one of the most influential and important of all the Platonists, Kurt Gödel, claimed that the objects of transfinite set theory "clearly do not belong to the physical world" (Gödel 1964: 271). Since the theorems of set theory are supposed to be independent of human desires, intentions, and control, nominalists find it difficult to conceive of how set theorists could have learned such alleged facts in a way that is consistent with the above teaching of science. Interestingly, Burgess, who has been a defender of a form of Platonism for a great many years, has never even attempted to address the question of how, in a way that is consistent with what we know about how humans acquire

Since the above argument was only published relatively recently, Quine cannot be expected to have responded to it. However, certain of his views expressed in *Word and Object* are relevant to the argument. How then might Quine have responded to Burgess's argument against the nominalist? One possibility is that, in trying to determine the sort of ontology he should adopt, Quine might have chosen to disregard how ordinary people, thinking in a natural language, tend to reason in common everyday situations. This is because he was convinced that natural languages are so vague and shot through with ambiguities that to determine the ontological implications of what ordinary people say in everyday situations is in general a shaky way to proceed. Thus, he might have reasoned that how ordinary people would justify claims about the number of books published by an author is simply not weighty, precise, or clear enough to be used in determining what a philosopher should include in the ontology of the hypothetical grand scientific theory of the project he was envisaging.

As some support for thinking that Quine might have taken such a position, it should be noted that, in describing the form of his canonical grammar to be used in formulating his grand scientific theory—a theory expressed in an *extensional* language, the vocabulary of which included no terms of propositional attitude, modality, or intensional abstraction—Quine wrote:

> Not that the idioms thus renounced are supposed to be unneeded in the market place or in the laboratory.... The doctrine is only that such a canonical idiom can be abstracted and then adhered to in the statement of one's scientific theory.   (Quine 1960: 228).

Quine held, in other words, that what is needed in the market place or the laboratory should not determine what kind of terms ought to be allowed in the language of his grand scientific theory. Similarly, one might argue that the sort of reasoning that is carried out in natural languages and that takes place in the market place or the laboratory should not determine what is to be included in the ontology of the grand scientific theory.

The above are only speculations about how Quine might have responded to Burgess's argument. I shall now give my own response

---

knowledge of the world, set theorists have obtained their knowledge of the (truth of the) axioms of set theory.

to the argument. Examining the overall structure of Burgess's reasoning, we see that, after describing a common method of justifying [1] in an ordinary everyday situation, he presents the nominalist with the choice either of maintaining that the common method of justifying the statement is insufficient for the assertion of [1], or else of denying that [1] implies that there are book types.

I wish to evaluate Burgess's reasoning here, but with respect to a slightly different example from the one he uses, because I wish to avoid the complications and subtleties that are involved in discussing books being published. Let us consider the case of the practice ("game" or "puzzle") of making tangrams: figures obtained by arranging on a flat surface the seven pieces obtained by cutting a square into five triangles, a square and a rhomboid (as pictured in Fig. 4.1).

Let us imagine a society in which the construction of memorable tangrams is considered a feat worthy of such notice and approbation that the discovery of a "new" tangram (one different in shape from all the tangrams that had previously been produced in the society) is not only rewarded monetarily but also recorded in the society's official tangram record book. Imagine that an organization had been formed to determine and record in an official record book each discovery of a "new tangram" (a tangram possessing a shape that had never previously been constructed by any member of the society and noted in the record book). The official record book would give the name of the discoverer and the date on which the new tangram was entered into the official record book. In the case of

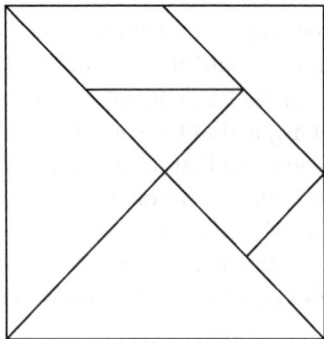

Fig. 4.1

each new tangram, the official record book would contain a single line drawing outlining the shape of the new tangram.
Consider the statement

> [3] There are now four tangrams which, according to the official record book, Jim Lee was the first in the society to have discovered.

The tangrams whose discoveries are being attributed to Jim Lee are not tangram tokens, since it is clear that the truth of the assertion is not dependent upon there being any particular tangram pieces in existence at the time of assertion. Thus, according to Burgess's method of reasoning, [3] must be the assertion of the existence of tangram types—things that are non-mathematical universals of some sort.

Now how might one gather, in ordinary circumstances, decisive evidence for [3]? One way would be go to the official record book and to search through the pages, actually finding the four citations crediting Jim Lee with the discoveries and giving the line drawings of the shapes in question (each shape drawn differing from all the others).

Then, the nominalist will be faced with the following choice:
Either

> (a) she can deny that the usual grounds given for asserting [3] are adequate;

or

> (b) she can deny that [3] implies that there are such things as tangram types.

Compare [3] with

> [4] There are now four line drawings in the official record book each of which is such that Jim Lee is credited with being the first in the society to have discovered a way of "forming-a-tangram" with the shape pictured in the citation.

where, the expression 'forming-a-tangram' is understood to be the act of forming a plane figure with seven tangram pieces that is (or would be) judged by the organization described above to be a tangram shape.

Does [3] mean the same thing as [4]? Absolutely not. Yet it would seem that, in the situation described above, any evidence one would give for [3] would be evidence for [4] and any evidence one would give for [4] would be evidence for [3]. How can that be, since nothing in assertion [4] implies the existence of an abstract entity that is a tangram type? To put the puzzle in another way, how can evidence that seems to be, in ordinary everyday situations, absolutely decisive for affirming [4] also be decisive grounds for affirming the existence of tangrams types, as Burgess's argument seems to suggest? (How did the rabbit get into the hat?)

Let us re-examine the evidence described above for justifying assertion [3] in common ordinary situations. Imagine that a wager has been made regarding the truth of [3] and that the betters set about to determine who the winner is. Suppose, now, that they search through the official record book as described above and find four distinct citations each one crediting Jim Lee with being the first in the society to have discovered a tangram possessing the shape pictured in the line drawing given there. Certainly, this evidence would be regarded as decisively determining that [3] is true. Surely no one would deny awarding the stake to the person who bet on the truth of [3] on the grounds that the evidence does not show that tangram types exist—to object on such philosophical grounds would be considered either a joke or an absurdity of the highest order. In the ordinary everyday situation described above, the question of the existence of non-mathematical universals is never considered as something at risk. In such situations, what is at stake is not the existence of universals or attributes, and the grounds for asserting [3] need not even address the question of the existence of such things as universals. Thus, just because we regard the evidence described above as decisively justifying [3] in ordinary everyday situations does not allow one to infer that this evidence provides us with decisive grounds for believing in the existence of tangram types. For this reason, I see no reason why the nominalist cannot allow that, in ordinary everyday situations, the kind of evidence described above can be taken to be a decisive justification for asserting [3], while at the same time denying that this evidence provides us with decisive reasons for asserting that tangram types (or other universals) exist. To some extent, then, the reasoning here agrees in spirit with the kind of reasoning hypothesized earlier to be attributable to Quine.

3. THE EXISTENCE OF MATHEMATICAL OBJECTS

One can see, from Burgess's argument for the existence of such things as book types, how some Platonists, who start out believing in mathematical objects, might come to believe in non-mathematical abstract entities as well. But like Quine, I feel that the case that has been made for believing in mathematical objects is, on the whole, significantly stronger than the one made for believing in non-mathematical "universals" or abstract entities. And also like Quine, I have focused my philosophical researches more on the question of the existence of mathematical objects than of the existence of non-mathematical things. This is not only because I have found the arguments put forward by Platonists for belief in non-mathematical abstract entities unconvincing. My main reason for concentrating on the dispute about mathematical objects, however, is because the mathematical case strikes me as being a more fruitful and more important area of research. More than a few distinguished mathematicians over the ages have been drawn to espouse some form of Platonism. That fact alone suggests that providing genuine insights into the disputed positions of the controversy may produce far-reaching advances in our understanding of the nature of mathematics and even of science. (As I shall indicate later, there are additional reasons why I believe it is important for philosophers to study the case for belief in mathematical objects).

My view of nominalism, however, differs considerably from Quine's, especially with regard to: (a) his characterization of the nominalist's motivation for eschewing abstract entities—his idea of what it is that motivates the nominalist to reject the existence of mathematical objects; and (b) his view of what positions about the nature of classical mathematics are open to the nominalist.

Examining (a) first, reconsider Quine's view that the nominalist is motivated to adopt an anti-Platonist position because she has a mentality similar to that of Lord Kelvin who supposedly could not understand a process unless it was reduced to terms of impact of bodies like billiard balls. As Quine describes the nominalist's thought processes, the nominalist is made to seem lacking in imagination or mental flexibility, and as a result, nominalism is made to appear to be a kind of superstition. I see nominalism as being motivated more by the conviction that the Platonic alternative is implausible and unworkable than it is by the attractiveness of Lord Kelvin's billiard ball model of physical interactions. To clarify and explain the sort of motivation I have in mind in more depth, I shall have to give a brief description of my views about the nature of philosophy itself.

The philosopher seeks an understanding of the world. But the sort of understanding sought, according to my view of the field, I like to call "Big Picture understanding". The philosopher seeks a kind of general view of the world that results from answering such questions as: What, in general and in broad outlines, is the universe like? What, in general and in broad outlines, is our place in the universe and how are we related to the things around us? How, in general and in broad outlines, are we humans able to gain an understanding of the things around us and of the universe? Of course, there are also many areas of philosophy that are researched by specialists. Indeed, for practically every area X of intellectual study, there is a philosophy of X. So there is philosophy of science, of mathematics, of psychology, of language, of history, of art, religion, etc. Someone working in the philosophy of X will seek a Big Picture understanding of the nature of X—one that will aid philosophers in achieving the goal of fitting X into the Big Picture of the relationship between humans and the universe they inhabit. Thus, the philosopher seeks ultimately to obtain an account of X that fits together with the accounts of the other Xs which she accepts, yielding a consistent and coherent account that is compatible also with the epistemology and natural sciences that she judges to be acceptable. The emphasis here is on consistency and coherence with the total picture. One wants one's account of X to be consistent not only with what one believes about Y, but also with R, T, and Z.

Consider, then, the specific area of philosophy that concerns us here: viz. philosophy of mathematics. The philosopher of mathematics, according to this conception of philosophy, wants to gain a Big Picture understanding of the nature of mathematics—one that will result in a conception and theory of mathematics which will be compatible with not only what science teaches us about how we humans acquire our knowledge and understanding of the world around us, but also with our views about, and knowledge of, science itself.

The above is an all too brief account of my view of philosophy, but hopefully enough has been presented to provide an intelligible background for the explanation to follow of what I take to be the chief motivation for seeking a nominalistic account of mathematics—the industrious reader can find a fuller and more adequate account of my view of philosophy elsewhere.[6]

The philosopher of mathematics wants to gain a Big Picture understanding of the nature of mathematics that yields a conception and theory of mathematics compatible with what science teaches us about how we humans acquire our knowledge and understanding of the world around us. Which side one chooses in the dispute between nominalists and Platonists regarding the existence of mathematical objects will determine to a large extent how one will attempt to fit mathematics into one's conception of human intellectual development and the relationship between the human mind and the world outside the mind. Thus, let us examine the Platonist's account of mathematics, starting with the idea that there really exist such things as sets and numbers. Mathematical theories, then, such as set theory and number theory, will be regarded as theories about these mathematical entities. Not surprisingly, Platonists (such as Quine) tend to see set theory as a theory like (and "on a par with") atomic physics: just as the basic principles and general facts about atoms formulated in atomic physics are regarded as truths discovered by physicists, so the basic principles and general facts about sets formulated by set theorists are regarded as truths discovered by mathematicians.

Now there are a number of serious problems with the above Platonic conception of mathematics. Imagine that the axioms of set theory are taken to be "truths about sets"—true statements that tell us various things about these abstract entities that are hypothesized to exist independently of our thoughts and desires. Then, since sets are not supposed to be objects that can be seen, touched, or detected even by our most sophisticated scientific instruments, the question arises: how have set theorists arrived at their presumed knowledge of the existence and properties of sets that are expressed in the axioms of set theory? Set theorists have not conducted experiments, as have physicists on the basis of which they have inferred the

---

[6] See the Introduction to my Chihara 2004.

existence and properties of such unobservable entities as positrons and quarks. What then rationally justifies the mathematician's (hypothesized) belief that she *knows* the truth of the axioms of set theory? Set theorists have supposedly come up with their axioms as a consequence of just thinking about sets. But how can they arrive at knowledge of the existence and properties of sets just by thinking about them? (After all, sets are supposed to be independent of the desires and intentions of humans.)

In courses in physics, experimental methods and ways of determining the various properties and features of the microscopic entities theorized about are presented and discussed. But no textbook on set theory that I know of provides any experimental methods and ways of determining the various properties and features of the sets about which the axioms of set theory are supposedly given as truths. And though I have sat through courses on set theory taught by very distinguished mathematicians, no instructor of any such course has explained how the axioms were discovered or found to be true. This suggests that there must be a non-Platonic way of understanding the nature of set theory.

There are other problems arising from the Platonic conception described above. No one doubts that a deep knowledge of mathematics is needed to develop, apply, and understand the mathematically sophisticated theories that contemporary physicists use in theorizing about the universe. Yet, if the Platonic view of mathematics is accepted, the fact asserted in the previous sentence implies that a deep knowledge of the existence and properties of esoteric abstract entities—the mathematical sets and numbers which, according to most Platonists, do not even exist in the physical world—is needed in order to discover facts about the physical entities described in the physicist's theories of the world. Why this should be is mysterious. Evidently, these mathematical entities must be playing some essential epistemic role in the physicist's theorizing. But what is this essential role? It is clear that mathematical objects are not involved in the causal processes that occur around us, since they are not supposed to interact causally with any physical entities.

Consider one very common way in which mathematics is used by the physicist theorizing about the physical world: a detailed description of evolving physical states of physical entities is given via reference to a type of mathematical structure. Then theorems proved by mathematicians about such structures are used by the physicist in the process of inferring verifiable facts about specific physical entities. (Here is one place at which the "deep knowledge of mathematics" alluded to earlier comes into play.) Now Platonists will conclude that the mathematical theorems so used have provided the physicist with information about relationships that obtain among the objects that inhabit the mathematical world. But this apparent reference to the kind of mathematical structure discussed by the physicist can be understood in a way that does not presuppose the existence of any mathematical objects.[7] So why is a detailed knowledge of relationships involving abstract mathematical objects required at all?

So far as I can see, no Platonist has as yet adequately explained why the physicist must refer to and discover facts about a realm of abstract objects, which no one can observe or detect, in order to theorize about concrete objects which we can observe or at least detect.

The above are only a few of the many deep problems that one faces if one accepts the classic Platonic account of mathematics.[8] One can, of course, attempt to solve these problems, perhaps by coming up with a new Platonic framework or by revising the classic account in various ways. But should not philosophers explore other completely different frameworks for viewing mathematics—accounts that do not picture mathematics as a science dealing with hypothesized esoteric entities that are beyond detection by our most sophisticated instruments? Such a strategy is especially worth pursuing since the history of philosophy has provided an ample fund of examples of philosophers who postulate some type of non-physical, undetectable substance or object in order to account for some feature of our language or our beliefs—postulates that are now regarded as dubious by most contemporary philosophers. The Platonist's postulation can be regarded as especially questionable, since the various attempts by Platonists to fashion

---

[7] For details about why I make such a claim, see Chihara 2004, especially the chapters on the Constructibility Theory and applications of mathematics.

[8] There is also the problem of how we are able to refer to mathematical objects that, evidently, do not even exist in the same universe we inhabit. See Chihara (2004: chapter 1, section 3), for more on this problem.

their views about mathematics into a coherent and intelligible system of beliefs have appeared to be fantastic or unbelievable to many philosophers of mathematics.[9] Why not then examine alternatives to the Platonic account of mathematics? Thus, that which motivates philosophers of mathematics to explore and develop a non-Platonic account of mathematics (that is, a nominalistic account) can be seen to be no more a superstition than is the impulse motivating statesmen to seek an alternative to a war policy that not only is not working but seems impossible to carry out without additional huge losses of lives, reputation, prestige, and resources.

4. HOW QUINE ARRIVED AT HIS RESTRICTED VIEW OF THE NOMINALIST'S OPTIONS

Let us now consider Quine's view, in *Word and Object*, of the possible positions about the nature of classical mathematics that are thought to be open to the nominalist. Recall Quine's argument, in his lecture, that the thesis of nominalism is false. The only option open to the nominalist, from the reasoning of the argument, is to hold that discourse adequate to the *essential* parts of science can be framed *without the inclusion of the whole of classical mathematics*—some weaker version of mathematics that can be understood without presupposing the existence of mathematical objects may be sufficient. However, by the time Quine published *Word and Object*, he had arrived at his Platonic view that the

---

[9] Thus, Gödel's account of mathematical intuition, proposed to explain our knowledge of sets, has seemed implausible to many philosophers (including this author: see my Chihara 1982). Penelope Maddy attempted in her Maddy (1990) to explain our supposed knowledge of the truth of the axioms of set theory by relying to a significant degree on speculative theories of neurophysiology (Donald Hebb's) and a philosopher's theory of perception (George Pitcher's), claiming among other things that we humans are able to literally see sets. Maddy's theories have also not received much support among philosophers (see Chihara 1990: chapter 10 for an exposition of her views and a series of criticisms). It should be mentioned that she has subsequently abandoned her Platonic views about the existence of sets. Another Platonist, James Brown, has argued: "We have mathematical knowledge and we need to explain it; the best explanation is that there are mathematical objects and that we can 'see' them" (Brown 1999: 45). But Brown's explanations are far from satisfactory. Cf. Chihara 2004: 13–15, and also chapter 10, section 2.

mathematics of the nominalist's scientific theory of the world would have to be limited to only trivial portions of arithmetic. How had Quine arrived at such a restricted view of the nominalist's options? Recall that, as Quine viewed the nominalism–Platonism dispute in *Word and Object*, the ontological options were discussed within the context of considering what should be required in formulating a satisfactory overarching scientific theory encompassing all of the sciences. A number of important decisions were made by Quine in that book before reviewing the nominalist's options. Here, I shall note two crucial ones: (i) it was decided that the canonical grammar of the grand scientific theory would have to be an extensional language, with no modal operators or modal terms; and (ii) Quine, in effect, accepted the thesis that the theorems of classical mathematics are truths. Keeping these two crucial decisions in mind, one will be able to see why Quine would conclude that the choices open to the nominalist, regarding the kind of mathematics she could employ, are limited to only trivial portions of arithmetic.

Having made choice (i), Quine never even seriously considers the option of utilizing modal notions in the development of a nominalistic version of mathematics. Since the little justification provided in *Word and Object* in support of (i) has not convinced many nominalists, Quine's claim (that the nominalist's mathematics must be limited to only trivial portions of arithmetic) has given rise to the development of accounts of mathematics utilizing modal concepts—accounts which allow there to be nominalistic versions of science that utilize systems of mathematics far stronger than elementary arithmetic.[10]

Let us consider choice (ii). Recall that Quine gave an argument, in his lecture, for the conclusion that the thesis of nominalism is false. One of the premises of the argument was that "classical mathematics is part of science". This thesis is repeated many years later in a more detailed form:

Mathematics—not uninterpreted mathematics, but genuine set theory, logic, number theory, algebra of real and complex numbers, differential and integral calculus, and so on—is best looked upon as an integral part of

---

[10] See Chihara 2004: chapter 5, section 3, for a discussion of some of the principal responses.

science, on a par with the physics, economics, etc., in which mathematics is said to receive its applications. (Quine 1966: 231)

Underlying, and presupposed by, this Quinean thesis is the thesis that the assertions (or theorems) of mathematics (i.e. "genuine set theory, logic, number theory,...") should be taken to be *truths* just as the assertions of physics, economics, etc. are taken to be truths. Since this thesis is one that Quine put forward as early as 1946 and, so far as I can see, held without deviations throughout his academic career, and since he never published anything like a reasoned justification for asserting it, it can be assumed that he took the thesis to be an obvious truth not in need of justification.[11] But from the nominalist's perspective, the thesis can and should be seriously questioned.[12] My own *structural account of mathematics* is based upon rejecting it.[13]

One frequent challenge to any philosopher questioning the thesis that mathematical theorems are truths is expressed: "If mathematical theorems are not true, then how is it that scientists and engineers successfully rely upon these theorems in applying mathematics to draw empirical conclusions from true empirical statements about the physical world?"

Consider the case of a mathematical theory T that is expressed as an axiomatized first-order theory. What feature can we attribute to a theorem s of T?

---

[11] An attempt has been made by Gideon Rosen and John Burgess to justify the thesis in question. See their Burgess and Rosen 2005: section 1. For criticisms of this attempt, see Chihara 2006.

[12] Hartry Field questioned this thesis in his Field (1980) by advocating the view that the theorems of contemporary mathematics—in particular, those of set theory—are simply false.

[13] This is the account of mathematics put forth in my Chihara (2004). An overview of the account can be found in "The Existence of Mathematical Objects" (forthcoming in a collection of essays to be published by the *Mathematical Association of America*, edited by Bonnie Gold and Roger Simons), sections 7 and 8. My rejection of the thesis in question is explicitly given and defended in Chihara (2006). My position on the thesis in question differs from Field's in several ways: (a) Field understands the theorems of set theory in the way Platonists do, viz. as genuine statements about what exists in the actual world (and hence as, in effect, metaphysical statements), whereas I keep open the possibility that the theorems of set theory may not be genuine assertions about the world—they may, for example, express something that can only be true in a structure; and (b) I claim that the theorems have a kind of content (see ensuing text) which can be used to explain how the theorems can be applied in science and everyday life.

[T]   Every model of the axioms of T will have to satisfy s.

In other words, s will have to be true in every structure that is a model of T. Sentence [T] expresses what I call the "structural content" of s. The structural content of a theorem does not tell us that the theorem is true; it merely tells us that the theorem is true in every structure of a certain sort. And I argue that one can explain applications of mathematics in terms of the structural content of the theorems—without making appeal to the supposed truth of theorems. By thus avoiding the need to explain applications of mathematical theorems in terms of the truth of the theorems used in the application (as is generally done by Platonists), one eliminates the need to explain how the set theorists have come to know the truth of the axioms and theorems of set theory. A fortiori, it eliminates the need to attribute special faculties or powers of "perception" to set theorists in order to explain how they have come to possess such knowledge.[14]

REFERENCES

Brown, J. R. (1999). *Philosophy of Mathematics: An Introduction to the World of Proofs and Pictures*. London: Routledge.
Burgess, J. (2005). Review of Chihara's *A Structural Account of Mathematics*. *Philosophia Mathematica* 13: 78–113.
——— and Rosen, G. (2005). "Nominalism Reconsidered". In S. Shapiro (ed.), *The Oxford Handbook of Philosophy of Mathematics and Logic*. Oxford: Oxford University Press, 515–35.
Chihara, C. S. (1973). *Ontology and the Vicious-Circle Principle*. Ithaca, NY: Cornell University Press.
——— (1982). "A Gödelian Thesis Regarding Mathematical Objects: Do They Exist? And Can We Perceive Them?" *Philosophical Review* 91: 211–27.
——— (1990). *Constructibility and Mathematical Existence*. Oxford: Oxford University Press.

---

[14] I discuss my overall strategy for using the structural content of theorems to explain how theorems can be applied to draw empirical conclusions from empirical statements in several of my recent papers, such as Chihara (2006: 326–29), "The Existence of Mathematical Objects" above, and "The Burgess-Rosen Critique of Nominalistic Reconstructions" (forthcoming in *Philosophia Mathematica*). A more detailed and comprehensive exposition of the strategy is given in Chihara (2004: especially chapters 7, 8, and 9).

Chihara, C. S. (2004). *A Structural Account of Mathematics*. Oxford: Oxford University Press.

——— (2006). "Burgess's 'Scientific' Arguments for the Existence of Mathematical Objects". *Philosophia Mathematica* 14: 318–37.

Feferman, S. (1998a). "Weyl Vindicated: Das Kontinuum Seventy Years Later". In *In the Light of Logic*. New York: Oxford University Press, 249–83.

——— (1998b). "Why a Little Bit Goes a Long Way: Logical Foundations of Scientifically Applicable Mathematics". In *In the Light of Logic*. New York: Oxford University Press, 284–98.

——— (2005). "Predicativity". In S. Shapiro (ed.), *The Oxford Handbook of Philosophy of Mathematics and Logic*. Oxford: Oxford University Press, 590–624.

Field, H. (1980). *Science without Numbers*. Princeton: Princeton University Press.

Gödel, K. (1964). "What is Cantor's Continuum Problem?" In P. Benacerraf and H. Putnam (eds.), *Philosophy of Mathematics: Selected Readings*. Englewood Cliffs, NJ: Prentice-Hall, 258–73.

Hellman, G. (1998). "Beyond Definitionism—But Not Too Far Beyond". In M. Schirn (ed.), *The Philosophy of Mathematics Today*. Oxford: Oxford University Press, 215–55.

Maddy, P. (1990). *Realism in Mathematics*. Oxford: Oxford University Press.

Quine, W. (1960). *Word and Object*. New York: John Wiley & Sons.

——— (1966). "The Scope and Language of Science". In *The Ways of Paradox and Other Essays*. New York: Random House, 215–32.

5. A World of Concrete Particulars

Joseph Melia

This chapter is not going to be a defence of Nominalism, but it is going to defend Nominalism from some Quinean worries. Like Quine, I find Nominalism congenial. Quine eventually abandoned the position. I shall urge that this was hasty.

1. A WORLD OF CONCRETE PARTICULARS

Quine characterizes Nominalism as the view that there are no universals, only particulars. Nowadays, Nominalism is frequently identified with the view that there are no abstract objects, only concrete ones and it is this aspect of Nominalism that I will mainly focus on in this chapter. Since Quine takes particulars, in both his Mental and Physical versions of Nominalism, to be concrete objects, it seems that the Quine of that time was partial to both views.

In Quine's hands, it is not part of Nominalism that something is yellow because it is called 'yellow', or that two things are the same type because they are both satisfied by the same predicate. It is right to free the Nominalist from these theses.[1] These should be avoided at all costs. Should it be impossible to stay within an ontology of concrete particulars without adopting such theses then I would reject Nominalism.

Strictly speaking, Quine's identification of the abstract and the universal is misguided. There's no reason for particulars to be identified with the causal or the spatio-temporal, and there's no reason to think that numbers or classes are universals, even though they are abstract and outside space and time. The two theses are logically distinct. Nevertheless, I am sympathetic to both versions. But is there anything that unifies the two theses, or are these just two views I, like Quine, happen to be partial towards? I suspect that the unification comes less from the content of the theses than

---

[1] Armstrong (1978) rightly criticizes those nominalists who have adopted these views.

from their motivation. The starting point is that the objects that I am immediately familiar with, the ones I have the most evidence for, the tables and desks and laptops of my surroundings, all appear to be concrete particulars. When this is coupled with a healthy parsimony, I then need to be given good reason to expand my ontology. Accept that scientific reasoning can give us good theoretical reason for expanding our ontology—as it does in giving us reason for believing in electrons and quarks. What the Nominalist thinks is that, at least at present, the theoretical reasons given for going beyond concrete particulars have not been successful—either for abstracta or universals.

I share Quine's warm feelings towards Nominalism. For Nominalism is a *parsimonious* theory. The universals, sets, numbers, propositions, and other metaphysical extravagances are avoided. Nominalism is a good theory for those like me who share Quine's taste for desert landscapes. However, parsimony alone can't be a reason for favouring Nominalism over other monistic theories. If it were possible to eliminate concrete particulars in favour of sets or true propositions or properties then the cause of parsimony would have been served equally as well. What Nominalism has in its favour over other monistic theories is that concrete particulars are overwhelmingly familiar objects—it would be a poor theory that denied their existence. The *second-hand laptop* I'm writing on, the *desk* at which I'm perched, the seven *books*, their *pages* frayed and *covers* worn, scattered haphazardly about the *floor*, the *chair* that supports me, the *half-eaten sandwich* left on the chipped *plate* perched beneath the *window*—all these familiar items are examples of concrete particulars. These items are concrete, in that they all have causal powers and are located in space and time. They are also particulars in that they are not multiply located or multiply instantiated.

Even if our ordinary thought and talk could somehow be paraphrased away in terms of talk of sets and true propositions, it would still be absurd to deny the existence of tables, chairs, and laptops. Concrete particulars are part of a safe and sane ontology: such things as tables and chairs obviously exist and we would need to have very good reasons before we rejected or replaced them. Concrete particulars are as familiar as could be, their existence uncontentious. By contrast, abstract objects, such as numbers and sets, are remote and unfamiliar. That tables and chairs exist is a truism. That numbers, sets, and functions exist is controversial. The philosopher who proclaimed the existence of tables and chairs at dinner parties would be regarded as an uninteresting specimen, confirming her listener's prejudices that philosophy has become a dull and dry subject. The philosopher who loudly proclaimed the existence of *abstracta* at the same dinner parties would be regarded as a fanciful and whimsical character, confirming his listener's prejudices that philosophers do not have a very robust grip on reality. A theory of the world that did without the controversial abstracta would be an attractive one.

It would be nice to go further and to show that there was something incoherent about Platonism. But strong anti-Platonist arguments are unconvincing. Once, Nominalists argued that abstract objects were unknowable or that we could never meaningfully refer to them. It would be nice to accept such arguments, but the trouble is that they are usually equally telling against the theoretical concrete particulars postulated by science. The objects postulated by science may not be part of common sense, but that doesn't make them problematic for the Nominalist. Like Quine, my attachment to Nominalism is tentative. Were it to be shown that there was good reason for accepting abstract entities, I would be moved to reconsider.

Abstracta may be unfamiliar—but what about universals? In this case, the situation is more complex, for the hypothesis that there are colours and shapes is, at least at first sight, not nearly as implausible as the hypothesis that there are abstract objects. But once concrete particulars are accepted, parsimony does at least favour the attempt to try and do without anything else. Moreover, I doubt that it is so intuitively plausible to reify colours and shapes. We are certain that there are coloured things and shaped things. Whether there are *also* colours and shapes is another question. And when one reads of the strange *instantiation* relation the realist believer in universals postulates in order to explain how particulars and universals 'come together', the position begins to lose its attractiveness. Calling *instantiation* a non-relational tie doesn't help—it just names the contradiction. Treating *instantiation* as an extra addition to reality leads to a regress which, though not clearly vicious, is certainly counter-intuitive. What should have been simple—the existence of a red thing or a charged thing, has turned out to be infinitely complex involving an infinite hierarchy of ever higher order relations binding very different things together.

It may be possible to make the story coherent, but getting involved in this story makes one question whether it's something we should ever have been involved with in the first place. The Nominalist has a simple way of avoiding such problems: deny the existence of properties. There just are the red things, the square things, the charged things. Don't think of something's being red as involving a relation between a particular and a property—it's scarcely natural to think of it in this way anyway. The Nominalist seems to have a natural and simple way of avoiding apparently intractable and unsolvable metaphysical questions. That speaks in the position's favour.

Some find this frustrating. They feel that such a Nominalist is somehow dodging serious metaphysics, sticking his head in the sand when he should be rolling up his sleeves and getting down to serious work. To leave things just red or square or charged is a kind of cowardice—it is to avoid the serious theorizing that is demanded from all who take an interest in the nature of the world. And, after all, as we have found, things are not simply red. There is a deep story to be told in this case. The Nominalist's unwillingness to theorize about such matters is really something to be ashamed of. But the nominalist can of course accept that there are deep explanations of what it is for something to be red. It's just that these are explanations that the nominalist can give too. The explanations do not involve the reification of properties—rather they involve the reality of electrons, of light beams of various frequencies. But these are explanations that require only the existence of the things that have been discovered by science.

The realist about universals may counter that the postulation of universals makes good explanatory sense or that he offers explanations where the Nominalist is silent. Even when it is allowed that the familiar scientific account of what it is to be red can be given by both the Nominalist and the realist alike; nevertheless, the Nominalist reaches a brute level where all he can say, for example, is that this thing is an electron, that thing is charged, this thing is five meters away from that thing... and that is the end of his account. By contrast, the realist can go further and give an analysis of these facts: this thing instantiates electron-hood, that thing instantiates charge, these things instantiate the five meters away from relation. The realist offers explanations where the Nominalist gives up. Isn't the explanatory superiority of his theory some reason for accepting his theory? The Nominalist shares Quine's unhappiness with empty theorizing. The difference between the kinds of entities with which the philosophers have populated the universe and the kinds of entities that the scientists have offered us is that it is, at the very least, far clearer that the scientists' entities do good explanatory work. Even if the Nominalist concedes that the realist has an account of what he takes as primitive, it doesn't follow that the realist's resulting theory has greater explanatory power. All explanations must come to an end somewhere, all theories have their primitives. Credence accrues to a theory only when the number of distinct primitives has been reduced. But this has not happened here. One group of unexplained truths has been replaced by another unexplained group of unexplained truths. The Nominalist's theory stops with a charged thing. The realist's theory stops with a's instantiating charge. The Nominalist's theory stops with a massive thing. The realist's theory stops with a's instantiating mass. There is no overall reduction in the number of brute unexplained truths. There is no overall increase of explanatory power. There is no overall increase of simplicity.

Both Mathematics and Universals play various theoretical roles in various enterprises. Examining all the applications to see whether there is good theoretical reason for believing in them would presently be too much. For now, I shall focus on Nominalism's denial of abstracta and largely set to one side the question of universals.

1.1 Nominalism and the authorities

The Nominalists are supposed to be in trouble with the authorities. Mathematicians, scientists, and other serious hard-nosed academics are allegedly in disagreement with the Nominalists. Mathematics and Science are both committed to mathematical objects. Mathematical and scientific books and papers are full of assertions that entail the existence of mathematical objects. Even if the nominalist tries to sweeten the pill, by offering some structuralist, formalist, or fictionalist reconstrual of mathematics and science, the worry is that it is still a revision. Who does the philosopher think he is to tell the scientists that what they say is literally false? Compare the failures of philosophy with the successes of science and mathematics, and we see that, where there is disagreement, it is philosophy that must yield.[2]

I'm unconvinced by this line of thought. It's wrong for the philosophers to ignore scientific and mathematical progress, but it's also wrong for us to think that scientists and mathematicians would even recognize various philosophical positions in the Philosophy of Mathematics as seriously competing with each other, or with their own views. It's not clear to me that mathematicians do take a clear stand on the ontology of Mathematics. It's not even clear to me that mathematicians do believe that there were such things as numbers. Many good mathematicians have publicly written things that suggest that they don't take a Platonist stance and there's been no very serious laughter or condemnation from the mathematical community. In a set-theory class, the lecturer told me that I shouldn't go as far as to *believe* anything that he said, as I would end up like Gödel.[3] There have been Platonists, for sure. Cantor and Gödel come to mind. But there have been plenty who clearly wanted to avoid Platonism. And, at least in my experience, there are plenty more who just don't really care, who want to be left alone to do their mathematics and who, as long as the philosophers respected the fact that what they were doing was very difficult and very clever, would be quite happy to leave it like that. There isn't a clear message coming from either the scientific or mathematical community about the existence of mathematical objects. There is a clear sign that they regard such questions as irritating, and as getting in the way of what they really want to do.

1.2 Nominalism and the folk

Some Platonists might complain that abstract mathematical objects are just as natural, just as much a part of common sense, as concrete

---

[2] See, for instance, Lewis (1991) and Burgess (2002).
[3] On further questioning, after the class, I made sure that the teacher meant 'mad' rather than 'brilliant'.

particulars. They'll argue their case by pointing to common and natural assertions that seem to imply the existence of abstract objects, and point to various truisms that, if they're Fregeans, contain singular terms for abstracta or, if they're Quineans, contain variables and quantifiers for things other than concrete particulars.

'The Number of dogs equals the number of cats'.
'There's nobody that can help'.
'His whereabouts are not known'.
'There are irreconcilable differences between us'.
'There has been a great lack of luck in his life'.

And so on. Though these are not pure existential statements—none of them is of the form 'Fs exist' or 'There are F's'—they all have fairly immediate existential consequences, existential consequences which are in tension with the view that the world contains only concrete particulars.

It has never seemed to me that the plausibility of concrete particulars and the strangeness of abstracta had its roots in the naturalness or otherwise of parts of ordinary thought and talk. One can accept that these sentences are natural and still say that the existence of abstract objects is, unlike that of concrete ones, controversial—even among the folk. The folk might not be completely consistent. Some of their beliefs might be in conflict with some of their other beliefs. Even if these statements are natural, the brute existential ones are not. 'The number of chairs equals the number of tables' may be as much a truism as 'there are chairs and tables' but, at least in my experience of discussing and teaching these issues, the existential consequence of the latter is uncontroversial whilst the existential consequence of the former is surprising.

There are many reasons why this might be so. The statements could be perfectly natural things to say, while the true logical form of the sentences might be quite different from their grammatical form. Do the folk think there's a significant difference between 'the number of dogs equals the number of cats' and 'there are as many dogs as cats'? If not, then it's not clear why the naturalness of the former sentence is reason for thinking that numbers are part of common-sense ontology.

Alternatively, one might share Quine's distrust of ordinary language. For ordinary language is full of apparently referential locutions that it is implausible to regard as existentially committing. Those who reject nobodies, differences, whereabouts, and lacks are not at all at odds with common sense. Even common sense is aware that you can't immediately read off our ontological commitments from the surface grammar of ordinary language. Drawing the analogous existential conclusions from these results in sentences that sound absurd—there are nobodies, nothings, and inflections. Getting from a truism to an absurdity in just one quick step is an indication that something has gone wrong. The fact that people are so willing to assert these sentences, yet so hesitant to assent to the 'obvious' existential implications is a sign that something is wrong. We have no such hesitation about the shoes, the offices, and the book. While it's true that we're not logically omniscient it is remarkable that, in such cases, many are unwilling to commit to the existence of things that are immediately entailed by their common-sense beliefs. The nominalist can say 'of course there are such things as tables and chairs and electrons' and not raise the ordinary folk's hackles. His opponents cannot.

Finally, reason itself gives us reason to distrust the commitments of ordinary language. Consider holes. For all the ink that's been spilled on them, it is a mistake to think that, as well as the bucket, there's such a thing as a hole in the bucket. It's not that, as a mad-dog nominalist, I have an aversion to holes. After all, it seems that holes are spatio-temporally located: the hole is located in the bucket. A believer in holes can make the case that his holes have causal powers: it's because of the hole that the bucket leaks. Moreover, our talk of holes seems to meet many of the relevant linguistic criteria. It's natural for us to existentially quantify over holes: there's a hole in the bucket. We're capable of counting holes: there are five in the bucket. There are true statements about holes involving their identity or distinctness: there's a new hole in the bucket that wasn't there yesterday. We can ascribe properties to holes: the new hole is at least smaller than the old holes. We can generalize about holes: most of the holes in the bucket are small. It may even be good theoretical practice in physics to reason about the behaviour of the holes rather than the background stuff in which the holes have formed, for the resulting theory may be simpler and more tractable in certain ways.

My worry about holes is similar to Lewis's worry about negative existentials.[4] The trouble with holes is that they are, in their very nature, not an *addition* to ontology but a *lack* of it. There is a hole in the shoe not because the world contains more than the whole shoe, but because the world contains *less*. Holes are the very opposite of an addition to ontology. They are merely what is missing in something else. It is perverse to think that we need to believe in something extra in the world in order to account for holes. There is a hole in the bucket because there is *less* in the world than there was before the hole was made—not because a new object has come into existence but because a part of something does not exist.

2. INDISPENSABILITY AND PARAPHRASE

Quine eventually abandoned Nominalism. In the accompanying lecture, he flirts with it, but seems uncommitted in the end. He presents an example of the kind of problem he thinks the Nominalist faces: What is the Nominalist to make of numerical statements? It's not that Quine is in the business of reading off ontological commitments from common sense but, in our more rigorous theorizing, we would like our theories to be capable of marking the fact that there are seventeen cats or that there are more cats than dogs. 'The number of Fs is n', can be dealt with by the Nominalist, says Quine. The appearance of the numeral 'n' can be eliminated in favour of 'There are n Fs'. But it is less clear what Quine thinks the situation is with statements of the form 'There are more Fs than Gs'. The Platonist has a place for this in his system. What is the Nominalist to do?

Quine makes a striking suggestion. The fact that there is a known finite limit on the number of concrete particulars allows the Nominalist a definition. 'There are more Fs than Gs' becomes the very large, but finite, disjunction 'either there is at least one F and no Gs, or there are at least two Fs and no more than one G or...'. Since the number of Fs and Gs are bounded, the ellipsis is, at least in principle, capable of being completed. But, it seems,

---

[4] Lewis (1992) objects to Armstrong's postulation of totality facts in order to provide truthmakers for negative existentials—it seems absurd to expand our ontology to account for a lack.

Quine is ambivalent about his suggestion. A few paragraphs later, he says that it is 'ridiculous' to make the statement dependent on the number of particulars and suggests that he would 'weep' for Nominalism if it couldn't be done some other way.

Quine doesn't consider the possibility that the Nominalist might just give up on 'more than' discourse. Presumably, this is too radical. 'There are more Fs than Gs' has Nominalist content, and could figure in the content of scientific theories. But if he is not to renounce such discourse, then it seems that the Nominalist must find a nominalistically acceptable language which can express it. We have a version of Quine's Indispensability argument: unless it is possible to find a language adequate for certain key purposes that doesn't involve commitment to abstract objects, we must renounce Nominalism. (What counts as *key* is a matter for debate—for Quine, it is the language of science; for others, it is the platitudes of common sense.) To deal with this argument on Quine's terms, a kind of technical linguistic programme needs to be carried out: the programme of finding definitions for various problematic but useful concepts within a Nominalist framework. And so philosophers turn to examine the power of theories that contain mereology, of theories that include a logic of plurals, of theories that postulate the existence of infinitely many concrete objects—or some combination of these. If *more than* can be defined in such a system, then the nominalist can be happy.[5] If not, then it seems that Quine would weep for Nominalism.

Even if the programme failed, I think it's far too early for weeping. There are plenty of promising possibilities open to the Nominalist. Here are five.

1. The Nominalist might simply take *more than* as a primitive, something that cannot be defined in simpler terms. The inspiration is Quine; this is the move that he suggests himself when dealing with the arguments for the existence of universals from truths of *similarity*. Instead of analyzing this notion in terms of shared universals, as the Realist suggests, the Nominalist can take it as a primitive. There is a worry that the availability of this kind of maneuver makes life

---

[5] Of course, given his suspicion of higher order logic, Quine himself would be unhappy with some of these suggestions. But his reasons for this are not due to his nominalism.

too easy for the Nominalist. Whenever the nominalist hits a brick wall, and finds himself unable to define the relevant terms in nominalistically acceptable ways, then he can take the relevant notion as primitive. But while this is an easy option, it's not clear what's wrong with it.

2. It might be open to the nominalist to employ *modal notions* in his analysis. Quine himself notoriously took a dim view of modality, but today, there are many who do not share Quine's skepticism. Of course, a possible worlds analysis would not be congenial to the Nominalist spirit, but a language that included modal operators might be able to find suitable paraphrase. Indeed, the use of modality may well give the Nominalist an easy way of piggy-backing on Platonist ontology: 'if there were numbers and the concrete world were just as it actually is, then the number of Fs would be more than the number of Gs'.[6]

3. It is not clear what counts as a successful analysis. Quine himself, with his attack on the notion of synonymy, has done much to loosen what is required here. Quine finds the fact that his suggested definition depends upon the number of particulars ridiculous. But why is it ridiculous? Is it any more ridiculous than the intuition that an analysis of *more than* should not make what seem to be quite concrete issues depend upon the existence of abstract numbers? If the number of particulars is indeed finitely bounded, then it is open for the hard-headed theorist to adopt an attitude towards 'more than' that Quine himself eventually adopted towards the upper echelons of set theory: the finite bounded statement is all that the nominalist will ever have need of—the disjuncts concerning numbers of entities greater than those that there actually are can be regarded as mere 'mathematical recreation'.[7]

If it is permissible for the Nominalist to use empirical knowledge as a bound on the number of Fs and Gs, then why not use further empirical knowledge to go and count the Fs and the Gs, and just write down their respective numbers—that there are a million Fs and just 10 Gs, for instance. That, too, fails to generate a sentence that is equivalent to the original. But if we're not offering *definitions*, then why is this not permissible? In general, the Nominalist might

---

[6] Field canvasses paraphrases such as these in his (1985), though he eventually rejects them.
[7] Quine (1986: 400).

do away with the concept of *more than*, preferring instead to state precisely how many Fs and Gs there are. Indeed, many of the normal cases of quantification arise precisely because we are ignorant of some feature of reality: there is some proposition that you and I believe; there is some colour that a and b have in common; there is some number that both numbers the Fs and numbers the Gs. A little empirical knowledge, and these could be replaced by 'you believe that snow is white and I believe that snow is white', 'a is blue and b is blue', 'there are three Fs and there are three Gs'.

Of course, this isn't always available to us. Without the relevant knowledge, we might not be able to state the precise numbers. Under such circumstances, we might have to use the *weaker* statement, that the number of Fs is greater than the number of Gs. Under such circumstances, we might not be able to formulate the claim in a way that doesn't involve numbers. But we use the language to characterize the Nominalist world as being a certain way, a way that would be best represented by a sentence containing an unknown number of existential quantifiers. The quantification might be indispensable, but the truth involves just concrete particulars.[8]

4. It may not always be necessary to find a paraphrase. It may be enough to show that the Nominalist's ontology has enough resources to make true the relevant statements. Consider, for instance, those who believe the "tenseless" theory of time. Many tenseless theorists concede that they cannot paraphrase away tenses. Instead, they argue that tensed tokens are always made true by *tenseless* facts.[9] In a similar vein, Armstrong does not paraphrase away statements referring to or quantifying over unnatural properties such as *grueness* or *bleenicity*.[10] Instead, he argues that the truth of such statements is grounded or dependent upon states of affairs that involve only natural properties. The Nominalist also can make sense of grounding—it may be possible for him to argue that, although he has no paraphrase, the relevant *more than* truths are always grounded in how many concrete particulars there are.[11]

5. The Nominalist can challenge the assumption that, because he must *use* sentences containing non-nominalist vocabulary, he must

---

[8] See Melia (1995).   [9] See, for example, Mellor (1998).
[10] Armstrong (1997: 44–5).   [11] See Melia (2005).

therefore believe the sentences that he uses. Van Fraassen believes that scientific theories are merely *empirically* adequate (van Fraassen 1980)—they are right about what they say about the empirical world—so the nominalist might say that these mixed sentences are merely *nominalistically* adequate—they are right in the implications that they have for the concrete part of the world. It may be that there is no way to correctly characterize the concrete world other than by using mathematics, that it is not possible to say *directly*, in purely Nominalist terms, what the concrete world is like. This certainly makes it tricky for the Nominalist to explain what he thinks the world is like, for he will find himself uttering sentences that imply the existence of abstracta along the way. But it doesn't mean that it's impossible for him to convey what the nominalist content of his theory is.[12]

There are many promising routes open to the nominalist to deal with this form of the Indispensability argument. However, there is a different way of developing the argument, one that stresses the *theoretical utility* of mathematical objects. I now turn to this version.

3. SIMPLICITY OF THEORY VS SIMPLICITY OF WORLD

Earlier, we emphasized the plausibility of the existence of medium-sized concrete objects, the tables and chairs that populate our immediate surroundings. But we have good reason to believe there's more. There are also microbes and bugs, there are black holes, there are distant stars and planets, there are subatomic particles—electrons, atoms, and protons. Though Nominalists are stringent about what they allow in their ontology, there's no reason why the nominalist who thinks that the world is a world of concrete particulars should, *qua* nominalist, have any trouble with the theoretical entities postulated by science.

Why go beyond the observable? The purely empirical reason, that theories which postulate such things make the right predictions, is inadequate. It seems possible to construct bizarre and convoluted theories postulating complicated and Byzantine laws or brute

[12] See Melia 2000.

coincidences that do away with the theoretical entities yet which make the same empirical predictions. Outright skepticism about theoretical entities is an overreaction. Instead, we should reject such theories precisely because of their complicated laws and their brute coincidences. The case for the theoretical entities is thus made not purely on the empirical success of the theories that employ them, but also on the overall theoretical virtues that they bring to a theory. The elegance, the simplicity, the unity that results from unobservables speaks in their favour. The better a theory scores on the theoretical virtues, the more reason we have to believe that the theory is true. Insofar as theories postulating the relevant unobservables score well, the theorist has good reason to believe in the relevant entities.

Without some appeal to theoretical virtues, scepticism about unobservables looks unavoidable. Without some appeal to theoretical virtues, all manner of deviant theories, all equally consistent with the data, cannot be discarded. (Perhaps even more radical scepticism cannot be avoided; perhaps even our reasons for believing in material objects are partly because of the simplicity and unity they bring to our experiences.) It is rational to expand our ontology if doing so results in an increase in the theoretical virtues. But now, the argument goes, the postulation of abstract and mathematical objects results in theories that score better in the theoretical virtues. Of course, there is extra ontology—as the postulation of electrons brings extra ontology—but this cost is more than balanced by the *simplicity* and *unificatory* power that the theory gains. The argument here is not so much that the mathematics is *indispensable*, but that postulating mathematical objects is just part of good methodology in general—even for concrete objects. There is parity between our reasons for believing in abstract objects and our reasons for believing in concrete ones.[13]

Earlier, we suggested that the Nominalist give up on finding an interesting analysis of *more than* and take it as a primitive. Now, though, the Platonist can object that this option comes at a cost: taking the concept as a primitive weakens the simplicity

---

[13] A recent interesting book examining the case is in Colyvan (2001), but these ideas appear in many discussions of the Indispensability argument. Field, in the Introduction to (1989), also treats the argument for mathematical objects as a kind of *inference to the best explanation*.

and elegance of our theory. This issue occurs in many places in philosophy. It has become part of the 'cost-benefit' model. Is it better to take *similarity* or *same-type* as primitive, or analyze it in terms of sharing the same universals or natural properties? Is it better to take *necessity* as a primitive or to analyse it in terms of *truth at all worlds*? Is it better to take *is an ancestor of* as primitive or to analyse it in terms of *is the parent of* plus set theory? Is it better to have a theory that has infinitely many one-place predicates for all the different lengths, or it is better to analyse these all in terms of the single two-place predicate 'x has length r'?

Of course, the Platonist will try to do more than show that just a single concept can be analysed successfully in terms of his ontology. A theory that takes *more than* as primitive seems conceptually no more complex than one which defines it in familiar number theoretic terms. The case is supposedly strong only when *many* things that the Nominalist takes as primitive can all be defined in Platonic terms. At that point, the number of primitives is clearly reduced and, though there may be a price to be paid in terms of ontology, the Platonist argues that the overall gain in simplicity is worth it. The Platonist claims that the fact that we are able to define many scientific concepts in a few terms brings a simplicity and unity to our theories. Not only should theories be ontologically parsimonious, they should be ideologically parsimonious too: they should cut down on the number of primitives. The Platonist argues that the postulation of abstracta allows us to analyse a wide range of concepts using these abstracta, and that the resulting analyses yield a theory which is not just more useful and easier to work with, but which results in a genuinely simpler picture of the world. In particular, the case for set theory is made, in part, because of the various ways in which set theoretic notions can be used to help us analyse various concepts, and this in terms of a theory which takes only one predicate as primitive.

While I accept that the theoretical virtues, such as simplicity, give us good reason to give credence to one theory over another, I think that the Platonist incorrectly applies the virtues. I do not think that the kind of utility that mathematical objects bring our theories is significantly different from the kind that is brought by the postulation of atoms and electrons. In particular, insofar as the taking of *more than* as a primitive is seen as resulting in an increase in the ideological economy of the theory, the kind of simplicity that comes with such a definition is not similar to the kind of simplicity that comes from the postulation of unobservables. Reducing the number of undefined terms within a theory may improve the simplicity of the *theory*, but it does not thereby give rise to a theory that describes a *simpler world*.

The point is masked by the different guises that *analysis* or *definition* can play within philosophy. When an analysis of P is offered as some kind of constitutive account of what it takes for P to be the case, then such analyses can result in a genuine simplification of our picture of the world. For instance, a theory which takes just *is an electron, is a proton,* and *is a neutron* as primitive does better than one which takes *is hydrogen, is helium* . . . as primitive. But the sense in which these are primitive is different—they are *metaphysically* primitive. The thought is that these predicates are used to say something about the way the world IS that is *fundamental*, that we have reached a bedrock in our explanations or account of the world, and that there is no interesting constitutive account to be told of what it takes to be an electron, or what it takes to be a proton.

It may be objected that there are cases where simplification of ideology, at the cost of a little ontology, is clearly good practice. Consider, for example, a theory of space that uses only *Betweenness* and *Congruence*.[14] Within such a theory, 'ab is as long as cd' is just 'abCongcd'. Within such a theory 'ab is twice as long as cd' can be analysed as '∃x(xBetab & xCongab & xCongcd)'. In general, for any rational number, the corresponding comparative ratio relation 'ab is m/n times as long as cd' can be analysed within the theory. There is the familiar ontological price to pay for this: we must accept substantivalism about space. If there is nothing at all between a and b, then the definitions won't work. But, the thought goes, the price is worth it. In the absence of such definitions, the various spatial relations have to be taken as primitive—with the availability of such definitions becomes available an account of the nature of space which, despite the extra ontology is, overall, *simpler*.

I agree that, understood in the right way, this account of space can result in genuine simplification. But the account results in a genuine simplification only if we take the left-hand sides of the analyses to

---

[14] Due originally to Hilbert (1902), but developed by Field (1980).

A World of Concrete Particulars | 115

be constitutive accounts of the right-hand side—if we take them to tell us *what it is* for ab to be m/n times as long as cd. When the analyses are understood as making a genuine metaphysical move, rather than as a way of defining within a theory predicates that apply to a pair of objects precisely when they stand in the right comparative ratio relation then the resulting theory can gain the right kind of simplicity. And when the extra ontology is concrete, as it is in this case, then the constitutive account may be plausible. It's not out of the question to suppose that the fact that ab is twice as long as cd *is* a matter of there being a point x midway between a and b, and ax being as long as cd. But to make this move is also to get embroiled in a metaphysical debate which goes beyond the question of whether the various predicates are merely definable. For instance, we might have thought that *distances* were intrinsic to pairs of points, that they didn't depend upon the existence of anything else. We might not have thought that comparative ratios didn't depend upon anything other than the four points being compared—that the fact that the distance between these ends of the ruler was twice the distance between your ends of the ruler didn't depend upon the existence of an occupied point midway between the longer ruler.[15] We might have thought that the structure of space was a contingent matter, that there could be holes in space—and we might have thought it possible that ab and cd stand in exactly the same comparative distance ratio, even when the point midway between a and b happened to be occupied. We might have thought it was *distances* that were really primitive, and comparative ratios were derivative on the distances. But double the distances and the Betweenness and Congruence truths remain unchanged. That, of course, doesn't refute the position—but it needs to be factored in as part of the debate. Issues of arbitrariness also arise. '$\exists x(cBetdx \& cdCongdx \& cxCongab)$' is an equally good candidate for 'ab is twice as long as cd'. In the two cases a very different point is mentioned, yet they can't both be constitutive accounts of what it is for ab to be twice as long as cd.

When terms for mathematical objects are used to reduce the number of primitive physical predicates (as, for instance, in the

---

[15] Note that this echoes Quine's worries about how his Nominalistic definition of *more than* depends on the number of quanta.

analysis of 'x is an ancestor or y' in set-theoretic terms or the analysis of 'x has *such and such* mass' in terms of real numbers) it is especially hard to construe these analyses in a constitutive spirit. For such a construal results in a very strange picture of the relationship between the abstract and the concrete. It's one thing to believe that we could not characterize the massive objects without using numbers; it is quite another to believe that *having mass* is, in part, a matter of being related to a number. It's one thing to think that there are abstract objects, outside space and time and acausal; it's another thing to think that objects have their causally efficacious properties by standing in relations to abstract objects.[16] That version of Platonism has such an implausible view of physical properties, it makes the nature of the relationship between the abstract and the concrete highly mysterious, that it is hard to believe.

Of course, such a constitutive account of the relationship between physical magnitudes and the numbers is not how the relationship is typically understood. Consider Putnam's discussion in his (1975). He points out that expressive power of purely nominalistic theories is limited. Putnam asks us to consider the Newtonian formula for force between two bodies, $F = gM_aM_b/d^2$, and says that the law has a content which 'quite transcends what can be expressed in Nominalist language'. In what follows, he emphasizes just how difficult it is for the Nominalist to express the relevant relationship that holds between the various quantities without the ability to use numbers. Yet, as he also admits, it's not that particular physical magnitudes such as distance *are* really relations to numbers. Rather, "the *concept* 'distance in meters' is an extremely complex one" (1975: 340) and the question for Putnam becomes the semantic question of how 'a physical magnitude such as distance can be coordinated with *real numbers*'. He then outlines a reasonable account of how this can happen: essentially, because the real numbers and points of space share a certain structure, various lengths can be indexed by various real numbers, given an arbitrary choice of unit.

---

[16] Such a position *may* be a version of the Heavy Duty Platonism that Field opposes in [1989]. But Field characterizes the position as the view that predicates such as 'x is r meters away from y' are primitive, and I'm uncertain which sense of primitive he has in mind: whether he means that there is no metaphysical account to be given or whether he means that it is an undefinable part of his theory.

A World of Concrete Particulars | 117

But the fact that the numbers serve merely to *index* various magnitudes indicates the way in which, at least in this case, the kind of theoretical utility that mathematics brings is not of the right kind: it doesn't make for a picture of a simpler world, though it may simplify our representation. Using numbers to index quantities may enable us to say much more complicated things about relationships between the various quantities, but it is nothing more than a labelling device. A labelling device is useful—maybe even indispensable—but it does not result in any simplification of reality: our picture of the world is no simpler because such relationships have become expressible. The actual correlation between the various magnitudes is unchanged whether it is expressed in a language where the predicates are taken as basic and the correlation is presented as an infinite disjunction or whether the correlation is presented finitely in a single mathematical formula. There is a kind of simplicity that mathematics brings our theories. But in the case considered here, it is not a simplicity of the right kind: it does not yield a picture of a simpler world. Simplifying the picture is not the point; it is the pictured that should be simpler.

Similar points hold of the example that troubles Quine: 'there are more Fs than Gs'. To remove the dependency that worried Quine, his definition needs to be extended infinitely—if it's part of a theory that there are more Fs than Gs, this should allow for the physical possibility that there are more things than there actually are. The right definition would involve an infinite conjunction. An infinite disjunction is hard to write down. But with a little set theory, the notion becomes definable. A finite sentence is simpler than an infinite sentence. A theory that contains only finitely long sentences is simpler than one which contains infinitely long sentences. But what is pictured becomes no simpler if it is represented using the finite sentence that refers to numbers than if it is done using the infinite disjunction. No simpler picture of the world emerges. Whether the theorist, God-like, uses the infinite disjunction, whether he introduces a new primitive of the theory, 'more than', or whether he uses set theory to characterize the Fs and the Gs, the relationship between the Fs and the Gs is no simpler. Alternatively, if the Nominalist takes *more than* as a primitive concept of his theory, he does not thereby end up with a picture of a more complex world than the Platonist. It's not as if, in taking *more than* as a primitive, he thereby thinks that *more than* truths are brute, incapable of further explanation. Rather, he may recognize that *more than* truths supervene upon how many Fs and Gs there are. The trouble is merely an issue about expressive power and *more than* is simply there to allow him to say more than he could before.

Mathematics has many different applications in science. Are there examples that would better fit the Platonist's purposes? I end by looking at some examples put forward by others explicitly designed to support this version of the indispensability argument.

4. MATHEMATICAL OBJECTS AND EXPLANATORY POWER

In the previous section I focused on Simplicity. But this is not the only theoretical virtue. The *explanatory power* of a theory is a theoretical virtue. Colyvan (2001, 2002) has argued that the Minkowski geometric explanation of certain relativistic effects gives us a clear example of an explanation which employs mathematical entities: 'the Minkowski geometric explanation of the Lorentz contraction is, arguably, a non-causal explanation (indispensably) employing mathematical entities such as the Minkowski metric' (Colyvan 2002).

But the Minkowski explanation is a *geometric* explanation of relativistic effects—not a *mathematical* one. For Minkowski, it is the structure and properties of *space-time* which accounts for the fact that moving bodies appear to suffer a contraction, which accounts for the fact that moving clocks run slowly, which grounds the difference between an inertial frame and a non-inertial one. True, it may be the case that the only way of picking out these geometric properties is by employing mathematical entities. Minkowski's insight was that, by dropping our old and familiar geometric explanations in terms of spatial and temporal separation and replacing them with a new notion of *spatio-temporal* separation, we could give a simple geometric explanation of relativistic effects. True, when we come to give the geometric explanation of a certain relativistic fact, we may find ourselves indispensably using mathematical objects. But here, the issues that appeared in our discussion of Putnam and Field repeat themselves. The mathematical entities are being used to *index* various geometric properties. It's not because o stands in a certain relation to number n that does the explaining. It's that o has a certain property (which happens to be indexed by number n) that does the explaining. By using mathematical objects, we are able to *pick out* a particular geometric property.

Starting with the fact that *unificatory power* is a theoretical virtue, Colyvan (2002) has argued that the postulation of complex numbers provides unification. Consider the differential equations: (1) $y - y'' = 0$ and (2) $y + y'' = 0$. The real algebra which can be used to solve (1) cannot be used to solve (2) and for that complex methods must be employed. Without complex methods, Colyvan writes, 'we would have no unified approach to solving the respective equations' (2002: 72). But having a unified approach to *solving equations* seems quite a different matter from having a unified account of apparently disparate phenomena. The kind of unification that, say, Newton succeeded in carrying out by explaining various phenomena in such simple terms is different from the kind of unification we get when we find a unified approach to solving different equations. On Newton's account, the tides, the planetary orbits, the trajectory of projectiles *are* all nothing more than examples of massive bodies evolving according to his gravitational and kinematic laws. The introduction of complex numbers does nothing to unify different phenomena in this way. Just because (1) and (2) turn out to be solvable by the same methods, it does not follow that systems described by these equations are manifestations of the same unified underlying reality.

Baker (2005) has argued that properties of numbers can and do play a genuine explanatory role. His main example is the lifestyle of the 'periodical' cicada. Roughly, certain species of cicada remain in a 'nymphal' stage for a long period of time, the adults all emerging, within days of each other, after either thirteen years in one species, seventeen years in another. They mate and die within two weeks before the cycle repeats itself.

Baker asks: 'why are the life cycles prime numbers?' An explanation of this fact is that cicadas will meet less frequently with predators if its cycle is prime. Baker cites Goles et al. (2001): "A prey with a 12-year cycle will meet—every time it appears—properly synchronised predators appearing every 1, 2, 3, 4, 6 or twelve years, whereas a mutant with a 13 year period has the advantage of being subject to fewer predators". A similar explanation applies to species of cicadas that have 17 year life cycles.

Baker fleshes out this explanation as follows:

1. Having a life cycle period which minimizes intersection with other (nearby/lower) periods is evolutionarily advantageous [biological 'law']
2. Prime periods minimize intersections (compared to non-prime periods) [number theoretic theorem]
3. Hence organisms with periodic life cycles are likely to evolve periods that are prime ['mixed' biological/mathematical law]

When the law expressed in (3) is combined with

4. Cicadas in ecosystem-type, E, are limited by biological constraints to periods from 14 to 18 years. [ecological constraint]

it yields the specific prediction

5. Hence cicadas in ecosystem-type, E, are likely to evolve 17-year periods. (Baker 2005: 233)

The point is not just that numbers are referred to or mentioned in these explanations—that wouldn't show that the numbers were playing an explanatory role. The mere appearance of number terms in, say, 1 and 4 are not supposed to be the problem for the Nominalist here. Rather, Baker thinks it is the purely mathematical (2), which he thinks is essential to the overall explanation, and genuinely explanatory in its own right, which makes problems for the Nominalist.

But the Nominalist can explain this specific prediction too without appealing to a general number-theoretic theorem. Begin with the biological fact that cicadas are limited by biological constraints to periods from fourteen to eighteen years. Again, the fact that numerals appear here is not reason for thinking that numbers are playing an explanatory role. Then let the Nominalist reason about how often the cicada with a life cycle between these years would intersect with predators of various life cycles. So, for instance, he will find that a cicada with a life cycle of fourteen years will intersect with a predator whose life cycle is ten years every seventy years. This can be done by long-winded but elementary counting procedures. By contrast, a cicada with a life cycle of seventeen years will intersect with the same predator every 170 years. Going through the cases, which is possible since the life cycle is bounded and since the relevant predators are those with nearby or lower life cycles, we can discover that, in general, when the life cycle is seventeen years, the length of time between overlapping cycles is greater—or, in Baker's words, that intersections are minimized. And this without the general number-theoretic theorem. Perhaps one might object that the existence of simple Nominalist explanations of the same fact doesn't change the point that the explanation given above, which does appeal to numbers, is still *an* explanation. But the Nominalist can say that's not enough. For the Platonist to win, he has to argue that there's been an *increase* in the relevant utility. Here, the Nominalist has at least as good an explanation of the relevant facts as the Platonist. Since he doesn't also have the extra ontology he can still maintain that, overall, he has the simplest theory.

However, even without this response, it is unclear how the *primeness* of an abstract object, a number, is playing a genuine *explanatory* role here. In particular, it is not clear what there is in this example that prevents the Nominalist from again thinking that the numbers are merely encoding information about the life cycles of cicadas. Consider an explanation of the role of mathematics along the following lines:[17] just as lengths share a similar structure to the real numbers, the years share a similar structure to the integers. The shared structure allows us to represent Nominalist facts about the years in terms of number-theoretic statements. In particular, it is possible to index certain periods of time with numbers—one year by the number 1, two years by the number 2, and so on. Certain number-theoretic facts then correspond to Nominalistic relations: if a period p is indexed by m and another period p* is indexed by n, and m < n, then period p is shorter than p*. Of course, the number-theoretic fact that m < n doesn't explain the fact that p is shorter than p*—it just encodes it.

Assigning numbers to years gives us a way of representing how much time has passed. If one point is indexed by m and another by n, then m − n represents how many years have passed. Addition on the integers corresponds to a certain operation on intervals of time. If p is indexed by n and p* is indexed by m, then, if we have an interval s of the same duration as p and an interval s* of the same

---

[17] As Field suggests in the early part of [1980], building on Representation Theory. Note that this part of [1980] is concerned not so much with the attempt to reformulate science without mathematics as with the attempt to show that the kind of utility that mathematical objects offer is different from that offered by concrete ones.

duration as p* sharing an endpoint with s, then the duration of the whole interval will be indexed by n + m. Similarly, multiplication of numbers corresponds to certain operations on intervals: if we have m successive intervals each indexed by n, then the duration of the whole interval will be indexed by the number m × n.

Admittedly, the ways in which the numbers code information is subtle and complex. As with all subtle and complex matters, there can be surprises. If a period p is indexed with a square number m^2, then there are m successive intervals, each indexed with m itself that fit *exactly* into p. But it would be wrong to think that the squareness of the index explains this. Rather, because the encoding is based on a shared structure between the mathematical and the concrete systems, periods indexed by square numbers will have this surprising property.

Similarly, because of the nature of the encoding, cicadas whose life-cycle periods are indexed with primes will coincide with creatures of other periods less frequently than those cicadas whose life-cycle periods are not. It can take some work to show how this correlation occurs, and the fact that there is this correlation may not be obvious from the way in which the initial coding is done. But the properties of the abstract objects are not explanatory of the properties of the concrete system—they are merely correlated with them.

I've talked of mathematics encoding features of the nominalist world. How does that happen in this example? Take a closer look at (2). Though Baker calls it a pure number-theoretic theorem, whether it is or not in fact depends upon how the phrase 'minimizes intersection' is interpreted. Interpreted as a pure number-theoretic relation, then (2) is a pure number-theoretic theorem. But, as such, it has nothing to do with the life cycles of cicadas. In order to apply (2) so that the prediction about cicadas can be made, 'minimizes intersection' must be interpreted as carrying information about the frequency with which cicadas with certain life cycles coincide. It is the connecting of these two senses of 'minimizing intersection' that forms the link between the abstract and the concrete.

It might be objected that, if there were real encoding going on, we should be able to adopt a different code, we should be able to link up the same periods of time with other objects. But of course, we can. We could count in terms of seasons rather than years. In such a

A World of Concrete Particulars | 123

case, the properties of physical systems would have been encoded in a different way. Using this encoding, it would have been periods of time indexed by numbers of the form 4xp, where p is a prime, that would be evolutionarily advantaged.

5. CONCLUSION

The arguments about Nominalism are still far from settled. Mathematics finds many different applications in science. On the basis of some of these applications it may well be possible to find cases where the postulation of abstract mathematical entities brings with it a genuine increase in the theoretical virtues.[18] So far, I see no reason as yet for the Nominalist to renounce his view that the world is a world of concrete particulars.

REFERENCES

Armstrong, D. M. (1978). *Nominalism and Realism: Universals and Scientific Realism*. Cambridge: Cambridge University Press.
____ (1997). *A World of States of Affairs*. Cambridge: Cambridge University Press.
Baker, Alan (2005). "Are There Genuine Mathematical Explanations?" *Mind* 114: 223–38.
Burgess, J. P. (2002). "Mathematics and *Bleak House*". *Philosophia Mathematica* 12: 18–36.
Colyvan, Mark (2001). *The Indispensability of Mathematics*. New York: Oxford University Press.
____ (2002). "Mathematics and Aesthetic Considerations in Science". *Mind*, 111: 69–74.
____ (forthcoming). "Mathematical Recreation Versus Mathematical Knowledge". In M. Leng, A. Paseau, and M. Potter (eds.), *Mathematical Knowledge*. Oxford: Oxford University Press.
____ and Lyon, Aidan (forthcoming). "The Explanatory Power of Phase Spaces". *Philosophia Mathematica*.
____ Field, Hartry (1980). *Science without Numbers: A Defence of Nominalism*. Oxford: Basil Blackwell and Princeton: Princeton University Press.
____ (1985). "Can We Dispense with Space-Time?" In P. Asquith and P. Kitcher (eds.), *PSA 1984: Proceedings of the 1984 Biennial Meeting*

---

[18] See, for instance Colyvan and Lyon (forthcoming) and Colyvan (forthcoming).

of the *Philosophy of Science Association*, ii. 33–90. and reprinted in Field 1989.

____(1989). *Realism, Mathematics & Modality*. Oxford: Basil Blackwell.

Goles, Eric, Schulz, Oliver, and Markus, Mario (2001). "Prime Number Selection of Cycles in a Predator-Prey Model". *Complexity*, 6: 33–8.

Hilbert, D. (1902). *Foundations of Geometry*.

Lewis, D. (1991). *Parts of Classes*. Oxford: Basil Blackwell.

____(1992). "Armstrong on Combinatorial Possibility". *Australasian Journal of Philosophy* 70: 211–24.

Melia, Joseph (1995). "On What There's Not". *Analysis* 55: 223–9.

____(2000). "Weaseling away the Indispensability Argument". *Mind* 109: 455–80.

____(2002). "Response to Colyvan". *Mind* 111: 75–80.

____(2005). "Truthmaking without Truthmakers". In Helen Beebee and Julian Dodd (eds.), *Truthmakers: The Contemporary Debate*. Oxford: Oxford University Press.

Mellor, Hugh (1998). *Real Time II*. London: Routledge.

Putnam, Hilary (1975). "Philosophy of Logic". Repr. in his *Mathematics, Matter and Method, Philosophical Papers*, vol. i. Cambridge: Cambridge University Press.

Quine, W. V. O. (1986). "Reply to Charles Parsons". In L. Hahn and P. Schilpp (eds.), *The Philosophy of W. V. Quine*. La Salle, Ill.: Open Court, 396–403.

Sklar, Lawrence (1974). *Space, Time and Spacetime*. Berkeley: University of California Press.

Van Fraassen, Bas (1980). *The Scientific Image*. Oxford: Clarendon Press.

6. Quine's 1946 Lecture on Nominalism

Peter van Inwagen

Quine has endorsed several closely related theses that I have referred to, collectively, as his "meta-ontology".[1] These are, roughly speaking, those of his theses that pertain to the topic "ontological commitment" or "ontic commitment". The *locus classicus* among Quine's early (that is, prior to the publication of *Word and Object*[2]) statements of his meta-ontology is his 1948 essay "On What There Is".[3] Hilary Putnam has said of this essay, "[I was bowled over] when I read it as a first-year graduate student in 1948–49, and I think my reaction was not untypical."[4] Indeed his reaction was not untypical, at least if I may judge by my own reaction to the essay as a new graduate student twenty years later. Although I enjoyed and agreed with the first part of the essay (the "anti-Meinongian" part), it was the second part that bowled *me* over, the part that begins "Now let us turn to the ontological problem of universals..." (p. 9). And what bowled me over was the ontological method on display in that part of the essay, not the particular things that Quine had to say about the problem of universals. (That is also the part, and the aspect, of the essay to which Putnam was describing his reaction.) But I think the 1946 lecture[5] is a *better* presentation of Quine's meta-ontology than "On What There Is". It would have been a good thing for the development of analytical ontology if Quine had written the lecture up and published it.[6]

---

[1] See my essay "Meta-ontology," *Erkenntnis* 48 (1998), 233–250. The essay is reprinted in *Ontology, Identity, and Modality* (Cambridge: Cambridge University Press, 2001), a collection of my papers on metaphysics.
[2] Cambridge, Mass.: the MIT Press, 1960.
[3] *From a Logical Point of View* (Cambridge, Mass.: Harvard University Press, 1953; 2nd edn., 1961), 1–19. (The essay was first published in *The Review of Metaphysics* in 1948.)
[4] *Ethics without Ontology* (Cambridge, Mass.: Harvard University Press, 2004), 79.
[5] W. V. Quine, "Nominalism," this volume, pp. 3–21. See the editor's introduction for an account of the circumstances of the lecture and the nature of the "manuscript".
[6] For one thing, if he had done that, his delightful coinage 'struthionism' might have become current. ('Struthionism' should not be confused with Armstrong's term

It's all there. (That is, all the meta-ontological theses that are on display in "On What There Is" are presented in the lecture.[7]) And it's set out—so it seems to me—more clearly and systematically than in "On What There Is". True, it is set out in the course of Quine's attempt to clarify certain questions of *ontology*—not meta-ontology, but ontology proper, the study that attempts to answer the question "What is there?"—but that's by far the best way to present a meta-ontology. The most effective way to present a meta-ontology is to display that meta-ontology at work, to use it to clarify ontological questions. The central ontological question that Quine addresses in the lecture is: What are the obstacles that face nominalism—the obstacles that face nominalism whether the nominalist recognizes them or not?

I will not discuss Quine's characterization of nominalism (<C5> – <C9>). This characterization consists in his attempt to say which sorts of entities the nominalist will wish to "countenance". In the discussion of the lecture that follows, I will speak very abstractly, and simply assume that certain sorts of entity are "nominalistically acceptable" and that other sorts are not. (Or, more exactly, I will assume that certain general terms are such that the nominalist—*qua*

'ostrich nominalism'. If I understand this term, Quine *is* an ostrich nominalist: a nominalist because he does not concede the existence of Armstrongian universals; a nominalist of the ostrich variety because—in Armstrong's view—he *refuses to see* that the fact that one predicate can apply to many objects implies the existence of universals.) And that would have been useful, for there has been a resurgence of struthionism in recent years. See, for example, Joseph Melia, "On What There's Not", *Analysis* 55 (1995), 223–9, Jody Azzouni, *Deflating Existential Consequence: A Case for Nominalism* (Oxford: Oxford University Press, 2004), and Putnam's *Ethics without Ontology*, cited in n. 4. My application of this dyslogistic term to Melia, Azzouni, and Putnam should not be taken to imply that I deny the following fact: the struthionism of Melia, Azzouni, and Putnam, like the earlier struthionism of Carnap, is philosophically very sophisticated and is informed by an awareness of Quine's arguments.

[7] But not all the meta-ontological theses that Quine would ever endorse. One such thesis, at least, is present neither in the lecture nor in "On What There Is": that the only "true" variables are nominal variables, that (despite appearances) there can be no such thing as quantification into non-nominal positions. An important consequence of this thesis (important for the ontology of universals) is this: an expression like 'There is an F such that for every x, x is F' is either meaningless or is a disguised way of saying either 'There is a y such that y is an attribute and for every x, y belongs to x' or 'There is a y such that y is a class and for every x, x is a member of y'. (A similar remark applies to apparent quantification into sentential positions.) See also note 12.

nominalist—will not object to anyone's affirming that those terms have non-empty extensions, and that certain other terms are such that the nominalist *will* object to anyone's affirming that they have non-empty extensions.) And I will assume, simply for the sake of the concrete illustrations of the Quinean meta-ontology at work that I shall present, that individual animals are "nominalistically acceptable entities", and that classes, attributes, relations, numbers, and biological species are not nominalistically acceptable. (That is, that any nominalist will maintain that there are no classes, attributes, etc.)

I will, moreover, refrain from discussing any matters relating to the following (very Quinean) thesis ("Nominalism", <C47> – <C52>):

Classical mathematics is irremediably committed to the existence of classes. And classical mathematics is a part of science. The nominalist will therefore wish to repudiate certain parts of science—at least those parts of classical mathematics that commit those who accept them to classes—as philosophically unsound. There is no reason to regard this repudiation as unacceptable, provided only that the nominalist "leaves us with" enough of science that our ability to predict experience is unimpaired. The problem that faces the nominalist, therefore, is this: to provide a nominalistically acceptable reconstruction of science that, while it discards much of classical mathematics, does not adversely affect our ability to predict experience.

Again, I will speak very abstractly and assume only that some of the declarative sentences we use (in science or in everyday life or in any other area or context) are regarded by the nominalist as indispensable. Indispensable, that is, to the nominalist's own projects and interests: sentences that the nominalist, for whatever reason, is not willing simply to discard, sentences that the nominalist will, for whatever reason, wish sometimes to use as vehicles of assertive utterance.

I will consider two sentences, each of which I will assume (without argument) that the nominalist will not wish simply to "discard".[8] Rather than simply recapitulate the meta-ontological theses

---

[8] In the end, it is the ontological implications of *theories* rather than of individual sentences that is the concern of the Quinean meta-ontology. But sentences play a special role in the meta-ontology, for, in Quine's view, a theory is identical with the set of sentences it "endorses", and the ontological implications of a theory are just the totality of the ontological implications of its constituent

presented in the lecture, I'll show them at work—that is, show how a nominalist (a nominalist who agrees with Quine about method in ontology) might deal with these two sentences. In the lecture, Quine himself gives several such examples (e.g. 'There are more dogs than cats'[9]). The examples I shall consider are rather more difficult—too difficult for Quine to have presented orally with much hope of his audience's being able to follow him—and, I think, more instructive.

My first example is taken from a much-quoted passage in "On What There Is":

[W]hen we say that some zoölogical species are cross-fertile we are committing ourselves to recognizing as entities the several species themselves, abstract though they are. We remain so committed at least until we devise some way of so paraphrasing the statement as to show that the seeming reference to species on the part of our bound variable was an avoidable manner of speaking. (p. 13)

Now why does Quine contend that saying that some zoological species are cross-fertile (although I yield to no one in my admiration of Quine's conservatism in matters of English usage, I'm going to omit the dieresis in the sequel) commits one prima facie—as one might put it—to the existence of species? The reason is simple: 'Some zoological species are cross-fertile' is, prima facie, represented in the idiom of quantifiers and bound variables like this:

(1) There is an x and there is a y such that x is a zoological species and y is a zoological species and x is not identical with y and x and y are cross-fertile.

sentences. It is individual sentences, moreover, to which the technique of "paraphrase" is applied. (What sentences *does* a given theory "endorse"? The question has a clear answer only if the "given theory" is an axiomatic theory: exactly those sentences that are logical consequences—first-order logical consequences, the only consequences that can properly be called "logical"—of its axioms. And that means that the question 'What are the ontological implications of Theory X?' may well have no clear answer if "Theory X" is not a first-order axiomatic theory.)

[9] Curiously, Quine's discussion of this example (<C72> - <C82a>) contains a trivial mathematical error—the only one, I'm sure, in the whole Quinean corpus. The error is his assertion that if there are k "quanta in all space-time," the number of particulars is 2^k. (The error made its first appearance at <C12>). A set with k members has 2^k subsets, true, but Quine apparently overlooked the fact that this count includes the empty set, which has no fusion. (If he had wished to affirm the existence of the "the null individual", he would certainly have said so.) The right number is therefore $2^k - 1$.

We could put the matter this way. All textbooks of "symbolic logic" contain exercises in "symbolization". Suppose one such textbook contained (in the section on predicate logic with identity) the following exercise:

Symbolize 'Some zoological species are cross-fertile'. Use these predicate-letters: 'Sx' ['x is a zoological species']; 'Cxy' ['x and y are cross-fertile'].

The student who produced '∃x ∃y (Sx & Sy & $\sim x = y$ & Cxy)' would, of course, be rewarded with a smiley face. We may therefore say that the student's sentence is a "symbolization" of 'Some zoological species are cross-fertile'. And we may say the same thing of sentence (1), for the fact that the student's sentence contains symbols that are not words of English does not mark any significant difference between that sentence and (1). After all, the English words are symbols, too, and "logical symbols" like '∃' and '$\sim$' are no more than abbreviations for words and phrases of English or of some other natural language.[10]

The rules of inference that will be found somewhere in the same imaginary (but typical) logic textbook in which we found our exercise in symbolization tell us that we may validly deduce

There is an x such that x is a zoological species

from sentence (1).[11] And 'There is an x such that x is a zoological species' is another way of saying—indeed, it is *the* way of saying—that at least one zoological species exists. And that statement is incompatible with nominalism. (The "variables" 'x' and 'y', Quine tells us, are simply third-person-singular pronouns. The sentence 'There is an x such that x is a zoological species' differs from

It is true of at least one thing that *it* is such that *it* is a zoological species

in no important way; the two sentences are notational variants. This example, however, illustrates only the simplest case of "variables

---

[10] The logic-text term 'symbolization', while it is convenient—and I shall continue to use it because it *is* convenient—is therefore not entirely appropriate. (Is 'Some zoological species are cross-fertile' not composed entirely of symbols?) An entirely appropriate, if rather cumbersome, phrase would be 'rendering into the canonical grammar of quantification'. (Cf. *Word and Object*, 231.)

[11] It is those rules that give "the canonical grammar of quantification" its point: the rules and the grammar are literally made for each other. See "Meta-ontology" (cited in note 1), 21. (The page citation refers to the reprint.)

as pronouns", for 'There is an x such that x is a zoological species' contains only one variable. And, one may ask, what about sentences like (1), sentences that contain more than one variable? If each of the occurrences of two or more variables in a sentence is to be "replaced by" an occurrence of the one pronoun 'it', it will be necessary to indicate the antecedent of each occurrence of 'it' explicitly. Here is a way to do this (illustrated in application to sentence (1)):

> It is true of at least one thing that it_1 is such that it is true of at least one thing that it_2 is such that it_1 is a zoological species and it_2 is a zoological species and it_1 is not identical with it_2 and it_1 and it_2 are cross-fertile.

But we need not invent a device to represent the antecedents of occurrences of third-person-singular pronouns, for the device already exists. Sentence (1) and the it_1/it_2 sentence differ only in details of notation: 'x' and 'y' *are* pronouns.[12])

How shall the nominalist who does not wish to "discard" the sentence 'Some zoological species are cross-fertile' (who wishes in fact to use it as a vehicle of assertive utterance) respond to this argument—this argument whose conclusion is

> A symbolization of 'At least one zoological species exists' follows by the rules of textbook logic from a symbolization of 'Some zoological species are cross-fertile'?

The answer is simple. The nominalist must insist that he or she *does not accept* sentence (1) as a symbolization of 'Some zoological species are cross-fertile'—as a rendering of that sentence into the canonical grammar of quantification.

"But," a critic of nominalism may reply, "the symbolization is the obvious one. After all, the student who offered it got the smiley face."

---

[12] If an argument is wanted for the thesis mentioned in note 7—that the only true variables are nominal variables—it would be the following. If there are non-nominal variables, they cannot be pronouns, for pronouns occupy nominal positions. But then what are non-nominal variables? "Pro-adjectives?" "Pro-verbs [as opposed to proverbs]?" "Pro-sentences?" No such items are to be found in natural language, and it is doubtful whether the idea of a pro-adjective (etc.) makes any sense. The premises of this argument can be, and have been, disputed. An evaluation of the argument lies outside the scope of this chapter.

"Well, yes. But the student was right only in relation to the two predicates that were given in the exercise.[13] The exercise in effect invites the student to suppose that those two predicates have non-empty extensions, a fact testified to by the fact that the student's sentence is true only if those two predicates have non-empty extensions—and I, nominalist that I am, deny that they have non-empty extensions. I would symbolize the sentence using other predicates than those two, predicates whose extensions comprise only nominalistically acceptable entities."

"And what would those predicates be? How would *you* render 'Some zoological species are cross-fertile' into the canonical grammar of quantification? (You can't just beg off doing that. If you don't endorse *some* rendering of this sentence into the canonical grammar, there will be no way for us, your critics, to determine what you take the logical consequences of the sentence to be. And you agree, don't you, that responsible philosophers will wish to make it clear what are the logical consequences of the sentences they use to make assertive utterances?)"

This question brings us to what Quine has said about "paraphrase":

We remain so committed [*sc.* to the existence of zoological species] at least until we devise some way of so paraphrasing the statement as to show that the seeming reference to species on the part of our bound variable was an avoidable manner of speaking.

("Some way of so paraphrasing the statement ...": some way of rendering the statement in the canonical grammar of quantification that employs only nominalistically acceptable predicates.) This, I will remark, is probably too strong a statement on Quine's part.

---

[13] Earlier, I said, "'Some zoological species are cross-fertile' is, prima facie, represented in the idiom of quantifiers and bound variables like this ..."—"this" being sentence (1). There is a certain tension between this statement and the words I have put into the nominalist's mouth, for the nominalist's words suggest that the two predicates specified in the logic-text exercise represent an arbitrary choice on the part of the author of the text—or of the graduate student who made up the exercise. We may reduce this tension a bit if we assume that 'Some zoological species are cross-fertile' can *naturally be supposed* to have a logical structure (whatever that means) analogous to that of 'Some people don't like each other' or of 'Some national capitals are less than 100 kilometers apart', and that the predicates specified in the exercise reflect this fact.

Suppose that a nominalist who wished to "retain" the sentence 'Some zoological species are cross-fertile' conceded that he or she had no such "paraphrase" to offer, and went on to say, "I'm sure there *are* such paraphrases,[14] but I'm unable to find any of them." (Or "... I'm unwilling to take the trouble to try to find any of them.") I think someone who said something along those lines could plausibly claim not to be "committed" to the existence of zoological species. But that sort of response to the argument seems rather lame, and there is no need for it in the present case, because nominalistically acceptable paraphrases of 'Some zoological species are cross-fertile' are not hard to come by. I will give an example of one. This example—purely illustrative—makes use of four predicates (abbreviated as indicated):

Ax x is a (living) animal
Cxy x and y are conspecific (animals)
Dxy x and y are fertile (sexually mature and non-sterile) animals of different sexes[15]
Ixy x can impregnate y or y can impregnate x[16]

And here is the paraphrase:

$\exists x \, \exists y \, [Ax \, \& \, Ay \, \& \, \sim Cxy \, \& \, \forall z \, \forall w \, (Czx \, \& \, Cwy \, \& \, Dzw \rightarrow Izw)]$.

Informally:

There are two living animals x and y that are not conspecific and which satisfy the following condition: For any two fertile animals of different sexes one of which is conspecific with x and the other of which is conspecific with y, one of those two animals can impregnate the other.

---

[14] That statement, too, is in prima facie conflict with nominalism, of course, but let that go.

[15] If anyone protests that this predicate could be satisfied by a pair of organisms only if there were objects—presumably they would not be nominalistically acceptable objects—called "sexes" such that the members of this pair were "of" distinct objects of that sort, we may reply that we could have written '(x is a fertile male animal and y is a fertile female animal) or (y is a fertile male animal and x is a fertile female animal)'.

[16] Quine, of course, does not like modal predicates, but we are trying to find a paraphrase of 'Some zoological species are cross-fertile' that is acceptable to the nominalist *simpliciter*—and not to the nominalist who also shares Quine's distaste for modality. It is certainly hard to see how the thesis that some zoological species are cross-fertile could be anything other than a modal thesis.

We observe that the paraphrase has a feature that renderings of natural-language statements into the canonical grammar of quantification often have: it resolves an ambiguity of the original. It is not obvious whether, for example, '*Equus caballus* and *Equus asinus* are cross-fertile' implies that *any* fertile horse can either impregnate or be impregnated by *any* fertile donkey—or only that *some* fertile horse can impregnate or be impregnated by *some* fertile donkey. But this is no more than a question about the intended meaning of 'cross-fertile'; it is of no ontological interest.

What is of some ontological interest is this. Our nominalistic paraphrase treats 'x and y are conspecific' as a primitive predicate. But if one were willing to "quantify over" zoological species, one could define this predicate in terms of 'x is a species' and '(the animal) x is a member of (the species) y'. Simplifying our ontology (adopting an ontology that includes animals but not species) has therefore led us to complicate our "ideology"—that is, has led us to expand our stock of primitive predicates.[17] (At any rate, it has led us to treat as primitive *one* predicate that we could define if we were willing to quantify over species.) The other three predicates used in the paraphrase are, of course, also undefined predicates that do not occur in sentence (1). But anyone with sufficient interest in biology to wish to assert that some zoological species are cross-fertile would probably find these predicates indispensable for making other biological assertions and would probably have to treat them as primitives.[18]

---

[17] See pp. 202–3 of W. V. Quine, "Ontological Reduction and the World of Numbers", in *The Ways of Paradox and Other Essays* (New York: Random House, 1966), 199–207. See also Quine's "Ontology and Ideology", *Philosophical Studies* 2 (1951), 11–15. A part of the latter essay (including Quine's remarks on "ideology") is incorporated in "Notes on the Theory of Reference" (*From a Logical Point of View*, 130–8). I have to say that I do not find the remarks on "ideology" in "Ontology and Ideology" and "Notes on the Theory of Reference" very enlightening. I would say the same thing about the brief discussion of the word in the final paragraph of "The Scope and Language of Science" (*The Ways of Paradox*, 215–32).

[18] 'Ax' might be defined as 'x is a member of some zoological species', but only by someone who did not wish to be unable to raise questions like 'Are all animals—hybrids, for example—members of some zoological species?' I note that, strictly speaking, 'A' is not necessary for the paraphrase: 'Ax & Ay' could have been replaced by 'Dxy'.

Our second example comprises all sentences of the form, 'There are n times as many dogs as cats' where 'n' represents the occurrence of a numeral ('1', '2', '3' ...). This example is similar to an example Quine considers in the lecture ('There are more dogs than cats') but more definite. (Quine mentions a similar case: "Other related idioms, e.g. 'there are more than twice as many dogs as cats'... can be handled in ways closely related to this example" <C78>). The example is taken from "Steps toward a Constructive Nominalism",[19] and the technique of paraphrase I shall present is an adaptation of a technique used in that essay. This technique is, I think, more interesting than the techniques Quine applies to 'There are more dogs than cats' in the lecture. It does not depend on an appeal to 'and so on' (the paraphrases are of finite length), and it does not depend on there being some particular finite number of individuals (or on the number of individuals being finite at all).

The object of the paraphrase is to eliminate the numerals from sentences of the form displayed above. Now one might well ask why nominalists would want to have such paraphrases at their disposal. Nominalists do not "countenance" numbers, of course—but *does*, for example, the sentence 'There are 3 times as many dogs as cats' imply the existence of numbers or at least the existence of *a* number (the number 3, if any, presumably)? Various considerations militate against supposing that it does. First, it is not at all clear that in this sentence '3' is a noun,[20] and, secondly, assuming that it is a noun, its being a noun does not entail that the position it occupies is subject to existential generalization. If the occurrence of '3' in our sentence is a noun, that fact does not entail that

There are 3 times as many dogs as cats

hence,

For some x, there are x times as many dogs as cats

---

[19] Nelson Goodman and W. V. Quine, "Steps toward a Constructive Nominalism," *Journal of Symbolic Logic* 12 (1947), 105–22.

[20] That '3' does not function as a noun in 'There are 3 times as many dogs as cats' is strongly suggested, if it is not entailed, by the fact that one cannot substitute the noun-phrase 'the number 3' for '3' in this sentence: 'There are the number 3 times as many dogs as cats' is ungrammatical. (Compare this case with the case of the occurrences of '3' in the sentences '3 is the square root of 9' and 'The number of planets is greater than 3'; these occurrences pass the "substitution test".)

is a valid argument. After all, as Quine observes, the undoubted fact that the final word of 'He did it for my sake' is a noun does not entail that

>He did it for my sake

hence,

>For some x, he did it for my x

is a valid argument. (To use a word that Quine was fond of, the occurrence of '3' in 'There are 3 times as many dogs as cats' may be syncategorematic.) These reflections show that the nominalist's interest in eliminating occurrences of numerals by paraphrase is not so straightforward as the nominalist's interest in eliminating apparent quantification over species by paraphrase.

Why, then, should Quine suppose that nominalists would be interested in "paraphrasing away" the occurrences of numerals in sentences of the form 'There are n times as many dogs as cats'? I suppose Quine would answer that the nominalist's vocabulary, like Caesar's wife, must be above suspicion. A nominalist who accepted this answer might present it in more detail as follows:

> Let us call a sentence *numerical* if it in any way involves numerical vocabulary. There are many numerical sentences that I, despite my denial that there are such objects as numbers, am not willing simply to discard, and (given that it is factually right) 'There are 3 times as many dogs as cats' is certainly one of them. Of the two options,
>
> - continue to use this sentence as a vehicle of assertive utterance, and insist, legalistically, that it has not been *demonstrated* that the assertions I make when I so use it are true only if there is such an object as the number 3
> - continue to use this sentence as a vehicle of assertive utterance, all the while having "in reserve" a paraphrase of the sentence that I should be willing to use in its place if anyone contended that the assertions I made by uttering 'There are 3 times as many dogs as cats' would be true only if there were such an object as the number 3—a paraphrase such that no one, the objector included, would suppose that its truth depended on the

existence of the number 3 or any other nominalistically unacceptable object,

the second is obviously superior to the first.

Now the paraphrase. The intuitive idea is this: we take an imaginary "bite" from each dog and an imaginary bite from each cat, all these bites being of the same size (= volume); if there are n times as many dogs as cats, then the fusion (sum) of the "dog-bites" will be n times the size of the fusion of the cat-bites; this will reduce our problem to the problem of expressing for each n the thesis that one object is n times the size of another in nominalistically acceptable terms.

The primitive non-logical vocabulary we shall use in the paraphrases comprises four items: 'x is a dog', 'x is a cat', 'x is a part of y', and 'x is the same size as y'. We shall make use of various items of mereological vocabulary that can be defined in terms of 'part'— 'proper part', 'overlap', 'fusion/sum of', and so on. We proceed to define some words and phrases in terms of our four primitives:

—an "animal" is either a dog or a cat

—a "dog-biter" is any object that overlaps every dog and overlaps nothing but fusions of parts of dogs; alternatively, a dog-biter is any part of the fusion of all dogs that overlaps every dog (and similarly for "cat-biter")

—a "biter" is either a dog-biter or a cat-biter

—for any biter x, an object y is "one of x's bites" or "an x-bite" if y is, for some animal, the *largest* part of x that is a part of that animal; that is, y is a part of x and a part of some animal, and y is not a *proper* part of anything that is both a part of x and a part of that animal[21]

—two biters x and y are "comparable" if everything that is either an x-bite or a y-bite is of the same size as any other such thing.

We note that it is obvious that, for any positive integer n, there are n times as many dogs as cats if and only if

For every x and for every y (if x is a dog-biter and y is a cat-biter and x and y are comparable, then x is n times the size of y).

---

[21] A biter is thus the sum or fusion of its constituent bites. (Cf. the statement of the "intuitive idea" behind the paraphrase in the text.)

What we must do, therefore, is to show how, for every numeral in the sequence '1', '2', '3', ..., to express in the vocabulary we have at our disposal the sentence that consists of 'x is' followed by that numeral followed by 'times the size of y'. We do this as follows. We express

x is 1 times the size of y

as

> For some z, z is a part of x and every part of x overlaps z and z is the same size as y. (This expression is equivalent to 'x is the same size as y'; we offer this elaborate paraphrase of 'x is 1 times the size of y' so that our paraphrase in the '1 times' case may be seen as an instance of the same technique we shall employ for '2 times', '3 times', etc.)

We express

x is 2 times the size of y

as

> For some z and for some w, z is a part of x and w is a part of x, and z and w do not overlap, and for all y (if y is a part of x, y overlaps z or y overlaps w), and z is the same size as w, and z is the same size as y.

We express

x is 3 times the size of y

as

> For some z, w, and v (z, w, and v are parts of x, and z, w, and v do not overlap, and every part of x overlaps z or w or v, and z, w, v, and y are all of the same size).

(In this last case, I have used a few informal abbreviations; the unabbreviated sentence would be well-nigh impossible to parse.) And so for each successive numeral in the sequence. Our paraphrase of 'There are 3 times as many dogs as cats' is thus,

> For every dog-biter x and every cat-biter y (if x and y are comparable, then for some z, w, and v (z, w, and v are parts of x, and z, w, and v do not overlap, and every part of x overlaps z or w or v, and z, w, v, and y are all of the same size)).

And the devices on display in this particular case can obviously be used to provide, for each sentence of the form 'There are n times as many dogs as cats', a paraphrase that does not contain a numeral.[22] There are two important things to note about this technique of paraphrase. The first is that the paraphrases it yields have ontological presuppositions—and ontological presuppositions that it seems highly doubtful are presuppositions of the sentences of which they are paraphrases. Suppose, for example, that there are no dog-biters. (A sufficient condition for there being no dog-biters is there being no object that overlaps every dog.) In that case, *all* our paraphrases of sentences of the form 'There are n times as many dogs as cats' are vacuously true—an untoward result.[23] I myself believe very firmly that there are no dog-biters (for I believe that nothing overlaps more than one dog). And I believe just as firmly (if you can follow this) that there are almost none of the objects that would be the bites of dog-biters if there were dog-biters for them to be bites of: I do not believe that dogs have "arbitrary undetached parts". And I believe even more firmly that the sentence 'There are 3 times as many dogs as cats' is true or false (whichever it is) quite independently of the question whether there are bites or biters.

The lesson is this: Although the sentences that are the fruit of our technique for eliminating numerals from sentences of a certain form are certainly consistent with nominalism in the abstract, they will not be automatically acceptable to just any nominalist: they will not be acceptable to nominalists (if such there be) who share my taste for desert landscapes. (*My* desert landscape, in contrast with the Quine–Goodman mereological jungle, contains very few fusions and very few undetached parts.)[24] And one would expect

---

[22] Note that these paraphrases make no use of the fact that nothing is both a dog and a cat. The same technique could be applied to, e.g., 'There are 4 times as many Britons as Scots'.

[23] Exercise for the reader: What are consequences of a parallel treatment of 'There are 6 times as many time machines as cabbages'? (Assume that there are all the cabbage-biters and cabbage-biter-bites that Quine and Goodman could wish for, but no time machines.) Hint: Although my dachshund Sonia overlaps every time machine, it is false that she overlaps nothing but sums of parts of time machines.

[24] It would be possible to avoid committing oneself to the strong mereological presuppositions of Quine–Goodman style paraphrases by investing in some ideology—in an extended sense of the word, for additional primitive predicates will be of no use toward this end. Suppose, for example, that we add "plural variables" ('the xs', 'the ys') to our logical apparatus, and that, having done this, we introduce two

that there will be many among the opponents of nominalism who will find these paraphrases ontologically objectionable for the same reason. This expectation is demonstrably satisfied in at least one case, for I am myself such an opponent of nominalism, and I say: All right, you've shown how to dispense with numerals (in certain contexts)—but at what cost! You've had to assume the truth of the Calculus of Individuals and the Doctrine of Arbitrary Undetached Parts; at any rate, you've had to assume the truth of *some* theories that share many of the bizarre ontological implications of those theories.[25]

And now the second point. While our technique of paraphrase provides, for each numeral in the sequence '1', '2', '3', ... a paraphrase of the sentence formed by writing 'There are' and then that numeral and then 'times as many dogs as cats', it does not provide a paraphrase of the open sentence 'there are x times as many dogs as cats'. (That open sentence may not be grammatical, for the reasons mentioned in note 20. It may be that the only grammatical open sentences "in the vicinity" of that sentence are sentences along the lines of 'the product of (the positive integer) x and the number of cats is the number of dogs'. Well, we certainly have not got a paraphrase of *that* sentence that contains no numerical vocabulary—although our technique does provide, for each numeral in the sequence '1', '2', '3' ... a paraphrase of the sentence formed by

---

"variably polyadic" predicates: 'x is one of the ys' and 'there are exactly as many of the xs as there are of the ys'. (For a discussion of plural variables and variably polyadic predicates, see my book *Material Beings* (Ithaca, NY: Cornell University Press, 1990), 22–8.) It is not difficult to construct "numeral-less" paraphrases of sentences like 'There are 3 times as many dogs as cats' using only this apparatus. It is, of course, always possible to insist that 'there are exactly as many of the xs as there are of the ys' is not "above suspicion"—and to insist on this while conceding that 'the xs' and 'the ys' range only over nominalistically acceptable objects.

[25] In note 16, I said, "... we are trying to find a paraphrase of 'Some zoological species are cross-fertile' that is acceptable to the nominalist *simpliciter*—and not to the nominalist who also shares Quine's distaste for modality." One might wonder whether that statement and what was said in the paragraph to which this note is appended are consistent with each other (as regards the ontology that it is permissible for a "nominalistic paraphrase" to presuppose). In my view, the two cases are not parallel. In the earlier case, a modal predicate was needed in the paraphrase because (this seems undeniable) "cross-fertile" is an inherently modal idea. In the present case—so I contend—the sentences to be paraphrased imply nothing about the existence of proper parts of dogs and cats or the existence of fusions of dogs, cats, and their parts.

writing 'The product of' and then that numeral and then 'and the number of cats is the number of dogs'.) The idea of "threeness" is expressed in our paraphrase of 'x is 3 times the size of y' by the number of existentially bound variables—three—that it contains. The paraphrase contains no noun or nominal phrase that denotes the number 3 (or that suggests "threeness" in any other way).

Of course, this is in one sense just what the nominalists want. But it has the consequence that our technique of paraphrase will not take them very far toward the realization of their program. It does not, for example, enable them to provide nominalistically acceptable paraphrases of 'The ratio of the number of dogs to the number of cats is 3 times the ratio of the number of lions to the number of tigers'—or none other than, '(There are 1 times as many lions as tigers and there are 3 times as many dogs as cats) or (There are 2 times as many lions as tigers and there are 6 times as many dogs as cats) or ... and so on'. (This device is, of course, applicable only to the case in which the ratio of the number of dogs to cats and the ratio of the number of lions to tigers are integers.) The nominalist paraphrase project becomes progressively more difficult as nominalists are forced to confront occurrences of numerals—and, worse, variables in numeral positions—in ever more recondite contexts. (What can nominalists say about 'For no integer n greater than 2 and no integer m greater than 3 does a central-force law according to which force varies inversely with the nth power of distance yield stable orbits in m-dimensional space'?) And, as everyone knows, positive integers are the least of the nominalists' mathematical worries, for they must also say something about fractions, negative numbers, irrational numbers, complex numbers, vectors, tensors, ..., all of which are everyday tools of applied mathematics—and all of which are more difficult to "paraphrase away" than integers. In point of fact, the nominalist paraphrase project, at least if it is to be carried out using tools at all like those employed in "Steps toward a Constructive Nominalism", is not simply difficult. It is hopeless.

In the 1946 lecture, Quine professes agnosticism about whether the nominalist project will ultimately be a success. But one might well ask why. In my view, the most interesting historical question about Quine's early advocacy of nominalism and his work on this topic with Goodman is this: Why didn't he concede at the outset that the nominalist project was hopeless?[26] It is true that—as he and Goodman showed—one can paraphrase various numerical sentences into sentences that contain no numerical vocabulary of any description (sentences that convey the idea of n-ness by their incorporation of n existentially bound variables or n bound variables flanking occurrences of the non-identity sign or some such device). But it is just obvious that one cannot do this for the whole class of such sentences. (Not at any rate by the use of devices at all similar to the devices Quine and Goodman used. For all I know, some technique vastly more powerful than any they consider—some technique that involved its advocates in some very serious and far-reaching ontological commitments indeed—might be successful. I am thinking of the devices employed by Hartry Field in *Science without Numbers*[27], a work I am not competent to evaluate.[28]) The "Quine–Goodman project" can be compared to an

---

[26] He certainly conceded this later—as everyone knows. (For a concise and straightforward statement of Quine's rejection of the possibility of providing nominalistically acceptable paraphrases for all scientifically indispensable sentences, see the article "Universals" in *Quiddities: An Intermittently Philosophical Dictionary* (Cambridge, Mass.: the Belknap Press, 1987), 225–9.) Quine's later remarks about his friendliness to nominalism in the middle forties seem evasive and disingenuous. (This friendliness went far beyond a hopeful agnosticism about the feasibility of the nominalist paraphrase project. "Steps toward a Constructive Nominalism" opens with the authors' statement that they think that nominalism is *true*, and anyone who accepts Quine's meta-ontology and thinks that nominalism is true is committed to the feasibility of the nominalist paraphrase project. Saying "Nominalism is true and I don't know whether the nominalist paraphrase project can be carried out" would be, from the point of view of Quine's meta-ontology, comparable to saying "Nominalism is true, but there is an objection to *accepting* nominalism that may be insurmountable.") Consider, for example, this remark, which was inserted as a parenthesis following the entry for "Steps toward a Constructive Nominalism" in the biographical references at the end of *From a Logical Point of View* (pp. 173–4): "Lest the reader be led to misconstrue passages in the present book by trying to reconcile them with the appealingly forthright opening sentence of the cited paper, let me say that I should now prefer to treat this sentence as a hypothetical statement of conditions for the construction in hand." The appealingly forthright sentence is 'We do not believe in abstract entities'. That sentence is given a similar gloss in a footnote in *Word and Object* (p. 243).

[27] Oxford: Blackwell, 1980.

[28] For an ingenious technique that dispenses with ontology altogether by introducing a powerful innovation in *ideology*, see Rolf Eberle, "Ontologically Neutral Arithmetic", *Philosophia* 4 (1974), 67–94. As in note 24, I use 'ideology' in an extended sense. Eberle's ideology overlaps the standard ideology of first-order formal theories only in that its items include the usual sentential connectives and sentences containing free variables. To this base Eberle adds a single very powerful variable-binding

attempt to reach the moon by climbing ever-higher trees (or, since Quine and Goodman have spoken of "steps", by walking toward the horizon at moonrise): not only should any reasonable person be aware at the outset that you can't get there that way, but that same reasonable person should be aware at the outset that the distance you can travel by that method is not even a significant portion of the distance you would have to travel to get there.

But attempts can be instructive even if they are failures—even if they are abject failures. The value of Quine's lecture is not to be measured by its failure to make any significant progress toward a goal that is—as he should have seen—impossible. It is to be measured by the enduring value of the tools that he introduced to define and clarify that goal. Its value is to be found in its demonstration, by example, of the way in which an ontological project should be undertaken, and not in the particular ontological project that provided the example. Its value lies in its contributions to meta-ontology, not in its contributions to ontology.

operator (he does not need quantifiers as separate items of his ideology, since they can be defined in terms of his primitive variable-binding operator). I think it probable that many nominalists will contend that this operator is not "above suspicion". It should be noted that Eberle's technique applies only to integers and that it is not obvious whether a parallel treatment of the real numbers (or even of fractions) is possible.

Part II

SOME PRINCIPLES CONCERNING DEPENDENCE AND NECESSITY

7. Ceteris Absentibus Physicalism

Stephan Leuenberger

1. INTRODUCTION

In a slogan, microphysicalism is the view that there is nothing over and above microphysical facts in our world. But how are we supposed to understand this slogan? There is a popular picturesque explanation: once God had created all the microphysical facts, He was done creating the world as it is; there was nothing left for Him to do. Clearly, this is merely a metaphor, since God's creating the universe is incompatible with physicalism. However, the metaphor has heuristic value, and can guide our search for an adequate formulation of physicalism.

The metaphor is often used to introduce the concept of supervenience, which in turn figures in typical definitions of physicalism.[1] Supervenience comes in different versions, but the standard template is as follows: a class of facts X supervenes on a class of facts Y if and only if there are no two worlds that differ in X-facts without differing in Y-facts. Supervenience physicalism is then the following claim:

SP All facts supervene on the physical facts.

However, SP goes substantially beyond what is suggested in the creation metaphor. For one thing, the metaphor says nothing about worlds in which God's creativity found a different expression on the first six days, while SP has implications for those worlds too. For another thing, the metaphor, unlike SP, is silent about those worlds in which He did not rest on day seven, or chose to resume his work on day eight. I want to focus on scenarios of this latter sort.

Many thanks to everyone with whom I discussed this material, in particular István Aranyosi, Karen Bennett, David Chalmers, John Cooper, Tim Henning, Philipp Keller, Colin Klein, Michael Fara, Jim Pryor, Gideon Rosen, Jacob Rosen, Daniel Stoljar, Robbie Williams, and audiences in Princeton and at the ANU.

[1] Unless indicated otherwise, I use "physical" and "physicalism" as shorthand for 'microphysical' and 'microphysicalism'.

In the actual world, untouched after day six, it is a fact that there is no ectoplasm in the region occupied by the table in front of me. Let this actually obtaining fact be called "$\neg Ectoplasm$".[2] In some other world w_{Ect}, God infused the table with the non-actual, non-physical substance ectoplasm on day eight, leaving all the physical facts unchanged. Thus $\neg Ectoplasm$, true in the actual world, is false in the physical duplicate w_{Ect}, and hence SP is false. But intuitively, the possibility of w_{Ect} ought not to conflict with physicalism as a claim about our world @. Its truth should depend entirely on what God actually did on the first six days, not on what He could have done had He resumed his work later.

This is a familiar problem for the attempt to cash out physicalism as a supervenience thesis, and various proposals have been made to get around it.[3] At bottom, the problem is that SP is non-contingent, while physicalism is contingent. In some possible worlds, there is nothing over and above physical properties. The possibility of worlds with ghostly, godly, ectoplasmic and suchlike features ought not to imply that physicalism, a thesis about the nature of a particular world, is necessarily false.

SP implies that the actual physical facts necessitate all actual facts. We have seen that they do not necessitate $\neg Ectoplasm$, or that there are no ghosts, or no gods. It seems that these are all examples of *negative* facts, as opposed to positive ones such as the fact that I have a non-zero mass. According to David Chalmers's definition, physicalism is true in a world w if all *positive* facts of w hold in every physical duplicate of w. The claim that the definiens holds in our world I call "necessitation physicalism", or "NP":

NP The actual physical facts necessitate all positive actual facts.

Since $\neg Ectoplasm$ and the other examples are negative facts, their failure to hold in some physical duplicate of @ is compatible with NP. Thus Chalmers's definition solves the familiar problem.

---

[2] I use "fact" roughly like some other authors use "state of affairs", or "proposition". A fact is the instantiation of a property by an individual, or of a relation by a sequence of individuals. I use "A is a fact of w" to mean that A holds, or obtains, in world w. Facts need not obtain in the actual world.

[3] For example, in Chalmers (1996: 39–40), Lewis (1983), and Jackson (1994). The first of these will be discussed shortly, and the latter two in section 3.

Ceteris Absentibus *Physicalism* | 147

But there is also a less familiar problem, illustrated by another alternative creation story.

In world w_{Alg}, God on day eight infused my foot with a non-physical substance different from ectoplasm—to be called "algoplasm". Algoplasm makes phenomenal properties disappear. In w_{Alg}, I do not feel an itch in my right foot, i.e. the fact *Itch*, that I have the phenomenal property of feeling an itch in my right foot, does not hold. Since *Itch* is a positive fact, the possibility of w_{Alg} is incompatible not just with SP, but also with NP. But it should be compatible with physicalism, for the same reason as the possibility of w_{Ect}: what God could have done after day six ought not to bear on the question whether our world is physicalistic.

In this second scenario, *Algoplasm*, the fact that there is algoplasm in my right foot, is a "blocker" for the positive fact *Itch*; less interestingly, it is also a blocker for the negative fact ¬*Algoplasm*.[4] Physicalism is compatible with the possibility, though of course not the actuality, of blockers for positive actual facts. After all, its distinctive claim is that the physical facts are sufficient for all actual facts. If God created only physical facts on the first six days and then stopped, the physical facts *are* sufficient. To be sure, the concept of sufficiency here is distinct from the one expressed by the locution 'sufficient condition' in logic and mathematics, where a sufficient condition is just a necessitating condition. It is *ceteris absentibus* sufficiency—sufficiency other things being absent.[5] The "other things", of course, are blocking facts such as the presence of Algoplasm. This concept of sufficiency is then deployed in the following definition: *ceteris absentibus* physicalism is true in world $w =_{df}$ the physical facts of w are *ceteris absentibus* sufficient for all facts of w.

How does this proposal classify w_{Ect} and w_{Alg}? World w_{Ect} comes out as non-physicalistic because Φ, the set of actual physical facts, is not *ceteris absentibus* sufficient for *Ectoplasm*; if other things than Φ

---

[4] The possibility of blockers was first discussed in the literature by Hawthorne (2002). Hawthorne also takes blockers to be conceivable, but thinks that if actual facts like *Itch* are blocked in some physical duplicate of our world, physicalism ought to be false. I briefly engage with his argument in section 3.

[5] Joseph (1980: 777) uses the term "*ceteris absentibus* clause". He explores, but does not endorse, the view that laws of nature should be understood with a *ceteris absentibus* clause.

are absent, then in particular Ectoplasm is absent. Likewise, world w_{Alg} gets classified as non-physicalistic because Φ is not *ceteris absentibus* sufficient for *Algoplasm*, the fact that my right foot is infused with algoplasm.

Ceteris absentibus physicalism is the following claim:

CAP   The actual physical facts are *ceteris absentibus* sufficient for all actual facts.

While I can define my own technical terms, I obviously lack the authority to stipulate what 'physicalism' means. It is a substantive claim that CAP is an adequate explication, i.e. that the truth of CAP vindicates physicalism. I try to make this claim plausible in section 3.

It is one thing to ask how physicalism ought to be defined. It is another thing to ask whether we ought to believe that it is true. Typically, belief in it is justified by extrapolation from the success of physical sciences in providing reductive explanations. However, the legitimacy of such extrapolation has been challenged. In particular, some aspects of the mind seem to resist reductive explanation in principle. This is the upshot of the so-called "Conceivability Argument", or "Zombie Argument", presented in its sharpest form by David Chalmers. The argument tries to establish that physicalism cannot account for phenomenal facts, such as *Itch*. For those, no reductive explanation, or even a plausible sketch of one, has been provided so far, and the argument aims to show that none can be achieved, since they are not even determined by the physical facts.

The Conceivability Argument asks us to conceive a world w_{Zom} that is physically exactly like ours, but differs with respect to facts involving phenomenal consciousness. In particular, I have a so-called "Zombie twin" in w_{Zom}, a molecule-for-molecule duplicate who does not feel an itch in his right foot.[6] It seems that I can easily conceive w_{Zom}; and most likely you can easily conceive a world where your physical duplicate lacks an aspect of your phenomenal experience. From the conceivability of w_{Zom}, the anti-physicalist infers its possibility. Hence there is a possible world w_{Zom} that differs phenomenally, but not physically from the actual world. From this, it follows that SP and NP are false.

---

[6] Usually the term "Zombie" is reserved for creatures that lack phenomenal consciousness altogether. In this example, I use the term more liberally, for a creature who merely lacks a particular phenomenal experience.

Physicalist folklore has two answers. The first is that our judgments about what we can conceive are not to be trusted. We may seem to be able to conceive zombies, but still fail to do so. The second answer is that conceivability does not entail possibility. Even if we conceive zombies, for all we know they are impossible. Both these responses are at least prima facie unsatisfactory.

A *ceteris absentibus* physicalist does not need to resort to either of these unattractive moves. Her answer to the Conceivability Argument is that physicalism is not committed to the claim that *Itch* is true in every physical duplicate of our world, for *ceteris absentibus* sufficiency is not necessitation.

However, an anti-physicalist can claim that in the conceived world w_{Zom}, there are no blockers present, and that CAP thus stands refuted as well. However, it is by no means clear that we can conceive Φ and ¬*Itch* and that there are no blockers present. In section 4 I will argue that we cannot. The upshot is that CAP can be defended against the Conceivability Argument.

In anticipation, my response to the Conceivability Argument can be summarized as follows. There is a possible world that is a physical duplicate of ours where nobody is conscious. But our conceiving does not show that there is a possible world that is a physical duplicate of ours where nobody is conscious, and where there is no blocking fact. The blocking fact prevents consciousness from arising; without it, the physical properties would be sufficient to give rise to consciousness. Thus the conceivability of zombies is compatible with *ceteris absentibus* physicalism.

In summary, this chapter makes two main claims. First, that physicalism is compatible with the possibility of blockers for actual positive facts. Secondly, that it cannot be positively conceived that there are no blockers. These two claims are independent of each other. Together, they entail that the Conceivability Argument fails.

The plan of the chapter is as follows: In section 2, I introduce the relation of *ceteris absentibus* sufficiency. In section 3, I defend the adequacy of CAP as a formulation of physicalism. Finally, section 4 defends CAP against the Conceivability Argument.

I end this introduction with flagging a few pertinent issues that I cannot address in this chapter. Claiming that physicalism ought to be compatible with the possibility of blocker falls short of showing that CAP ought to be accepted as a formulation of physicalism. Some other proposed definitions also are compatible with the possibility of blockers.[7] However, I do not have the space here to discuss in detail what these rival definitions are, what problems they face, and why I take CAP to be preferable to them.

Moreover, I remain uncommitted in this chapter on a number of questions concerning physicalism and *ceteris absentibus* sufficiency. First, on whether physicalism is actually true. While I am sympathetic to the view and think that science has accumulated a great deal of evidence for it, I acknowledge that rebutting arguments against it falls well short of establishing physicalism. Secondly, on whether only phenomenal facts could possibly be blocked. It is a widely shared view that the actual microphysical facts are enough to give rise to the actual macrophysical, chemical, and biological facts. For all I claim here, the actual physical facts might merely be *ceteris absentibus* sufficient for those facts, or they might necessitate them. Thirdly, on what sort of epistemic access we have to the relation of *ceteris absentibus* sufficiency. I do want to claim that it counts as evidence for the physical facts being *ceteris absentibus* sufficient for A if science offers a reductive explanation of A in terms of physical facts. Beyond that, I remain uncommitted. Physicalists are sometimes classified according to whether they think it is a priori or at best a posteriori that the actual physical facts necessitate the actual biological or mental facts. We can likewise distinguish between a view on which the relation of *ceteris absentibus* sufficiency is a priori from one on which it is only a posteriori accessible. What I say here ought to be neutral between these views.

2. THE RELATION OF *CETERIS ABSENTIBUS* SUFFICIENCY

I claim that even if some facts actually give rise to me feeling an itch, they need not do so unimpeachably. Other facts could interfere and block what would otherwise have been given rise to. I then say that the former set of facts is *ceteris absentibus* sufficient for me feeling an itch. For brevity, I introduce another, synonymous technical term 'afford' for 'is *ceteris absentibus* sufficient'. The notion of a blocker is

---

[7] An example is the definition proposed by David Lewis, as noted by Hawthorne (2002).

Ceteris Absentibus *Physicalism* | 151

then defined in terms of *ceteris absentibus* sufficiency, or affording: B is a blocker of A relative to Φ if Φ affords A, but $\Phi \cup \{B\}$ does not.[8] In this chapter, I do not offer a theory of the relation of *ceteris absentibus* sufficiency. In particular, I do not deal with three important questions about it. First, what formal conditions it satisfies. It is non-monotonic, unlike necessitation; but are there any interesting weaker conditions that it satisfies? Secondly, how it relates to possibility and necessity. Affording is not definable in terms of them; but are they definable in terms of affording? Thirdly, whether affording can be analysed in other terms. It might appear promising to specify a "totality function" *Total* on sets of facts such that Γ affords A if and only if $Total(\Gamma)$ necessitates A. However, it turns out to be very difficult to implement this proposal, and I thus prefer to take the concept of affording as primitive.

While I gloss over these theoretical questions, I want to quell some preliminary doubts. *Ceteris absentibus* sufficiency is supposed to be a genuine relation of sufficiency. A *ceteris absentibus* physicalist is committed to the claim that Φ is sufficient for *Itch*, even though it does not necessitate it.[9] Somebody might be skeptical about whether anything short of necessitation deserves to be called a relation of "sufficiency".

Against this objection, I want to appeal to paradigm cases: intuitively negative and universally quantified facts. Suppose F is an alien property. Then no actual positive facts entail that I do not have F. Yet there is a sense in which the totality of actual positive facts is sufficient for that negative fact. Likewise, if ϕ applies to all actual, but not to all possible individuals, then $\{\phi x : x$ is an actual individual$\}$ does not necessitate $\forall x \phi(x)$. Nonetheless, there is a sense in which it is sufficient for $\forall x \phi(x)$.[10]

---

[8] This is a technical term, and does not capture all connotations of "blocker" in ordinary language. A stronger notion of a blocker would require that $\Phi \cup \{B\}$ affords $\neg B$.

[9] *Algoplasm*, the fact that there is algoplasm in my right foot, is just one of the many possible blockers of *Itch*. Moreover, for every actual phenomenal fact Q, there are possible blockers of Q relative to Φ. If B is such a blocker, then Q does not hold in physical duplicates of our world where B holds. According to *ceteris absentibus* physicalism, Φ is sufficient for Q, but not for any of these blockers.

[10] Russell (1956) points out that general facts are not entailed by particular facts. Bricker (2006) and McLaughlin and Bennett (2006) note that although general facts are not entailed by particular facts, they supervene on them.

Another sort of skeptic may grant that sufficiency does not entail necessitation, but object that only negative facts can be afforded but not necessitated. What I call the "unblockability objection" appeals to what is alleged to be an obvious truth about positive facts such as itches and pains: that they are not blockable, unlike negative facts. This is not an objection against the claim that there is such a relation as *ceteris absentibus* sufficiency, but against its relevance for the debate about physicalism.

My own view is only committed to facts such as *Ectoplasm* and *Algoplasm* being positive. Thus it is open to me either to deny that *Itch* is positive, or that positive facts are unblockable. If the objector stipulates that only unblockable facts are positive, she may do so; but then I would deny that *Itch* is positive. If it is not supposed to be true merely by stipulation that positive facts cannot be blocked, then I challenge the objector to argue for it. As long as no such argument is forthcoming, I respond by soliciting intuitions against the principle invoked, using examples outside the disputed terrain of conscious experience.

Prima facie, constituting a statue is a positive property.[11] Consider the piece of marble that constitutes Michelangelo's *David* in the actual world. In a different world, it is an interior part of a marble cylinder. The presence of the mereological difference between that cylinder and the piece serves as a blocker for the positive fact that the piece constitutes a statue.[12]

Being red is a positive property. Imagine that according to the color physics of world w, basic color-making properties superpose to produce different colors. In w, object o has property ρ, which makes it red. In w', with the same color physics, o has ν in addition to ρ, making o orange. Thus the presence of ν blocks the positive fact that o is red.[13]

---

[11] Here and in the following examples, I try to get the hypothetical objector to admit that a given property is positive by her own light. To repeat, this is not a commitment of my own view.

[12] Since this example is meant to serve merely as an intuition pump, I have taken the liberty to ride roughshod over subtle issues about material constitution.

[13] This example suggests the intriguing possibility that blockers may themselves be physical. Except in note 19, I will ignore this in the rest of the chapter. When I talk about the totality of physical facts Φ holding at w, this is meant to include all facts, positive and negative, that involve possible physical properties and relations.

Being disposed to reflect photons is a positive property. Suppose that in the actual world, *o* has that disposition, but is never reached by a photon. In a physical duplicate of the actual world, *o* is infused by photon-absorbing gunk. The fact that there is gunk blocks the positive fact that *o* is disposed to reflect photons.[14]

No doubt there are disanalogies between these examples and the case of conscious experience. But it seems to me that the burden of proof is on those putting forward an impossibility claim. So far, I have not seen an argument against the possibility that non-negative facts are blocked.

3. CAPTURING PHYSICALISM

Suppose that I am right that there is conceptual space for a bona fide sufficiency relation weaker than necessitation, and that *ceteris absentibus* physicalism is actually true. Can we conclude that *physicalism* is true? There might still be a worry that my proposal fails to capture the real content of that notion. My elaboration of the creation metaphor in the beginning of the chapter was intended to allay such suspicions in a preliminary way. Here I address them again.

It is hardly controversial that the term 'physicalism' has different uses among philosophers, and that the question what physicalism is has a terminological component. However, philosophers do not typically vie for the best account of the meaning of a word. Rather, they look for an interesting and fruitful articulation of the ideas associated with it. The concern is that my notion leaves too far behind what philosophers typically have in mind when they use the term 'physicalism'. In this section I discuss objections to the effect that CAP is inadequate because it does not entail certain claims about modality and about explanation.[15] Then I defend the most prominent feature of CAP, its compatibility with the possibility of blockers, by pointing out that it is

---

[14] An example of that kind is suggested in Prior et al. (1982: 253). On some views, the disposition is still present in this scenario, and merely masked by the presence of the gunk. For my purposes, it is not crucial whether what I describe really counts as having a disposition, as long as it counts as a positive fact.

[15] I am fairly loose with my use of the terms "definition", "formulation", and "explication"; they are mostly interchangeable.

also a feature of other, independently motivated definitions of physicalism.[16]

The strength or weakness of claims is often assessed by their inferential role. Typically, only deductive inferences are considered. *Ceteris absentibus* physicalism is deemed weak because it does not imply certain modal claims. However, it is a rather strong claim if we also consider its role in non-deductive inferences, or even more generally what I call its "doxastic role". I briefly sketch important aspects of the doxastic role of physicalism, and then argue that they are captured by CAP.

Physicalism is a claim that is mind-boggling for the scientific neophyte. On the one hand, there is the world of microphysics. It is just a bunch of particles aimlessly swirling around, of only very few different types. There is hardly any diversity, and there are no colors on that scale. On the other hand, the macroworld is motley, rich in variation, and seemingly organized. How could the microworld be enough to give rise to the macroworld? Is there not some extra ingredient needed? Even when we take into account that modern physics posits more than just particles, physicalism may initially be little more plausible than pre-socratic hypotheses to the effect that everything is at bottom just water, air, or fire. *Ceteris absentibus* physicalism is designed to encapsulate exactly that initially astonishing claim: the microphysical facts are enough for the world to be as it is.

Another aspect of the doxastic role of a claim concerns the degree of conceptual sophistication required to understand it. It seems to me that physicalism is meant to be a surprising answer to a fairly unsophisticated question. CAP is a simple claim about the actual microphysical facts and other actual facts, and a non-accidental relation between them. NP is less simple, once it is parceled out. It implies that whatever else there could be besides microphysical facts, none of the actual positive facts could fail to obtain given the actual microphysical facts. This stronger claim implicitly quantifies over all possible facts, and rules out that any

---

[16] I am concerned with physicalism as a claim about the nature of a world. Sometimes, restricted versions of physicalism are discussed, most prominently physicalism about the mental. Analysing such restricted claims raises further issues, which are discussed in Leuenberger (2006).

Ceteris Absentibus *Physicalism* | 155

of them could be a blocker. Intuitively, physicalism is not a claim about such merely possible facts. It seems to me that on that score, *ceteris absentibus* physicalism is more adequate than a formulation which requires necessitation.

A further crucial feature of the doxastic role of physicalism is that it is made more and more likely by the accumulation of scientific knowledge. CAP shares this feature. It has the form of a universal generalization: all actual facts are afforded by the actual physical facts. Whatever is the right story about how universal generalizations are confirmed by their instances should apply to it. Any time science reductively explains a fact A, this is evidence that Φ affords A, and hence the credibility of *ceteris absentibus* physicalism rises incrementally.[17] Thus in this respect, too, my proposed formulation does a good job at capturing the doxastic role of physicalism.

It seems to me that the considerations about its doxastic role make a good case for *ceteris absentibus* physicalism being an adequate explication of the pre-theoretical notion. However, it is not my main concern whether it deserves to be called 'physicalism'. Some philosophers will find that it fails to capture an essential aspect of what they understand that word to mean. What I do want to insist on, though, is that *ceteris absentibus* physicalism is a claim about the relation between physical and non-physical facts that is strong and ambitious, and that has a fighting chance of being true. To be sure, claims that are stronger than CAP are certainly interesting and worth investigating. But if somebody is inclined towards physicalism, but persuaded by the Conceivability Argument that NP is untenable, then CAP ought to be particularly attractive.

I have defended CAP against the objection that it does not honor all the modal commitments of physicalism. I briefly want to address what I call the "objection from explanation", according to which my definition fails to ensure that physicalism meets its explanatory commitments. John Hawthorne describes scenarios

---

[17] I neglect the complication that science also discovers new non-microphysical facts for which it does not immediately have a reductive explanation. In such a case, the credibility of *ceteris absentibus* physicalism arguably decreases. Since it is plausible that the credibility of physicalism decreases, too, this does not count against the adequacy of my proposed explication.

where consciousness is blocked, and argues that their possibility is incompatible with physicalism:

> What spells trouble for materialism is the following circumstance: Some negative fact having to do with immaterial beings [i.e. that no blocking property is present] explains some fact about our world that is itself a positive fact [i.e. a phenomenal fact]. Insofar as a putative definition of materialism is consistent with there being positive facts of this latter variety, it will not do justice to the materialist's commitments. (Hawthorne 2002: 108)

Presumably, what is meant to be incompatible with physicalism is not just that a non-physical fact would figure in an explanation of some positive fact. Physicalism can allow that actual mental facts are cited in explanations of macrophysical facts, as long as those mental facts supervene. Rather, Hawthorne can be read as relying on the premise that if physicalism is true, then no non-physical fact is indispensable for explaining some positive fact about our world.[18]

In response, we can accept that it is a commitment of physicalism that non-physical facts are dispensable in explanations, but deny that the absence of blockers needs to be part of an explanation of a positive fact about our world. There is a complete explanation of the positive facts that does not invoke the negative fact about blockers. To argue for this, I want to set up a dilemma. There are two ways in which we can take the demand for explanation, which I label "epistemic" and "metaphysical".

In the epistemic sense, an explanation of a fact is a story that allows us to understand why it obtains. Scientific explanations in that sense routinely rely on implicit background assumptions, which would clutter our minds and hinder understanding if they were made explicit. In particular, they rely on *ceteris paribus* assumptions. *Ceteris paribus* assumptions take many different forms, and one special case is a *ceteris absentibus* assumption. To be sure, I have not presented an analysis of such a *ceteris absentibus* clause, or totality clause that could be appended to an explanation, and I am skeptical about the possibility of such an analysis. But philosophers of science have not managed to satisfactorily spell out other versions of *ceteris paribus*

---

[18] It is clear why this assumption is restricted to positive explananda: even if physicalism is true, the negative fact that there is no ectoplasm does not need to have a physical explanation.

clauses either, and this failure has not cast any doubt on whether a story relying on such a clause may count as an explanation. Many facts can be explained without citing some of the negative facts on which they counterfactually depend. For example, an explanation of why the planets remained in their orbits for millions of years need not mention that no evil demon came into existence and diverted them. The scope of my claim is very limited: in some explanations, not all facts to which the explanandum is counterfactually sensitive need to be invoked. This does not rule out that some, or even all, facts can only be explained by invoking negative facts. Maybe it ought to be part of the explanation for the stability of the orbits that no bodies apart from the sun and the planets exert gravitational influence above a certain threshold. But while some negative facts may be needed, surely not all of them are.

In the metaphysical sense, an explanation of a fact is a story that tells us what makes it the case that it obtains; it does not need to make us understand why it obtains. In that sense, asking for an explanation of A is asking about what determines A, or what is sufficient for it. Taken that way, the objection from explanation is really an objection against taking affording to be a bona fide relation of determination, or sufficiency. This brings us back to objections addressed in section 2. Assuming that the case for affording can be made, it does not follow on either horn of the dilemma that a negative fact like $\neg Algoplasm$ is indispensable in an explanation of *Itch*.[19]

---

[19] In addition to those mentioned, there is a concessive response that gives up on the letter of CAP. An alternative definition restricts the range of facts that may act as blockers to (non-actual) physical ones: *ceteris physicalibus absentibus* physicalism.

    CPAP   The actual physical facts are *ceteris physicalibus absentibus* sufficient for all actual facts.

My response to the Conceivability Argument in section 4 could arguably be made on behalf of this stronger explication as well, with some adjustments.

A defender of CPAP who rejects NP in effect claims that while there could be physical blockers, there could not be any non-physical blockers. The question arises whether this is a stable position. Is it ad hoc to require that any possible blockers would have to be physical? In defense of this proposal, there is a way to motivate the restriction to physical blockers. Think of the totality of actual physical facts, and that they give rise to certain non-physical facts. These non-physical facts result, in some way, from the physical facts, and may therefore in an extended sense count as physical—let us call them *physicalistic* facts for the moment. (*Being physicalistic* is a world-relative property of facts.) Then we might have the intuition that what

My proposed definition of physicalism is by no means the only one that makes the view compatible with the possibility of blockers. While Hawthorne objects to some definitions on these grounds, I would like to turn the tables on this issue: the fact that it follows from independently motivated definitions ought to support the view that physicalism does not rule out the possibility of blockers.

When introducing definitions due to David Lewis and Frank Jackson, I will assume that there are fundamental properties and relations, and fundamental facts. Fundamental properties and relations form a minimal supervenience base for everything and obey certain recombinatorial principles. Fundamental facts are instantiations of fundamental properties and relations. Ultimately, I deny the legitimacy of the assumption that there is such a class of fundamental properties and relations, and for that reason, I prefer my own definition to Lewis's. But it would require another article to spell out my reasons for this. For the purposes of this chaper, what matters is the claim that physicalism is compatible with blockers, not whether we take it to be CAP or another claim that shares this features.

Lewis (1983: 364) defines physicalism as a contingent supervenience claim. A world w' is *alien* to a world w if some fundamental property not instantiated in w is instantiated in w'.[20] According to Lewis, physicalism is true in world w if among worlds that are not alien to w, no two differ without differing physically. As a claim about the actual world, physicalism becomes:

CSP   Among non-alien worlds, no two differ without differing physically.

is physicalistic can only be blocked by something physical. It is a closure principle reminiscent of one that plays a crucial role in debates about mental causation: physical effects always have physical causes. In the present context, the claim would be that physicalistic differences must have physical grounds—i.e. only differences in physical fundamental properties make for differences in physicalistic properties. The idea is that the physical cannot be interfered with by the non-physical, that it can only be impeached by other physical facts. However, I myself cannot see a reason why blockers would have to be physical, or why we ought to accept the closure principle gestured at above.

[20] Three remarks about this: First, Lewis himself applies the term "alien" to properties and relations, not to worlds, but nothing hangs on this. Secondly, he uses the term "natural" where I use "fundamental". I think he is committed to accept the definition with "fundamental" in its place, but I cannot argue that here. Thirdly, Lewis allows that there might be other features of a world that make a world alien (Lewis 1994: 475).

Suppose that worlds where *Itch* is blocked, such as w_{Alg}, are alien to the actual world. Then even though there are physical duplicates that differ from the actual world, there is none among the non-alien worlds, and hence CSP is true. When Lewis motivates his definition, he does not mention the possibility of blockers. But it turns out that CSP, just like CAP, is compatible with them.

Frank Jackson's definition of physicalism in terms of minimal physical duplication is popular among philosophers. The informal remarks with which Jackson (1994: 28) motivates his definition are in the same spirit as those I have given. He uses the metaphor of a recipe: when God had created the physical facts and stopped there, everything fell in place. This captures the intuition behind *ceteris absentibus* physicalism nicely. Following a recipe carefully might be sufficient to produce a delicious cake; but it is only sufficient *ceteris absentibus*, since if you add a second helping of salt despite not being instructed to do so, the cake is not going to be delicious.

Jackson proposes the following definition: physicalism is true in w if every minimal physical duplicate is a duplicate *simpliciter* (Jackson 1994: 28) Accordingly, minimal duplicate physicalism is the following claim:

MDP   Every minimal physical duplicate of the actual world is a duplicate *simpliciter*.

MDP raises the question what it is for a physical duplicate to be *minimal*. Jackson's definition presupposes that there is a partial ordering among the members of the equivalence class $E_@$ of physical duplicates of our world, i.e. a relation $\leq$ that is reflexive, antisymmetric (i.e. $x \leq y$ and $y \leq x$ imply $x = y$), and transitive. A world w is then minimal in $E_@$ if there is no $w' \neq w$ such that $w' \leq w$. To understand MDP, we need to know what this ordering relation is. Jackson does not tell us much in that respect. Perhaps $\leq$ could be taken as a primitive concept, but if so, we would need to be told much more about it. Alternatively, the relation could be defined. I will consider two approaches below.

Whether MDP is compatible with the possibility of blockers depends on whether $@ \leq w_{Alg}$ holds, where w_{Alg} is the physical duplicate of @ where *Algoplasm* blocks *Itch*. If indeed $@ \leq w_{Alg}$, then w_{Alg} is not minimal among the physical duplicates of @, and we have no reason to think that the possibility of w_{Alg} is incompatible with MDP. Otherwise, we can argue that MDP is false.

How do we assess whether $@ \leq w_{Alg}$? Intuitively, it says that everything that is true at $@$ is true at w_{Alg} as well. This only defines a non-trivial relation if the universal quantifier is restricted to a privileged class of facts. The question whether $@ \leq w_{Alg}$ then boils down to the question whether *Itch*, which is false in w_{Alg}, belongs to the privileged class. There are two obvious candidates for delineating this class, and accordingly two definitions of the relation $\leq$.

$\leq_F w \leq w' =_{df}$ every fundamental fact of w holds in w'.[21]
$\leq_P w \leq w' =_{df}$ every positive fact (whether fundamental or not) of w holds in w'.[22]

If the relevant ordering relation is defined by $\leq_F$, then MDP is compatible with the possibility of blockers.[23] For every fundamental fact of $@$ holds in w_{Alg}, and therefore $@ \leq_F w_{Alg}$. Thus for the purpose of this chapter, I can accept MDP, supplemented by $\leq_F$, as a definition of physicalism.[24]

Is MDP supplemented with $\leq_P$ also compatible with the possibility of blockers? Given $\leq_P$, it is not the case that $@ \leq_F w_{Alg}$, since *Itch* does not hold in w_{Alg}.[25] Since *Algoplasm* is arguably a positive fact, it is likewise not the case that $w_{Alg} \leq @$. Hence the worlds $@$ and w_{Alg} are incomparable with respect to $\leq$. We may assume that for every physical duplicate w of the actual world, there exists a minimal world w' such that $w' \leq w$.[26] Hence there is a minimal physical duplicate w of $@$ such that $w \leq w_{Alg}$. Since *Itch* is a positive fact, it does not hold in w, and hence w is not a duplicate *simpliciter* of $@$. Hence if blocker-scenarios are possible, MDP and $\leq_P$ together yield the verdict that physicalism is false.

---

[21] This is obviously reflexive and transitive. It is also anti-symmetric given that any two distinct worlds differ in fundamental facts, i.e. that the fundamental facts are a supervenience base for everything.

[22] This is anti-symmetric given that any two distinct worlds differ in their positive facts.

[23] Hawthorne (2002: 105) also claims that MDP is compatible with blocker-scenarios. When he argues for this, he does not use the official formulation, however, but rather the informal gloss that Jackson provides.

[24] As noted in section 1, I prefer CAP because it does not carry a commitment to the existence of properties that are fundamental in the sense explained above.

[25] If $\leq$ is defined by $\leq_P$, NP and MDP turn out to be equivalent.

[26] Unless this condition is fulfilled, Jackson's proposal may well give the wrong verdicts. If there is an infinitely descending chain of physical duplicates of $@$ that is not bounded below, then MDP comes out as true, regardless of whether there are immaterial spirits or not in $@$.

4. CONCEIVABILITY, POSSIBILITY, AND ZOMBIES

We should understand physicalism as the claim that the actual physical facts afford all actual facts. But ought we to believe that it is true? In this section, I argue that it can be defended against the Conceivability Argument, or Zombie Argument, according to which conscious experience cannot be accounted for by physical facts.[27]

In section 1, I briefly sketched the Conceivability Argument. It relies on the two premises that we can conceive a world w_{Zom} where I have a Zombie-twin, and that conceivability implies possibility. Rejecting either premise seems unattractive.

Prima facie, it seems that we can conceive that some physical duplicate of us lacks one or all of our phenomenal properties. It is true that although we have privileged access to what is in our minds, we are not infallible in that respect. We are sometimes wrong about what we believe or desire, and presumably also about what we can conceive. But exceptions to the default principle that we know our own minds require an explanation. Kripke (1980) provides examples of how we can go wrong about what we can conceive. As argued by many philosophers, including Kripke himself, those examples do not provide a model for how we could go wrong in the particular case relevant to the Conceivability Argument. The first response is thus undermotivated.

Admittedly, the implication from conceivability to possibility is non-trivial. Conceivability comes in different varieties, and some fail to imply possibility. But zombies seem to be conceivable in pretty much every sense, and hence to resist the argument one would have to deny the implication for conceivability in pretty much every sense. However, a blanket rejection of the implication tends to lead to skepticism about our judgments of possibility.[28]

An adequate response would not just show where the argument goes wrong. In addition, it would account for its seductive

---

[27] I take it that this argument provides the most substantial challenge to physicalism, but I cannot defend that assumption here.
[28] These last two paragraphs evidently do not constitute an adequate response to what I take to be the standard responses. There is a large and growing literature about conceivability, a posteriori necessities, phenomenal concepts, etc. which I am not doing justice to here. I simply assume here that the standard responses are not fully satisfactory.

potential. It is a striking feature of the Conceivability Argument that it seems to us that we will always find its premises compelling. Indeed, they would arguably remain compelling even under the supposition that we had an explanation of the phenomenal in terms of the physical. I here try to offer a response that accounts for this. It relies crucially on my claim that physicalism is compatible with the possibility that phenomenal facts are blocked.

The dependence is not mutual: one could accept my account of what physicalism is while rejecting my answer to the Conceivability Argument, either taking that argument to be sound or diagnosing its flaw differently. Nonetheless, my explication of physicalism is more attractive in a package with the answer I offer here.

Physicalists appear to face the unappetizing choice between denying that we can conceive that *Itch* does not hold while all physical facts are as they actually are, and allowing that something impossible could be conceivable. But they ought not to resign themselves to this predicament. For the argument above does not formulate the relevant conceivability claim properly, since it says of a particular world that it is conceivable. It is not literally true that we can conceive the world w_{Zom}. However, something very much in its spirit is true: we can conceive the proposition $\Phi \land \neg$ *Itch*, which is true in w_{Zom}.

It appears natural to predicate conceivability of situations, as in the passage by David Chalmers below. He distinguishes positive from negative conceivability, and explains what he takes the former to be:

Positive notions of conceivability require that one can form some sort of positive conception of a situation in which S is the case. One can place the varieties of positive conceivability under the broad rubric of *imagination*: to positively conceive of a situation is to imagine (in some sense) a specific configuration of objects and properties. It is common to imagine situations in considerable detail, and this imagination is often accompanied by interpretation and reasoning. When one imagines a situation and reasons about it, the object of one's imagination is often revealed as a situation in which S is [the] case, for some S. When this is so, we can say that the imagined situation *verifies* S, and that one has *imagined that* S. Overall, we can say that S is positively conceivable when one can imagine that S: that is, when one can imagine a situation that verifies S. (Chalmers 2002: 150)

On this account, you are mentally latching onto a situation, as it were, when you are positively conceiving something. Positively conceiving is a relation between a thinker and a situation that is in important ways akin to the relation you bear to a scene you perceive. Such a scene is a particular, a region of space-time, and you can presumably have a *de re* attitude toward it. There is a difference between misperceiving it, and hallucinating another, merely possible scene. When you perceive it first with little and later with more detail, you are all the time perceiving the same scene. Chalmers's passage suggests that you can likewise have a *de re* attitude toward a situation, that it makes sense to ask what is true in *the* situation you are imagining.

Provided that we understand it correctly, ascribing attitudes toward merely possible situations is no more problematic than ascribing attitudes toward propositions that are only possibly, but not actually true. For we can go back and forth between talk of situations and of propositions. Situations are partial worlds, where parthood is understood in a generalized sense, not just spatial or spatio-temporal. A partial world can be associated with a proposition: the class of worlds of which it is a part. Conversely, a proposition can be associated with a partial world: the greatest common part of all its members. Thus even if it takes situations as its objects, positive conceiving can be understood as a propositional attitude. But care is needed if we shift from talking about attitudes toward situations or propositions to talking about attitudes toward worlds.

It is illegitimate to move from "I am positively conceiving a situation in which A" to "I am positively conceiving the world completely described by A". It is not part of the content of the positive conception that the imagined situation is not merely a partial, but a total world.[29] By imagining a situation, or a proposition, we do not latch onto one particular world among the many of which the situation is a part, or one among the many members of the proposition.[30]

---

[29] Yablo (1993: 29) also allows that "I can imagine a world that I take to verify p", but as I understand him, he does not suggest that if I do, there is one fully determinate world that is the object of the imagination.

[30] Henceforth, I omit the alternative formulations in terms of situations.

Can we understand "w_{Zom} is positively conceivable" simply as shorthand for "$\{w\}$ is positively conceivable", and thus as predicating conceivability of a proposition? If the premise were true under that reading, the distinction I just made would not be relevant for the present discussion. However, I will argue that we cannot conceive such propositions with only one non-actual world as a member.

It is a well-known objection to the positive conceivability of maximally specific propositions that worlds are too complex. The relevant worlds, in the context of the Conceivability Argument, are physical duplicates of ours. It is hard to see how we could pull off the feat of conceiving $\{w\}$, if w is of as much physical complexity as our universe. Thus it seems that 'conceiving a world w' cannot be taken to stand for 'conceiving $\{w\}$'. However, I do not want to rely on the objection from complexity. I allow that in a discussion of the Conceivability Argument we can idealize away from that contingent limitation of our cognitive powers. After all, the intuition driving the argument, that given a class of microphysical facts Γ, we can conceive that Γ holds and *Itch* does not, is robust with respect to enlargement of Γ.

Nonetheless, the theory of positive conceivability to be sketched provides a diagnosis of why the Conceivability Argument fails. It is not merely due to our limited cognitive processing powers that we cannot positively conceive a maximally specific proposition $\{w\}$, for a non-actual w. Cognitively enhanced counterparts of us might have attitudes toward this proposition. They could believe or disbelieve it, perhaps. However, I claim that they could not positively conceive it.

Before analyzing the Conceivability Argument in more detail, it is useful to reconstruct it formally. Throughout, I take it for granted that eliminativism about phenomenal facts is false: there actually are facts such as *Itch*. Let M be some phenomenal fact, and Φ the proposition that is true in all and only the physical duplicates of our world.[31] The premises C (for "conceivability") and E (for "entailment") imply that NP is false:

---

[31] I will often use the same expression to stand for a class of facts, a conjunctive fact (possibly with infinitely many conjuncts), and a proposition, when no harm can result. For example, the same symbol "Γ" may sometimes stand for $\{Itch, Ectoplasm\}$, sometimes for $\{w: Itch$ and *Ectoplasm* are true in $w\}$, and sometimes for $Itch \wedge Ectoplasm$. (Occasionally it also expresses rather than names that conjunction.)

C   It is conceivable that $\Phi \wedge \neg M$.
E   If $\Phi \wedge \neg M$ is conceivable, it is possible.[32]

Most physicalists have focused on undermining one or both of these two premises. However, CAP is entirely compatible with C and E. Given that reflection on the creation metaphor gives a physicalist independent reason to commit only to CAP, but not to NP or SP, she has answered the challenge from the argument using premises C and E.

Unsurprisingly, though, we can construct versions of the Conceivability Argument that target CAP. Let B be the proposition that some fact obtains that blocks M relative to Φ. The following modifications of C and E imply that CAP is false:

C*   It is conceivable that $\Phi \wedge \neg M \wedge \neg B$.
E*   If $\Phi \wedge \neg M \wedge \neg B$ is conceivable, it is possible.

The problem with this version of the argument is that C* is far less plausible than C, as I now argue.

I have already noted that different notions go under the label "conceivability". David Chalmers usefully classifies them in his attempt to back up the Conceivability Argument by a theory of conceivability. Here I focus on what he calls "positive conceivability".[33] Above I quoted a passage where he introduces that notion.[34] How should we model the propositions that are objects of acts of conceiving? If we take them to be classes of possible worlds, we lose distinctions among impossible propositions. In a context in which it is at issue whether certain propositions are possible, it is helpful to model them simply as classes of worlds, possible or impossible. Possibility of propositions is then a derivative notion, defined in terms of possibility of worlds:

A proposition is possible if it is true in at least one possible world.

---

[32] Admittedly, this is not an entailment claim. I choose to call it "E" because that premise typically relies on the claim that for a certain class of propositions, conceivability entails possibility. My formulation as a conditional sidesteps the issue how to characterize such a class for which the entailment holds.

[33] I think that if the Conceivability Argument is formulated using the notion of negative conceivability, it is less threatening to physicalism, although I do not have the space here to discuss the reasons for this. Likewise, I cannot discuss a different, but related influential anti-physicalist argument, the Knowledge Argument.

[34] I often use "conceivable" as shorthand for "positively conceivable".

My main claim about positive conceivability is limitative: it puts a restriction on what sorts of propositions are positively conceivable. In the background, there is an "atomist" conception of positive conceivability, according to which we positively conceive complex facts only in virtue of conceiving atomic facts. A full articulation of that conception would require a paper of its own, but I hope what I say here at least makes the claim somewhat plausible.

To state my claim, I define a few technical terms, deploying the notion of a positive fact.[35] Say that a world w' is an *extension* of w if all that facts obtain at w' but not at w are positive. Further, a proposition A is *closed under extension*, or *closed* for short, if whenever $w \in A$, then every extension w' of w is also in A. In logical rather than set-theoretic terms, closed propositions are conjunctions of positive and neutral facts only, not of negative facts. A provisional principle then reads as follows: only closed propositions are positively conceivable. That some positive properties or relations are absent is not part of the content of our positive conceiving.

However, the provisional principle is in need of qualification. If you form a mental image, it may be part of its content that there is no apple on the table. Thus arguably you can positively conceive that negative fact. But this seems to be the case only because you know what it would be for there to be an apple on the table. I propose the following qualification of the provisional principle: we can only positively conceive a negative fact $\neg A$ if A concerns properties of our acquaintance, such as being an apple. To put it differently, we can positively conceive negative facts involving properties and relations about which we have *de re* thought. Such properties I call *familiar*. Being an apple or feeling an itch are familiar properties, while being in a region with ectoplasm or being in a region with algoplasm are not. The distinction between familiar and unfamiliar properties induces corresponding distinctions among facts and propositions. A fact is familiar if it is the instantiation of a familiar property or relation; and a proposition is familiar if it is a Boolean combination of familiar facts. Given these

---

[35] In my elucidation of affording, the notion of a positive fact was just used heuristically. We do not need it as a primitive in an account purely about the fundamental features of the world, as opposed to an account of our epistemic access to it. I merely claim that positive facts play an ineliminable role in our theory of positive conceiving.

definitions, we can formulate the following qualified principle INC ("inconceivability"):

> INC If A is positively conceivable, there is a closed proposition A' and a familiar proposition A'' such that $A = A' \wedge A''$.

In effect, INC denies that we can positively conceive the absence of facts that are both positive and unfamiliar. Informally, the idea is that in imagination, whatever is not specified by you does not get specified by default. In particular, the negation of a fact or the absence of a property does not get specified by default. The limiting case is illuminating: if you do not imagine anything, you do not count as imagining that there is nothing. Unless you make the mental image very specific, what the image represents is indeterminate between many different worlds. With respect to facts that you are not acquainted with, you are not in a position to make the image specific.[36]

Of course, we can accompany a mental image with a commentary, e.g. "no other positive properties are instantiated" or "no blocker of *Itch* relative to Φ holds". This might be one way of having an attitude toward a proposition that is not a conjunction of a closed and a familiar proposition. We may call this attitude "annotatedly conceiving". But the Conceivability Argument with "annotatedly conceive" in the place of "conceive" is not successful. Unless there are restrictions on what the commentary can be, annotated conceivability does not imply possibility. I can positively conceive that Thomas Hobbes is drawing figures and writing symbols on a piece of paper, and add the commentary "Hobbes squares the circle". In this example, the commentary is impossible by itself. The commentary may be possible, but not compossible with what I positively conceive: I can positively conceive that a particle travels at 500 million meters per second, and add the commentary "The particle obeys the laws of Special Relativity". Obviously, requiring that the commentary be compossible with what is conceived does not help if we want to take annotated conceiving as a guide to possibility. I cannot see what other restriction would ensure that it implies possibility.

---

[36] Marcus (2004) argues that we cannot positively conceive negative facts about consciousness (for a response, see Alter forthcoming). Since such facts count as familiar, my account allows that their absence can be positively conceived.

What are the consequences of INC? Suppose that *Ectoplasm* and *Algoplasm* are positive and unfamiliar, and that *Itch* is familiar. Then INC allows that we can conceive that $\Phi \wedge \neg Itch$, that $\Phi \wedge Ectoplasm$, or that $\Phi \wedge Algoplasm \wedge \neg Itch$. But it rules out, for instance, that $\Phi \wedge \neg Algoplasm$ is conceivable.

The falsity of C* follows from INC together with a further premise: that there is at least one possible blocker for *Itch* (relative to Φ) that is both positive and unfamiliar. Without loss of generality, we can take *Algoplasm* to be positive and unfamiliar. Let w_{Zom} be a (possible or impossible) world where $\Phi \wedge \neg M \wedge \neg B$ is true. Let w_{Alg} be a world where $\Phi \wedge \neg M$ is true, but where $\neg B$ is false because *Algoplasm* is true. These worlds do not differ from each other with respect to any familiar proposition. The argument is now this: By INC, every positively conceivable proposition that is true in w_{Zom} is also true in w_{Alg}.[37] However, $\Phi \wedge \neg M \wedge \neg B$ is true in w_{Zom} but not in w_{Alg}. Hence, $\Phi \wedge \neg M \wedge \neg B$ is not positively conceivable, i.e. C* is false.

The assumption that at least one of the blocking facts is both positive and unfamiliar is rather weak. In fact, it would not be too implausible to claim that *all* blocking facts are positive and unfamiliar. $\neg Algoplasm$ and the like are paradigmatically negative facts of the actual world, and hence their negations are positive. Moreover, they involve properties that are alien, i.e. not instantiated in the actual world. How could we be acquainted, or have *de re* thought about, alien properties? If we cannot, facts involving them are unfamiliar.

Although there is a good prima facie case for it, the stronger claim that all blocking facts are positive and unfamiliar is open to challenge. To be sure, we do not stand in any causal relations to alien properties. But I do not wish to deny that there could be modes of being acquainted that do not require causal contact. After all, hallucination and certain forms of imagination might familiarize us with alien properties.[38] Maybe a more gifted writer

---

[37] As noted above, no familiar proposition is true in w_{Zom} but not in w_{Alg}. Since *Algoplasm* is positive, w_{Alg} is an extension of w_{Zom}, and thus there is no closed proposition A' that is true in w_{Zom} but not in w_{Alg}.

Thus we get the following for both closed and familiar propositions: if they are true in w_{Zom}, they are true in w_{Alg}. By INC, a positively conceivable proposition is a conjunction of a closed and a familiar one. Hence every positively conceivable proposition that is true in w_{Zom} is true in w_{Alg} as well.

[38] Johnston (2004) defends the claim that in hallucination, one can perceive properties that are actually uninstantiated.

than me could make algoplasm appear so vivid to your mind that its presence would be a familiar fact. Thus it bears emphasis that in the above argument, *Algoplasm* just functions as a placeholder for whatever blocker of M is unfamiliar. It takes just one unfamiliar B such that the argument goes through with w_B in the place of w_{Alg}. Whatever our imaginative capacities, and however frequently we hallucinate, surely we are not relevantly acquainted with *every* possible blocker. We can safely conclude from INC that no proposition with the relevant features is positively conceivable, and hence that the Conceivability Argument does not threaten *ceteris absentibus* physicalism.

I conclude by highlighting an attractive feature of my account. Not only does it appear that we are now able to positively conceive $\Phi \wedge \neg Itch$, but also that we will be able to do so in the future, independently of how science develops. Consider the following future scenario: science has finally found a reductive explanation of conscious experience. Philosophers admit that they can understand how the actual physical facts give rise to the phenomenal facts. However, they find it just as easy to conceive $\Phi \wedge \neg Itch$ as they did before they learned the new scientific theory. I am optimistic that this scenario describes our future. On my account, those philosophers need not have a false belief either about what they understand or about what they can conceive. I take this to be one of its virtues. It is not irrational to be more confident now about the claim that $\Phi \wedge \neg Itch$ will always remain conceivable than about the claim that consciousness will never be explained. If the former proposition entailed the latter, it would be irrational. It is often taken for granted that what can be positively conceived is limited by what reductive explanations there are, and *vice versa*. On my account, these things may be largely independent.

REFERENCES

Alter, Torin (forthcoming). "Imagining Subjective Absences". *Disputatio*.
Bricker, Philip (2006). "The Relation between General and Particular: Entailment vs. Supervenience". In Dean Zimmerman (ed.), *Oxford Studies in Metaphysics*, vol ii. Oxford: Oxford University Press.
Chalmers, David J. (1996). *The Conscious Mind: In Search of a Fundamental Theory*. Oxford: Oxford University Press.

Chalmers, David J. (2002) "Does Conceeivability Entail Possibility?" In Tamar Szabo Gendler and John Hawthorne (eds.), *Conceivability and Possiblity*. Oxford: Oxford University Press, 145–200.

Hawthorne, John (2002). "Blocking Definitions of Materialism". *Philosophical Studies* 110: 103–13.

Jackson, Frank (1998). *Mind, Method and Conditionals*. London: Routledge.

—— (1994). "Armchair Metaphysics". In John O'Leary-Hawthorne and Michaelis Michael (eds.), *Philosophy in Mind*. Dordrecht: Kluwer. Reprinted in Jackson 1998.

Johnston, Mark (2004). The Obscure Object of Hallucination". *Philosophical Studies* 120: 113–83.

Joseph, Geoffrey (1980). The Many Sciences and the One World". *Journal of Philosophy* 77: 773–91.

Kripke, Saul A. (1980). *Naming and Necessity*. Cambridge, Mass.: Harvard University Press.

Leuenberger, Stephan (2006). "*Ceteribus Absentibus* Physicalism". PhD. dissertation, Princeton University.

Lewis, David (1983). "New Work for a Theory of Universals". *Australasian Journal of Philosophy* 61: 343–77. Reprinted in Lewis 1999.

—— (1994). "Humean Supervenience Debugged". *Mind* 103: 473–90. Reprinted in Lewis 1999.

—— (1999). *Papers in Metaphysics and Epistemology*. Cambridge: Cambridge University Press.

Marcus, Eric (2004). "Why Zombies are Inconceivable". *Australasian Journal of Philosophy* 82/3: 477–90.

McLaughlin, Brian and Bennett, Karen (2006). "Supervenience". *Standford Encyclopedia of Philosophy*.

Prior, Elizabeth W., Pargetter, Robert, and Jackson, Frank (1982). "Three Theses about Disposition". *American Philosophical Quarterly* 19: 251–7.

Russell, Bertrand (1956). "The Philosophy of Logical Atomism". In *Logic and Knowledge*. London: Routledge, 177–28.

Yablo, Stephen (1993). "Is Conceivability a Guide to Possibility?" *Philosophy and Phenomenological Research* 53: 1–42.

8. Truthmakers and Predication

Daniel Nolan

A theory of truthmakers has often gone hand in hand with a theory of facts, or states of affairs. In one direction, this seems understandable: if, for whatever reason, one thinks that there are facts in the world, and especially if they are abundant, so that whenever a proposition p is true, there exists a fact that p (and if no "false facts" or other such things exist), then facts make for tempting truthmakers: whenever a proposition is true, then necessarily there is something which makes that proposition true: there is a fact that p. Truthmaker theorists would typically like something stronger: they would like the necessity connecting the existence of truthmakers and the truth of the corresponding proposition to be *de re* rather than *de dicto*: not just that necessarily, when p is true there is a fact that p, but also that for any fact that p, necessarily when it exists p is true. (This would not be the case, were facts to have their truth-making features contingently, as in Parsons 1999.) One dream is to have a theory in which truth supervenes on being, in the sense that there can be no difference in what propositions are true without a difference in what exists (the converse would also presumably hold, but this is uncontroversial, or should be). In this sort of theory, the facts, or states of affairs, can be identified with truthmakers.

I will leave to others for now the task of explaining why we might want a world of states of affairs (a world of facts, and *therefore* things). But it is tempting for a few reasons: it copes well with our pre-theoretical habit of employing quite general linguistic procedures to use expressions apparently referring to states of affairs in subject positions in sentences and employing quantification over them; it provides a smooth theory of events—if we are going to have a thing every time there is a change, then why not when things stay the same? (Shouldn't we think that persistence and stability are events, albeit boring ones?) And it provides for causal relata which are much easier to systematically fit into a theory of causation (see Menzies 1989). Finally, there is the push to truthmakers, or facts, from a correspondence theory of truth—where true claims correspond to pieces of the world. If the world must have different pieces in order for different claims to be true, then facts seem to be an appropriate sort of building block to think of the world as being made of.

With facts in place, all sorts of claims can have ontological underpinnings—all sorts of claims can have facts as their truthmakers. The truth of "The electron is spin up", for example, is not merely underpinned by the electron (the existence of which is presumably a necessary condition for the truth of the statement): it is also underpinned by the fact that the electron is spin up. This fact is something in the world, and in an obvious respect the assertion of the existence of this fact amounts to much the same as the assertion that the electron is spin up, given a background theory of facts. (I have deliberately picked a very simple example: if there are complex, non-fundamental facts of the sort we believe in—e.g. that a given chair is wooden—this fact will itself be constituted from more simple facts.) Note, however, that we need not say that the claims "the electron is spin up" and "the fact that the electron is spin up obtains (or exists)" literally *mean* the same thing, when the latter claim is intended literally as the assertion of the existence of a fact of a certain sort. I take a fact's obtaining and a fact existing to amount to the same thing. This is not a universal usage: there are those who take talk of the existence of facts to be a category error, and those who think that all possible facts exist, but only the privileged actual few obtain (see e.g. Plantinga 1974). My usage of "fact" here is also at variance with those who use "fact" to refer to true propositions.

Of course there will be those who will want to claim the two sentences mean the same thing. But there are all sorts of reasons someone may deny that "the electron is spin up" and "the fact that the electron is spin up obtains" mean the same thing. A nominalist, for instance, may accept the former and reject the latter: presumably they will thus want to distinguish the meanings of the two. Or one might think that the reference of the noun phrases of the two sentences are different: the former may *express* a fact, while the latter explicitly refers to it, for example. Or one might think it a matter of synthetic metaphysical discovery (albeit perhaps one implicit to some degree in our pre-theoretic metaphysics) that the former is true just in case the latter is: in which case one will not want to identify the meanings of the two, and make the connection an analytic one. I in fact favour taking the two claims to mean different things, partly for the sorts of reasons I outline. (I do not agree with the nominalist objection, of course, but I think nominalism is at least a prima facie coherent position.) Or at least I want to say this if "fact" talk is to be taken at all robustly. What is the connection, then? I think it is at least as strong as strict bi-implication—one could not be true without the other being true.[1] This modal connection between the two is not brute, however, so there may be some stronger connection. Identity of truthmakers is one attractive connection which appears to obtain[2]—and we are all familiar with the accounts according to which postulated identities do not need to rest on a priori semantic connections between the names for the objects, but are instead discovered a posteriori. So might it be with truthmakers: despite its "philosophical" nature, there is nothing to stop metaphysics from being an a posteriori investigation.

One way to have a comprehensive truthmaker theory would reject the existence of "bare" truths: reject the existence of any truths not corresponding in the appropriate way to a truthmaker. (For example, "the electron is spin up" as understood by a nominalist—there is an electron, all right, which is an ontological correlate of the claim, and the existence of which is hardly irrelevant to its truth, but its existence does not guarantee the truth of the claim.) Truth would supervene on being, in John Bigelow's apt phrase: it would not be possible for there to be exactly the same things, but some proposition being true in one place and false in another (there could not be truths which did not correspond to facts which made them true).[3]

---

[1] Maybe this is too strong: suppose that there was more than one possible fact which would make it true that a particular electron was spin up. It may be that the former could then be true while the latter be false. If the actual spin-up fact is S_1, and a merely possible spin-up fact for the very same electron is S_2, then the claim "the fact that the electron is spin up obtains", at least interpreted *de re* and as actually uttered is false in a world where the electron exists with the S_2 fact. However, "the electron is spin up", even interpreted *de re*, is true in such a world.

[2] Again this may be slightly too strong, for the reason given in the previous footnote.

[3] Bigelow himself does not understand the supervenience of truth on being in this way: he rather intends the weaker claim that the truth supervenes on what there is *and how it is*. This is rather closer to being trivial.

This kind of rejection of "bare" truths amounts to something even stronger than "truthmaker maximalism": the claim that for every truth there is a truthmaker.[4] What it adds is that the truth depends on the truthmaker for its truth—something that may often be implicit in truthmaker talk in any case, but might seem more dubious to someone who thought of "facts" as highly dependent entities, ontologically depending on what is true about things. It also includes the claim that a truthmaker's existence "guarantees" the truths that it truthmakes: one traditional way to try to ensure this is to insist on truthmaker essentialism, that the existence of a truthmaker necessitates any of the truths it makes true. (It does not make them necessary, but the claim that a given truthmaker exists strictly implies the related truths.) Perhaps this guarantee can be cashed out in some other way (for one motivation, see the discussion on p 187), and perhaps something more fundamental than the mere modal covariation is required, but I will not try for more specificity here. Once we have added this conception of facts as fundamental, we have the opportunity to "ground out" many truths ontologically—and so in some sense, to offer an ontological analysis of what it is for various different truths to be true. The sense in which this is an analysis will be discussed further below.

It should be noted, however, that the rejection of bare truths does not commit us to thinking there is a distinct truthmaker for every truth—only that every truth has some truthmaker or other. A standard thought here is that existential statements, for example, are made true by each of their witnesses, and do not need any special "existential facts" in addition. The fact that Rover is a dog is enough of a truthmaker for "there is at least one dog", for example: once we have this fact we do not need to hunt further for "some-dog" facts, somehow less specific than any of the facts about the existence of particular dogs. Some truths will thus have many truthmakers (every fact that so-and-so is a dog will do to truthmake "some dogs exist"). Furthermore, one and the same truth might have different truthmakers in different worlds in which it is true: again, "there is at least one dog" may be true in a world lacking all the actual dogs, provided that some other dogs exist there (the fact that non-actual Petunia is a dog will do, for example). While it would be convenient

---

[4] For an extended discussion of truthmaker maximalism, see Armstrong 2004.

Truthmakers and Predication | 175

for some purposes to have a one-one correspondence between truths, on the one hand, and facts or truthmakers, on the other, I will be following contemporary orthodoxy about truthmakers and suppose that many truths can share a truthmaker, and one truth can have many truthmakers.

What has been sketched is one picture of the role of truthmakers: it is of course not the only picture available, but the fact that it is particularly expansive in its claims makes it useful as background to the topic I wish to discuss in this chapter. I wish to address one question about how far the realm of facts, or truthmakers, can be made to do their ontological work. Truths involving the straightforward predication of "spin up" can be accounted for in terms of the existence of facts: the fact is all you need to exist for the electron to be spin up. There is a question of whether this can be extended to all predicates (and other pieces of language—whether an ontology of facts or truthmakers can adequately handle "negative truths", or modal truths, or moral truths, or subjective truths, or quantified truths...). One of the challenges is a question about whether property possession can be handled ontologically: whether a particular object having a property, or in particular some particular objects standing in a relation, can be "analyzed" ontologically: whether we can take this to be a matter of the obtaining of a fact of a certain sort (the fact that the object has the property, or stands in the relation): a fact, the obtaining of which does not have to be analyzed in terms of predication.

Several people appear to have answered this in the negative. David Lewis, in "New Work for a Theory of Universals" (1983: 353 and n. 14), denies that predication in general, and in particular predication involved in saying that objects have properties, can be reductively analysed ontologically. "For how could there be a theory that names entities, or quantifies over them, in the course of its sentences, and yet altogether avoids primitive predication? Artificial tricks aside, the thing cannot be done." Nobody seems to have specifically disputed this verdict, though as I will argue the materials to dispute this verdict have been supplied now and again by those providing truthmakers for claims about instantiation (see Armstrong 1997: 118–19). Primitive predication can be avoided, at least in this case, and so the suspicion that "bare" truths lurk at the heart of a truthmaker theory can be avoided. David Lewis uses the claim that everyone is committed to primitive predication to defend nominalism and various moderate realist views from needing to answer a question posed by the "problem of predication". No doubt it will still remain controversial whether we need any general answer to the question of what it is for an object to merit the application of a predicate. But I think it is interesting that there is an alternative to the usual strategy of treating some predication as primitive, basic, and unanalysable.

The way to avoid it is very simple. Take the case of the electron's being spin up. What is the truthmaker for the predication in this case? Obviously, just the fact that the electron is spin up. The way the world is which, together with the meanings of our words, makes the claim "the electron is spin up" true is just the fact obtaining. This looks like a reductive analysis: for what were putatively two 'truths', a truth about the spin of the electron and the truth about the obtaining of a certain fact, turn out to be only one. And the second truth can be expressed merely as an existence claim—if we have a constant to denote the fact, it can be expressed in first order logic using only an existential quantifier, and identity. There is no need for a non-logical predicate of any sort. Of course, if saying of something that it exists, or that it is self-identical, is to indulge in "primitive predication", then by that standard, I have not done away with primitive predication. When the question is whether there are theoretical commitments which cannot be treated as being merely ontological ones, however, it should be clear that imputing existence is a different matter from ascribing more standard properties.

I should stress some of the things that this "ontological reduction" does not achieve. I am not claiming that it is a semantic reduction: that one could infer, from the meanings of the words alone, from the statement that a certain named fact exists to the truth of the proposition that the electron is spin up, unless the fact is described as "the fact that the electron is spin up", or some such. Furthermore, this is by no means intended as any sort of eliminative reduction: it would be foolish to deny that the electron was spin up, simply on the grounds that it is a fact that the electron is spin up.[5] Finally, one

---

[5] Perhaps it is one of these senses which Lewis intended in his rejection of primitive predication. If he did intend one of these, however, then it does not seem to be the

need not suppose that the fact itself is simple or unsusceptible to further analysis—it may well have internal structure of some sort, either of simpler facts, or perhaps of non-facts (the electron and the property of being spin up, perhaps). Nevertheless, in this case at least primitive predication has been rejected in favour of ontological commitment. Furthermore, if this is to count as an analysis (trading in primitive predication for ontological commitment), there seems no reason why it cannot be perfectly general.

Lewis's comment about the impossibility of doing without primitive predication occurs in a discussion of a particular case of predication, one which has been thought to be a particular problem possibly since the middle ages, and certainly for much of the twentieth century. (And there may be hints of it in Plato and Aristotle.) It is the problem of the predicate for instantiation. Objects, we want to say (well, I want to say), have properties and stand in relations. However, saying what the connection between objects and their properties and relations is is notoriously difficult. Some have found in this talk a motive to eschew property and relation talk altogether (though with the usual theoretical schizophrenia: as soon as they begin speaking with the vulgar, nine times out of ten they forget their nominalist scruples). Among the rest of us, however, this much is uncontroversial: noun phrases standing for properties and relations (e.g. their names) appear with noun phrases referring to their objects connected with dyadic predicates in true sentences, in these sorts of cases. For example, "My father and I stand in the relation of parent to child", or "This table has the right shape", or the old chestnut "Socrates has wisdom". These sentences, and the predicate "has", or the triadic (or higher-adicity) predicate "stand in" are parts of ordinary English. More technical jargon which metaphysicians use also does this job. "The apple instantiates redness" or "Bill and Mary jointly instantiate the loving relation", for example. At the very least, dyadic predicates, or predicates with higher adicity, are employed in true utterances in these sorts of cases. (In fact, for ease, the predicate of instantiation in the case of relations is often taken to hold between an ordered n-tuple of

---

tu quoque intended against Armstrong's relation regress, since Armstrong, unlike at least some of his nominalist targets, seems to be in the business of providing an ontological analysis of predication rather than an eliminative reduction of predication, or a semantic hypothesis about the meanings of predicate applications.

objects and a relation: so in the loving case, instantiation would hold between the ordered pair <Bill, Mary> and the relation of loving. While this may not be the most metaphysically perspicuous way of talking, I'll talk this way as shorthand, since dealing with one dyadic instantiation predicate, or its relatives, is easier than dealing with a host of multi-adic instantiation predicates).

The metaphysical analysis of these cases is more controversial. One obvious attempt is to suppose that, when these predicates are satisfied by the relevant objects, a relation holds between those objects: that is, a relation holds between a property and an object, or a relation and some objects. After all, that's what realism is all about—taking there to be an ontological correlate to predicates (or some privileged predicates) as well as to noun-phrases. Doing this, however, brings on a regress: the dreaded regress of instantiation. For, as the argument goes, if we need a relation (call it Instantiation) to relate a relation and its relata (e.g. if we need Instantiation to hold between Bill and Mary, on the one hand, and Loving on the other), then we will need another relation (Instantiation2, let us call it) to relate Instantiation with the things it relates (in this case, Loving and its relata). And we will need another relation again (Instantiation3) to relate Instantiation2 with its relata, and so on forever (see Ryle 1939). Or so the objection goes.[6]

It is not transparent how this is meant to be an objection: the charge that this is inconsistent is false, and people often withdraw to the charge that it would be uneconomical. Fortunately the argument does not work as it stands: no reason has been offered so far (nor is standardly offered)[7] for assuming that the Instantiation relations at each stage must be distinct. (One possible reason is if each has a different adicity—ordered collections vs multiadic Instantiation.)

---

[6] This objection is sometimes called "Bradley's Regress", but I think this is a mistake. There is a regress argument in Bradley, and it is interesting, but I believe it is different from this one. Here is not the place for Bradley exegesis, however.

[7] This is not always true: in my opinion a version of the "copy theory" of instantiation discussed in Plato's *Parmenides* would justify this distinctness assumption. Objections are sometimes raised on type-theoretic grounds for a relation to relate itself to anything: but these objections are no stronger than the type-theoretic assumptions which support them, and while some might endorse type-theoretic restrictions on relations, one need not—and I think should not, since the mathematical paradoxes of self-reference can be avoided without it, and the paradoxes of self-reference cannot in general be solved merely through type-theoretic devices.

The regress of relations need not get started. However, there does seem to be a regress of token cases of the relation of Instantiation: the Instance <<Bill, Mary>, Loving> seems distinct from the Instance <<<Bill, Mary>, Loving>, Instantiation>, which is distinct from the Instance <<<<Bill, Mary>, Loving>, Instantiation>, Instantiation>, and so on. If we are to handle the predicate of Instantiation ontologically, and take there to be for each case of a true predication of Instantiation some thing in the world, the existence of which guarantees the truth of that predication, then one might think that an infinite regress looms.

Whether a genuine regress looms, and if so whether there is anything wrong with that, I will leave aside for a moment.[8] First, I should point out that this problem is not particularly a problem for a believer in universals (as one might have thought from my discussion, since "Instantiation" is often a technical term reserved for that link between universals and the things which have them). Other conceptions of relations are just as liable to problems with the connection between relations and their relata. Take perhaps the best known account of relations, as being sets of some kind. They may be no more than the sets beloved by extensionalists, or they may be only a restricted sort of set: those hallowed by the aura of naturalness, or being in some other sense "special" (see Lewis 1986, though he is prepared to use the name "relation" for unnatural and non-special sets of various sorts). The sets are sets of ordered n-tuples, and an Instance of a relation is an ordered n-tuple which is a member of that relation. (For simplicity I shall restrict my attention to dyadic relations—so I shall treat relations as being sets of ordered pairs.) What ordered pairs are is itself something people can disagree on: they may themselves be reduced to sets (e.g. in the Wiener-Kuratowski way), or one could even if one wanted treat ordered-grouping of objects as being on a par with set-grouping, and not reducible to it. Or one could reduce sets to ordered collections, as von Neumann (1925) can be interpreted as doing if his functions are considered as functions in extension.

Such theories can be interpreted as giving a partially ontological cashing out of what it is for a relation to hold between some

---

[8] For a general discussion of infinite regresses and what might be wrong with them, though, see Nolan 2001.

objects: for a standard relation to hold between two objects, the objects must exist, they must belong to an ordered pair, and that ordered pair must be a member of the relation, which is a set. So we have reduced e.g. loving to the existence of various objects plus the holding of membership relations.

In this sort of theory, however, there is a (putative) "relation" which resists treatment in these terms. It is of course the "relation" of membership. (Or several membership relations if the relationships of belonging to ordered n-tuples are not reduced to set membership. At the risk of simplicity, I shall assume that some reduction to set membership is possible for these relationships—via the Weiner–Kuratowski method, for example.) To all appearances, it cannot be that an object is a member of a set just in case there is a set of ordered pairs, the first member of each is a set and the second one of its members. For a start, there is no such set in orthodox set theories. It would violate the axiom of foundation, having itself in its transitive closure. Employment of a few standard ZF axioms can derive all sorts of fun paradoxes from it: the paradox of the Russell set, and Cantorian paradox, most straightforwardly. The move to classes (treated ontologically) only pushes the problem back a step: while there is a class of all the relevant pairs for the set-membership relation, there is no class for the pairs needed for the class-membership relation (many classes cannot be members of ordered pairs, according to standard class theories like Kelly Morse, or Gödel–Bernays–von Neumann). One might try to handle this by invoking categories consisting of categories which are pairs of classes and members of those classes, but the same sorts of problems are still, it seems, only deferred, not dealt with.[9]

Even if the issue of the existence of a suitable collection of the needed ordered pairs is somehow coherently dealt with, there is still a problem which I think more properly analogous to the regress of Instantiation. The relation of Membership is explicated, on the view I am discussing, as being a matter of membership holding between ordered pairs and Membership (and indeed Membership holding between those pairs and certain objects). And that is a matter of

---

[9] It is in part for these sorts of reasons that David Lewis, for example, rejects a "relation" of membership, and treats "is a member of" as a piece of ideology: see Lewis 2002: 7–10.

membership holding between Membership and an ordered pair of another ordered pair together with Membership. And that is a matter of Membership holding between an even more complex ordered pair and Membership, which is a matter of... An immediate worry is that of circularity: that membership has not been accounted for ontologically after all. This regress is the same problem, with "membership" standing in place of Instantiation.

Finally, an analogy to the regress of Instantiation can be produced in a trope theory which does not rely on unanalysed ideology. Trope theories come in many different varieties, but since space is short, I ask pardon from those proponents whose theories will be neglected in my comments. A trope theory's fundamental ontology consists of property-instances: Socrates's whiteness, my thirst, electron Fred's spin. What the relationship between tropes and individual objects (like Socrates, me, or the electron Fred) is varies from theory to theory: it may be a matter of mereology, or of set membership, or some *sui generis* internal relation ('constitution', or some such). However, a trope theory worth its salt will also make room for more general properties and relations: when I am thirsty and you are thirsty, then we have something in common (or, if "thirst" is not a genuine property, pick a sparser, more worthy candidate). What these *general* properties or relations (whiteness, as opposed to Socrates's whiteness) are will also vary. Some trope theories accept full-blown universals as well, so they have the problems of a defender of universals. Others take general properties and relations to be sets of tropes: thus embracing the difficulties of the set-theoretic approach I mentioned. One can avoid both in various ways, e.g. via a relation of exact similarity, or a dyadic predicate of co-troping. Normally a similarity predicate or co-troping predicate would be taken as primitive, and not cashed out in ontological terms, but clearly if they were a regress would likely ensue: there would be co-troping tropes relating tropes of the same kind, and further co-troping tropes holding between the first level co-troping tropes, and so on.

Now we have seen that the regress of Instantiation, or an analogous problem, arises for those theories attempting to handle predication without primitive non-ontological resources. As far as finding truthmakers goes, though, the regress need cause no special problem (as some will have been wanting to point out since I raised it).

Remember that at each step there must be a fact: there must be a fact that Bill loves Mary, a fact that the ordered pair of Bill and Mary Instantiate Loving, the fact that the ordered pair of <Bill, Mary> and Loving Instantiate Instantiation, the fact that the pair <<<Bill, Mary>, Loving>, Instantiation> Instantiates Instantiation, and so on. However, we have no reason to suppose each of these facts is distinct. Indeed, nothing we are so far committed to stops us from saying that the fact that <<<Bill, Mary>, Loving>, Instantiation> Instantiates Instantiation is identical with the fact that <<<<Bill, Mary>, Loving>, Instantiation>, Instantiation> Instantiates Instantiation, and that <<<<Bill, Mary>, Loving>, Instantiation>, Instantiation>, Instantiation> is also the same fact, and so on ad infinitum. Ontology for each truth, and no infinite regress of facts, but only of descriptions of facts: and it should never be thought that an infinite regress of descriptions is something to worry about per se.

It was once fashionable to mutter that facts had no clear principles of individuation, and were suspect. Unfortunately, it turned out that very little had clear principles of individuation, and few mutterers thereupon turned into thoroughgoing ontological skeptics. But my identification of most of the hierarchy of instantiation facts will worry some who do not necessarily demand necessary and sufficient (and non-trivial) identity conditions for every entity mentioned. Others might suspect the maneuver of being ad hoc (though what it is exactly for a maneuver to have this feature is unclear, and how much of a disadvantage this is likewise). So let me adduce some reasons why one might welcome the identity conjecture.[10]

The first is that some sort of reduction is very desirable here, for supervenience reasons. According to the theory, when one has one stage of the hierarchy, one must have the stages above it: it can't be a fact that a pair and Instantiation together Instantiate Instantiation unless the pair of that pair and Instantiation Instantiate Instantiation, and so on up the ladder. These further facts are

---

[10] Armstrong (1997: 118–19) seems to endorse the identity conjecture: perhaps surprisingly, since his instinct in the 1997 work is often to allow additional supervenient things (additional properties and relations, states of affairs etc.) and attempt to establish that they are an "ontological free lunch". Here I will try to articulate some reasons for the identity conjecture.

Truthmakers and Predication | 183

all supervenient, and we would like an explanation of this supervenience. Armstrong supposes that supervenient facts like these should not be among the fundamental furniture of the universe: that they should be "no real addition to being" and an "ontological free lunch". I find the thought attractive, though it is very hard to satisfactorily spell out the details. One cannot just postulate a necessity and then declare "free lunch", of course (and Armstrong agrees—see Armstrong 1997: 156–7, where he rejects "brute necessities"), but Armstrong is not always careful to explicitly provide the explanation which his ontological free lunches require (and after all, as we know from everyday life, the cardinal rule is that if you think you're getting a free lunch, that means you've already paid for it somewhere else). Identity is always a good internal relation to invoke to explain supervenences, where it is available: for a case where there can be no change in Bs without change in As is not mysterious if each B is identical to an A, for there can be no change in something without a change in that thing. Similarly, the existence of the bottom of the hierarchy necessitating the existence of the rest is no longer mysterious if the fact described by the description at the bottom of the hierarchy (or near the bottom) is identical to the facts picked out at each of the other stages: for it is not mysterious that the existence of something should entail the existence of itself.

Another, lesser consideration is that the hierarchy after <<<Bill, Mary>, Loving>, Instantiation> Instantiating Instantiation consists of orderings of the same elements—while the relation of "constitution" between "components" of facts should not be that of mereology, and while different facts with the same "components" may need to be admitted (to handle non-symmetric relations: the fact of Bill's loving Mary tragically need not be accompanied by the fact of Mary loving Bill), one may still not wish to postulate "relations that generate", in Goodman's phrase, more than necessary: metaphysical relationships which produce more than one object from the same "components". In any case, it is surely a necessary condition for identifying putatively different facts that all of the components of one are components of the other, by the indiscernibility of identicals.

The last is a point that I am still groping at. Consider the facts of Bill, Mary, Loving, Instantiation taken all together—the whole hierarchy, whether real or putative. It is this whole mess which captures something important: to speak in what is possibly an unhelpful metaphor, the "glue" that holds the ontological commitment together. It is other tokens of this sort of hierarchy which "glue" the ontological commitments together. If we take it to be a genuine hierarchy, it has a great deal of internal structure. This great deal of internal structure contributes little to our theory: perhaps the most that can be said of it is that it preserves the analogy between Instantiation and relations like Loving (just as a case of Loving must have a putatively distinct fact of Instantiation "above" it, so must a case of Instantiation). Simplicity grounds (which I take to be the reason people intuitively reject all of that unparsimonious and complicated internal structure) count against this internal structure—and one of the easiest way of simplifying the whole thing is taking the whole mess to be a matter of a single fact. The explicit invocation of simplicity in this context is just to employ a familiar argument from a perspective external to the hierarchy, rather than the perspective from "the bottom of the ladder", so is probably not a distinct argument from the first one offered. In an area where methodology is so far from explicit, though, the fact that the point has intuitive force from more than one perspective might have persuasive power even if it adds nothing to the justificatory scales.

Perhaps an argument is this: the only advantage, so far as I can see, for treating the facts of instantiation as a genuine hierarchy, is the analogy with other, more normal relations, like Loving (or pick some sparser, more fundamental relation if you prefer). If this is the only reason, it seems likely it is the only reason why treating Instantiation differently from the "normal" relations might merit the charge of ad hocery. But Instantiation, if it operates in this way, is disanalogous to two other "connections"—the classic "internal" relations of identity and part-to-whole. In the case of the "relation" of identity (or perhaps better property, since while it is often thought to have two argument places, they have to be occupied by the same object), we do not normally think that everything needs to have a distinct "self-identity" fact tagging along to be the ontological ground of the claim that it is identical to itself: though I suppose this has sometimes been held, for instance by some of those who commit themselves to heccaeties or "thisnesses" of objects, where these are supposed to be the object's particular self-identity. It seems to me that we do not need a numerically distinct existent to guarantee my self-identity: I am of course a perfectly adequate truthmaker for it, but I see no particular reason to find a constituent of me (necessarily dependent but non-identical) to be a more minimal truthmaker for the identity claim. Furthermore, if we did, we would be off on a regress of identity facts, since that constituent would have to be self-identical, and so would require an identity fact, which would be self-identical... The most natural way of locating a truthmaker for an identity statement, I feel, is to say that the minimal truthmaker for it is the object involved itself.[11]

(Note: you might think that finding truthmakers for identity statements is just part of the more general problem of finding truthmakers for necessary truths. If, however, you think a true identity statement is existentially committing, and you also reject Barcan formulae, this is not the same problem, since Daniel Nolan = Daniel Nolan is then contingent: it fails in any world in which I do not exist. I am interested here primarily in what truthmaker corresponds to truths expressed using an existentially committing sense of the identity predicate, which makes the issue one of truthmakers for contingent truths. The relation is still internal, however, since it necessarily holds when its relata exist: I cannot exist without being self-identical.)

Similarly, there is a problem of the truthmakers for claims about mereological relationships. When X is a part of Y, my intuition, at least, suggests that all that is needed is X and Y: we do not need a distinct case of a part–whole relationship. (At least this is so when we are employing the generous standard of part–whole given by

---

[11] This is so for positive identity statements, at least: whether either relatum of a non-identity statement is a sufficient truthmaker, or both are required, or none (but merely the absence of a (necessarily non-existing) truthmaker for the negation thereof), is a matter I need not address here.

A problem related to the "problem of the many" might arise here: one may think that less than all of me is enough for the identity statement to be true: me minus my hair is arguably a truthmaker for Daniel Nolan = Daniel Nolan, since it would be enough for me to exist (and *a fortiori* be self-identical). The problem that there are arguably many truthmakers for the claim that "Daniel Nolan = Daniel Nolan" is similar to the problem that there seem to be many objects which have a claim to be Daniel Nolan (the undetached hairless part, the undetached legless part, the maximal one with hair and legs, and at least millions more). A story which works for the latter will hopefully be adaptable for the former. This problem by itself does not seem to give us much reason to take a truthmaker with no claim to be me to be a truthmaker for my self-identity, however.

classical mereology: if being a part of something requires some proximity or external relations to other parts of that thing, then some more external relationships may need to hold as a constituent of the part–whole relationship.) The part–whole relationship also seems to be an internal relationship, though less so than identity: unless mereological essentialism is true (and it does not seem to be), things can have more or fewer parts than they actually do.[12] Nevertheless, there is some connection: plausibly an object cannot have too many of its parts be different,[13] and plausibly this necessity is grounded in the existence of the actual nature of the whole, rather than anything extrinsic. Again, "part-whole facts", numerically distinct from the whole and the part but necessarily connected to them seem otiose: and in addition they will generate infinite regresses, given generous composition principles. Take the classic example of a car and a part of it, say a wheel: given those two, there will be a fact of part–whole holding between them: so (with a generous principle of composition) there will be a whole consisting of the car, its wheel, and the part–whole fact, and so there will be part-to-whole facts of their all being related to the new fusion, and these facts, together with the previous fusion, will

---

[12] Being four-dimensional about objects makes mereological essentialism slightly more palatable, and removes temporal counter-examples, depending on how we describe cases (I can, and do, lose hairs—but if all that means is that my four-dimensional "worm" only partially overlaps the "worms" of my hairs, this is not a case of my four-dimensional totality being different at different times).

[13] Again, I am mostly concerned with the modal case, and I think this proposal is most plausible across times. Near the end of its life, an organism may have very few atoms in common with the organism at the beginning: but in another possible world where there was a similar organism which never had any atoms in common, we are more likely to think that that organism must be a distinct one. This is especially true if we consider organisms which are different in character as well. Take an actual dog, Fido. Now, we are tempted to think that there may be a possible world where Fido is treated very differently, comes to have a very different personality, eats different food, and so on. A case where there all of this happens, but the dog in that world comes from the same initial parts as Fido (e.g. the same fetus) is clearly a possibility for Fido. When we have a case of a similar fetus, but one with no atoms in common or only a few atoms in common, and which grows up to be a dog with a very different character and lifestyle from our actual Fido (but the same as our previously mentioned counterfactual Fido), we are much more likely to think that that isn't a possibility for our actual Fido—that is just a different dog, albeit one with interesting early similarities to Fido. Some take this to merely reflect a Kripkean essentiality of origin. I do not think that origin is quite so central, but I would not be surprised if we tended to count early overlap as more important than later overlap.

form a new fusion.... Mereology is powerful, and adopting classical mereology multiplies the entities one is committed to, but not, one would think, to the extent of generating infinite commitments from finite materials.

The mereology case is less straightforward, since, once we reject mereological essentialism, we are likely to think that the whole can exist without the part, the part without the whole, and we may even accept that both the whole and the part can exist without the part being a part of that whole. (Think of a bicycle assembled of slightly different parts—a gear that is actually a part may be left on the shelf in another world, co-existing with the bicycle without ever being a part of it.) This suggests that some other condition is needed besides the existence of the whole and the part, and so suggests the need for a "further fact" beyond the existence of the whole and the part. Perhaps this should drive us to give up the intuition that nothing else is needed, or this observation together with the intuition may drive us back into the arms of mereological essentialism. Another option would be to reject the modal criterion for when a further fact is required, at least in its full generality: to allow that sometimes a fact F can be a truthmaker for p even if F could exist but p be false. (This would be a denial of truthmaker essentialism.) If we then wanted to retain the view that all truths were to be accounted for ontologically, in something like the sense developed in this chapter, then it would not be so much that truth supervenes on what exists (i.e. no difference in what is true without a difference in what exists), but rather that it stands in some other intimate relation to existents (saying that truth is "constituted" by what exists, or that truths hold "in virtue of" what exists, might be labels for this, though both expressions tend to be weasel-words). I will suppose the intuition that the part–whole relation requires nothing more than the existence of its relata can somehow be vindicated, and so the regress of mereological facts does not arise. Those who do not want to follow me in this supposition need not, for present purposes—the case of identity is enough to establish an analogy for instantiation, and if mereology is not analogous to identity in this respect, we still have one analogue to work with.

In both of the cases of the "classic" internal relations, the facts of their obtaining are better seen as not being like the facts of the obtaining of external relations between objects (even the most simple case of external relations: relations intrinsic to their relata). In both cases, I think the most plausible identification of the relevant truthmakers are the objects themselves: the object itself, in the case of the identity relation, and the whole (or the whole and the part) for the part-whole relation. The analogous thing to do in the case of finding facts of instantiation is to identify the instantiation fact with the first order fact: (so that the fact that Loving holds between Bill and Mary is identical with the fact that Instantiation holds between Bill and Mary, on the one hand, and Loving on the other). This is not to deny that there are facts of instantiation, let alone deny that there are truthmakers for claims concerning instantiation, any more than identifying Hesperus with the planet Venus is a denial that Hesperus exists. But it does deny the existence of numerically distinct instantiation facts, let alone an infinite hierarchy of them every time something has a property or stands in a relation.

If we did something analogous here, and denied that the facts of instantiation were anything over and above the first order fact, we would still have avoiding predication which could not be analysed ontologically. For we would still have facts, the existence of which amounted to an object instantiating a property (or some objects instantiating a relation): the existence of the first order fact is all that is needed for the "instantiation fact", and to assert the existence of this fact is enough to assert something which is sufficient to guarantee the truth of the relevant proposition concerning instantiation. Again, it may not be a priori that the existence of this very thing is the existence of the fact that Bill loves Mary, and we are not in the business of attempting to supply a non-enthymematic inference of the form "A exists, therefore Bill loves Mary", where "A" is a placeholder for some or other proper name.

Identifying instantiation facts with ground-level facts faces some difficulties: we have the puzzling question of what the status of the supposed "relation of Instantiation" is. These puzzling questions extend to other internal "relations". Is the relation of identity a constituent of everything? Is the relation of part-to-whole something numerically distinct from a given whole and one of its parts? If so, we have ontological multiplication, and odd-looking regresses. If not, we struggle to find a "one through many" uniting these cases, as well as a semantic value for expressions like "the relation of identity". Perhaps we should just embrace "Logical Forms", as the Plato of the *Parmenides* and *Sophist* would have us do, or perhaps we should reopen the Pandora's box of searching for non-committing paraphrase of claims apparently about such relations. (I'd like it to be true that Identity is an equivalence relation, for example, but it's tricky to see how this could be so if there were no such thing as Identity.) I think the question of what to say about whether there are genuinely "ones through many" in cases where things putatively have similar mereological structures, or through many different facts of instantiation, is a question which I will not attempt to answer here.

As an alternative to taking the ground-level fact to be the Instantiation facts, one could take there to be an Instantiation fact as well as the ground-level fact. Thus, one could have two facts in the example I was using: the fact that Bill and Mary stand in the relation of Loving, and the fact that Instantiation holds between Bill and Mary on the one hand, and Loving on the other. This would have some advantages: Instantiation can more smoothly be taken to be a component of the second fact than of the first, and it would preserve a distinction between Instantiation facts and all sorts of other facts. Instantiation facts would be ones in which objects (or-tuples of objects) were related by Instantiation, whereas basic ones like Bill and Mary being related by Loving would not be facts of this sort. Instantiation could be more of a genuine one-through-many in this approach, since there would be a relation of Instantiation which would be present in all and only the instantiation facts. If the second fact is identified with all of the rest of the facts in the putative hierarchy, the infinite regress of instantiation facts can still be avoided, as before. And this regress would have been of Instantiation facts with the same ultimate constituents (in my example, Bill, Mary, Loving, and Instantiation), so it is a tempting candidate for a reduction such as this identification to be carried out. This approach has the final advantage of confining the "oddity" of the identification of so many facts described differently to specifically Instantiation facts, rather than having to say that every fact we come across is also an Instantiation fact with this feature. Confining oddity to an area of our theory which has traditionally thought to need an unusual solution may be thought to be an advantage over changing our conception of ordinary facts as well.

The main flaw with this alternative is that it requires necessary connections between distinct existences: for there must be Instantiation holding Bill and Mary together with Loving, though the fact that Bill and Mary stand in the relationship of Loving is distinct from the fact that Bill and Mary, together with Loving, stand in the relationship of Instantiation. It seems that the necessity of the existence of an instantiation fact, given the first order fact, would need to be taken as brute—whereas, of course, if the instantiation fact is identical to the first order fact, the necessity of their coexistence is anything but mysterious. I am reluctant to postulate brute necessities beyond necessity (a principle Peter Forrest has called Hume's razor in Forrest 2001), so I do not find this approach attractive. From the point of view simply of providing truthmakers for instantiation statements, though, this theory would serve adequately also.

I doubt that I have quietened all worries on the score of treating Instantiation facts in an ontological manner. Many people have the idea that there is something wrong with the Instantiation regress, and showing that some putative problems are not insurmountable does not by itself quell this worry. One avenue of exploration is an avenue which hopes to show that paradox analogous to the semantic or set-theoretic paradoxes flow from supposing that instantiation is a genuine relation—whether this is successful depends not only on establishing that useful theories of properties and relations must have the features suitable to raise paradox, but also on what responses are best for paradoxes of this sort (and I, for one, am not sanguine about my preferred approaches to semantic and set-theoretic paradoxes). Wholesale rejection of semantic language or set-theory have so far (thank goodness) not been the only options in those areas, so even if Instantiation has problems like that of Truth or Membership, that may not be its doom.

Finally, one may question the whole project of seeking an ontological treatment for our theoretical commitments—or in particular extending ontological commitments to areas where commitments are more comfortably expressed through use of predicates. This debate, however, is a bigger philosophical debate, and touches on an entire rationale for a truthmaker theory in the first place, so I hope I may be excused if it is not thoroughly addressed here. There is a lot of talk of "trading ideology for ontology", in David Lewis (e.g. Lewis 1986: 4) and elsewhere, but it is often unclear what is meant.

I think a theory of truthmakers can serve as part of a theory of what it is to cash out theoretical commitments ontologically, and *contra* Lewis, such a theory need not leave some ideology unanalyzed, in at least one interesting sense of "unanalyzed".

In this chapter, I have hoped to establish that a "truthmaker" principle can handle truths about the instantiation of properties, and in at least one sense, an ontological reduction (ontological explanation?) of an object's having a property can be had, without primitive predication. As well as demonstrating the possibility of applying a truthmaker principle to a difficult case, this result has the potential to show more. I am interested in a larger project of seeing how far our theoretical commitments can be understood ontologically (or how adequate a theory can be made while minimizing non-ontological commitments), and how such theories measure up to non-ontological, "nominalist" schemes.

Instantiation is a classic trouble spot, and needs to be dealt with if the overall metaphysic is to be acceptable. Another "large" task of which this is a small part is the task of making sense of, and establishing, a correspondence theory of truth—a smooth account of what it is that corresponds to predications should extend to the predications of "having", property possession, instantiation, or whatever. Treating Instantiation ontologically has another specific benefit—it disarms the *tu quoque* Lewis 1986 levels against Armstrongian rhetoric against unanalyzed predication in the debate about realism about properties and relations: to the extent that Armstrong's intuitive considerations support realism, they need not be undermined by primitive predication at the heart of a realist theory of properties.[14]

REFERENCES

Armstrong, D. M. (1978). *Nominalism and Realism* (vol. i of *Universals and Scientific Realism*). Cambridge: Cambridge University Press.
____ (1997). *A World of States of Affairs*. Cambridge: Cambridge University Press.
____ (2004). *Truth and Truthmakers*. Cambridge: Cambridge University Press.

[14] Thanks to many people for discussion of these issues, including David Armstrong, Andre Gallois, Carrie Jenkins, Roger Lamb, and Josh Parsons.

Forrest, P. (2001). "Counting the Cost of Modal Realism". In G. Preyer and F. Siebalt, *Reality and Humean Supervenience*. Lanham, Md.: Rowman & Littlefield, 93–103.

Lewis, D. (1983). "New Work for a Theory of Universals". *Australasian Journal of Philosophy* 61: 343–77.

―――― (1986). *On The Plurality of Worlds*. Oxford: Blackwell.

―――― (2002). "Tensing the Copula". *Mind* 111/441: 1–14.

Menzies, P. (1989). "A Unified Account of Causal Relata". *Australasian Journal of Philosophy* 67: 59–83.

Nolan, D. (2001). "What's Wrong with Infinite Regresses?" *Metaphilosophy* 32/5: 523–38.

Parsons, J. (1999). "There is no Truthmaker Argument against Nominalism". *Australasian Journal of Philosophy* 77: 325–34.

Plantinga, A. (1974). *The Nature of Necessity*. Oxford: Clarendon Press.

Ryle, G. (1939). "Plato's Parmenides". *Mind* 48/190: 129–51.

Von Neumann, J. (1925). "The Axiomatisation of Set Theory" in van Heijenoort (ed.), *From Frege to Gödel*. Cambridge, Mass.: Harvard University Press, 1967, 393–413.

9. On Locating Composite Objects

Jacek Brzozowski

INTRODUCTION

The world contains a number of objects composed of other objects. A table is composed of a few pieces of wood and some nails; an H_2O molecule is composed of two hydrogen atoms and an oxygen atom; and some say there is something composed of the table and the H_2O molecule. When some things compose some further thing, the former are proper parts of the latter. (A proper part of a thing is a part that is not identical to that thing.) The proper parts compose a composite object and a composite object decomposes into its proper parts.

Composite objects (at least some of them, in our world) are located in space-time.[1] The question I will pose is the following: does the location of a composite object derive from the location of its proper parts, or not? I will argue that either way, there are unappealing consequences. We face a dilemma. Either:

1. If the location of composite objects is derived from their proper parts, we must deny the possibility of spatio-temporal gunk objects: composite objects each of whose parts is itself composite, or,

2. If the location of composite objects is not derived from their proper parts, we must posit brute metaphysical necessities connecting the location of composite objects with the locations of their proper parts.

Thanks to Karen Bennett, Hud Hudson, Brendan Jackson, Theodore Sider, Daniel Stoljar, Dean Zimmerman and an anonymous referee for helpful comments and discussion. Special thanks to David Chalmers. In addition, I would like to thank an audience at the ANU.

[1] I am assuming that composite objects (or at least some of them) are located in space-time. I suspect that if we 'discovered' that composite objects could not be located in space-time, what we would have discovered is that there are no composite objects. I am also assuming that composite objects exist, though for some doubts about the existence of composite objects see Dorr and Rosen (2002).

In what follows I will develop this dilemma. In the first section I will argue that if locations for composite objects are derived, there can be no spatio-temporal gunk objects, on pain of an infinite regress. In the second section I will argue that if the location of composite objects is not derived, we need to posit brute restriction on possibility (though I leave room for escaping the dilemma if we undertake a substantial change in our ontological scheme). In the third section I shall choose the first horn, give three reasons to accept that the location of composite objects is derived, and offer a way to explain away the alleged possibility of spatio-temporal gunk objects. I conclude that whether or not you accept my reasons in section 3, what is important is that the dilemma stands. I also suggest that the dilemma may extend more generally to most or all properties of non-fundamental objects.

It should be noted that the dilemma we face is the same regardless of which of the main competing theories of space-time we adopt. There are two main competing philosophical theories of space-time. The first is substantivalism, whereby space-time exists as an entity distinct from the objects located in space-time. Objects are then located in space-time via a fundamental location relation to space-time. The second theory is relationism. Relationists deny that space-time exists as a distinct entity that objects are related to by a fundamental location relation. Rather, their view is that space-time is constructed out of certain fundamental spatio-temporal relations that objects stand to one another. Objects are thereby located in space-time via the fundamental spatio-temporal relations they stand to other objects. For simplicity, in what follows I shall speak as if substantivalism about space-time is true, but the main points I make would hold just as well if it turned out that relationism were true. (I will relegate the translations into relationism to footnotes.)[2]

---

[2] There are two other views of space-time that are quite prominent. First is supersubstantivalism. On this view space-time exists as a fundamental entity, and objects that are in space-time are identical to regions of space-time. Second, whereas supersubstantivalism, and both substantivalism and relationism are realist views about space-time, there are also anti-realist views of space-time (see Dainton 2001 for a good discussion of the various views on space-time). I shall not discuss either supersubstantivalism or anti-realism in what follows. I suspect that the former faces

1. DERIVED LOCATION: THE FIRST HORN

If composite objects derive their location from their proper parts, then it is in virtue of these proper parts that composite objects are located. For composite objects then, being located reduces to having proper parts that are located.

To illustrate, a spatio-temporal composite object that has only two proper parts, each of which is located in space-time can be represented as:

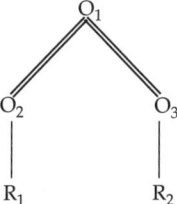

(O is an object (with numbers to keep track); R is a region of space-time (with numbers to keep track); double lines are parthood relations; single lines are location relations).

Where O_1 is a composite object that has two objects, O_2 and O_3, as proper parts. Each of O_2 and O_3 stand in a location relation to space-time and thereby are located in space-time. O_1 then derives a location in region R_1 from O_2 and derives a location in region R_2 from O_3. Thereby both O_2 and O_3 locate the composite object at regions of space-time, so the composite is located in virtue of O_2 and O_3 being located.[3]

---

similar problems to that which relationism is faced (except instead of fundamental space-time relations between objects that are at a spatio-temporal distance from each other, here there are extra fundamental mediating objects between the objects that are at a spatio-temporal distance from each other), while I simply take anti-realism to be false (or at least that the cost of a more general physical anti-realism that it seems to entail (Foster 1982), to be unacceptably high).

[3] Arguably regions R_1 and R_2 compose a region R_3. The whole composite object O_1, by having proper parts O_2 and O_3 located at R_1 and R_2, would then be located at R_3. This does not entail that the whole composite object is located in three distinct regions. It is important to remember that it is not the whole composite object that is located at R_1, and the whole composite object that is located at R_2, as the composite has a proper part O_3 that is not located in R_1, and has a proper part O_2 that is not

Proper parts of composite objects, if themselves composite, can also derive their location from their proper parts. But it seems plausible that if composite objects derive their location from their proper parts, then for them to be located, they must have at least some proper parts that are located, but not in virtue of their proper parts. If this is right, then it follows that if composite objects are located, then there must be some objects that have a location not derived from their proper parts, or in other words, that have underived location.[4]

From the assumption that the location of composite objects is derived, together with the assumption that for composite objects to have derived location in space-time they must have some proper parts that have underived location, it follows that all spatio-temporal composite objects have simple objects (objects lacking proper parts) as parts. The reasoning is as follows. If a composite object is located, it follows from the two assumptions that it has a proper part with underived location. But from the first assumption it follows that any object with underived location is a simple object. So any composite object that is located must have a simple object as a part.[5]

But many people hold that it is an open empirical question whether decomposition terminates at some proper parts that no longer have proper parts. That is, they hold that it is an open question whether composite objects are ultimately composed of simples, or whether decomposition goes on ad infinitum. Such

---

located in R_1. The composite object is thereby only partly located in these regions. But as the composite object is located in R_3, and has no parts not located in R_3, the composite object is wholly located in R_3. But to not make the discussion overly complex and as this does not affect the points made, I shall ignore this in the main text, and speak merely of the composite object being located at the regions where its proper parts are located.

[4] On the relationist picture, the location of a composite object would be derived by composite objects having simple objects as proper parts that stand in underived spatio-temporal relations to other simple objects.

[5] The same would hold if relationism were true. If composite objects do not stand in underived spatio-temporal relations to other objects, and if for a composite object to be located in space-time it must have a proper part that stands in an underived location relation to some object, then as every part of a composite object that does not have simple proper parts is composite, no part of that composite object stands in an underived spatio-temporal relation to any other object, so such composite objects are not located in space-time.

objects that are not ultimately composed of simples, but rather are composite all the way down, are often called "gunk objects".

The history of science is such that on many occasions when scientists thought they had discovered fundamental simples, it was soon discovered that in fact these objects had proper parts after all.[6] All that was required was that more powerful scientific devices be invented (or more sophisticated theories devised) that detect these smaller parts.[7] It seems possible that every time we think we have found the fundamental objects of our world, further parts will be discovered, by looking just a little closer. So, perhaps the objects that we now think of as fundamental such as leptons and quarks, will in time, with advances in scientific technology, turn out to have proper parts that are themselves composite. And even if it turns out that in our world there are objects that have no further proper parts, it can be argued that this is only a contingent matter, and that there are at least some possible worlds where every proper part of an object has proper parts.

So if it is possible for there to be gunk objects located in space-time, then at least one of the two assumptions from above must be false. Either it is possible after all that some composite objects have underived location in space-time, or we were mistaken to think that for a composite object to have derived location in space-time it must have at least some proper parts that have underived location in space-time. Denying the first assumption, that composite objects have derived location, would move us onto the second horn (discussed in the next section). So if we are to maintain that composite objects have derived location, and allow for the possibility of spatio-temporal gunk objects, we must deny that for a composite object to be located in space-time it must have some proper parts that have underived location in space-time.

However, if we accept that composite objects always have derived location and yet deny that for a composite object to be located in space-time it must have some proper parts that stand in an underived location in space-time, we are led into regress. For a

---

[6] See Lewis (1991), Sider (1993), Schaffer (2003).
[7] I am not however claiming that a proper part has to be smaller than the object it composes. In fact I deny this in section 3 where I accept the possibility of a composite object and its proper parts being the same size. Thanks to an anonymous referee.

composite object to derive a location from its parts and be located in space-time, at least some of its proper parts must be located in space-time. In the case of composite objects with simple proper parts, as we saw above, the composite is located in space-time by standing in a parthood relation to the simple which stands in an underived location relation to space-time. But in the case of composite objects without simple proper parts, the composite must derive its location from its composite parts, which derive their locations from their composite parts, and so on. None of these objects stands in a parthood relation to an object with an underived location. But without a part standing in an underived location relation to space-time, it seems none is. At best, we have an endless regress of derived locations that is never grounded in an underived location, and that therefore is not grounded at all.

A believer in gunk may suggest that there can be an infinite regress of location for gunk objects, while holding that this regress is benign rather than vicious. They may complain that it is a mistake to think of the location of a gunk object in the way we have been thinking of the location of composite objects that have simple proper parts. In particular, they may say it is a mistake to think that since a gunk object has no part that stands in an underived location to space-time, it cannot be located in space-time. Rather, the gunk theorist may say that we can pick a composite part at any one of the levels of decomposition of a gunk object, and then state that it has a location, and that its location is derived from its proper parts, which are themselves located in space-time. If we then ask how these latter parts are located, the gunk theorist can reply that their locations are derived from their own proper parts, which are themselves located in space-time. And so on, ad infinitum. At each level of decomposition, the gunk theorist says that that composite part at that level of decomposition is located as it has a proper part and that proper part is located in space-time.

The problem for the location of gunk objects remains, however. Offering this kind of piecemeal story is only half of the explanation required, and it would be a mistake to conclude from it that the regress is not vicious.[8] Even though the believer in gunk can tell us

---

[8] Thanks to Hud Hudson and David Chalmers for helpful discussion here.

at each level that that composite derives its location from a proper part, it is still not clear what can ground the fact that *any* of these objects is located in space-time.

Of course, not all regresses are vicious.[9] Consider Bradley's regress.[10] The idea is that if there is a thing a, and a property F, then a has the property F by standing in an instantiation relation R to that property F.[11] The problem then is supposed to be, for R to hold, there must also then be an instantiation relation R* (which can either be the same as relation R, or be different) that must hold between a, F, and the first instantiation relation R. And then so too must there be an instantiation relation R** that holds between a, F, R, and R*, and so on, ad infinitum. Most who believe that the regress does get off the ground nevertheless do not believe that this is a real problem for the instantiation of properties.[12] Rather, they merely accept this entails that if an object instantiates a property then there are an infinite number of instantiation relations. And barring a denial of actual infinites, the regress, as it stands, leaves us with no problem.

If this kind of regress was all that the believer in gunk faced, then accepting that the location of composite objects was derived would not rule out the possibility of spatio-temporal gunk objects. But the problem for gunk objects is not that the view that the location of composite objects is derived entails that if there were gunk objects then we would be forced to accept that there are an infinite number of derived location relations. Rather, the worry is that even if there were an infinite number of derived location relations, this would still not be sufficient to locate gunk objects in space-time.

A closer analogy here would be a second version of Bradley's regress. Imagine someone who holds that whenever a is F, a's being F is *derived* from a's standing in an instantiation relation R to F. And

---

[9] Thanks to Dean Zimmerman and an anonymous referee for pushing me on this point.

[10] Bradley (1893).

[11] Or that the pair a and F have the relational property of instantiation. You can substitute relational properties for relations in the main text if you prefer. Nothing important hangs on this for the point being made.

[12] Though of course many may deny that the regress even gets up and running, by either denying that instantiation is a relation, or denying that an object then needs to stand in some further instantiation relation R* to the former instantiation relation R.

then they add that a and F standing in the instantiation relation R is derived from a, F, and R standing in the instantiation relation R*; and that a, F, R, standing in R* is derived from all those standing in R**, and so on ad infinitum. This regress would certainly be vicious, as the entire infinite series of instantiations would be grounded in nothing at all. In effect, this story leaves open the explanatory task of telling us how the instantiation of F by a even gets off the ground.

The problematic regress here arises only if someone claims that instantiation always *derives* from some higher fact of instantiation obtaining. To avoid the regress, one should accept that the instantiation relation R holds between property F and object a, and deny that R holds in virtue of higher order instantiation relations. One may likewise optionally hold that a's being F does not hold in virtue of a's bearing R to F at all. Either way, while higher order instantiation relations obtain, they need not play a role in grounding lower order instantiation.

Here we can distinguish a regress of *entailment*, where facts about each element of an infinite series *entail* facts about further elements of the series, from a regress of *derivation*, where facts about each element of an infinite series obtain wholly *in virtue of* facts about further elements of the series. It is plausible that regresses of entailment, as on the first way of looking at Bradley's regress, are benign.[13] But it is also plausible that regresses of derivation, as on the second way of looking at Bradley's regress, are vicious.

To see that regresses of derivation are vicious, consider the following analogy. Let us suppose that someone is royal only in virtue of their father being royal, and never in virtue of anything else. Then if there is only a finite series of people, no one is royal. And even if there is an infinite series, still no one is royal. In effect, there is nothing in the world that makes it the case that *someone is royal* in the first place, rather than no one being royal. Equivalently: there is nothing in the world that distinguishes it from a qualitatively identical situation in which no one is royal. For something to distinguish this world from a world in which no one is royal, one would need it to be the case that somewhere along

---

[13] Truth regresses and certain arithmetic regresses seem to be further examples of such benign regresses, see Nolan (2001).

the line, someone's royalty is not wholly derived from their father's royalty.[14]

The problem for the location of gunk objects should now be clear. The regress in this case is a regress of derivation. Even though at each level of the series of decomposition we can explain the location of a composite object by appealing to the location of a proper part, it is left unexplained how *any* object in the series is located in space-time. Given the piecemeal story, there is no way for the totality of location relations to be grounded, any more than there is a way for the totality of royalty properties to be grounded in the example above. So the regress is vicious. Something extra needs to be added to anchor the gunk object into space-time. What needs to be added is an *underived* location relation that holds between some part of the object and space-time. But if so, then we must accept that at least some composite objects have underived location.

If composite objects do not have underived location, but rather derive their location, then we are unable to anchor gunk objects in spacetime. So we reach the first horn of our dilemma. If we hold that composite objects have derived location, we must deny the possibility of spatio-temporal gunk objects.

If instead we allow that spatio-temporal gunk objects are possible, it follows from above that it is possible for composite objects to have locations in space-time that is not derived. This moves us to the second horn of the dilemma.

2. UNDERIVED LOCATION: THE SECOND HORN

If the location of composite objects is not derived from their proper parts, and yet composites are located in space-time, then composite objects have underived location. For composite objects, being located in space-time does not depend on having proper parts located in space-time. In other words, the relation that composite objects stand in to space-time does not reduce to (and thus ontologically depend upon) standing in parthood relations to objects and the location relations in which these parts stand, and thereby the location

---

[14] Thanks to David Chalmers for this analogy.

of composite objects cannot be explained solely in terms of these objects and the relations between them.

To illustrate, consider again a spatio-temporal composite object that has only two proper parts, this can now be represented as:

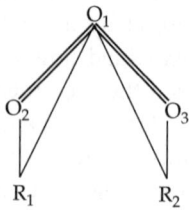

The composite object O_1 has the objects O_2 and O_3 as proper parts. O_2 and O_3 have underived location in regions of space-time R_1 and R_2 respectively. Where things differ from the view that composite objects derive location, is that the composite object O_1 itself has a location that is not derived from its proper parts, and is located in regions R_1 and in R_2 (or perhaps in the sum of R_1 and R_2) independently of its proper parts being there located.

The thesis that composite objects have underived location in space-time is consistent both with the existence of spatio-temporal composite objects that have a decomposition into simples and with the existence of spatio-temporal gunk objects. In the former case both composite and its simple proper parts are located in space-time by having underived location. In the latter case, despite not having simple proper parts that have underived location, the composite gunk object and its proper parts are located in space-time by themselves having underived location.

The problem is that this view leads to the consequence that, unless there are brute restrictions on possibility, it is possible that a composite object be located somewhere where none of its proper parts is located.

If composite objects and their proper parts each have underived location in space-time, the location of each in space-time is logically independent of the others. Therefore it is logically consistent that the composite object and its proper parts are located in disjoint (non-overlapping) regions of space-time, despite the objects being related by parthood relations to one another. That is, the composite object may be located in a region of space-time where none of its proper parts are located. Of course (assuming that having proper parts located is sufficient for a composite to be located in space-time[15]), the composite would also be located where the proper parts are located, as having proper parts that are located in space-time will determine that the composite is located in space-time. But the composite would then also be located in a region where none of its proper parts are located, for example the composite could be located 10 meters away from where its proper parts are located. If the location of composite objects in space-time is underived, then a composite object could be displaced, in that it may be located where none of its parts are located.[16]

The possibility of displaced composite objects can be represented in a diagram as:

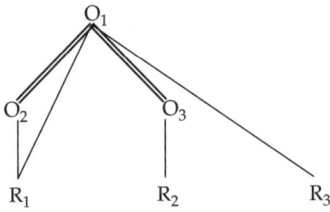

In the diagram we have the composite O_1 that has objects O_2 and O_3 as proper parts. O_2 and O_3 each have underived locations in regions of space-time R_1 and R_2 respectively. O_1 is also located in region R_1 by having an underived location, but then instead of having an underived location in region R_2 (though perhaps being derivatively so located), as in the previous diagram, it now has underived location in a region R_3, disjoint from regions R_1 and R_2,

---

[15] Though this has little consequence for the central problem of the location of composite objects under discussion here.

[16] The same problem would arise on the relationist picture. The proper parts would stand in certain underived spatio-temporal relations to other objects, and the composite object would stand in underived spatio-temporal relations to objects. As the spatio-temporal relations of the composite are logically independent to those of its proper parts, these spatio-temporal relations could differ from each other. The proper parts could stand in spatio-temporal relations of 20 meters to some object, while the composite could stand in a spatio-temporal relation of 10 meters from that object. The composite would, just like its proper parts, be located 20 meters from the object (by having a location determined by its proper parts) but would also stand at 10 meters from that object (unlike any of its proper parts), so the composite would be located somewhere where its proper parts are not located.

where none of O_1's proper parts are located. The composite object is thereby located in the regions where the proper parts are located (assuming that having a proper part that is located in a region of space-time is sufficient to locate that composite in space-time) and also located where none of its proper parts are located.[17]

If composite objects have underived location in space-time, then it would be possible for a composite object to be located in a region of space-time where none of its proper parts is located. But it is not possible for a composite object to be located in a region of space-time where none of its proper parts is located.[18] So composite objects do not have underived location in space-time.[19]

If the locations of a composite object and its parts are underived and thereby logically independent of each other, it seems it would have to simply be a brute fact that composite objects are located where and only where their proper parts are located. A necessity being brute is not automatically problematic, as arguably nomological necessities are such brute necessities. But it seems to be a

---

[17] Note, the same problem would arise if in the previous example we had the composite object standing in a location relation to the sum of R_1 and R_2, for this location relation, as it is underived, would be logically distinct from the fundamental location relations of that composite object's parts, thereby it would still be possible that that composite object stands in that location relation to R_3 (or perhaps the sum of R_1 and R_2 and R_3), despite the composite object not having any proper parts located in R_3.

[18] I have no argument that displaced composite objects are not possible, but it seems that having this possibility as a consequence of one's metaphysical view would be a highly counter-intuitive price to pay.

[19] Pointing out that composite objects undergo change in parts as they persist through time, and therefore are at one time located where certain of their proper parts are located, while at another time are not located where those proper parts are located, would not be a counter-example to the impossibility of displaced composite objects. In the persistence case (and here I remain neutral between endurance and perdurance theories of persistence), when the composite object is located in a region of space-time where its proper parts are not located, this is because the composite object, at that time, no longer stands in parthood relations to the objects that it did at an earlier time stand in such relations to, rather it now has different proper parts where it is located. So in the persistence case there is not a composite object standing in parthood relations to objects, and while standing in these parthood relations being located where none of its proper parts located. And this is what we seem to have to accept as possible if composite objects stood in underived location relations to space-time. So whereas the persistence case is unobjectionable, the case of a composite object standing in an underived location relation to space-time and thereby being located in a region of space-time where none of its proper parts are located, is objectionable.

metaphysical necessity that composite objects are located where and only where their proper parts are located, so appeal to a merely nomological tie is too weak. A brute fact that binds the location of the composite to that of its proper parts would have to be a brute metaphysical necessity. And here, the problem is that many people do not believe that there are any such brute metaphysical necessities. Brute necessities seem plausible only if they are nomological necessities. If we are to hold that all objects have underived locations, we must deny that brute necessities are only nomological, and accept that these brute necessities are metaphysical primitive restrictions on possibility. And this is a high methodological price to pay.

Now someone may resist the need for brute necessities by insisting that it is an analytic or conceptual truth that composite objects are located where and only where their proper parts are located. But as the relations we are dealing with are underived, appeal to analyticity or conceptual truth would simply be misplaced. How could analyticity or anything about our concepts bind such relations in the world?

It may well be analytic to or a conceptual truth about 'located' that a composite object is located where and only where its proper parts are. If so, then if a composite object bears a relation R to space-time without any of its parts bearing R to space-time, it follows that R is not a location relation. But this does not explain how there can be *any* underived relations R such that a composite object stands in R to a region if and only if one of its parts stands in R to a region. This thesis makes no appeal to location, so explaining it requires going beyond analytic truths about "location". Instead, it seems to require a brute metaphysical necessity between underived relations.

Perhaps it is analytic (or a conceptual truth) about 'parthood' that a composite object is located where and only where its proper parts are located. One way this may go is that something is a part of something else if it is located in a sub-region of the region where the other thing is located. But this seems inadequate. As the composite object has an underived location, it follows that by simply moving from the region where its parts are located to a region where none of its parts is located, the composite becomes a simple. Further, it will leave behind a number of simple objects that do not compose any object. This consequence cannot be avoided by moving to a four-dimensional framework, for the view would still have the consequence that it is possible for the composite to become a simple by moving, and that it is possible that it leaves behind a number of simple objects that compose nothing.[20]

The general worry that arises by appeals to analytic or conceptual truth for the view that composite object have underived location, is that given that we are accepting that the composite object and its proper parts stand in relations to space-time that are logically independent of each other, the question will always be why can those relations not stand to distinct regions of space-time? No matter what conceptual or analytic restrictions you put in place, given that the composite and its parts have underived locations, there will always be something further that needs to be explained.

Another temptation may be to insist that it is not possible that composite objects are located where none of their proper parts is located is because the composite stands in the very same relations as its proper parts. So any relation that locates the composite in a region locates the proper parts in that region, and any relation that locates a part in a region locates the composite in that region. But it seems unless one holds the highly controversial view that composition is identity, this move is bound to fail.[21]

There remains a way to resist appeal to brute necessity while denying that composite objects derive their location from their proper parts. This is to allow that composite objects derive their location, but that this location is derived from something other than the location of their proper parts. I can see two ways this might then go. The location might be derived from facts about the world

---

[20] Thanks to David Chalmers and Brendan Jackson for helpful discussion here.

[21] For composition being identity to avoid brute necessities one would have to hold the strong thesis that a composite object is strictly identical to its many parts. Versions of such a view are defended by Baxter (1988), and Wallace (ms). Most tempted by such a view, find it ultimately implausible, embracing the weaker view of composition as only analogous to identity. See Lewis (1991) and Sider (2007b). And the weaker view would not be able to escape the bruteness of the necessity in this way, as the composite and the proper parts would ultimately be distinct, and thereby, under the view we are considering, stand in distinct location relations. Sider (ibid.) appeals to 'the intimacy of parthood', but I cannot see how this gets him off the second horn, unless he embraces the derived view of location, which then places him on the first horn.

as a whole, or the location might be derived from the *stuff* that constitutes the object.

The first way then to deny that composite objects derive their location from their proper parts is to hold that the only composite objects that have underived location in space-time are those that are not proper parts of any other composite objects. It is from these composites that all the proper parts, whether they be composite or simple, derive a location in space-time. But it is plausible that the only composite object that is not a proper part of any other object is the whole world. If so, this view leads to the consequence that the location of both simple and composite objects is derived from facts about the whole world.

If we take this route, we then need to give a reason why only composite objects that are not proper parts of some composite object have underived location, while other composites don't. The only reason I can see would be to hold that certain composite objects are more fundamental than other composite objects, and that only the most fundamental objects have underived location, while less fundamental objects derive their location from these fundamental objects. Thereby as the world composite is the only object that has underived location, and as only fundamental objects have underived location, a consequence of the view is that the world composite is a fundamental object, with all the proper parts as less fundamental. We thereby reach an ontological view known as priority monism.[22]

The priority monist now has to tell us how both the existence and particular location of the proper parts are derived from the world composite. A promising approach is to hold that the world composite has underived location and instantiates fundamental *distributional* properties, and it is from these that the proper parts derive both their existence and particular location. Distributional properties are properties of the whole object that can have either homogeneous or heterogeneous property distributions, where being uniformly coloured blue throughout would be an

---

[22] Schaffer (forthcoming) defends priority monism in far greater detail. He contrasts it with what he calls existence monism. Both priority monism and existence monism hold that the whole world is the most fundamental object; where they differ is that the former holds that the world is composite, while the latter believes it is simple. In what follows I sketch one version of priority monism.

example of a homogeneous distributional property, while being black and white checkered would be an example of a heterogeneous distributional property.[23] If the world has the distributional property of being black and white checkered, and this is a fundamental property, then the priority monist can say that the existence of some black checks located at certain sub-regions of the region where the world object is located are derived, and the existence of some white checks located at certain sub-regions of the region where the world object is located are derived. This common derivation of both the existence of proper parts and their location from the fundamental distributional properties of the located whole should then guarantee that the problem of displaced composites does not arise.

This is an interesting proposal, which we should look at more closely. The fundamental distributional properties would not involve a distribution of macro-physical properties (as in the checkered example) from which we then derive the proper parts and their properties, for as the literature on multiple realization has taught us, such macro-physical properties do not entail any particular micro-physical properties (they tell us nothing about the nature of the micro-physical properties).[24] For example, with the black and white checkered world, if this is a fundamental distributional property, then even if the black checks and the white checks can be derived, this tells us nothing about the properties of the proper parts of the checks (or whether they even have proper parts). If the distributional properties simply had distributions of macro-physical properties, then we would not have a supervenience of the micro-physical properties on the fundamental distributional properties (as two worlds could be the same in respect to distributional properties

---

[23] Parsons (2004) introduces distributional properties, which he argues are not in general equivalent to non-distributional properties. Schaffer (forthcoming) adopts fundamental distributional properties as his preferred view in defending priority monism, though allows that if one denies the existence of fundamental heterogeneous distributional properties, the priority monist can instead hold that the distributional properties are derived from homogeneous properties that are either a complex of property and location (i.e. derived from the properties black-here and white-there), or from monadic properties that have location built into their instantiation (i.e. black instantiated-here and white instantiated-there).

[24] Here the distinction between macro-physical and micro-physical is supposed to be something like qualitatively micro and qualitatively macro. Hopefully this is intuitive enough.

that had macro-physical distributions, yet differ in micro-physical properties), and supervenience is required for the derivation of the existence of the proper parts from the fundamental distributional properties of the whole. It thereby seems that the fundamental distributional properties of the world composite must involve a more fine-grained distribution of micro-physical properties, upon which macro-physical properties of composite objects (including certain properties of the whole world, such as the mass of the world) supervene, and from which these properties are derived. For the priority monist then, the world has fundamental distributional properties with certain micro-physical distributions, from which all the parts of the world and their properties are derived. We can then add that if the fundamental distributional properties of the world have a simple micro-physical distribution then the world has a decomposition into simple objects, while if the micro-physical distribution is gunky, the world is a gunk world.

The second way to deny that composite objects derive their location from their proper parts is to introduce a new ontological kind, stuff. In addition to quantifiers for things such as simple or composite objects, we now also introduce quantifiers for stuff.[25] Objects are then derived from or constituted by stuff that has underived location, and it is from this stuff that both simple and composite objects derive their location.[26]

However, it seems that stuff itself could have compositional structure: if there is some stuff and some more stuff, then under certain conditions there will be stuff that has these as proper parts.[27] In which case the problem of the location of composite objects just re-emerges at the level of stuff. The stuff theorists have two possible replies. Either they can deny that stuff has compositional

---

[25] Markosian (2004) is one defender of a stuff ontology. Chalmers (forthcoming) expresses some sympathy to a stuff ontology, and motivates an anti-realism for objects.

[26] I am here assuming that the stuff theorist accepts the existence of objects as well as stuff. Though of course this can be denied, in which case we could accept nihilism about all material objects, both simple and composite. Jubien (1993) argues that quantification over things can be eliminated in favor of quantification over stuff.

[27] Markosian (2004) accepts that stuff has compositional structure, and that the composition of stuff is unrestricted (though holds that for objects composition is restricted), so whenever you have some stuff and some more stuff, there will be stuff that has these stuffs as proper parts.

structure and accept that it is only objects derived from this stuff that have compositional structure, or they accept that stuff does have compositional structure, just that the stuff proper parts are derived from the stuff whole.[28]

If we take the first option then there is a distribution of properties across stuff that has underived location, from which the existence and location of all objects are then derived. If we take the second option then once again there is a distribution of properties across stuff that has underived location, but here it is stuff proper parts that derive their existence and location from the location and distribution of properties of the stuff whole, and these stuff parts then constitute objects that derive their location (and perhaps existence) from the stuff parts that constitute them. Both options are analogous to the priority monist view in that the existence and location of proper parts (whether they be object proper parts of stuff proper parts) is derived from the distributional properties of the whole (whether this be an object or stuff). And in addition, if the distributional properties have a simple micro-physical distribution, then objects have a decomposition into simples, while if the distribution is gunky, objects are gunky. These stuff theories, however, differ from priority monism in that the priority monist has the world object as fundamental, while the stuff theorist has no obvious priority of one object over any other.

It thereby seems that if we accept either a priority monism, or we include fundamental stuff in our ontology, we have a way to escape the dilemma. But to many, the acceptance of such non-standard ontological views would seem too high a price to pay. Many will find that giving up the possibility of spatio-temporal gunk objects, or accepting brute metaphysical necessities is a lesser evil than upholding the priority of the whole over that of the parts, or of accepting the addition of the extra ontological kind of stuff. The general intuitive worry is that certain facts about objects, such as facts about their intrinsic nature, are intuitively facts only about those objects and their parts, and not ultimately facts about the whole world (or about how properties are distributed across the stuff). And the same goes for many relations between objects, where

---

[28] A third option would be to accept the stuff has compositional structure, deny that stuff is gunky, yet allow that the objects that the stuff constitutes are gunky. This seems to me to be the least promising of the options.

these just seem to be facts about those objects related, and not facts about how the whole is.[29] Related to this, an intuitive worry for priority monism in particular is that for any object in a world, all that God would have to do to make that object a fundamental object is to destroy all objects that are not parts of that object. Being fundamental therefore becomes an extrinsic property of objects. On the other hand, a problem for stuff is that as the stuff theory becomes more analogous to priority monism, it becomes less clear why exactly stuff is taken to differ from priority monism, or at least why it is taken to be different from a view that denies stuff as an extra ontological category. So more needs to be said exactly how stuff differs from objects, and what benefit is gained by introducing the extra ontological category of stuff provides. Finally, a general worry is that it is unclear whether distributions of properties across a whole are sufficient to determine the existence of the proper parts. Consider a sphere that has the homogeneous distributional property of being uniformly pink throughout. Does this sphere have a decomposition into simples, or is it gunky, or perhaps it has no proper parts at all?[30] Given the homogeneous pink distribution it does not seem that any one reply is preferable to any other. The problem is that without appeal to proper parts, it is hard to see how to make sense of a gunky versus simple distribution, or a distribution from which you don't derive parts. Adding the parthood structure seems to be an extra step. This is not to say that either priority monism or a theory of stuff is obviously false. Both research projects are well worth pursuing further than I can in this chapter. But more does need to be said in their favour.

Henceforth I will put aside the option of accepting such a non-standard ontology. If we put this option aside, we are faced with our original dilemma: either we must deny that spatio-temporal gunk objects are possible, or we must accept that the location of composite objects is restricted by a brute metaphysical necessity.[31]

---

[29] Sider (2007a) raises this intuitive worry for priority monism, and goes on to raise arguments against priority monism, two from possibility, and one from intrinsicality. I won't recreate or assess these arguments here. See Schaffer (ms) for a response.

[30] Parsons (2000) (2004) uses distributional properties as a tool in motivating the possibility of extended objects that lack proper parts. I discuss a different case of the possibility of extended simples in the next section.

[31] If one prefers, one could of course instead set things up as a trilemma, whereby either you have to deny the possibility of gunk objects, or you have to accept brute

3. TAKING THE FIRST HORN

I believe the right choice is to take the first horn: we should deny the possibility of spatio-temporal gunk objects. There are three reasons that motivate this. I will present these in order from what I see as the weakest to the strongest reason.

First, the view that composite objects derive their location is preferable on Occamist grounds. In cases where composite objects do have an ultimate decomposition into simple objects that stand in underived location relations to space-time, positing a further underived location relation between the composite object and space-time would seem redundant and ontologically excessive, as such relations, not being derived, would be genuine ontological additions to the world.

Second, it seems we can weaken the intuition for the possibility of gunk objects. A large part of the alleged conceivability of spatio-temporal gunk objects lies in the idea that it seems at least possible that scientists could keep discovering smaller and smaller objects, located in sub-regions of the regions where larger objects are located. And as we are able to conceive of this process of discovery going on ad infinitum, we seem to be able to conceive of the possibility of spatio-temporal gunk objects. But this description is incomplete. To it we need to add that every one of these objects that we discover, on closer inspection, is a *composite object such that each of its parts is itself composite*. For we should not confuse the possibility of gunk objects with a related possibility that is also consistent with the picture above, that certain composite objects may be infinitely divisible, or may be discovered to have an infinite number of parts. For even though if spatio-temporal gunk objects are possible then these will be infinitely divisible, if an object is infinitely divisible, this does not mean that it is a gunk object. The idea of infinite divisibility and the discovery of an infinite number of parts is compatible with the existence of composite objects that have an infinite number of un-extended, pointy, parts that do not themselves have any proper parts. For example, in a geometry based on points, a line

necessities between the location of a whole and its proper parts, or you accept a non-standard ontology.

is said to be infinitely divisible into smaller lines, yet ultimately composed of an infinite number of points.[32] And such possibilities *are* compatible with the location of composite objects being derived from simple proper parts that stand in underived location relations to space-time. So it seems that accepting that a composite object is infinitely divisible does not entail that the object is a gunk object. And I think this takes away much of the intuitive force from the conceivability of gunk objects.

Finally, the view that the location of composite objects is derived has an important explanatory advantage over the view that the location of composite objects is underived. For if composite objects do not stand in underived location relations but rather derive their location in space-time, then we can explain why it is necessary that composite objects are not located somewhere where none of their proper parts is located. If the location of a composite object is derived, then for a composite object to be located in a region of space-time it must have a proper part that stands in an underived location relation to that region of space-time from which the composite object derives its location. If a composite object does not have a proper part that stands in an underived location relation to a region of space-time, then the composite object is not located in that region of space-time. So in every region that a composite object is located it must have at least one proper part that is located in that region. If composite objects derive their location then the possibility of a composite object being located somewhere where none of its proper parts is located is ruled out structurally. The metaphysical necessity of composite objects being located where and only where their proper parts are located is thus explained. And being able to explain such metaphysical necessities is a great theoretical benefit.[33]

I think that, in light of the dilemma, the above is reason enough to deny the possibility of gunk objects, and endorse the view that composite objects derive their location. But some may still

---

[32] See Nolan (2006).

[33] It may seem that the view that locations of composite objects are derived also faces a problem of brute necessity, namely, it needs to explain why it is not possible for composite objects to stand in fundamental location relations to space-time. I think this can be best answered by looking closer at the very nature of composite objects. This needs to be argued for, but that I will have to leave for another paper.

hold that it seems possible that there could be a world with ever smaller objects at sub-regions of the regions where certain extended objects are located, without there being any point-sized objects. For the rest of the chapter I shall develop a picture that allows for this possibility, and yet does not commit us to the possibility of gunk objects. I shall thus develop a substitute for gunk objects.[34] These are spatio-temporal objects that are structurally similar to gunk objects, without committing us to the possibility of gunk objects.[35]

Let us begin by considering a simple object that stands in an underived location relation to a point of space-time. We allow what should be an unobjectionable amount of combinatorial reasoning about possibility, whereby we allow for any recombination of *fundamental* objects and relations.[36] As a simple is a fundamental object, and as underived locations are plausibly fundamental, with the combinatorial principles we then have the possibility of the simple standing in a one–many pattern of location to space-time. We thereby have a single simple object, and we have a number of fundamental location relations, each with the simple as one of their relata and each with a distinct point of space-time as the other. We thereby have a simple standing in location relations to a number of distinct regions of space-time. This simple would be located in more than one region of space-time, thereby be extended through space-time. It would thus be an extended simple, an object that is located in distinct regions of space-time without having proper parts at each of those regions.[37] Such a simple would arguably be homogeneous, instantiating uniform properties, but would then stand in relations to itself across the various regions where it is located, creating relational complexity. To see this, think of a composite object composed of a number of simple objects all located at distinct regions of space-time each of which has the same

[34] After writing this I discovered that J.R.G Williams (2006) introduces a similar gunk substitute.

[35] What I say below is largely independent of what has been argued up until this point; thus even if one denies the picture I now present (which admittedly, is extremely controversial), the dilemma above still stands, and so do the points in favor of taking the first horn over the second.

[36] For a more thoroughgoing combinatorialism about possibility see Armstrong (1989), (1997: 148–184), and Lewis (1986).

[37] See Sider (2007b).

intrinsic properties as the others. By having these properties and standing in various spatio-temporal relations to one another, they will have created a certain complex pattern. It is then simply by having these objects that instantiate such properties and stand in such relations as parts, that the composite instantiates the properties that it does (barring non-reductive properties or truly emergent properties, if there be such). So in the case of extended simples, we have the simple in each of those regions, instantiating the intrinsic properties that the qualitatively identical simples instantiated, and standing in the relations to itself at distinct locations as the simples stood to one another. The difference being that even though the simple is in all these locations, it is nonetheless still a single simple, so would not compose anything that has the properties that the composite composed of the many simples would have. The two scenarios would however be qualitatively indiscernible. Extended simples seem conceivable. Perhaps our world does not contain any such extended simple (as quarks and leptons are arguably pointy simples), but surely simples with extension are possible.[38]

So the extended simple can be represented as:

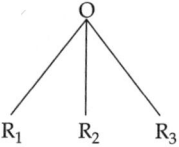

Second, just as by our combinatorial reasoning we allowed the possibility of a single simple standing in fundamental location relations to a number of distinct regions of space-time, so too can we redistribute the simples and the fundamental location relations to space-time. This time, instead of having a simple standing in a one-many pattern of location to a number of regions of space-time, we now have a single region of space-time related in a one-many pattern of fundamental location relations to a number of distinct

---

[38] Friends of extended simples include Braddon-Mitchell and Miller (2006), McDaniel (2007), Parsons (2000), and Sider (2007b). Though see Hudson (2005: 106–21) for a number of problems that those who accept the possibility of extended simples face.

simples. So we have a single fundamental point of space-time, and we have a number of fundamental location relations with the point of space-time as one of their relata, and each with a distinct fundamental simple object as the other relata. We thereby have the possibility of a number of disjoint simple objects co-located at a single region of space-time.[39]

The possibility of co-located disjoint objects can be represented as:

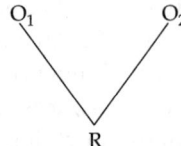

And the possibility of such co-location of disjoint objects does appear plausible. Some scientists have believed that Bosons (which unlike Fermions do not obey the Pauli Exclusion Principle) can have the very same location of space-time. Whether or not it is actually the case that bosons can be located in the same region of space-time, such co-location at least seems conceivable (and that such scientific theories were treated seriously gives further evidence that the co-location of composite objects is conceivable), thereby good evidence that such co-location is at least possible.[40] And it seems that what would rule out the co-location of objects in our world would be a mere nomological necessity, rather than any deep metaphysical necessity.

Finally, denying the possibility of two disjoint simples located in exactly the same region of space-time amounts to a positing a brute *de re* modal fact between distinct existences. For to exclude the possibility of simples from being located in exactly the same region of space-time, there must always be some event (a swerving, or a ceasing to move by one or both of the simples) that occurs upon their approaching the same region that prevents them from co-locating at this region.[41] So to deny such co-location, we must

---

[39] Note that these simples remain *disjoint* despite being located at the same region of space-time; this thus differs from other alleged possibilities of co-location discussed in the literature, such as those that arise in discussion of constitution, where there are two distinct objects that share a decomposition yet apparently remain distinct (due to temporal or modal differences).
[40] See McDaniel (2007).   [41] See McDaniel (ibid.).

deny the Humean dictum that there are no necessary connections between distinct existences.[42]

With the possibility of extended simples and the possibility of the co-location of disjoint simple objects, by combining these two possibilities, we are in a position to give our gunk-substitute.

We have an extended simple O_1 located in a number of regions of space-time that form a region that has these as sub-regions. We then have an extended simple O_2 that is located only at half of the sub-regions that O_1 is located at and nowhere else. We then also have a third extended simple O_3 located at the other half of the sub-regions and nowhere else.

This can then be represented as:

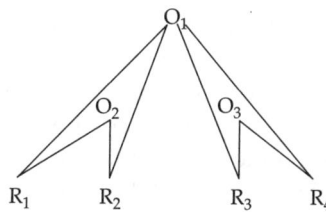

We can then have four more extended simples, each of which is only located at a quarter of the sub-regions of the regions at which O_1 is located. And we continue this process ad infinitum, by adding more and more extended simples located at sub-regions of the regions where we have extended simples, occupying smaller and smaller regions of space-time, without any ever located at only a single pointy region of space-time.[43]

---

[42] The Humean dictum can take many forms, depending on what you mean by "distinct existences". Many would deny that distinct means numerically distinct, as the hold that there can be necessary connections between objects that are numerically yet not mereologically distinct, or that there are necessary connections between numerically distinct properties such as being red and being colored. The Humean dictum I am appealing to is in a pretty weak form, in that it merely does not allow necessary connections between distinct fundamental existences, and thereby, given the assumption that a composite is not a fundamental object, allows necessary connections between numerically distinct objects that are not mereologically distinct, and given the assumption that being coloured is not a fundamental property, allows a necessary connection between the property of being red and the property of being coloured.

[43] On a relationist picture of space-time, O_1 would stand in a number distinct spatio-temporal relations to O_2, some at zero distance, others at various distances, and

So imagine that the simple O_1 occupies a region of space-time that is table shaped. Faced with O_1, it would look as if there was a table in that region of space-time. Imagine then that the regions of space-time that O_2 and O_3 were located in were half-table shaped regions. Each of these half-table shaped regions is a sub-region of the table shaped region. And then imagine that there were five regions shaped like pieces of wood, and some regions shaped like nails, and that each of these regions had an extended simple, disjoint from all the other simples, located in (and only in) that region. And so on, for atom-shaped sub-regions of the table shaped region, and even smaller shaped sub-regions, ad infinitum. Faced with the extended simple that looks like a table, if we look closer we see two objects that look like half-tables, and then look closer and see objects that look like pieces of wood and some nails. And we look closer and we see some objects that look like atoms, and so on. This process of discovery of ever smaller looking objects in smaller regions of space-time would (in principle) go on ad infinitum. This process of discovery would look to us like the discovery of ever smaller proper parts of a table, with each of the smaller objects looking like it had proper parts.

The picture described would be structurally similar to what we would expect of spatio-temporal gunk objects, thereby would for epistemic purposes match gunk at a time. In fact, we could strengthen the picture above by introducing certain laws that, at the world described, nomologically yoked the co-located simples into this structure, thereby matching gunk objects across time. This would still fail to match gunk objects modally, but would match spatial-temporal gunk objects for all epistemic purposes at these worlds as (1) there would be an object O_1 that is located at some region of space-time with an infinite number of ever smaller objects located at sub-regions of that region, so the closer you look the more objects you would discover; (2) the object O_1, due to the nomological necessities posited, would be located where and only where these objects are located. This would however not be a gunk object, as: (1) each of the infinite number of objects is simple; (2) each object is located in space-time by an

so too for O_3. O_2 and O_3 would then stand in spatio-temporal relations to one another. These various spatio-temporal relations would then build the spatio-temporal structure for partially co-located extended simples required.

underived fundamental location relations; (3) the largest object is only contingently located where and only where these other objects are located.[44]

These considerations bring out an important asymmetry between parthood and location that is not always appreciated: if something is a proper part of a composite object it is located in a region where the composite is located, yet it is not the case that if something is located in a region where the composite is located then it is a proper part of that composite.

With the example of the infinite number of co-located extended simples we are able to explain away the seeming conceivability of spatio-temporal gunk objects by offering a substitute that would, for epistemic purposes, match spatio-temporal gunk objects at a world. The conceivability of spatio-temporal gunk, and the conceivability of this infinity of co-located extended simples would be indiscernible. This thereby allows us to deny the appeal to the alleged conceivability of spatio-temporal gunk objects as a counter-example to the derived location view of composite objects. As the example makes use only of simple objects, it does not commit us to the possibility of spatio-temporal gunk objects, nor does it undermine the derived location of composite objects.

If the substitute I have given for spatio-temporal gunk objects is plausible, then, even if we were to discover that our world has a gunk-like structure, this would still not show that spatio-temporal gunk objects are possible. At most we would have discovered either that our world has spatio-temporal gunk objects, thereby spatio-temporal gunk objects are possible, or that our world contains infinite numbers of co-located extended simples held together in a gunk-like structure by some law in our world. We would have to decide the issue on other theoretical grounds, such as appeal to simplicity and explanatory power. But it is on such theoretical grounds (in considering the location of composite objects) that we have been led to denying the possibility of spatio-temporal

---

[44] If unrestricted composition is true, then there would also be a composite object that was composed of all these ever decreasing simples, though this object would not be a gunk object, these simples of ever decreasing size would not stand in the right parthood relations to one another, and the composite would still have a decomposition into simples, just that these would all be extended.

gunk objects. On theoretical grounds, we should thereby decide against the possibility of the existence of spatio-temporal gunk objects.

CONCLUSION

The view that the location of composite objects is derived is superior to the view that a composite object can have underived location, for the three reasons I put forward at the beginning of section 3. So I suggest that we embrace the theory that composite objects derive their location from their proper parts, and accept the consequence that it is impossible for there to be any spatio-temporal gunk objects.

Whether or not you agree with this, what is important is that the dilemma stands. Either the location of composite objects is derived from their proper parts or it is not. If it is derived, then it is not possible for there to be gunk objects located in space-time. If it is not derived, then (unless we embrace a non-standard ontology) we must appeal to brute metaphysical necessities in order to rule out the possibility of objects being located where none of their proper parts are located. A choice must be made.

As a parting thought, it is now an interesting question whether the dilemma holds only for the location of objects, or whether it extends to the properties of objects more generally. If high-level objects have properties that supervene with metaphysical necessity on the properties of low-level objects, we can ask whether those objects derive those properties from the low-level objects, or not? If they do, then unless those low-level objects have a decomposition that terminates in fundamental simple proper parts, we seem to be left with a regress of derivation. On the other hand, if the properties of high-level objects are not derived from the properties of the low-level objects upon which they supervene, it seems that unless we accept a non-standard ontology, there must be brute necessities to guarantee that the supervenient and subvenient properties line up. It seems plausible to me that the dilemma holds not only for the location of objects, but more generally for any properties of high-level objects that supervene with metaphysical necessity on the properties of low-level objects. But I shall not defend this claim here.

REFERENCES

Armstrong, D. M. (1989). *A Combinatorial Theory of Possibility*. Cambridge: Cambridge University Press.

―― (1997). *A World of States of Affairs*. New York: Cambridge University Press.

Baxter, D. (1988). "Many-One Identity". *Philosophical Papers* 17: 193–216.

Braddon-Mitchell, D., and Miller, K. (2006). "The Physics of Extended Simples". *Analysis* 66: 222–6.

Bradley, F. H. (1893). *Appearance and Reality*. Oxford: Clarendon Press.

Chalmers, D. J. (forthcoming). "Ontological Anti-Realism" in D. J. Chalmers, D. Manley, and R. Wasserman (eds.), *Metametaphysics: New Essays on the Foundations of Ontology*. Oxford: Oxford University Press.

Dainton, B. (2001) *Time and Space*. Montreal: McGill-Queen's University Press.

Dorr, C., and Rosen, G. (2002). "Composition as a Fiction". In R. M. Gale, (ed.), *The Blackwell Guide to Metaphysics*. Oxford: Blackwell Publishers

Foster, J. (1982). *The Case for Idealism*. London: Routledge & Kegan Paul.

Hudson, H. (2005). *The Metaphysics of Hyperspace*. Oxford: Clarendon Press.

Johnston, M. (2005). "Constitution". In F. Jackson and M. Smith (eds.), *Oxford Handbook of Contemporary Philosophy*. Oxford: Oxford University Press, 636–77.

Jubien, M. (1993). *Ontology, Modality, and the Fallacy of Reference*. Cambridge: Cambridge University Press.

Lewis, D. (1986). *On the Plurality of Worlds*. Oxford: Basil Blackwell.

―― (1991). *Parts of Classes*. Oxford: Basil Blackwell.

Markosian, N. (2004). "Simples, Stuff, and Simple People". *Monist* 82: 405–28.

McDaniel, K. (2007). "Brutal Simples". *Oxford Studies in Metaphysics* 3: 233–266.

Nolan, D. (2001). "What's Wrong with Infinite Regress?" *Metaphilosophy* 32/5: 523–38.

―― (2006). "Stoic Gunk". *Phronesis* 51/2: 162–83.

Parsons, J. (2000). "Must a Four-Dimensionalist Believe in Temporal Part?" *The Monist* 83: 399–418.

―― (2004). "Distributional Properties". In F. Jackson and G. Priest (eds.), *Lewisian Themes: The Philosophy of David K. Lewis*. Oxford: Oxford University Press, 173–80.

Schaffer, J. (2003). "Is there a Fundamental Level?" *Noûs* 37: 498–517.

Schaffer, J. (forthcoming). "Monism: The Priority of the Whole".
____ (ms.). "For (Priority) Monism: A Reply to Sider".
Sider, T. (1993). "Van Inwagen and the Possibility of Gunk". *Analysis* 53: 285–89.
____ (2007a). "Against Monism". *Analysis* 67: 1–7.
____ (2007b). "Parthood". *Philosophical Review* 116.
Wallace, M. (ms). "On Composition as Identity".
Williams, J. R. G. (2006). "Illusions of Gunk". *Philosophical Perspectives* 20/1: 493–513.

Part III

GUNK AND BLOBS

10. Gunk, Topology, and Measure

Frank Arntzenius

1. INTRODUCTION

It is standardly assumed that space and time consist of extensionless points. It is also a fairly standard assumption that all matter in the universe has point-sized parts. We are not often explicitly reminded of these very basic assumptions. But they are there. For instance, one standardly assumes that one can represent the states of material objects, and of fields, by functions from points in space and time to the relevant point values. Electric fields, mass densities, gravitational potentials, etc. ... are standardly represented as functions from *points* in space and time to *point* values. This practice would seem to make no sense if time and space did not have points as parts.

There is an alternative that has not been much explored. The alternative is that space and time and matter are 'pointless', or 'gunky'. The idea here is not that space and time and matter have smallest finite-sized bits, that space and time and matter are 'chunky'. Rather the idea is that every part of space and time and matter has a non-zero, finite, size, and yet every such part can always be subdivided into further, smaller, parts. That is to say, the idea is that every part of space and time and matter has a non-zero size, and yet there is no smallest size.

Let me emphasize how radical this idea is. It is very natural to think that any thing decomposes into some ultimate collection of fundamental parts. And it is very natural to think that the features of any object are determined by the way that object is constructed from its ultimate parts, and by the elementary features of these ultimate parts. Indeed, much of the history of science can be seen as an attempt to break down complex objects and processes into ultimate parts, and to find the laws that govern these ultimate parts.

But if there are no smallest regions, and if there are no smallest parts of objects, then a spatial or temporal decomposition of a region, and of an object, cannot bottom out at an ultimate level. The idea that the features of large regions and large objects are determined by the features of minimal-sized regions and minimal-sized objects cannot work if space and time, and the objects in it, are gunky, i.e. pointless. Space, time, and objects would simply not have ultimate parts. There would just be an infinite descending chain of ever-smaller parts. A somewhat dizzying prospect.

Well, let's not get ahead of ourselves. Not only would it require a fairly radical revision of our atomistic intuitions, it would also require a fairly radical and extensive reworking of standard mathematical methods for doing physics. If we cannot use real numbers to coordinatize locations in space and time, what can we use? If we cannot use ordinary functions to describe the states of things, what can we use?

All things in good order. We will get started on the business of rewriting physics a bit later on. First we will consider arguments for undertaking this seemingly mad enterprise. To preview: we will find no utterly compelling arguments against the existence of points. But we will find non-compelling reasons to explore the mathematics of gunky space and time.

2. THE POSSIBILITY OF MOTION AND DETERMINISM

Zeno argued that if time consists of instants of zero duration, then during each such instant an object cannot move. But if time consists entirely of a series of such instants then objects can never move. In view of this problem Aristotle proposed that there are no instants, no 0-sized intervals of time, indeed no smallest sized, atomic, intervals of time. Rather, time consists of smaller and smaller intervals. To put it another way: the world is a true movie, not a sequence of snapshots. To put it even more suggestively: becoming is not reducible to being.

One may not be impressed by Zeno's argument. One may for instance respond, as did some commentators in the middle ages, that to be in motion is just to be at different locations at different times, so that it simply is not true that just because one occupies only one location at one time one never moves.

Indeed, this is a perfectly coherent way to respond to Zeno's problem. However, one can then formulate a new worry, which is closely related to Zeno's worry. For if motion is just a matter of being at different locations at different times, then the intrinsic state of an object at an instant does not include its velocity. How then does an object at an instant 'know' in which direction to continue and at which speed? Less anthropomorphically: if the instantaneous states of objects do not include their velocities, then how could the instantaneous state of the world determine its subsequent states? That is, how could determinism hold? The world may in fact develop in a deterministic fashion, and it may not, but surely whether it does or does not should depend on the character of the laws of evolution of the world, rather than that the atomicity of the structure of time alone should imply that the world cannot be deterministic.[1]

One might attempt to respond to this argument by claiming that even if time consists of 0-sized instants, nonetheless the intrinsic state of an object at a time does include a velocity. Such an 'intrinsic velocity' would not be defined (as in ordinary calculus) in terms of (limits of) the position development of an object. Rather, it would be a primitive intrinsic feature of an object at a time, which *causes* the object to subsequently move in the direction in which the intrinsic velocity is pointing.

This does not strike me as a plausible response. For according to this response the intrinsic velocity at an instant and the direction in which the trajectory in space continues are not definitionally related, but are merely causally related. So it should be logically possible to have an object whose spatial trajectory continues in a direction that differs from the direction in which its intrinsic velocity points. Now, one might claim that such a bizarre non-alignment of direction of trajectory and intrinsic velocity is ruled out by the laws of nature. However, the mere conceptual possibility of such a misalignment seems puzzling, to say the least. Furthermore, if the laws of nature are to connect the directions in which primitive velocities point and the directions of trajectories in space, as they

---

[1] Well, it could still be deterministic if the equations of motion were first order, as they are in quantum mechanics. Still, one might like to think that even if the equations of motion are second order, as they are in classical mechanics, the world could be deterministic.

must do, then there is going to have to exist some further primitive relation, 'parallelhood', which obtains, or fails to obtain, between intrinsic velocities and spatial directions. Other things being equal it seems undesirable to add 'intrinsic velocities' and 'parallelhood' to one's stock of primitive quantities and relations, when one has no real need for them. In short, this response on behalf of points does not seem plausible to me. (For more detail on this line of argumentation, see Arntzenius 2000.)

However, a more plausible response to Zeno can be made on behalf of points. For one could simply claim that determinism should not be understood as the idea that the state at an instant determines states at all other times. Rather it should be understood as the idea that *any finite history* of states determines states at all other times.

Indeed, it seems to me that Zeno's arrow provides no compelling argument against point-sized instants. Let's turn to another argument.

3. CUTTING THINGS IN HALF

If space consists of points then one cannot cut a region exactly in two halves. For if one of the two regions includes the point on the cutting line, i.e. if it is closed at the cut, then the other does not include the points on the cutting line, i.e. it is open at the cut. Imagine, for instance, that we have x and y coordinates which are parallel to the sides of a rectangle. Suppose that the horizontal, x coordinate, of the rectangle runs from 0 to 2, and suppose that we cut the rectangle at $x = 1$. The question then arises: do the points that have x coordinate $= 1$ belong to the left-hand side after we have made our cut, or to the right-hand side? If they belong to the left-hand side, then the left half is closed at the cut, and the right half is open. If vice versa, then the left side is open. So the two parts would not be identical. So one cannot cut a region exactly in half if regions are composed out of points. One might reasonably conjecture that such a difference between open and closed regions is an artefact of our mathematical representation of regions, that does not correspond to a difference in reality. I, for one, find it hard to believe that there really are distinctions between open and closed regions in nature. But I agree that this is hardly a knock-down argument.

4. PARADOXES OF SIZE

If there exist points in space, and space is continuous, then it can be shown that there must be regions that have no well-defined size. For instance, there will be a part of any wall in any room such that it has no well-defined size. If you wanted to paint such a part of a wall in your house blue, there would be no possible answer to the question: "How much paint will I need to paint that part of my wall blue?" The problem is not that you would not know how much paint you would need, or that you would need 0 quarts of paint. Rather, the problem is that there just exists no quantity r of paint such that you would need exactly that quantity to paint that region. Let me be a bit more precise.

One can prove that in a continuous, pointy space there must exist regions that have no well-defined measure, if one assumes the axiom of choice and one assumes that the measure is countably additive. One can also prove that in a continuous pointy space of three or more dimensions there must exist regions that have no well-defined measure, if one assumes the axiom of choice and one assumes that the measure is finitely additive and invariant under (distance preserving) translations and rotations.[2]

There is even more weirdness about points and sizes: Banach and Tarski have shown that the existence of points implies cost-free guaranteed increases in size. That is to say, they showed that in a continuous pointy three-dimensional space one can take a sphere, break it into a finite number of pieces (five pieces in fact), move those pieces around rigidly (i.e. while preserving distances between the parts of the pieces), and rearrange those pieces to form a sphere of twice the size! That is to say, by breaking an object into five parts, and merely rearranging these parts spatially, without any stretching or changing of shapes, one can make an object larger or smaller, as one desires.

There is in fact a close relationship between this result and the fact that there are regions which have no well-defined size. Some of the parts into which we must break the sphere must have no well-defined sized. It is not hard to see that this must be so, for

[2] See e.g. Skyrms (1983) and Wagon (1985).

rigid motions preserve size, and the size of an object that consists exactly of five non-overlapping parts is just the sum of the sizes of those parts. So Banach and Tarski's result depends essentially on the existence of size-less regions.

How might one respond on behalf of points? Well, in the first place, one might simply deny the axiom of choice. This is an issue that could take us deep into philosophy of mathematics and mathematical physics, to which I have nothing new to contribute. I merely wish to point out that denying the axiom of choice implicitly commits one to (being part of) a large project, namely that of rewriting that part of mathematics and mathematical physics that one wants to retain, in such a way that it makes no use of the axiom of choice. My only comment on this project is that I am interested in a different project, namely that of doing physics without points. My project has several independent motivations, only one of which concerns the measure theoretic paradoxes.

A second possible response to the measure theoretic paradoxes is: who cares? Surely we will not as a practical matter get our hands on measureless parts of objects. Surely size-altering de-compositions and re-compositions are not practically achievable. So why worry?

Indeed, since one needs the axiom of choice to prove the existence of measureless regions, one cannot have explicit constructions of measureless, or of measure-altering, de-compositions and re-compositions. Nonetheless the mere existence of regions and/or parts which have no measure, and the mere possibility of size-altering de-compositions and re-compositions, remains rather bizarre, and prima facie implausible.

A third possible response to the measure theoretic paradoxes (on behalf of points) starts by making a distinction between sets of points in space-time, which are mathematical entities, and physical regions. One could, for example, suggest that all physical regions are Borel regions.[3] If that is so, then all physical regions are (Lebesque) measurable, and no size-altering de-compositions and re-compositions are possible.

Indeed, one could say this. But note that this means that regions fail to satisfy the standard axioms of mereology. For one is denying

---

[3] Borel regions of the real line: start with the collection of all open intervals, then close this collection up under countable union and intersection, and complementation.

that the fusion of any arbitrary collection of regions is a region. (Some collections of points are such that their fusion is a non-Borel region.) It seems hard to motivate this failure independently.

Nonetheless, yet again, we have found no devastating argument against points. We have simply found one more reason to try to see how far we can go without points. Let us turn to another argument against points.

5. QUANTUM MECHANICS AND POINTS

In non-relativistic quantum mechanics one can represent the state of a single particle by a wave-function. The probability that a particle will be found in a particular region upon measurement is given by the integral of the square of this wave-function in this region. If one has two functions whose values differ on a set of points of measure 0, then integrating them over any region will always yield identical results. Thus, as far as probabilities of results of measurements are concerned, functions that differ on a set of points of measure 0 are equivalent. This provides motivation for the claim that functions that differ on a set of points of measure 0 correspond to the same wave-function, i.e. the same quantum state.

A slightly more formal motivation for this derives from the fact that in a Hilbert space there is a unique null vector, a unique vector whose inner product with itself is 0. Thus, if one wishes to represent vectors in a separable Hilbert space (with a countable infinity of dimensions) by (complex) functions on space (or configuration space), and one wishes to represent the inner product of vectors by integration of the corresponding functions, then one has to represent vectors not by functions, but by equivalence classes of functions whose values differ on up to (Lebesque) measure 0 points. Indeed, although it is not often brought to the fore, it is a standard assumption in quantum mechanics that wave-functions correspond to equivalence classes of (square integrable) functions that differ up to Lebesque measure 0.

This ignoring of measure 0 differences between regions in space suggests that quantum mechanics should be set in a gunky space, not in a pointy space. (We will flesh out this claim in more detail when we examine the measure theoretic approach to gunk.) But, as always, there are responses possible on behalf of the point lover.

In the first place one might respond that the above is a false claim: quantum mechanics standardly uses wave-functions that are eigenfunctions of position, so-called 'delta functions', which differ from each other only on measure 0 sets of points. This line of response takes us into a tricky area. So-called 'delta functions' are not functions at all. Indeed position operators, on the standard separable Hilbert space approach to quantum mechanics, simply cannot have eigenstates. Nonetheless, it is true that there are (non-standard) ways of rigorizing the notion of an eigenstate of position, and thereby sanctioning states that in a clear sense are confined to a single point, while departing from the standard formalism of separable Hilbert spaces. (See e.g. Böhm 1978 and Halvorson 2001.) Not only does one have to depart from the standard formalism of separable Hilbert spaces in order to do so, but position eigenstates also have the feature that observables such as momentum and energy have no well-defined expectation values in such position eigenstates. In Arntzenius (2004) I have discussed whether it is worth paying this price for the acquisition of position eigenstates, and argued for a cautious 'no'. Let me here merely say that it is far from clear that it is worth paying this price, and leave it at that.

There is of course another possible response that can be made on behalf of the point lover. One could simply accept that quantum mechanics happens not to make use of measure 0 differences, and argue that this is all good and well, but this does not mean that such differences do not exist. Not every theory needs to make use of all the features that nature has on offer.

Indeed, I agree that both of the above two responses (on behalf of points) are perfectly coherent and possible. Nonetheless it seems to me that nature is piling up the hints that there just might be no points out there in space and time. Let's look at one more problem with points.

6. CONTACT BETWEEN OBJECTS

In the nineteenth century some people started worrying about the possibility of contact between solid objects if space consists of points. Here is a sketch of such worries. Let us suppose that solid objects cannot interpenetrate, i.e. that solid objects cannot occupy overlapping regions. Now consider two solid objects which always occupy closed regions, i.e. regions which include their own boundary. Such objects can never be in contact, for closed regions either overlap or are a finite distance apart. In order to avoid interpenetration such objects must decrease their velocities when they are still a finite distance apart, so some kind of action at a distance would have to occur. It seems strange and objectionable that the mere existence of solid objects should imply action at a distance. Alternatively suppose that solid objects occupy open regions. Then there must always be at least one point separating them. So they still cannot be in genuine contact, and they still must change their velocities without ever being in genuine contact.

The impossibility of genuine contact seems to provide an objection to the existence of points. However, there are a number of decent responses that one can give on behalf of points.

In the first place, one could respond that one would not want such 'genuine contact' anyhow, since collisions would lead to sharp, undifferentiable, kinks in the trajectories of objects. One could plausibly argue that a more realistic physics has objects interacting through fields. Then there will never be 'genuine contact', so there is no 'problem of contact'. One could amplify this line of thought by claiming that it is even more realistic to suppose that quantum mechanics, with an ontology of wave-functions (or perhaps wave-functions plus point particles), is correct, and that given such an ontology there is no problem of contact.

Secondly, one could argue that even if one wants to countenance solid objects which interact by contact, one could just have a slightly different account of what it is to 'be in contact' and what it is to 'interpenetrate'. One could, for example, just say that two objects are 'in contact' if and only if the boundaries of the regions that they occupy overlap. (A point p lies on the boundary of region R if any open set containing p intersects both R and the complement of R.) And one can say that objects do not 'interpenetrate' unless they overlap on more than just their boundaries. Physics can then proceed as usual. Of course, this would mean that objects occupying open regions (in a three-dimensional space) that are separated by a two-dimensional surface are in contact, and that bodies occupying closed regions which overlap on a two-dimensional surface do not interpenetrate. But so what. It does not lead to any trouble in formulating physics, or any trouble with experiment. It only leads to trouble with philosophers who think that it is a priori that 'genuine contact' is possible, where 'genuine contact' means having not even a single point in between, and who think it is a priori that 'interpenetration' is not possible for solid objects, where 'interpenetration' means not overlapping even on a single point. I don't know whether to respond to such philosophers that in a Newtonian collision world there are, in their sense of 'solid', no solid objects, or whether to respond that in their sense of 'genuine contact' there is no genuine contact, and in their sense of 'interpenetration' there is interpenetration. But one can do Newtonian collision physics when one defines contact as having overlapping boundaries, and interpenetration as overlapping on more than a boundary.

Both of the above responses on behalf of points seem adequate. Nonetheless note that neither of the responses requires a physics that makes essential use of points, or of measure 0 differences. So one is still left with the suspicion that points, and measure 0 differences, are artefacts of the mathematics, and do not exist in reality.

7. NOW WHAT?

It appears that every problem associated with the existence of points can be overcome; there appears to be no single devastating argument that space and time (or matter) have to be gunky. Nonetheless it remains of interest to examine the possibility of doing physics in gunky space and time in more detail.

There have been a number of approaches to the mathematics of gunky spaces. These approaches divide into three categories: the measure theoretic approach (see Skyrms 1993 and Sikorski 1964), the topological approach (see Roeper 1997), and the metric approach (see Gerla 1990). In this chapter I will not look in any detail at the metric approach. The reason I will not is that in the metric approach one assumes from the start as fundamental notions the notion of the 'diameter' of a region and the notion of the 'distance' between regions. This approach is prima facie ill-suited for the purposes of modern physics since in general relativity the notion of distance is local and path-dependent rather, it is not a non-local path-independent relation between regions. It would seem preferable to first be able to build a pointless differentiable manifold, and then to be able to put a metric tensor field on such a differentiable manifold. The measure-theoretic and topological approach to gunk are prima facie more amenable to this idea, since they do not start by presupposing the existence of non-local metric structure. Let's look at these two approaches in more detail and let's start with the topological approach.

8. THE TOPOLOGICAL APPROACH TO POINTLESS SPACES

My strategy for constructing a pointless topological space will be as follows. I will start with an ordinary pointy topological space. I will then put on blurry spectacles which wash out differences in regions which, intuitively speaking, are differences in the (pointy) mathematical representation of space that do not correspond to differences in actual physical space. This will yield a pointless topology. Once I have a pointless topology, I, of course, no longer have ordinary (point to point) functions. But there are still maps from pointless regions to pointless regions. We will see that a rather natural set of such maps corresponds 1–1 to pointy functions that map regular closed region to regular closed regions. Unfortunately this does not include functions which are constant on a finite region, so that we do not appear to have enough materials to do physics with. Furthermore, one would like to be able to put a measure on a pointless topological space. We will find that there is also a problem in putting a measure on a pointless topological space. I will therefore advocate switching to the measure theoretic approach. But first some of the details of the topological approach.

Let us start with an ordinary pointy topological space which is a 'locally compact T_2 space'. A topological space is a 'T_2 space' if and only if for any distinct points x and x' there are disjoint open subsets O and O' containing x and x' respectively. This is a very mild separability condition. A topological space is 'locally compact' if and only if for every point x there exists a 'compact' closed set C such that x lies in the 'interior' of C. A set S is 'compact' if and only if for every collection of open sets $\{O_a\}$ such that S is a subset of the union of these open sets, $S \subset \cup\{O_a\}$, there is a finite subcollection of these open sets such that S is a subset of the union of that subcollection: $S \subset O_{a1} \cup O_{a2} \cup \ldots \cup O_{an}$. The demand that a space be locally compact is very mild and roughly speaking amounts to the demand that each point is contained in an open set whose closure is not 'very large'. (The closure of a set S is the union of S with its boundary.)

Now let us put on our blurry spectacles, and ignore differences between sets that 'differ only on their boundaries'. We will say that two sets A and B 'differ only on their boundaries' if and only if the closure of the interior of A is equal to the closure of the interior of B, i.e. if $ClInt(A) = ClInt(B)$. (The interior of a set consists of the points of that set that do not lie on its boundary.) Here are a couple of examples of sets that, by this definition, differ only on their boundaries. Any set and its interior differ only on their boundaries ($ClIntInt(A) = ClInt(A)$). Any set consisting of finitely many points and any other set consisting only of finitely many points differ only on their boundaries, since the closure of the interior of each of them is the empty set.

Now, let us divide up all pointy regions (all sets of points) into equivalence classes R of regions that differ only on their boundaries. The motivation for doing this is that our 'blurry glasses' cannot distinguish regions that are in the same equivalence class, so we can regard these equivalence classes as corresponding to pointless regions. (From here on the symbols 'R' and 'R_i' will be always taken to denote pointless regions rather than pointy regions.)

Now let us give these equivalence classes R mereological structure. (This mereology will be standard except that it will include a 'null region', i.e. it will be a complete Boolean algebra.) In order to do this, let me first note that every equivalence class of pointy regions will include exactly one 'regular closed' pointy region, where pointy region S is said to be 'regular closed' if and only if $ClInt(S) = S$. For, take pointy region S in some equivalence class. Now consider $ClInt(S)$. It will be in the same equivalence class as S, since $ClInt(S) = ClIntClInt(S)$. For the same reason $ClInt(S)$ is regular closed. It is also the *only* regular closed pointy region in that equivalence class. For suppose S' is regular closed and in the same equivalence class as S. Then $ClInt(S) = ClInt(S') = S'$, so S' is the same as $ClInt(S)$. So there is a 1–1 correspondence between pointless regions R, and regular closed pointy regions PR. So we can define a mereological structure on the equivalence classes R by defining a mereological (Boolean) structure $(\leq, \neg, \wedge, \vee)$ on the corresponding regular closed pointy regions PR. This we can define in the following way:

(1) The empty set is the null region
(2) $PR_i \leq PR_j$ if and only if $PR_i \subset PR_j$. ('$\leq$' stands for the 'part of' relation.)
(3) $\neg PR = Cl(Co(PR))$. (Co(PR) is the set theoretic complement of PR.)
(4) $PR_i \vee PR_j = PR_i \cup PR_j$
(5) $PR_i \wedge PR_j = Cl(IntPR_i \cap IntPR_j)$
(6) If S is a set of regular closed pointy regions then $\vee S = Cl \cup \{PR | PR \in S\}$
(7) If S is a set of regular closed pointy regions then $\wedge S = ClInt \cap \{PR | PR \in S\}$.

Next let us give the pointless regions topological structure. The topological structure we will give pointless regions cannot be given in the same way that we gave pointy spaces topological structure, namely in terms of a distinction between open and closed regions. For that is exactly the kind of distinction that we do not believe exists if reality is pointless. Instead we will give the topological structure of pointless regions in terms of the primitive notions of 'part of', 'connectedness', and 'limitedness'. And again, we will use the 1–1 correspondence with regular closed pointy regions to determine the topological structure of the pointless regions. In particular, we stipulate that

(1) Two pointless regions are 'connected' if and only if the closed regular pointy regions that they correspond to have non-empty intersection,
(2) A pointless region is 'limited' if and only if the closed regular pointy region that it corresponds to is compact.

Now we can make use of a result that Peter Roeper proved (in Roeper 1997). He has shown that any collection of pointless regions that is constructed in the above way (i.e. by taking equivalence classes of pointy regions in a locally compact T_2 space which differ only on their boundaries) will satisfy the following axioms of pointless topology:

A_1 If pointless region A is connected to pointless region B, then B is connected to A

A_2 Every pointless region that is not the pointless 'null region' is connected to itself. (The pointless 'null region' corresponds to the equivalence class of regions which differ only on their boundaries from the null set.)

A_3 The null region is not connected to any pointless region

A_4 If A is connected to B and B is a part of C then A is connected to C

A_5 If A is connected to the 'fusion' of B and C, then A is connected to B or A is connected to C. (The 'fusion' of B and C is the smallest pointless region that has B and C as parts.)

A_6 The null region is limited

A_7 If A is limited and B is a part of A then B is limited

A_8 If A and B are limited then the fusion of A and B is limited

A_9 If A is connected to B then there is a pointless limited region C such that C is a part of B, and A is connected to C

A_{10} If A is limited, B is not the pointless null region, and A is not connected to the 'complement' of B, then there is a pointless region C which is non-null and limited, such that A is not connected to the 'complement' of C, and C is not connected to the 'complement' of B. (The 'complement' of a pointless region A is the pointless region −A such that A and −A have no parts in common, and every non-null pointless region has some part in common either with A or with −A.)

From a philosophical point of view it might seem that it would have made more sense to start with the axioms of pointless topology, and then to explain that any collection of pointless regions which satisfies these axioms will correspond 1–1 to equivalence classes of pointy regions in the unique corresponding locally compact T_2 space. After all, I certainly do not want to say that pointless regions *just are* equivalence classes of pointy regions, for that would mean that pointless regions just are mathematical constructions out of entities (pointy regions) which I believe not to exist. And that would not make much sense. No, the pointless view that I am here exploring is that pointy regions really do not exist, let alone that equivalence classes of them exist. The things that really exist are pointless regions, the primitive predicates and relations that are needed are the 'part of' relation, the 'limitedness' predicate, and the 'connected to' relation, and the axioms that characterize the true topology of space are A_1 through A_{10}. However, not only is it much easier to introduce the machinery of pointless topologies via a construction out of pointy topologies, it is also very important to see that pointless regions behave exactly the way that our blurry spectacle motivation wants them to behave. That is why I constructed pointless topologies in the way that I did. OK, on to the next tasks: placing material objects and fields in such a pointless topological space, and giving this space more structure than topological structure.

9. OBJECTS IN A POINTLESS TOPOLOGY

If space is pointless then one cannot specify the locations of material objects by indicating for each point in space whether that object occupies it or not. So how should we conceive of the locational properties of objects in a pointless space? Well, here's a suggestion. We specify the locational state of a material object by specifying for every pointless region whether the object is entirely contained in that region or not.

This suggestion is problematic. The problem is that, despite the fact that space is pointless, one could nonetheless have point particles if one followed this suggestion. How? Well, imagine that a material object is such that it is entirely contained in each of a collection of smaller and smaller pointless regions. Now, if for any pointless region within which the object is contained there is an arbitrarily small pointless subregion within which the object is contained, the object could not have any finite size. So it must have size zero.[4] This is surprising. For it means that one can have pointless space containing point particles! However, allowing such a thing seems to defeat most of the reasons we started on this whole business of gunk. We wanted neither points in space nor point particles.

---

[4] This doesn't quite mean that it has to be a point particle, since it could still be a line, or an infinitely thin surface. But one can define a notion of 'a converging set of regions' in such a way that the particle does indeed have to be a point particle if it is entirely within each of the regions in the 'converging set of regions'.

Moreover, allowing such point particles also leads to a formal feature that seems objectionable, namely a violation of 'countable additivity'. Here's what that means in this context and why it fails. Consider the following plausible looking principle: if an object is wholly outside each of a countable collection of regions R_i, then it is also wholly outside the fusion of these regions. Now consider our example. If a particle is entirely contained in each of a collection of converging regions, then it is wholly outside the complements of these regions. Now consider the fusion of the complements of these regions. Intuitively speaking the only thing that this fusion does not contain is the point that the converging collection is converging to. But remember that we are in a pointless space, and there exists no such point. So one should expect that the fusion of this countable collection is the whole space, for there is no pointless region that it misses out on, as it were. And indeed, this is correct: the fusion of these complements is the whole space. But a material object cannot lie entirely outside the whole of space. So we have a countable collection of regions such that the object lies wholly outside each one of the regions in the collection, but is wholly contained in their fusion. This is a failure of countable additivity, and seems bizarre and objectionable. So it seems that one should not allow a specification of the locational properties of a material object by specifying for each region whether it is entirely contained in it or not.

The obvious alternative is the following. One specifies the locational properties of a material object by specifying which region the object exactly fills. It will then, of course, be entirely contained in any region that includes this region, etc. But it could not be entirely contained in a converging collection of regions, for there is a minimal region, such that it is not contained in anything smaller than that region. No problem.

10. FIELDS IN A POINTLESS TOPOLOGY

How about the states of a field such as the electric field in a pointless topology? Here's a very natural suggestion. We specify the state of a field by specifying for each pointless region in space the exact range of values that the field obtains in that region. This brings up a further issue. Should we think of the possible ranges of values of the field as pointless ranges or as pointy ranges? Should we think that fields can have exact point values, or that the value spaces of fields are as gunky as the physical space that they inhabit? I don't know. In what follows I will make the weaker assumption, i.e. I will assume that the value space of a field is a pointless space, and see how far we get.

Following Peter Roeper (Roeper 1997), let us call a map h from a pointless physical space S to a pointless field value space VS a 'bounded continuous mereological' map, if it satisfies the following constraints:

(1) h(R) is the null region in VS if and only if R is the null region in S
(2) If R_1 is part of R_2 then h(R_1) is part of h(R_2)
(3) If V is non-null and part of h(R_1) then there exists a non-null R_2 such that R_2 is part of R_1 and h(R_2) is part of V
(4) If R_1 is connected to R_2 then h(R_1) is connected to h(R_2)
(5) If R is limited, then h(R) is limited.

One can prove (see Roeper 1997) that there is a 1–1 correspondence between bounded continuous mereological maps (between two pointless spaces) and continuous pointy functions (between the two corresponding locally compact T_2 spaces) which map regular closed sets of points to regular closed sets of points. That is to say, if we specify the state of a pointless field in a pointless space by means of a bounded continuous mereological map h, then this is equivalent to specifying the corresponding pointy field in the corresponding pointy space by means of a function f from points in space to pointy field values, where f must satisfy the constraint that it maps regular closed sets of points in space to regular closed sets of field values.

Now, suppose that it were the case that every pointy field function f that one ever is likely to need when doing standard pointy physics has the feature that it sends regular closed sets to regular closed sets. Then one could suggest that even though physical space and field value spaces in fact are pointless, one can still continue the standard practice of using ordinary pointy functions f when doing one's calculations in physics, since the possible gunky field states in gunky space correspond 1–1 to such pointy functions in pointy space.

Unfortunately, though, this is not true. For consider a pointy function f that has a fixed constant value v over some pointy region

PR. It will map every subset of PR, and hence every regular closed subset of PR, to the singleton set {v}. And a singleton is not a regular closed set. So a function that is constant over some (finite) region PR does not preserve the property of being regular closed. But clearly physics needs to make use of such functions. So we have a problem.

And there is more trouble. It seems clear that we will need to put a measure on pointless regions. For how else are we going to be able to talk of the sizes of regions, and how else are we going to be able to do the pointless analogue of the integration of functions, something that we surely have to be able to do. Unfortunately when one tries to put a measure on a pointless topological space one will run into difficulties that appear to be insurmountable.

Let me start on the project of putting a measure on a pointless topological space by considering a very simple case. We know that there is a 1–1 correspondence between pointless topological spaces and pointy locally compact T_2 spaces. Let us now consider the pointless topological space that corresponds to the pointy one-dimensional continuum, i.e. the real number line. We know that there is a 1–1 correspondence between the pointless regions R in the pointless one-dimensional continuum and the regular closed sets of real numbers. Given this fact, the obvious way to try to put a measure on the pointless regions in the pointless continuum is to identify the measure of any pointless region R with the Lebesque measure of the corresponding closed regular set of real numbers PR. The problem now is that this will turn out to yield a measure on the pointless regions which violates countable additivity. We can see this by looking at a 'Cantor-set', or rather, the complement of a Cantor set.

Start with the set [0,1]. Call this set S_0. It is a regular closed set with Lebesque measure 1. Now consider the middle quarter of this set, i.e. the set [3/8, 5/8]. Call this set S_1. S_1 is a regular closed set with Lebesque measure 1/4. Now consider the set S_2 which consists of two parts which fill the middle of the gaps left by S_1 and which has Lebesque measure 1/8. That is to say $S_2 = [7/32, 9/32] \cup [23/32, 25/32]$. Keep on doing this, i.e. set S_n has parts which are slotted halfway between all the parts of all the previous sets, and S_n has half the Lebesque measure of set S_{n-1}. Since each set S_n is a regular closed set, each such set corresponds to a pointless region R_n in the pointless one-dimensional continuum. Let us now ask what the fusion $\vee\{R_n\}$ of all these pointless regions is.

Gunk, Topology, and Measure | 243

Well, by our previous account of the mereology of pointless regions, this is going to be the unique pointless region that corresponds to the regular closed pointy region $Cl \cup \{S_n\}$. The union of all pointy regions S_n is dense on the set [0,1]. So its closure is just [0,1]. So the pointless region $\vee \{R_n\}$ corresponds to the equivalence class of regions that differs by measure 0 from the pointy region [0,1].

Now we can see why we are in trouble if we assign measures to pointless regions by assigning them the Lebesque measure of the unique regular closed regions that they correspond to. For $\vee \{R_n\}$ will be assigned measure 1 by this method, while the measures of the R_n will sum to $1/2$. That is to say, this measure will not be countably additive. This is a terrible problem, for we need a countably additive measure.

Now one might suggest that the problem here is that I simply suggested the wrong rule for assigning measures to pointless regions. However, not only is there no other obvious candidate for such a measure, one can in fact prove that there can be no such measure. That is to say, one can prove that there cannot exist a countably additive measure that is defined on every element of an algebra if that algebra is isomorphic to the algebra of closed regular regions of a continuum.[5] So our attempt to do physics in this kind of pointless topological space is in big trouble. Combined with the implausibility of our account of the possible states of fields in this kind of topological space, this provides us with a good reason to try our luck instead with the measure theoretic approach to pointless spaces.

11. THE MEASURE THEORETIC APPROACH TO POINTLESS SPACES

Let's concentrate on a simple case: the real number line. As before, we are going to create a pointless space by putting on blurry glasses. On the measure theoretic approach what we are going to blur out

---

[5] This is so because the algebra of closed regular regions of the real line is not 'weakly distributive', and one cannot have a 'semi-finite' countably additive measure that is defined on every element of an algebra that is not weakly distributive. A measure is said to be 'semi-finite' if every element that has infinite measure has a part that has finite measure. For the definition of weak distributivity and a proof of the fact that one can not put a semi-finite measure on an algebra that is not weakly distributive, see chapters 32 and 33 of Fremlin 2002.

is differences of Lebesque measure 0. In order to do that, we first have to restrict ourselves to Lebesque measurable sets. So let's start by restricting ourselves to the Borel sets. One gets the collection of all Borel sets on the real line by starting with the collection of all open intervals (open sets of the form (a,b) for any real numbers a and b), and closing this collection up under complementation, countable union, and countable intersection. Now let us put on our blurry glasses and define pointless regions R of the pointless real line to be equivalence classes of Borel sets of the pointy real line that differ up to Lebesque measure 0. Note that forming such equivalence classes preserves complementation, countable union, and countable intersection. Indeed one can show that the algebra of such equivalence classes is a complete Boolean algebra, i.e. a standard mereology (with a null region) which is closed under arbitrary fusion. (See Sikorski 1964: 73–5.)

As before we would like to be able to recover standard physics, and we would therefore like to be able to recover a large collection of pointy functions from pointy space to a pointy field value space from some suitable collection of mappings between the corresponding pointless spaces. Luckily there already exists a nice and well-known account of how to do this. In particular, one can prove the following (see Sikorski 1964: section 32). There exists a 1–1 correspondence between equivalence classes of pointy 'Borel-measurable' functions *from* real line A *to* real line B that differ on up to Lebesque measure 0 sets of points, and 'σ-homomorphisms' *from* pointy regions on the pointy real line B *to* pointless regions on the pointless real line A. A function is said to be 'Borel measurable' if it sends Borel sets to Borel sets. A mapping h between Boolean algebras that are closed under countable union and intersection is said to be a 'σ-homomorphism' if :

(1) $h(\neg R) = \neg h(R)$
(2) $h(\vee R_i) = \vee h(R_i)$, for any countable collection $\{R_i\}$
(3) $h(\wedge R_i) = \wedge h(R_i)$, for any countable collection $\{R_i\}$.

That is to say, if we make the very simple and natural assumption that the state of a pointless scalar field in a pointless continuum (the above generalizes to n-dimensional continua) can be given by a σ-homomorphism from pointy value ranges to pointless regions in space, then we can recover all Borel measurable pointy functions (including highly discontinuous ones) up to differences of Lebesque measure 0. This is a great result. Not only can one recover all the functions that one could reasonably be expected to ever need in physics, one can also only recover these functions up to the kind of differences that one would expect not to correspond to real differences in nature.

What about topology though? We have just put a measure on an atomless mereology of pointless regions, but that tells us nothing about which pointless region is connected to which pointless region. For, loosely speaking, cutting out a segment of the real line, and pasting it in somewhere else along the real line does not alter the mereology of the real line, nor the measure theoretic structure of that mereology. So we need to add a topology separately. How could we do that? Well, what we could try to do is to start with the pointy real line, and then use its pointy topology to define a topology on the pointy real line which is invariant under differences of up to Lebesque measure 0. Let's try that.

Let's say that pointy Borel sets A and B are 'connected' if and only if there exists a point p such that any open set containing p has an overlap of non-zero measure both with A and with B. And let us say that pointy Borel set A is 'limited' if and only if for some compact Borel set B we have that A $\cap$ Complement(B) has measure 0.

Clearly these definitions are invariant under differences in regions A and B up to measure 0. So we can use it to define a topology on the pointless regions of the pointless real line. The resulting structure will satisfy Roeper's axioms A1 through A9, but it will violate axiom A10. Let me remind you what this axiom says: if R_a is limited, R_b is not the pointless null region, and R_a is not connected to the complement of R_b, then there is a pointless region R_c which is non-null and limited, such that R_a is not connected to the complement of R_c, and R_c is not connected to the complement of R_b.

To see that this axiom fails consider a Cantor-type pointy set, for instance the pointy set B = $(0, 1) \cap$ complement($\cup S_n$) where the S_n are the gap-filling sets that I defined in the previous section. Set B is a measure $1/2$ Borel set, so we can consider the corresponding non-null pointless region R_b to which it corresponds. Now let R_a be the null region. R_a is limited and not connected to the complement of R_b since the null region is not connected to anything. So there should be a non-null and limited R_c such that R_c is not connected to the complement of R_b. Now the complement of R_b is the union of three pointless regions: $\{-\infty, 0\}, \cup R_n$, and $\{1, \infty\}$. Now, any pointy non-null open set has an overlap of non-zero Lebesque measure with any pointy set in the equivalence corresponding to this pointless region, so this pointless region is connected to every non-null pointless region. So there can not be such an R_c.

The problem is the following. The basic idea of axiom A10 is that there is a topological notion of pointless region R_1 being 'strictly inside' pointless region R_2. The idea is that R_1 is strictly inside R_2 if R_1 is disconnected from the complement of R_2. And then the idea of 'pointlessness', or the idea of 'non-atomicity' suggests that if R_1 is strictly inside R_3 then there ought to be an R_2 such that R_1 is strictly inside R_2 and R_2 is strictly inside R_3. In particular for any non-null R there should be a non-null region R' which is strictly inside R. This axiom fails given the way that I have defined connectedness on the measure theoretic approach, since there are Cantor type non-null regions such that there are no regions that are strictly inside such a Cantor type region, since the complement of such a Cantor type region is connected to every non-null region.

Now one might think that the failure of this axiom shows that we do not really have a *pointless* space. However, the fact that our space is pointless is still unambiguously represented in two different ways:

(1) The algebra of regions is non-atomic
(2) Other than the null region, every region has non-zero measure, and for every non-zero measure, no matter how small, there are regions that have that measure.

So I am not terribly worried about the failure of axiom A10. However, it is interesting to note that the fact that there exists a pointless region R_b corresponding to a pointy Cantor set shows that one should not think that each pointless region can be decomposed into a collection of extended 'solid islands'. The pointless region R_b, for instance, is not so decomposable. Ah well, so be it.

There is a question that I have not yet answered. Namely: to what extent does a measure algebra with a topology satisfying axioms A1–A9 uniquely correspond to a pointy topological space plus measure? Part of the answer is well known: every atomless separable measure algebra is isomorphic, and hence corresponds uniquely to the mereology of the continuum with the Lebesque measure on its Borel algebra. (See Royden 1968: chapter 15.) But I do not yet know to what extent the pointless topological structure uniquely determines the corresponding pointy topological structure. So there is interesting work left.

And, of course, this is only a beginning. We also need to add differential structure and then metric structure in order to be able to do modern physics. But that is work for the future. For now let me simply conclude that the measure theoretic approach to gunky, or pointless, spaces is the most promising.

REFERENCES

Arntzenius, F. (2000). "Are There Really Instantaneous Velocities?" *The Monist* 83/2: 187–208.

―― (2004). "Is Quantum Mechanics Pointless?" *Philosophy of Science* 70/5: 1447–58.

Böhm, A. (1978). *The Rigged Hilbert Space and Quantum Mechanics*. Berlin: Springer.

Fremlin, T. (2002). *Measure Theory, Vol 3*. Published by Fremlin himself. Available at <http://www.essex.ac.uk/maths/staff/fremlin/mtsales.htm>.

Gerla, G. (1990). "Pointless Metric Spaces". *Journal of Symbolic Logic* 55/1: 207–19.

Halvorson, H. (2001). "On the Nature of Continuous Physical Quantities In Classical and Quantum Mechanics". *Journal of Philosophical Logic* 30: 27–50.

Roeper, P. (1997). "Region-Based Topology". *Journal of Philosophical Logic* 26: 251–309.

Royden, H. (1968). *Real Analysis*. London: MacMillan.

Sikorski, R. (1964). *Boolean Algebras*. Berlin: Springer Verlag.

Skyrms, B. (1983). "Zeno's Paradox of Measure". In R. S. Cohen and L. Laudan (eds.), *Physics, Philosophy and Psychoanalysis*. Dordrecht: Reidel, 223–54.

―― (1993). "Logical Atoms and Combinatorial Possibility". *Journal of Philosophy* 90/5: 219–32.

Wagon, S. (1985). *The Banach-Tarski Paradox*. Cambridge: Cambridge University Press.

11. The Structure of Gunk: Adventures in the Ontology of Space

Jeffrey Sanford Russell

1. POINTS AND GUNK

Here are two ways space might be (not the only two): (1) Space is 'pointy'. Every finite region has infinitely many infinitesimal, indivisible parts, called *points*. Points are zero-dimensional atoms of space. In addition to points, there are other kinds of 'thin' boundary regions, like surfaces of spheres. Some regions include their boundaries—the *closed* regions—others exclude them—the *open* regions—and others include some bits of boundary and exclude others. Moreover, space includes *unextended* regions whose size is zero. (2) Space is 'gunky'.[1] Every region contains still smaller regions—there are no spatial atoms. Every region is 'thick'—there are no boundary regions. Every region is extended.

Pointy theories of space and space-time, such as Euclidean space or Minkowski space, are the kind that figure in modern physics. A rival tradition, most famously associated in the last century with A. N. Whitehead, instead embraces gunk.[2] On the Whiteheadian view, points, curves, and surfaces are not parts of space, but rather abstractions from the true regions.

Three different motivations push philosophers toward gunky space. The first is that the physical space (space-time) of our universe might be gunky. In Quinean terms, spatial regions are posits, invoked to explain what goes on with physical objects; the main reason to believe in point-sized regions is the role they play in our

---

Dean Zimmerman has been a relentless source of suggestions and criticism throughout the writing of this chapter. Thanks are also due to Frank Arntzenius, Kenny Easwaran, Peter Forrest, Hilary Greaves, John Hawthorne, and Beatrice Sanford for helpful comments.

[1] David Lewis coined the term 'gunk' to describe infinitely divisible atomless objects (1991).
[2] For historical background, see Zimmerman 1996b.

physical theories. So far it looks like points are doing well in that regard despite their uncanniness: all of our most successful theories represent space-time as a manifold of points. But do the points really do important theoretical work, or are they mere formal artefacts, scaffolding to be cast off of our final theory? Modern physics does offer some evidence for the latter. Frank Arntzenius observes that the basic objects of quantum mechanics are not fields in pointy space, but instead equivalence classes of fields up to measure zero differences: point-sized differences between fields are washed out of the theory (2007). This is suggestive: perhaps the points don't belong in the theory in the first place.

A second motivation is interest in possibility rather than actuality. For some metaphysicians, whether or not our own universe's space is pointy or gunky is of only incidental interest; the real question is what ways space *could* be—in the sense of metaphysical rather than epistemic possibility. This question is pressing due to the role of *material* gunk in recent debates. Many philosophers have the intuition that atomless material objects are genuinely possible, even if atomism happens to be true in the actual world, and certain views have been criticized for failing to accommodate this intuition.[3] Furthermore, there are reasons to think that gunky space is the right environment for material gunk. One road to that conclusion is by way of 'harmony' principles that link the composition of material objects to the composition of the spatial regions they occupy.[4] Another route to gunky space is by way of contact puzzles.[5] Suppose two blocks are in perfect contact. If space is pointy, then there is a region of space at the boundary between the two blocks. Either this region is empty—which apparently contradicts the assumption that the two blocks are touching—or else it is occupied by both blocks—which looks like disturbing co-location—or else some strange asymmetry is at work. Perfect contact may not take place in the actual world, but to the extent that one thinks it a genuine (metaphysical) possibility, this should incline one toward gunk. (It's plausible, for instance, that gunky space is the right environment for corpuscular Newtonian mechanics, where collisions are taken seriously.)

---

[3] E.g. in Sider 1993.
[4] Cf. Gabriel Uzquiano, "Mereological Harmony" (unpublished draft).
[5] Cf. Zimmerman 1996a.

A third reason to investigate gunky space is to formalize the psychology of space. Regardless of whether phenomena like perfect contact are physically or even metaphysically possible, they surely play into 'common sense' spatial reasoning. Rigorously capturing this kind of reasoning is important for formal semantics, cognitive science, and artificial intelligence.

These different motivations all call for a clear account of space without points. My interest is in framing theories of gunky space that are as formally adequate and precise as the theories of pointy space on offer—an ambition many share. One pioneer is Alfred Tarski, who presents an elegant formalization of Whiteheadian geometry, which he describes as 'a system of geometry destitute of such geometrical figures as points, lines, and surfaces, and admitting as figures only solids—the intuitive correlates of open (or closed) regular sets of three-dimensional Euclidean geometry' (1956). (Note, though, that the issues in this chapter are independent of space's particular dimension or curvature.)

In addition to framing precise theories, it is useful to construct models of gunky space. The open regular sets are a model for Tarski's geometry, since they satisfy his axioms.[6] This demonstrates that his theory is logically consistent—as long as the Euclidean theory, in whose terms the model is couched, is consistent. (Of course, the model is not meant to show what space really *is*. If gunky space were really an abstraction from pointy space, then the gunky space would only exist if the pointy space did as well—this would make things awfully crowded.)

Recently, though, Whiteheadian space has been threatened Peter Forrest (1996) and Frank Arntzenius (2007) have independently offered parallel arguments that challenge the coherence of some gunky accounts.[7] Theories like Tarski's run into serious trouble when we ask questions about the precise sizes of regions. In this chapter I present a generalization of the Forrest–Arntzenius argument that makes clear which features of space are incompatible.

---

[6] An open regular set is an open set which is the interior of its closure. The interior of x (int x) is the largest open set contained in x (equivalently, the set of x's *interior points*). The closure of x (cl x) is the smallest closed set that contains x (equivalently, the set of x's *limit points*). For example: the open interval $(0, 1)$ is an open regular set; the union of open intervals $(0, 1) \cup (1, 2)$ is not.

[7] John Hawthorne and Brian Weatherson present a related argument (2004).

The Structure of Gunk | 251

The objection thus sharpened, I take up gunk's defense, considering three responses: Arntzenius's, Forrest's, and a new response. The Forrest–Arntzenius argument requires some concessions, but it does not force us to give up gunky space.

2. THREE KINDS OF SPATIAL STRUCTURE

Before presenting the main argument in Section 3, I need to lay some formal groundwork for the relevant spatial structures. Along the way I isolate three different constraints on Whiteheadian space.

2.1 Mereology

The first of these structures is mereology: a region x may be *part* of a region y (for short, $x \leq y$); synonymously: y contains x, or x is a subregion of y, in the weak sense where every region is a subregion of itself.[8] My main argument only requires two properties of this relation (x, y, and z are arbitrary regions throughout):

(1) $x \leq x$. **(Reflexivity)**
(2) If $x \leq y$ and $y \leq z$, then $x \leq z$. **(Transitivity)**

These are very weak conditions: any two-place relation at all has a transitive and reflexive extension.

Some results other than the main argument depend on slightly more structure. Adding one further proposition yields the axiom system of Ground Mereology (**M**):

(3) If $x \leq y$ and $y \leq x$, then $x = y$. **(Antisymmetry)**

Throughout this chapter I invoke the three axioms of **M** without apology. I don't make use of any mereological principles beyond these without due warning.
I also use the following definitions:

(D1) x and y **overlap** iff there is a region z such that $z \leq x$ and $z \leq y$. Regions that do not overlap are **disjoint**.
(D2) x is a **proper part** of y ($x < y$) iff $x \leq y$ and $x \neq y$.

---

[8] The definitions and axioms in this section are adapted from Varzi 2006.

Intuitively, a proper part must have something 'left over'—something that 'supplements' it. This intuition has formalizations of various strengths:

(4) If $x < y$, then y has a part that is disjoint from x. **(Weak Supplementation)**

(5) Unless $x \geq y$, y has a part that is disjoint from x. **(Strong Supplementation)**

An even stronger formulation is that x must have some *remainder* in y—some part which exactly makes up the difference between them.

(D3) A region z is the **remainder** of x in y (or the **mereological difference** of y and x, denoted $y - x$) iff: for every region w, $w \leq z$ iff w is a part of y that is disjoint from x.

A remainder is a *maximal* supplement. This gives rise to the third and strongest supplementation principle:

(6) Unless $x \geq y$, x has a remainder in y. **(Remainder Closure)**

Besides taking differences between regions, we can also take sums of regions.

(D4) A region f is a **fusion** (or **mereological sum**) of a set of regions S iff: for every region x, x overlaps f iff x overlaps some $y \in S$.

Intuitively, the fusion of the y's is the region that includes all of the y's and nothing more. If Strong Supplementation holds, then any set of regions has at most one fusion. As we have various supplementation principles, we also have various composition principles. This is one standard principle:

(7) For any x and y, some region is a fusion of x and y (denoted $x \vee y$). **(Sum Closure)**

The principles listed so far are together equivalent to the axioms of *Closure Extensional Mereology* (**CEM**). A much stronger composition principle is the following:

(8) Any set of regions has a fusion. **(Unrestricted Composition)**

Under this principle, mereological sums exist for arbitrary finite or infinite collections of regions. Adding Unrestricted Composition to **CEM** yields the system of *General Extensional Mereology* (**GEM**), also called simply 'standard mereology'. Euclidean and Tarskian geometry both satisfy **GEM**, but (to reiterate) I don't assume standard mereology in what follows.

Points have a distinctive mereological feature: they are *atoms*, regions with no proper parts. Pointless space has a corresponding feature: it is atomless.

(9) Every region has a proper part. **(Mereological Gunk)**

2.2 Topology

Topology describes general shape properties such as connectedness, continuity, and having a boundary. Mathematical orthodoxy casts topological structure in terms of properties of point-sets: the *open* sets are taken as primitive, and other structures are defined in terms of them. This is of little use if there are no points. Instead I'll follow the tradition of Whitehead, Bowman Clarke (1981), and Peter Röper (1997), which instead characterizes topology in terms of a primitive relation of *connectedness*. Intuitively, two regions x and y are connected ($x \bowtie y$) if they are adjacent, including if they overlap. The corresponding notion in point-set topology is sharing a limit point; i.e. having overlapping closures.[9]

With connectedness on hand, we can define a number of other important notions.[10]

(D5) x is a **boundary** of y iff every part of x is connected to y and also to some region disjoint from y.

A boundary region is tightly sandwiched between some region and its complement.

(D6) x is **open** iff no part of x is a boundary of x.

---

[9] Tarski does not take connection as primitive in his geometry. Instead, Tarski treats *sphericality* as a primitive property of regions. The spheres impose a *metric* structure on the space, which induces a topology. With some ingenuity, Tarski frames a purely mereological condition for two spheres to be *concentric*. We can then define 'x and y are connected' as 'There exists some sphere s such that every sphere concentric with s overlaps both x and y'. This parallels sharing a limit point in point-set topology: the set of concentric spheres is an ersatz point.

[10] The following connection axioms suffice to prove the claims in this section:
(i) $x \bowtie x$. **(Reflexivity)**
(ii) If $x \bowtie y$, then $y \bowtie x$. **(Symmetry)**
(iii) If $x \bowtie y$ and $y \leq z$, then $x \bowtie z$. **(Monotonicity)**

(D7) A region x is an **interior part** of y iff $x \leq y$ and x is not connected to any region disjoint from y.[11]

It follows from the definitions that for any $x \leq y$, either x is a boundary of y, or else x contains an interior part of y. In particular, every open region has an interior part. Moreover, except when a region is disconnected from the rest of space, every interior part is a *proper* part.

Whiteheadian space isn't just mereologically distinctive, but also topologically distinctive: there are no boundary regions. We can formulate this as a second condition on gunk:

(10) No region is a boundary. **(No Boundaries)**

Or equivalently,

(11) Every region is open.

This entails, and in the presence of Strong Supplementation is equivalent to,

(12) Every region has an interior part.[12]

I call space that satisfies No Boundaries *topologically gunky*. Topological Gunk is a natural extension of Mereological Gunk: not only does every region have a proper part, it has a part which is strictly inside of it.

I draw on one further topological notion. A *topological basis* is a collection of open regions out of which all of the open regions can be built up: any open region is a mereological sum of basis regions. An important topological basis in Euclidean space is the set of *rational spheres*: the open spheres with rational center coordinates and rational radii. This basis is *countable*. Any space that is shaped like Euclidean space, whether pointy or gunky, has a countable basis. For instance, the regions in Tarski's geometry that correspond to the rational spheres make up a countable basis there. Since in topologically gunky space every region is open,

[11] When Strong Supplementation holds, the clause '$x \leq y$' is redundant.
[12] (11) entails (10) because if x is a boundary of an open region y, then x is disjoint from y and connected to y at every part, hence not open. (12) entails (10) by the following argument. Suppose x is a boundary of y. *First case:* $x \not\leq y$. By Strong Supplementation, some $z \leq x$ is disjoint from y. But every part of x—and so every part of z—is connected to y, so z has no interior part. *Second case:* $x \leq y$. Every $z \leq x$ is connected to some w disjoint from y, and thus disjoint from x as well—so x has no interior part.

(13) If space is topologically gunky and B is a topological basis, every region contains an element of B.

This is important.

2.3 Measure

Besides mereology and topology, regions have sizes. This feature is formalized using a *measure function*, m, which assigns sizes—represented by non-negative real numbers up to infinity—to regions of space (Munroe 1953). A measure function should satisfy this condition:

(14) If x and y are disjoint and $f = x \vee y$, then $m(f) = m(x) + m(y)$. **(Finite Additivity)**

Finite Additivity has an important generalization, which is an axiom of standard measure theory:

(15) For any countable set of pairwise-disjoint regions S, if f is a fusion of S then $m(f) = \sum_{x \in S} m(x)$. **(Countable Additivity)**

With Remainder Closure, this has an important consequence:

(16) For any countable set of regions S, if f is a fusion of S then $m(f) \leq \sum_{x \in S} m(x)$. **(Countable Subadditivity)**

The whole is no larger than the sum of its parts. I discuss this condition further in Section 4.2.

Now we turn to measuring gunk. In pointy space, there are *unextended* regions—regions (like points, curves, and surfaces) that have measure zero. Gunky space is supposed to be free of unextended regions:[13]

(17) Every region has positive measure. **(No Zero)**

Gunky space also shouldn't have discrete 'chunks', regions with no parts smaller than some finite size. Rejecting chunks means committing to the following principle:

(18) Every region has an arbitrarily small part: i.e., for every region x, for any $\varepsilon > 0$ there is some $y \leq x$ such that $m(y) \leq \varepsilon$. **(Small Regions)**

---

[13] Arntzenius and Hawthorne propose this condition (2005).

Small Regions holds automatically in pointy space: every region contains a point with size zero. It also follows from Mereological Gunk, given Remainder Closure and Finite Additivity.[14] The conjunction of No Zero and Small Regions entails (and again given Remainder Closure and Finite Additivity, it is equivalent to):

(19) Every region has a strictly smaller part. **(Measure-Theoretic Gunk)**

As having an interior part is a natural topological elaboration on having a proper part, having a smaller part is a natural measure-theoretic elaboration. Note that since each of the three ways of being gunky constrains a different sort of structure, they need not all stand or fall together.

3. DISASTER

In fact, these structural constraints can't all hold. The following argument by Arntzenius (in this volume), gives a picture of why not. (Forrest (1996) offers a parallel argument using a different construction.) For simplicity, consider one-dimensional gunky space—a line—and let the *Big Interval* be a one-inch interval in this space. Let a be the $\frac{1}{4}$-inch segment in the middle of the Big Interval. Then consider the two subregions of the Big Interval flanking a, and let b_1 and b_2 be two $\frac{1}{16}$ inch intervals in their respective middles. This divides r into a, b_1, b_2, and four equal regions surrounding them. In each of the latter four regions, pick out a region that is $\frac{1}{4}$ of $\frac{1}{16}$ inch long (i.e. $\frac{1}{64}$ inch); call these c_1 through c_4. And so on. Call $a, b_1, b_2, \ldots$ the *Cantor Regions*.

The Cantor Regions include one $\frac{1}{4}$-inch interval, two whose lengths add up to $\frac{1}{8}$ inch, four whose lengths add up to $\frac{1}{16}$ inch, etc. So the sum of their lengths is $\frac{1}{4} + \frac{1}{8} + \frac{1}{16} + \ldots = \frac{1}{2}$ inch—strictly less than the length of the Big Interval. And yet if space is topologically

---

[14] Except in the degenerate case where some infinite region only has infinite subregions. *Proof.* Consider an arbitrary region x with positive finite measure. By Mereological Gunk, x has a proper part y, and by Remainder Closure (it's easy to show) $x = y \vee (x - y)$, so by Finite Additivity $m(x) = m(y) + m(x - y)$. It follows that at least one of $m(y)$ and $m(x - y)$ must be less than or equal to $\frac{1}{2}m(x)$. Repeating this n times procures a part of x no larger than $m(x)/2^n$, which is eventually smaller than any positive ε.

gunky, then the Big Interval is the fusion of the Cantor Regions (I'll defer the details to the main argument below). We have a set of regions whose lengths add up to half an inch, but whose fusion is a whole inch long: this is serious trouble.

Before responding to this predicament, I want to sharpen the troubling feeling with my own more general argument.[15]

Theorem. *The following five theses are inconsistent:*

1. *Space has a transitive and reflexive parthood relation.*
2. *Space has a topology with a countable basis.*
3. *Space is topologically gunky.*
4. *Space has a non-trivial countably subadditive measure.*[16]
5. *Every region has an arbitrarily small subregion.*

Proof. Consider a region with positive finite measure—the *Big Region*—and call its measure M. Let the *Insiders* be the basis elements that are parts of the Big Region. Since the basis is countable, there are countably many Insiders, so we can enumerate them. For $i = 1, 2, \ldots$, pick a subregion of the ith Insider whose measure is less than $M/2^{i+1}$; call these subregions the *Small Regions*. The Small Regions' sizes add up to strictly less than M.

Even so, the Big Region is a fusion of the set of Small Regions. To show this, we need to show that every region that overlaps a Small Region overlaps the Big Region, and vice versa. The first direction is obvious: each Small Region is part of the Big Region. Now let x be any region that overlaps the Big Region, so x and the Big Region have a part in common, y. Topological Gunk implies that y contains a basis element b, which must be one of the Insiders, and so b contains a Small Region. Since $b \leq x$, x overlaps a Small Region.

Therefore the Big Region fuses the Small Regions, as advertised. But the Small Regions are too small for that! This means that Countable Subadditivity fails, Q.E.D.

Standard mereology, topology, and measure theory, even when stripped to a bare skeleton, are inconsistent with topological gunk.

---

[15] My argument is more closely analogous to Forrest's variant than Arntzenius's. Forrest's construction, though, depends specifically on pointy representations of regions: he appeals to regions that are well-represented by neighborhoods of points with rational coordinates. Moreover, both Arntzenius's and Forrest's constructions depend on assumptions about the geometry of space. By contrast, my construction is purely topological.

[16] By 'non-trivial' I mean that at least one region has positive finite measure.

Any account of gunk that commits to all five theses is incoherent—so things look bad for Whiteheadian space.

3.1 Aside: measurability

My argument officially requires a measure function that is defined for *every* region of space. This may seem too strict a requirement; the Vitali theorem and the more notorious Banach–Tarski theorem show that in Euclidean space there are sets of points that cannot be consistently assigned a measure (these theorems require the Axiom of Choice). Thus the standard measure function in Euclidean space (Lebesgue measure) is defined only on a distinguished collection of sets, which are called *measurable*. Here are two metaphysical interpretations of the mathematics: one might say that some regions in Euclidean space have no sizes; or one might say that the true regions in Euclidean space correspond to just the measurable sets.[17] (On the latter interpretation, Unrestricted Composition fails: an arbitrary set of regions does not necessarily compose a region—for there are sets of point-sized regions which do not. Fusions of arbitrary *countable* sets of regions still exist, but all bets are off for the *uncountable* sets.)

We hope that gunky space will free us from such discomforts. Arntzenius and Hawthorne propose a requirement on gunk to this effect (they call it 'Definition') (2005):

(20) Every region is measurable. **(Measurability)**

Note that my argument requires no composition principles, so Measurability can be had cheaply by banishing any supposed exceptions, as in the latter response to Banach–Tarski. But even admitting non-measurable regions gives no relief from my argument. Small Regions guarantees the existence of regions with small measures, which are *a fortiori* measurable, and this supplies enough measurable regions to make the argument work. Even if we revise this thesis to say only that every *measurable* region has an arbitrarily small part (so we don't get measurable regions for free) the argument still succeeds with an unobjectionable extra premise: every basis element (e.g. every sphere) is measurable. This permits restricting the measure function far beyond what would suffice to

---

[17] Arntzenius discusses these options (2007).

accommodate Banach and Tarski's results, without escaping an inch from my argument. Measurability is not the culprit.

4. ESCAPE

The generalized Forrest–Arntzenius argument doesn't leave very many places for the gunk theorist to turn. One way out is to reject one of the three kinds of structure: in fact space does not have, or (for the theorist who only wants the *possibility* of gunk) does not necessarily have measure, topology, or mereology. Deleting any of these is dizzying; perhaps sizeless or shapeless spaces are broadly possible even so, but henceforth I assume that our gunk theorist wants to hold onto at least the rudiments of parthood, size, and shape. This theorist has to deny one of the five inconsistent conditions on these structures.

The mereological condition—that parthood is reflexive and transitive—is so weak as to be beyond reproach.

What about giving up a countable topology? There are topological spaces that do not have countable bases, but generally speaking they are exotic infinite dimensional affairs. Such space would be shaped nothing like Euclidean space or any other ordinary manifold. There may still be interesting possible spaces to be explored in this direction, but for now I leave that exploration to others.

And Small Regions? We could imagine 'chunky' space with some smallest volume—say on the Planck scale—which is a floor on the size of regions. But for space like this to be *gunky* it would have to be non-standard—for as I observed in Section 2.3, denying Small Regions while holding Mereological Gunk entails that either Remainder Closure or Finite Additivity fails. In what follows I consider some revisions to standard mereology and measure theory in their own right, but none of them gain appeal for the gunk theorist by being conjoined with the denial of Small Regions. So I pass over this route, too.

This leaves two claims open to scrutiny: Topological Gunk and Countable Subadditivity. Rejecting either of these bears a serious cost, but does present live options for the gunk theorist. Arntzenius's response denies Topological Gunk, while Forrest's response (in a roundabout way involving non-standard mereology) denies Countable Subadditivity. I will discuss each of these avenues, as well as a third response that appeals more directly to non-standard measure theory.

4.1 Gunk with boundaries

Arntzenius (following Roman Sikorski and Brian Skyrms) proposes a conception of gunky space that departs rather dramatically from Whitehead's (Arntzenius 2007; Sikorski 1964; Skyrms 1993). Arntzenius's space obeys standard mereology, it has a topology with a countable basis, it has a countably additive measure function, and, moreover, it is both mereologically and measure-theoretically gunky. It is not, however, topologically gunky, and thus escapes the problem at hand.

To motivate Arntzenius's construction of a model for this kind of space, let's revisit Tarski's model—the open regular sets—from another angle. We start with orthodox pointy Euclidean space and then 'smudge' it, leaving out some distinctions the pointy theory makes but retaining the most important structure. There is a general method for 'smudging' certain unimportant elements out of a mereology[18]—Arntzenius's metaphor for this is 'putting on blurry glasses'. The method works as long as the unimportant elements form an *ideal*: any part of an unimportant element must be unimportant, and the fusion of any two unimportant elements must be unimportant. To model Tarski's space, we smudge the boundaries of regions; it's not hard to check that the boundary regions are an ideal.

Once we have picked an ideal of unimportant elements, we define an equivalence relation on the original space: two regions x and y are considered equivalent just in case $x - y$ and $y - x$ are both unimportant.[19] (It is easy to show that for any ideal this is indeed an equivalence relation.) This presents us with a natural collection

---

[18] Assuming **CEM**, i.e. that the mereology forms a Boolean algebra. The result is called a *quotient algebra* (Sikorski 1964: 29 ff.).

Note: a Boolean algebra conventionally includes 'bottom' and 'top' elements: a 'null region' contained by everything and a 'universal region' containing everything. There are trivial translations between mereology with a null region and without it: for instance, in the presence of a null region, disjoint regions have exactly *one* common part. Introducing a null region is a technical convenience on par with introducing '∞' as a value for functions that increase without bound, or 'a third truth-value' to indicate truth-value gaps.

[19] Including when $x - y$ (or $y - x$) is null—i.e., when $x < y$ (or $y < x$).

of 'smudged' objects: the equivalence classes under this relation represent regions of gunky space.[20] In the case of Tarskian space, this amounts to considering two Euclidean regions equivalent if they agree up to their boundary points.

The representatives inherit mereology from the original space: if gunky regions r and s are represented by equivalence classes X and Y, then $r \leq s$ iff for every $x \in X$ and $y \in Y$, $x - y$ is unimportant. They also inherit topological structure from the Euclidean topology: $r \bowtie s$ iff for every $x \in X$ and $y \in Y$, $x \bowtie y$. Showing that these satisfy the standard axioms is straightforward.[21] (Choosing a measure for Tarskian space is more involved; I discuss this in Section 4.4.) Each Tarskian equivalence class contains a unique open regular set, which we can treat as a region's canonical representative; in fact, the model we have just constructed is isomorphic to Tarski's.

This model gives primary importance to the topological gunk condition: we use blurry glasses that can't see boundaries, ensuring that the No Boundaries condition will be met. As we have seen, this condition is problematic. Arntzenius responds by instead privileging the measure-theoretic features of gunk, in particular No Zero. His model is constructed using blurry glasses that are blind to Euclidean regions with (Lebesgue) measure zero. These regions also form an ideal, so we can follow exactly the same construction: gunky regions are represented by equivalence classes of regions that have measure zero differences. We obtain mereology and topology as in the preceding paragraph,[22] and we can set the size of a region

---

[20] One of these equivalence classes—the ideal itself—represents the null region. This class can simply be discarded from the final structure.

[21] More carefully: in general this process results in a Boolean algebra; whether the algebra is *complete*—i.e., whether Unrestricted Composition holds—needs to be checked in individual cases. In the instances I consider, it does hold.

It's not clear what the 'standard axioms' are for connection, but at any rate the defined relation is reflexive, symmetric, and monotonic (note 9), as well as obeying Röper's decomposition principle,

(iv)   If $x \bowtie (y \vee z)$ then $x \bowtie y$ or $x \bowtie z$.

Finding a full adequate set of topological axioms in terms of connection remains a major undertaking. Röper offers a set of ten axioms, but his tenth axiom is equivalent to the problematic Topological Gunk condition (and thus is not satisfied by Arntzenius's space); removing this axiom undoes his method of recovering points from pointless topology.

[22] Arntzenius uses a different definition of connection. Say p is a *robust limit point* of x iff for every open neighborhood $u \ni p$, $m(u \cap x) > 0$. (Measure-equivalent

to be the (Lebesgue) measure of any member of its representative equivalence class, since equivalent regions have the same measure. This yields a model of measure-theoretically gunky space couched in the terms of standard pointy space. It follows that the consistency of the one reduces to the consistency of the other: the prospects look bright for Arntzenian space.

On the other hand, this space has some surprises for the gunk theorist. Consider again the Cantor Regions from Section 3. Arntzenian space harbors both the Big Interval and a proper part of it that fuses the Cantor Regions—the *Cantor Fusion*. Moreover, it has a third region making up the difference between them—the *Cantor Dust*. This is a peculiar region. While it is extended (its size is positive), it has no interior, and it is a boundary of the Cantor Fusion: true to form, Arntzenian space violates the topological gunk condition. Furthermore, the Cantor Dust is entirely scattered: every part is divisible into disconnected parts. It is tempting to describe the region as a fusion of uncountably many scattered points—but of course this is the wrong description, since there are no points.

In Euclidean space, one can completely characterize a region in terms of the points that make it up: the points are a *mereological basis*. Likewise in Tarskian space, the rational spheres are a mereological basis. Arntzenian space has no analog to either the points or the spheres in this respect. The points are an *atomic* basis for Euclidean space; the spheres are a *countable* basis for Tarskian space. If Arntzenian space has any set of 'fundamental parts' it must be neither atomic nor countable. This isn't a crippling deficit, but it helps explain why regions like the Cantor Dust are difficult to get an intuitive grip on.

Arntzenian space is gunky, but in a weaker sense than full-blooded Whiteheadian space. Space could be gunky in a weaker

---

sets have the same robust limit points; we can treat the 'robust closed sets' as canonical representatives.) Arntzenius's condition for the connectedness of regions represented by X and Y is that some p is a robust limit point of every $x \in X$ and $y \in Y$. This is equivalent to my condition. (Say x and y have no robust limit points in common. Then every point in $\mathrm{cl}x \cap \mathrm{cl}y$ has a neighborhood u such that $m(u \cap x) = 0$ or $m(u \cap y) = 0$. Since the Euclidean topology has a countable basis, there are countable collections of open sets $\{v_i\}$ and $\{w_i\}$ such that $\mathrm{cl}x \cap \mathrm{cl}y \subset \bigcup v_i \cup \bigcup w_i$ and for each i, $m(v_i \cap x) = m(w_i \cap y) = 0$. By countable additivity, $x - \bigcup v_i$ and $y - \bigcup w_i$ are measure-equivalent to x and y (respectively) and they have disjoint closures—that is, they are not connected. The converse is clear.)

sense still, satisfying Mereological Gunk but neither the topological nor the measure condition. The now-familiar smudging method produces a model for such space: we look at Euclidean space through blurry glasses blind to regions made of *finitely many points*, and define mereology, topology, and measure in parallel fashion to Arntzenius's space. The resulting space underscores how separate the different gunk conditions are from one another: this space is very much like ordinary Euclidean space in that it has boundaries, unextended regions, zero-dimensional regions, distinctions between open and closed spheres—but even so, it has no *atomic* regions—no points. For those whose interest in gunk springs from purely mereological concerns, this 'bare-bones' gunk should suffice.

4.2 Interlude: foundations of measure

One way to save gunk is to give up the topological condition and settle for a weaker kind of gunkiness. But some gunk theorists—for instance, those who turn to gunk to solve contact puzzles—may be less willing to admit violations of No Boundaries. For these theorists, the main alternative is to deny Countable Subadditivity. This is a natural response for those in the Whitehead–Tarski tradition: the Forrest–Arntzenius problem arises because Whitehead and Tarski simply didn't take measure into account in their theories.

Since in standard mereology Countable Subadditivity follows from Countable Additivity, I turn to the latter principle. Is there a plausible theory of full-fledged measurable space without this condition? Answering this question requires a detour into the philosophical foundations of measure theory. So far I have treated sizes as if they were fundamental numerical tags on things. This is obviously a fiction; the numbers and arithmetic operations on them arise from other features of the world. Treating sizes as numbers is convenient, but can mislead: it gives the illusion that numerical operations are automatically meaningful, obscuring underlying assumptions.[23] We must make sense of sums of sizes, and specifically infinite sums.

---

[23] Compare Ernest Nagel's comments (1931: 313).

Say we have some determinable property of regions. For this property to be *size*, it has to have quantitative structure. First, the determinates should at least be ordered: it must be sensible to say that this object's size is greater or less or the same as that object's size. This guarantees only a fairly weak kind of quantitativeness—in the medieval jargon, that of *intensive qualities*. Size, though, is an *extensive quality*: it has algebraic structure such that sizes can be *added*. This operation isn't literally numerical addition, but it's structurally analogous.

The algebra of sizes does not float free: it must correspond to a natural relation on the objects that have sizes; I'll call this relation *aggregation*.[24] Aggregation imposes an algebraic structure on things that have sizes; this structure is what underpins addition of sizes. The sum of two things' sizes is the size of their aggregate.

(21) If x is the aggregate of y and z, then the size of x is the sum of the size of y and the size of z. **(Finite Additivity)**

This additivity condition, I claim, has the status of a conceptual truth: without it there is no intelligible talk of adding sizes at all.

What is aggregation? It's natural to say it's mereological structure: x is the aggregate of y and z just in case y and z are disjoint regions whose mereological sum is x. Then the Finite Additivity condition above amounts to the condition by that name in section 2.3: the sum of two sizes is the size of the mereological sum of disjoint regions that have those sizes. Composition is what gives additive structure to sizes. For now, though, I'll go on saying 'aggregation' without committing to which relation it is.

This accounts for finite sums of sizes; but before we can evaluate Countable Additivity, we need to make sense of infinite sums. One way would be to define infinite sums of sizes directly in terms of another primitive relation: aggregation of an infinite collection of regions. This would put Countable Additivity on par with Finite

---

[24] Why think this? One reason is *operationalism*, the view that physical quantities like size must be defined in terms of measurement procedures, and operations like addition of sizes must likewise reduce to some mechanical procedure that can be performed on the things that are measured. Another reason is *nominalism*: if size properties aren't reified, then their algebraic structure must latch directly onto the things that bear the properties, as there isn't anything else for that structure to describe. I don't find either of those reasons compelling, but even so I think the principle is true.

Additivity as a defining condition for sums of sizes. But there's another way of spelling out infinite sums of sizes, which is the standard way of making sense of infinite sums of *numbers*. This way leverages the account we already have of finite sums. First we precisely explicate the *limit* of a sequence of determinates.[25] Then we define the value of an infinite sum of sizes to be the limit of the sequence of finite sums. Using numbers to represent sizes and operating on them with the '$\sum$' symbol tacitly calls on precisely this definition; so it was implicit in the original statement of Countable Additivity.

This definition of an infinite sum of sizes makes no appeal at all to *aggregation* of infinitely many things. Still, there is such an infinite aggregation relation—for mereological sums, we have this in Definition 4. This raises a substantive question: is the size of an aggregate of infinitely many things always equal to the infinite sum of their sizes? That is, is the following true?

(22) If x is the aggregate of a countable set of regions S, then the size of x is the sum of the sizes of the members of S. **(Countable Additivity)**

This principle could go either way. Infinite sums of sizes are defined apart from infinite aggregations of regions; there is no conceptual reason why the two need coincide. Unlike Finite Additivity, Countable Additivity does not spring from the requirements for extensive qualities: it might fail and yet leave size structure intact.

The present escape route involves denying Countable Additivity in the particular case where aggregation is the disjoint fusion relation. One could deny this by rejecting additivity—the limit of a sequence of sizes might not reliably yield the size of an infinite aggregate—or by rejecting fusions—the mereological sum might not be the right relation to play the aggregation role for sizes. I'll consider each of these options.

4.3 Non-standard mereology

Forrest levels his version of the argument against standard mereology; in particular Weak Supplementation (2002). This move

---

[25] We can define 'limit' in terms of the ordering of sizes. Denote this order $\preceq$, and let the *interval* $[p, q]$ be the set of sizes $\{r : p \preceq r \preceq q\}$. Then we say $\lim p_k = p^*$ iff for every interval $[q, r]$ that includes p^* ($p^* \neq q \neq r$, unless p^* is $\preceq$'s bottom or top), there exists some integer K such that for all $k > K$, $p_k \in [q, r]$.

appears to miss the point: my strengthened argument does not depend on any supplementation principle, so how could rejecting Weak Supplementation constitute a response? Only if this denial is followed by another: denying that fusions have countably additive sizes. If Weak Supplementation fails, then the definition of 'fusion' (Definition 4) pulls apart in many ways from its usual theoretical role—and so in particular it becomes plausible that the fusion relation so defined does not play the *aggregation* role for measure theory.

When Weak Supplementation fails, some sets of regions have more than one fusion; a region may fuse a set and yet fail to contain any of its members; indeed, the fusion may be a proper part of some member. These bizarre consequences suggest that in the absence of Weak Supplementation, the standard definition of fusion fails to capture a theoretically important natural relation, and fails to capture the ordinary intuitive concept of *composition*.[26] This is not terribly surprising, seeing as Definition 4 was framed with standard mereology in mind.

Let's distinguish 'fusion' from another, closely related concept:

(D8) A region u is the **least upper bound** of S (for short: lub$S$) iff: for every region x, $x \geq u$ iff x contains every $y \in S$.

(Antisymmetry guarantees uniqueness.) The least upper bound of S is the smallest region that contains every element of S. If Remainder Closure holds, then x is a fusion of S if and only if x is the least upper bound of S. So in standard mereological contexts, the two concepts have the same extension. This fact, I submit, is the main motivation for the standard definition of 'fusion'. But when supplementation principles fail, these two concepts pull apart from one another. In that case, we lose our reason for thinking that the definition captures the right relation to ground our measure theory.

Instead we should turn to the least upper bound. This relation gets along without Weak Supplementation better than the fusion relation: a least upper bound is unique and contains its members, at least. This suggests that we should replace our original statement of Countable Additivity with this one:

---

[26] Cf. Forrest 2007. Kit Fine argues for a general conclusion along the same lines (2007).

(23) For any countable set of pairwise-disjoint regions S, $m(\text{lub}S) = \sum_{x \in S} m(x)$. **(Lub Additivity)**

This revision makes room for a consistent theory of topologically gunky space—at the price of adopting (in Forrest's words) a 'semi-standard' mereology.

Forrest's model for such space is the open sets with measure-zero differences 'smudged' (i.e. measure-zero equivalence classes of open sets). The ontology of Forrest's space is richer than Tarski's but poorer than Arntzenius's. We can see this by considering the Cantor Regions from Section 3 once again. Arntzenius's space includes the Big Interval, the Cantor Regions, the Cantor Fusion (the mereological sum of the Cantor Regions), and the Cantor Dust (the difference between the interval and the Cantor Fusion). Tarski's space, meanwhile, includes the Big Interval and the Cantor Regions, but countenances neither the Cantor Fusion (as an entity distinct from the Big Interval) nor the Cantor Dust. Forrest's space includes the Big Interval, the Cantor Regions, and the Cantor Fusion (better called 'the Cantor Lub')—but there is no 'dusty' region making up the difference between the Cantor Fusion and the interval. This might strike some as the right balance, since the Cantor Dust is the most bizarre of the regions under consideration. But accepting this ontology sacrifices Weak Supplementation: without the Dust, the interval has a proper part with nothing left over. If you paint each of the Cantor Regions in Forrest's space, you thereby succeed in painting the Cantor Fusion but fail to paint the Big Interval—and there's no way to finish the job without repeating some of your work, since every part of the Big Interval has paint on it. This is an unnecessarily drastic concession.

4.4 Finitely additive gunk

Returning to more hospitable mereology, why think that additivity holds for countably infinite fusions? One might motivate this with an infinite 'supertask', such as the *Pudding Task*.[27] Say we have a countable set of disjoint regions $r_1, r_2, \ldots$ which together compose a finite region s, all in a world entirely free of pudding. At step

---

[27] Forrest argues along these lines (1996). For a more elaborate example, see Hawthorne and Weatherson 2004.

one, fill r_1 with chocolate pudding; at step two fill r_2, and so on. When all of the steps have been carried out, s is entirely filled with chocolatey goodness. So the total amount of pudding in the world is $m(s)$. The total amount of pudding served is $m(r_1) + m(r_2) + \ldots$. So if $m(s)$ is greater than the sum, then there is more pudding in the world than was served. Whence this extra pudding?

Intuition presses us toward this principle: the sizes of the finite fusions should converge to the size of the infinite fusion. If we think of the regions involved as also forming a convergent sequence—the finite fusions converge to the infinite fusion—then there's another way to say this: intuitively, the measure function should be *continuous*.

Intuition favors continuous functions, yet continuity often fails in our dealings with the infinite.[28] Consider, for instance, the *Painting Task*. Suppose we have an infinite sequence of blank pages labeled with the natural numbers, and a large can of paint. At step one, paint the first page; at step two paint the second page, and so on. After any finite number of steps, there are infinitely many blank pages. Yet when the supertask is complete, there are no blank pages left at all. Again continuity fails: the limit of a sequence of infinities is certainly not zero, so the limit gives the wrong result for this supertask. Why shouldn't the Pudding Task be similar to the Painting Task in this respect? As the number of steps carried out approaches infinity, the amount of pudding approaches a particular amount—but when the number of steps reaches infinity, there is a different amount. There is a 'break' at infinity. Surprising, but hardly impossible.

One might worry that completing such supertasks would make it possible to violate certain physical principles: a one-mile bridge could be built with only half a mile's worth of concrete, by building it up from the right set of parts. One available reply is that such physical principles *can* be violated: in worlds with the kind of space in question, it may be physically possible to build a bridge on the cheap in just this way. If the world has the right conservation laws, though, then the supertask cannot be carried out. It is a little puzzling that a law of physics might rule out an infinite sequence of operations without ruling out any finite subset of them, but this kind

---

[28] This line of thought is influenced by conversation with Frank Arntzenius.

of thing happens. For instance, in a Newtonian world, conservation of momentum rules out an infinite sequence of collisions between vanishingly small balls at vanishingly small distances from one another, without ruling out any particular collision (Laraudogoitia 1996). The physical law is inconsistent with the initial conditions that give rise to the infinite collision scenario—and so the law rules the scenario out. Similarly, in worlds where conservation of concrete is a law of nature, the bridge-building supertask can't be carried out. Whatever initial conditions might give rise to it are physically impossible.

One might also worry because measure *supervenience* fails. If the size of a region is not determined by the sizes of a collection of disjoint things that exhaustively compose it, doesn't that make its size a sort of spooky, free-floating thing? One reply is *tu quoque*: we are already accustomed to exactly this situation in pointy space, since an uncountable collection of point-sized regions may be rearranged to make up a region of any size whatsoever. If this is acceptable, we might equally well learn to live without size supervenience for countably infinite fusions of gunky regions. But the 'spookiness' worry might be raised more generally: what fixes the size of a region, if not the sizes of its parts? For pointy space, the answer to this question is written in the annals of classical measure theory. For topologically gunky space it turns out to be a difficult question.

The natural place to look for a model for finitely additive, topologically gunky space is Tarski's open regular sets. Tarskian regions have the mereology and topology of their representative open sets; it would be nice to similarly fix the size of a region to be the (Lebesgue) measure of its representative. But this won't do.[29] To see why not, consider once more the Cantor Regions, labeled a, b_1, b_2, c_1, c_2, c_3, c_4, ... Recall: the size of a is $\frac{1}{4}$, the combined sizes of the b's is $\frac{1}{8}$, the combined sizes of the c's is $\frac{1}{16}$, and so on; all of these together add up to $\frac{1}{2}$; and the fusion of the Cantor Regions is the unit interval. Now let the *Big Pieces* be a, the c's, the e's, etc., and let the *Little Pieces* be the b's, the d's, the f's, etc. Since the Big Pieces are twice as big as the Little Pieces, and all together they add up to $\frac{1}{2}$, the Big Pieces' sizes add up to $\frac{1}{3}$ and the Little Pieces'

---

[29] Thanks to John Hawthorne for forcing me to get clear on this.

sizes add up to $\frac{1}{6}$. Now consider *Big Cantor*, the fusion of the Big Pieces, and *Little Cantor*, the fusion of the Little Pieces. How big are they? According to the proposed rule, the measure of Big Cantor is $\frac{1}{3}$ and the measure of Little Cantor is $\frac{1}{6}$.[30] But note: the fusion of Big Cantor and Little Cantor is the unit interval. So on this account of size, *Finite* Additivity breaks down!

Fixing sizes based on the open regular sets was a bad idea. The closed regular representatives do no better—the closed representative of Big Cantor has size $\frac{5}{6}$, and the closed representative of Little Cantor has size $\frac{2}{3}$; these don't add up to 1 either.[31] Appealing to a region's representative equivalence class is even less helpful: by adding and subtracting regions like the Cantor Dust, we can find members of each equivalence class with any given positive size. Which of these should we choose? The pointy representatives don't pin down the sizes of Big and Little Cantor.

Here's another way of characterizing this problem: Tarskian space includes regions that are not *Jordan-measurable*.[32] To define Jordan measure, we start with a collection of elementary regions whose sizes are already well understood—typically rectangles (in one dimension: intervals). We can calculate the measure of any finite fusion of disjoint rectangles by addition. Call these finite fusions the *blocks*. We then define the *outer measure* of a region x as the lower limit of the sizes of the blocks that contain x, and the *inner measure* as the upper limit of the sizes of the blocks that are part of x. If the outer and inner measure agree, then x is Jordan-measurable, and their common value is the Jordan measure of x. Jordan measure is finitely additive; in effect, Jordan measure starts with the sizes of elementary regions and unrolls the consequences of Finite Additivity for the rest. But there are regions whose sizes

---

[30] Let I, U_1, U_2, ..., and V_1, V_2, ... be the representative open sets for the unit interval, the Big Pieces, and the Little Pieces, respectively, and let $U^* = \bigcup U_i$ and $V^* = \bigcup V_i$. U^* is an open regular set. This is because every point in I is either (i) a member of U^*, (ii) a member of V^*, or else (iii) a boundary point of both U^* and V^*. So the closure of U^* is $I - V^*$, and the interior of clU^* is U^*. Thus U^* is Big Cantor's representative. Furthermore, since Lebesgue measure is countably additive, $m(U^*) = \sum m(U_i) = \frac{1}{3}$. Similar considerations hold for Little Cantor.

[31] The closed representatives of Big Cantor and Little Cantor are the closures of their open representatives: namely $I - V^*$ and $I - U^*$, respectively.

[32] Jordan measure is to the Riemann integral as Lebesgue measure is to the Lebesgue integral (Frink 1933).

can't be determined in this way—and, sadly, Big Cantor and Little Cantor are among them. Big Cantor's inner measure is $\frac{1}{3}$, and its outer measure is $\frac{5}{6}$. In pointy space, Lebesgue measure captures these regions by going beyond finite collections of rectangles to *countable* collections—but since Countable Additivity fails here, this won't help.

One response to this failure is to cut the offending regions loose, either by admitting that Tarskian space includes peculiar regions that lack sizes, or else by restricting the space to include just the Jordan-measurable regions. The latter option involves giving up Unrestricted Composition for infinite collections of regions. These are costs we hoped to escape in gunky space, but at any rate they aren't much worse than the costs faced by points: these two options parallel the two responses to non-measurable sets in Section 3.1. For a model following the latter option, represent gunky regions with *Jordan-measurable open regular sets*, and assign regions the same parts, connection, and sizes as their representatives. The mereology of this space is not quite standard: while every *finite* set of regions has a fusion, some *infinite* sets do not: for instance, neither the Big Pieces nor the Little Pieces have a fusion.[33]

A second response to the failure of Jordan measure is to introduce 'spooky' sizes which are not pinned down by elementary regions and additivity considerations. In fact, there are infinitely many finitely additive measures that extend Jordan measure to all of the Tarskian regions.[34] We can assign Big Cantor any size between its

---

[33] The mereology satisfies the system **CEM**: it forms a Boolean algebra, but not a *complete* Boolean algebra.

[34] This is an application of a general result that Garrett Birkhoff (1967: 185 ff.) attributes to Tarski: if S is a subalgebra of a Boolean algebra A, then any finitely additive measure function defined on S has a finitely additive extension over all of A.

If $a \in A$ and $a \not\in S$, we can extend the measure on S to the larger subalgebra of elements of the form $(b \wedge a) \vee (c - a)$ (where $b \wedge a = b - (b - a)$). We set the size of such an element to be outer$_{m,S}(b \wedge a)$ + inner$_{m,S}(c - a)$, where outer$_{m,S}(x) = \inf\{m(s) : x \leq s \in S\}$ and inner$_{m,S}(x) = \sup\{m(s) : x \geq s \in S\}$. Birkhoff shows (it isn't difficult) that this is finitely additive and agrees with m on S. The measure is extended to the entire algebra A using an induction principle (When A is uncountable this relies on the Axiom of Choice).

Note that in this argument inner$_{m,S}(b \wedge a)$ + outer$_{m,S}(c - a)$ would yield a measure just as well, and any weighted average of measures is itself a measure. Therefore as long as there is some element of A whose outer and inner measures disagree, m has infinitely many finitely additive extensions.

inner measure of $\frac{1}{3}$ and its outer measure of $\frac{5}{6}$, and go on to fix sizes for the rest of the unsized regions in a consistent fashion. All of the measure functions we obtain agree on simple cases like rectangles, and all of them obey additivity. What could favor one of these measure functions over any other? For instance, what might determine that Big Cantor is truly bigger than Little Cantor, rather than the other way around? The truth about the sizes of such regions might be a matter of 'brute fact', but this introduces a host of brute facts where on the classical story about measure we have very few. There is, then, a model of Tarskian space with a finitely additive measure function; in fact, there are infinitely many non-isomorphic models. The problem is not that there is no way of assigning sizes—it is that there are too many.

This leaves us with two kinds of finitely additive space. The first kind requires giving up either Measurability or an infinite composition principle, and the second kind requires giving up a supervenience principle. These costs are considerable, but not unthinkable—remember, the point lover faces analogous compromises. Besides these costs, merely finitely additive sizes lead to counter-intuitive discontinuities, but intuitions are untrustworthy when it comes to questions about continuity at infinity. Note finally: *uncountable additivity* (insofar as uncountable sums make sense) is a principle that pointy space has long since abandoned. Are *countably* infinite sets more sacred? Finitely additive space is closer to the Whiteheadian picture than either Arntzenius's or Forrest's alternatives—it is full-fledged gunk in the mereological, topological, and measure-theoretic senses. In it we have a reasonable candidate for at least some of the gunk theorist's purposes.

5. CONCLUSION

I have presented a strong argument against naive Whiteheadian space: a small set of independently plausible conditions on gunky space turns out to be inconsistent. The gunk theorist can respond in several ways. The options on the table include Arntzenius's measure-theoretic gunk that violates the No Boundaries principle, Forrest's space that introduces revisionary measure theory by way of revisionary mereology, and a version of Tarski's geometry where sizes disobey Countable Additivity. Each of these options goes against certain intuitions: roughly, Arntzenius's space sacrifices an intuitive bit of topology, Forrest's space an intuitive bit of mereology, and Tarski's space an intuitive bit of measure theory. But I insist: the usual pointy models of space violate intuition as well, as curiosities like the Banach–Tarski theorem (among many others) go to show. We have to live with a bit of counter-intuitiveness in any case.

How we choose among these theories will depend on what we are choosing them for. If the goal is a theory of space that is adequate for actual-world physics, Arntzenius's measure-theoretic gunk seems far and away the most satisfactory. If on the other hand the main concern is capturing commonsense spatial reasoning, one of the finitely additive models may be better. And if the question is what spatial structures are broadly possible, then (short of further argument to the contrary) possibilities abound.

One lesson to draw from this discussion is a reminder that innocent-seeming premises can lead quickly into hidden incoherencies—we should heed Hume's admonition to "be modest in our pretensions".[35] An account may be intuitive without being consistent, especially when extrapolations to infinity are involved. But there are babies as well as bath-water in intuition's tub: while the naive conception of gunk is problematic, the core idea displays a hardy resilience. In particular, my argument certainly does *not* rule out gunky space as a physically interesting candidate for our actual universe's space-time, as a metaphysical possibility, or as a consistent framework for spatial reasoning. Avoiding contradictions does force certain counter-intuitive results on us—any theory of space has its puzzles and surprises—but we should expect that much.

REFERENCES

Arntzenius, Frank (2007). "Gunk, Topology, and Measure." In this volume.
____and Hawthorne, John (2005). "Gunk and Continuous Variation". *Monist* 88 (Oct.): 441–65.
Birkhoff, Garrett (1967). *Lattice Theory*. Colloquium publications. Providence: American Mathematical Society.

---

[35] *An Enquiry Concerning Human Understanding.* IV.ii

Clarke, Bowman (1981). "A Calculus of Individuals Based on 'Connection'". *Notre Dame Journal of Formal Logic* 22 (July): 204-18.

Cohn, Anthony, and Varzi, Achille (2003). "Mereotopological Connection". *Journal of Philosophical Logic* 32: 357-90.

Fine, Kit (2007). "Misuses of Mereology". *Mereology, Topology, and Location*. New Brunswick, NJ: Rutgers University, October.

Forrest, Peter (1996). "How Innocent is Mereology?" *Analysis* 56 (July): 127-31.

—— (2002). "Nonclassical Mereology and Its Application to Sets". *Notre Dame Journal of Formal Logic* 43/2: 79-94.

—— (2007). "Mereological Summation and the Question of Unique Fusion". *Analysis* 56 (July): 127-31.

Frink, Orrin (1933). "Jordan Measure and Riemann Integration". *Annals of Mathematics* 34 (July): 518-26.

Hawthorne, John, and Weatherson, Brian (2004). "Chopping up Gunk". *Monist* 87: 339-50.

Laraudogoitia, Jon Perez (1996). "A Beautiful Supertask". *Mind* 105 (January): 81-3.

Lewis, David (1991). *Parts of Classes*. Cambridge: Blackwell.

Munroe, M. E. (1953). *Introduction to Measure and Integration*. Reading: Addison-Wesley.

Nagel, Ernest (1931). "Measurement: Mit deutscher Inhaltsangabe". *Erkenntnis* 2: 313-33.

Röper, Peter (1997). "Region-Based Topology". *Journal of Philosophical Logic* 26 (June): 251-309.

Sider, Ted (1993). "Van Inwagen and the Possibility of Gunk". *Analysis* 53: 285-9.

Sikorski, Roman (1964). *Boolean Algebras*. Berlin: Springer Verlag.

Skyrms, Brian (1993). "Logical Atoms and Combinatorial Possibility". *Journal of Philosophy* 90 (May): 219-32.

Tarski, A. (1956). "Foundations of the Geometry of Solids". In J. H. Woodger (ed.), *Logic, Semantics, and Metamathematics*. Oxford: Clarendon Press, 24-9.

Varzi, Achille (2006). "Mereology". In Edward N. Zalta (ed.), *The Stanford Encyclopedia of Philosophy*.

Zimmerman, Dean (1996). "Could Extended Objects Be Made Out of Simple Parts? An Argument for 'Atomless Gunk'". *Philosophy and Phenomenological Research* 56 (March): 1-29.

—— "Indivisible Parts and Extended Objects: Some Philosophical Episodes from Topology's Prehistory". *Monist* 79 (Jan.): 148-80.

12. Beware of the Blob: Cautions for Would-Be Metaphysicians

Mark Wilson

> *And as for the mixed mathematics I may only make this prediction, that there cannot fail to be more kinds of them, as Nature grows further disclosed*
>
> —Francis Bacon

1.

In this chapter, I will voice a discomfort that some of us have entertained with respect to the waves of philosophical speculation about the constitution of matter that have become abundant within the past fifteen years or so (for want of a better term, I'll dub this literature "the new metaphysics"[1]). In rough measure, such investigations revolve around sweeping questions of the sort, "How might an extended object be comprised of smaller parts?" In many ways, musings of this general character appear familiar enough, for they display many affinities with discussions found in noted savants of the past such as Leibniz, Kant, Bolzano, and Whitehead. Nonetheless, that was then and this is now, a consideration that leaves the discomfited puzzled by the fact that the modern discussions forge ahead relying upon the *strongly classical terminology* of older days.

---

[1] This labeling may sound more prejudicial than I intend. Judging from conversations I've had with other philosophers of science, a fair number of us have been puzzled by the manner in which various writers in the Saul Kripke–David Lewis tradition now frame their projects. The latter often begin by outlining topics in which physics and applied mathematics have long taken an interest, yet the ensuing discussions frequently head in directions (e.g. "Are gunky spaces possible?") whose exact motivations seem obscure to us outsiders and to run tangential to what the world before us demands. For better or worse, the present chapter attempts to express this unease by outlining a particular conceptual pathway that scientists have painfully learned to follow with respect to continua and to raise the methodological question, "Why should we expect that philosophy should proceed any differently here?" We critics do not raise such concerns out of any bias against metaphysics proper, but rather from the sense that the subject should not be following some radically different drummer of its own concoction.

Consider the following passage from J. R. G. Williams, typical of this literature:

> People once took atoms to be physically indivisible units sitting at the most fundamental level of reality. Advances in science showed that atoms could be decomposed into further micro-particles; and, on the standard model, quarks, bosons and leptons are held to be indivisible units. But just as the atoms' role was supplanted by quarks, future discoveries may reveal that the quarks decompose into yet more fundamental entities: sub-quarks. And below the sub-quarks there could lie further layers of reality. Imagine this process of discovery proceeding *ad infinitum*; in such a scenario, every kind of micro-particles would be underlain by smaller entities. This would be a world of "infinite descent": in such a scenario, there is no "most fundamental layer" of particles.[2]

This characterization serves as a prelude to a strange (in my estimation) debate whether a certain thesis of "metaphysical nihilism" is wholly necessary, viz., that the only physical entities that truly exist are nature's most fundamental and smallest physical parts. I don't propose that we follow Williams into these mists; let us linger with the conception of "smallest part" that propels him onward.

From modern physics' point of view, the most striking feature of this passage is that it employs strongly *classical terminology* quite freely—specifically, in its unshaded appeal to "part"—in application to inherently *quantum phenomena* such as the behavior of quarks et al. Yet one of quantum mechanics' many foibles lies in the fact that its basic phenomena do not appear to be neatly localizable: critical events occur only within some loose and relatively ample "effective volume" that can be spatially sharpened only at the cost of gaining ruinous uncertainty with respect to momentum. True: to the best of our knowledge, electrons and quarks act as "dimensionless scattering centers", but this phrase encapsulates a technical concept that does not align neatly with trackable, localized positions. A better analogy for thinking of the compositional "parts" of a quantum system is to consider the overtone "components" found within a vibrating string. To

---

[2] "Illusions of Gunk", *Philosophical Perspectives* 20 (2006), 493. Dean Zimmerman correctly observes that Williams writes of "smallest particles" and that he may have intended some measure of "smallness" other than size. Perhaps, but it would have been better to make these matters more explicit when considering the sub-atomic realm. I thank Dean for his helpful comments on this paper throughout.

unravel its complicated patterns, physicists (under the heading of "Fourier analysis") allocate different packets of energy to sundry vibrational modes hidden in the string: firstly, to its simple back and forth sine wave movements that transpire at, for example, 440 cycles per second; secondly to the doubled octave movements that leave the halfway point of the string fixed;—and so on, running through a spectrum of increasingly rapid patterns of movement, in an infinite ascent that runs through its possible overtones. Scientists often describe this energy decomposition in "particle" terms: they declare that the string is composed of "phonons", here regarded as the quanta of an acoustic disturbance. However, in the case at hand, it should be recognized that such "phonons" are not unique (other manners of "decomposition" can prove salient) nor are they *spatially smaller* than the original string; they coexist over exactly the same region as its entire cord. Their "part of a string" nature is explicated in terms of the smaller *quantities of energy* that each phonon mode stores, not because these specialized patterns display any further measure of spatial localization. Within a true quantum setting, the entire "particle" notion becomes considerably stranger, for many of these only exist in a "virtual" manner that manifest a large array of utterly queer features. But if we wish to debate the "ontology" of the real universe, we should be wary of leaning upon "part" in Williams's manner.

In truth, few scientists (except impetuous dogmatists) pretend that we understand the ontology of quantum mechanics well at the present time. A few splinter groups (e.g. the school of David Bohm) assign quantum behaviors more sharply localized trajectories than meet the eye, but such views are scarcely accepted as orthodoxy today. Surely, as long as such substantive interpretational difficulties persist, our new metaphysicians should be wary of hastily importing *classical assumptions* about "fundamental particles", their "spatial parts" and "trajectories" into the quantum realm. Yet, to all appearances, Williams has done precisely that in the passage quoted above. It would also seem, from my limited sampling of the literature, that many allied philosophers freely imitate Williams in his classically biased rashness, evoking classical "spatial part" in contexts where basic quantum experience would advise greater caution.

Such morose reflections suggest that prudent metaphysicians might set some of their favorite projects on hold until the happy day that we unravel quantum behavior in a more satisfactory manner. Yet no such restraint seems evident. Why?

A popular manner of reply appeals to the fact that we still evoke the classical notion of "spatial part" quite profitably at the macroscopic level in both everyday life and engineering; indeed, "spatial part" proves exactly the stuff of which the substantial branch of modern engineering known as "continuum mechanics" is made. "The continuum approach captures a *possible way* the world might be," a reply to our doubts elaborates, "so we metaphysicians, in our wide ranging toleration of possible circumstance, should wish to understand how 'part of' behaves in classical possible worlds like these." Indeed, the story of how modern continuum mechanics addresses the classic worries about continuous matter found in the great philosopher/scientists of the past is both fascinating and informative (this chapter will outline its basic contours).

In this regard, however, such philosophers fail to appreciate that the modern technical work suggests surprising conclusions that often do not conform happily to their "possible world" expectations. In particular, applied mathematicians usually rationalize their conceptual innovations as the mathematical tools that naturally emerge when one "anti-averages", on a macroscopic level, over an underlying base of quantum fact. The expectation is never to produce the complete "worlds" anticipated in metaphysical speculation, but merely to extract useful descriptive fragments that can successfully clock a complex macroscopic system over a certain range of behaviors (outside of that range, it is expected that direct attention to phenomena at a lower size scale will be required). Nonetheless, insofar as any hope remains for providing precise mathematical accounts of the "classical possible worlds filled with continuously distributed matter" prized by our metaphysicians, these constructions must utilize technical innovations akin to the delicate procedures fashioned by modern experts in continuum mechanics for their own purposes (for brevity's sake, let us dub the desired constructions "blob worlds" in the sequel). In other words, a self-consistent "blob universe" suitable for metaphysical speculation will need to be fitted out with shock fronts, Young's measures and the allied innovations to be surveyed in this chapter. But such supplements frequently render Williams-like appeals to "smallest spatial parts" murky or problematic. My primary aim in this chapter is to provide a gentle introduction to some of these unfamiliar constructions for a philosophical audience.

Let me reframe these motivating observations in more general terms. When we probe our ordinary conceptions of "what physical object X might possibly do" carefully, our answers actually open out into a hierarchy of claims structured in a scale-sensitive manner that I elsewhere call "the lousy encyclopedia phenomenon".[3] That is, we normally provide *partial answers* $S_1, S_2, S_3, \ldots$ whose validity obtains only locally and up to a certain scale of resolution. When we require "possibility" answers with a larger range of validity, we find that we must often override our old answers with a substantially altered set $S_1^*, S_2^*, S_3^*, \ldots$. In many natural situations (including classical blob talk), this series of replacements never reaches a stable bottom. But new metaphysicians rarely anticipate that everyday "possibility talk" will prove structured in this *localized*/"lousy encyclopedia" manner, but instead adopt tacit *globalized assumptions* of the sort outlined in section (ii). The chief moral of this chapter is to warn against philosophical tropisms of this ilk.

However, there is an interesting wrinkle that complicates this simple dichotomy about "possibility" talk in the case of classical blobs. Twentieth-century mathematicians have discovered a wide range of sophisticated ways in which the utility of basic S_1, S_2, S_3 talk can be maintained far beyond the old-fashioned limits where we would be otherwise forced to adopt S_1^*, S_2^*, S_3^* replacements. But as these "stay on the S_1, S_2, S_3 level" extensions are tolerated, our naive conceptions of a blob's "point-based behaviors" often become obscured within the functional analysis details (such mathematical constructions represent some of the "mixed mathematics" that emerge "as Nature grows further disclosed"). Metaphysicians who still hope to construct global "blob possible worlds" may require these unexpected conceptual innovations to complete their projects with any satisfaction, in which case many

---

[3] See my *Wandering Significance*, (Oxford: Oxford University Press, 2006), 180. The phrase alludes to an encyclopedia my family owned that never provided a complete entry for any subject, but forever tempted gullible readers onward with endless "for more details, see..." endnotes. More generally, my (very long) book offers a detailed account of how everyday possibility talk can be semantically supported in a localized manner alternative to the globalized "possible world" view criticized here.

standard philosophical assumptions about "blob parts" will need to be radically rethought.

Before we turn to specifics, a quick outline of continuum mechanics' vexed history is in order. From late medieval times through the end of the Victorian era, great thinkers struggled to develop coherent mathematical models for the simpler behaviors of continuous classical stuffs such as fluids and flexible solids. In many specific cases, successful models were developed that remain widely in use today (e.g. Navier's equations for an elastic solid; the Navier–Stokes equations for a viscous fluid). However, such formulae could be developed only in a context where the relevant scientists were willing to hurry brusquely through foundational territory where a large number of confusing and seemingly contradictory assumptions about physical infinitesimals need to be adroitly juggled. The conceptual anomalies inherent in these procedures were often noted by clear thinking philosophers and mathematicians of the period, although with scant prospect of providing an adequate cure (such woes demand more advanced mathematical techniques than were then available). The inability to render their procedures lucid sometimes pushed physicists into anti-realism out of despair. This unsatisfactory state of affairs persisted through the entire heyday of classical physics, i.e. well past 1910 or so.

Let me stress that the conceptual anomalies native to blob behavior do not represent "philosophical puzzles" alone, but directly correlate with substantial mathematical barriers that impede the development of practical models for garden variety forms of blob behavior (such as the "gliding and sliding"[4] of asphalt or molasses). Unless these barriers can be somehow surmounted, there is little hope of developing adequate accounts for complex materials like asphalt or molasses, rubber or paint or even articulating a rational treatment of how iron bars manage to fracture or fuse. Accordingly, motivated by the needs of industry and taken up in earnest by skilled applied mathematicians in the 1940s,[5] a distinguished

---

[4] Cf., "It creeps and leaps and glides and slides...," The Five Blobs, "The Blob," Columbia 41250.

[5] In *Supersonic Flow and Shock Waves*, R. Courant and K. Friedrichs poignantly observe, "During the last few years, however, when the barriers between applied and pure science were forced down, a widespread interest arose in...shock waves and expansion waves" (New York: Wiley Interscience, 1948), 2. They refer to the

list of investigators carefully scrutinized the foundational mess bequeathed to them by nineteenth-century practice, in the hope that more *reliable cords of guidance* could be found for macroscopic classical materials. These modern researches have revealed a substantially altered mathematical landscape in which classical blob behavior is now described and successfully modeled within engineering practice.

For reasons we'll explore in greater detail, most modern experts ultimately rationalize their sometimes strange constructions as macroscopic averagings (or "anti-averagings") over quantum behaviors upon a microscopic scale. As we observed, it seems likely that metaphysicians who wish to consider "possible blob worlds" independently of these lower-scale underpinnings will still require the mathematical tools developed in the modern research for their own philosophical purposes. This is because *the only known methods for maintaining a "blob universe" in coherent order require the innovations characteristic of modern applied mathematics.* That is, the only adequate "cures" for the long-lingering anomalies of classical blobs, both within the historical record and in the ongoing ruminations of present-day metaphysicians, require that a self-standing "blob possible world" be fitted out with additional entities such as shock waves and Young's measure interfaces. Or so this chapter will argue.

Insofar as I am aware, no recent metaphysicians have paid significant attention to the mathematical constructions indicated. At best, such thinkers discuss continuously extended matter more or less under the sheltering umbrella of *point set topology*, as that subject was developed in the 1880s.[6] But this mathematical topic, as admirable and important as it otherwise is, simply represents the

Second World War, in which many great "pure" mathematicians were forced to ponder physical phenomena allied to bomb design.

[6] In truth, relatively few writers pay explicit attention to boundaries et al. although it is hard to see how one can coherently adjudicate the plausibility of proposed "mereological principles" within a classical context unless these matters are addressed (for an excellent survey of the latter, see Achille Varsi, "Mereology", *Stanford Encyclopedia of Philosophy* (an online journal)). Writings in (what I consider to be) an explicitly "point set topology" format include Achille C. Varsi, "Boundaries, Continuity and Contact", *Noûs* 31 (1997) and Barry Smith, "Mereotopology: A Theory of Parts and Boundaries," *Data and Knowledge Engineering* 20 (1996). Throughout this chapter I shall simply take it for granted that philosophers have not addressed the problems of everyday blob talk adequately unless they discuss how we must conceive

wrong setting for the blobs of everyday experience. In fact, this inadequacy was fully recognized from point set topology's first beginnings.[7] Notions like "limit point" do play important roles within the fancier constructions of the modern blob experts, but these also demand tools from functional analysis that were not developed until the 1950s. Adequate mechanisms to govern fracture and phase change remain active research topics and fresh innovations continually emerge from the ongoing literature.

Why do contemporary metaphysicians maintain a confident faith that an unsuitable setting as point set topology provides an adequate arena in which the standard anomalies of classical blob behavior can be fruitfully discussed? Some of the explanation traces to the misleading instruction offered in most undergraduate physics classes. Professional physicists are rarely interested in classical continua as such and, insofar as such topics get taught in their classes at all, they are still approached in the slapdash and incoherent manner of the Victorians, often with a false pretension that foundations have been addressed rigorously. To learn of the better modern work, a student must visit the department of applied mathematics or enroll in an advanced course in engineering. Few philosophers are likely to have strayed into such arcane realms (although I fancy that experts in modern continuum mechanics outnumber academic philosophers in the world today!). This educational compartmentalization deprives our writers of the very mathematical tools from which they might optimally profit (as long as they remain inclined to muse upon "classical blob worlds" at all). Indeed, as long as we mistakenly presume that the basic mathematical setting relevant to continua is point set topology, we are likely to assume that delicate questions of "what might a blob possibly do?" can be adequately resolved from the philosophical armchair.

In any case, this persistent reliance upon inadequate mathematical tools leaves one with the collective impression of a squad of

---

their sundry "parts" when they fuse, fission, and otherwise display slithery skills of that ilk.

[7] See, for example, Hilary Putnam's introduction to Charles Sanders Pierce, *Reasoning and the Logic of Things* (Cambridge: Harvard University Press, 1993). Pierce is influenced by algebraic geometry in which figures need to be modeled as "varieties" rather than "point loci". This recognition was coeval with the birth of point set topology.

knights who set out to slay a dragon armed only with slingshots ("Be advised: before you venture into those woods, take along more formidable weapons"). At this stage, I would like to acknowledge an excellent article by Sheldon Smith[8] that neatly documents the faulty conclusions that metaphysicians often reach through following the miscues of point set presumption (indeed, I first learned of the degree to which modern metaphysicians have become interested in classical blob behavior from Smith's report). In my own contribution to this discussion, I will mainly concentrate upon some of the chief reasons why self-coherent "blob worlds" need to be tricked out with additional entities unrecognized by most new metaphysicians.

2.

It is helpful to begin our study with a simple logical observation, a homespun maxim that might be rendered as "Little acorns do *not* always into mighty oaks grow." It represents a moral that we should bear firmly in mind whenever we muse of blobs and "possible worlds". As noted before, the canonical models bequeathed to us by the great physicists of the eighteenth and nineteenth centuries were generally *incomplete* and *partial* in their scope: at best, they can apply to plausible materials for a short portion of their lifetimes. Such modeling limitations prompted the modern reconsiderations of foundations described in the previous section.

In such a context, one must be wary of succumbing too readily to blandishments of the following sort, exemplified in a celebrated passage from Saul Kripke's *Naming and Necessity*:

An analogy from school—in fact, it is not merely an analogy—will help clarify my view. Two ordinary dice (call them die A and die B) are thrown, displaying two numbers face up. For each die there are six possible results. Hence there are thirty-six possible states of the pair of dice.... The[se] thirty-six possible states of the dice are literally "possible worlds", as long

---

[8] "Continuous Bodies, Impenetrability and Contact Interactions," *British Journal for the Philosophy of Science* (forthcoming). It was Sheldon who introduced me to this metaphysical literature and helped guide me through it (we had originally hoped that we might write this chapter collaboratively). Thanks as well to Anil Gupta for other helpful advice.

as we (fictively) ignore everything about the world except the two dice and what they show.... Only one of these mini-worlds... is the "actual world", but the others are of interest when we ask how probable or improbable the actual outcome was.... "[P]ossible worlds" are little more than the mini-worlds of school probability blown large.[9]

Scott Soames enlarges upon this claim in terms of *maximality*:

A possible world is a possible world-state—a way that everything could have been. It is, in effect, a maximal property that the universe could have had.[10]

In physics, we should never posit such global "possible worlds" (or "maximal properties") merely upon the basis of local fragments alone, for a formalism can easily encode useful data of a counterfactual type locally, yet fail to provide maximal information of the type proposed (i.e., the formalism tells us about Kripke's "mini-worlds", but tolerates no "maximal worlds" at all). The following situation is rather common in continuum mathematics (and elsewhere). Let us begin with a wad of plastic that we'll call "Lulu". Engineers extract their modeling equations for Lulu by subjecting similar specimens of plastic to various laboratory regimes of pushing, pulling, and heating. In analogy to Kripke's "mini-world" dice rolls, these experiments teach us how Lulu will counterfactually behave if she were to be pulled or stretched in sundry directions for short periods. Modern technique inserts these localized experimental behaviors (expressed as so-called "constitutive equations") into a group of formulae **F** that predict how Lulu will evolve over larger spans of time. Now consider a hypothetical blob (whom we'll call "Tubby") that differs slightly from Lulu in exactly the same way as one of those stressed laboratory specimens differs in condition from the actual Lulu (in other words, Lulu and Tubby represent exactly similar materials except that Tubby's initial conditions differ slightly from Lulu's). Picture Lulu's and Tubby's present configurations as two dots that lie close together in what physicists call a "phase space". Utilizing the modeling equations **F**, we can ask, "How rapidly will Tubby's trajectory depart from Lulu's?" The answer can tell us much about Lulu's own stability and predictability, for she

---

[9] *Naming and Necessity* (Cambridge: Harvard University Press, 1972), 16–18.

[10] *Philosophical Analysis in the Twentieth Century*, vol. ii (Princeton: Princeton University Press, 2003), 355.

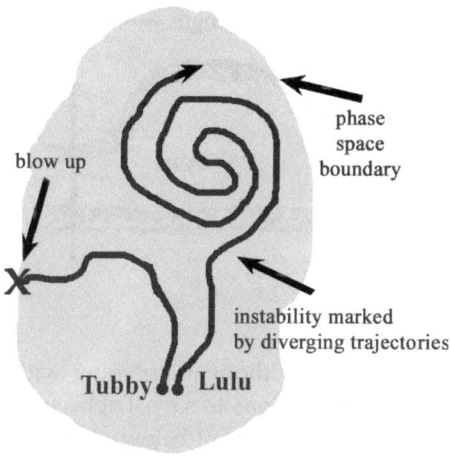

Fig. 12.1

should be considered inherently *unpredictable* if Tubby's behavior diverges from hers too swiftly. For this purpose, we only require information on Tubby's local (or "mini-world") behavior; we do not need to know how he behaves over a longer span. However, demanding a "maximal possible world" in this context suggests that Tubby's trajectory can be *extended indefinitely far into the future and past*. But such maximal extensions are rarely possible in a continuum physics context, for Tubby's traits commonly display mathematical "blowups" (= develop descriptive inconsistencies) if extended beyond moderate spans of time (we'll examine such "blowups" in more detail below). Such premature terminations do not impede Tubby's ability to tell us useful things about Lulu on a "mini-world" basis, but we should not automatically presume that any coherent "maximal world" can be extrapolated from his localized qualities.

The philosopher who regards "classical mechanics" as an armory of "possible but non-actual worlds" should be more vividly aware that such *internally generated failures* often attend the otherwise valuable modelings found in undergraduate textbooks.[11] In most cases, there is no hope of extending Tubby's "mini-world" quantities

---

[11] For more details, see my "Determinism: The Mystery of the Missing Physics," *Phil Sci Arch* (2007).

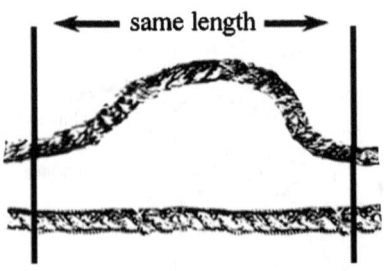

Fig. 12.2

to a greater span of time without intervening with rather fancy functional analysis constructions to save Tubby from his blow up (I'll discuss such remedies in detail below). These considerations illustrate a general lesson about classical blobs: their behaviors will seem straightforward and rosy only if examples are considered in an offhanded and contextually restricted manner. Probe the finer details and many nasty difficulties crawl forth.

Beside such blow-up problems, the stock continuum models supplied in elementary textbooks frequently reveal straightforward contradictions when their features are inventoried in detail. Consider the standard linear wave equation for a vibrating string found in every elementary primer. Working with this model further, we discover that its scope is patently *partial* (it only handles strings that wiggle just a little and can't transmit their vibrations to an instrument's sound box). Worse yet, the qualities it assigns are clearly *incoherent*, for the model describes a string that can adjust its shape from a straight line to a bow without either changing length or contracting its horizontal span! How does it manage that?[12]

Such problems are typical of virtually all of the familiar modelings inherited from earlier eras and reveal the depths of the conceptual problems that our twentieth-century reformers were forced to confront. A proper cure for these miseries necessitates a careful scrutiny of blob basics (the sources of these anomalies must be tracked down before there's much hope of developing sensible equations for the behavior of paint). From these foundational

---

[12] These anomalies become quite pronounced within classical beam theory, which essentially enlarges our string problem to three dimensions.

studies, it has emerged that a proper accounting of the mechanical factors relevant to a small element of string are quite complicated and that a quite lengthy derivational story is needed to wend a just path to the usual linear wave equation (a derivation that accurately identifies where the anomalous length properties creep into its story and how they can be remedied). As I warned above, readers should *not* expect to find the requisite care exemplified within a run of the mill college physics text. Even today, introductory primers evade the daunting complexities of a simple stretch of continuous string by summonsing a "Taylor's series" (or allied expedient) to the rescue. Sir Taylor swiftly rides in, kicks up considerable dust, and, when the air clears, a conceptual dragon lies prostrate next to a differential equation modeling ready to accommodate our scientific desires. But subsequent experiences with our modeling gradually reveal its unhappy limitations and inconsistencies. When we reflect upon what went awry, we gradually realize that our Taylor's series knight has hacked away with his sword quite indiscriminately and the old reptile is not quite dead. We will improve our modeling successes only by treating old conceptual obstacles with a far greater delicacy.[13]

In a recent book, I have complained of the philosophical dangers of "the irrelevant possibility unwisely emphasized".[14] If we wish to understand difficult phenomenon X, it really doesn't help when someone suggests, "Let's look at the simpler possibility Y instead. True, nothing about Y provides useful data about X, but talking about Y will be more fun." Accordingly, I fail to see the utility of searching for self-devised "cures" for a comparatively small subset of the collection of woes long associated with continua, when far better mathematical remedies have been known to applied mathematicians for over fifty years. Yet that project, it seems, is precisely the enterprise in which many present day metaphysicians are now

---

[13] Less metaphorically, the tasks of setting up the stress tensor, inserting constituitive assumptions and linearization have been historically confused, but these distinct chores must be distinguished if better modelings are to be found. For a vivid contrast between old and new treatments, compare a standard textbook approach to the vibrating string with that recommended by S. Antman in "The Equations for the Large Vibrations of Strings", *American Mathematical Monthly* 80 (1980). Besides Taylor's series, a number of allied dodgy moves have been utilized to the same purpose.

[14] *Wandering Significance*, 57.

engaged. In this chapter, I hope to demonstrate, through direct comparison, that we will learn more about "what is really possible" with respect to classical blobs by attending to the engineers than we are likely to extract from the philosophers.

3.

In our everyday thinking, the full extent of the conceptual difficulties connected with blobs is often masked by the *scale dependent* manner in which we usually consider their qualities. In this regard we might recall an old Mel Brooks/Ernie Pintoff cartoon entitled *The Critic*. On the screen some tedious exercise in abstract art is displayed, comprised of the comings and goings of sundry colored blobs. On the soundtrack we hear the elderly voice of an unseen kibitzer struggling to make sense of what he sees. A brightly colored patch appears on the screen. "What is this?" demands our onlooker. "It must be a *Thing*." A crevice forms and widens: "The Thing is breaking into two Things," he opines. Two colored patches seem to merge into one another but later separate: "Two Things having sex." And so on. We regularly make judgments of this sort based upon a diagnosis of where blob boundaries should be allocated, often relying upon our estimates of likely blob behaviors. (A protuberance on a spindly stalk forms: is the Thing forming a new head or spawning a baby?[15])

Certain blob behaviors automatically prompt a spontaneous shift in *scale size* to rationalize what we observe. Let us recall a few blob behaviors typical of the eponymous protoplasm honored in my title. The Thing ingests an elevated train car, but how did it manage to pull the entire contraption inside without destroying it altogether? Well, in its celebrated 1958 movie biography the Thing flowed in upper and lower sheets around the contours of the vehicle and joined up on the other side. But what happens, I wondered as a kid, to the *exterior skin* of the upper half of this flow when it

---

[15] Here I allude indirectly to a real dilemma that arises in the mathematical treatment of ocean spray: how do we *mathematically decide* when protuberances on the surface of an agitated sea will break into droplets and leave the main body of the fluid? See Christopher E. Brennan, *Fundamentals of Multiphase Flow* (Cambridge: Cambridge University Press, 2005).

Fig. 12.3

rejoins the flow around the bottom of the car? How does this stretch of skin manage to disappear? To resolve this quandary, we are instinctively inclined to shift the *size scale* in which we describe the blob and begin to *redescribe* the Thing's skin as an assembly of much smaller attracting blobs (or "molecules"). That is, we exchange a large scale modeling (where only one continuous blob is present) with a smaller scale model involving a population of much smaller blobs. Employed this revised description, we can easily explain the rail car consumption as follows: "The large blob is actually comprised of tightly attracting yet separate smaller blobs. When situated along an exterior surface, these smaller blobs pull tightly together through surface tension to form a skin, yet when two patches of such skin abut, their molecules can interlace and assume the surface tension-less condition of regular interior molecules. *Ergo*: the skin disappears, leaving the engulfed transit car neatly cocooned inside." Although perhaps not a process feasible for an extraterrestrial life form, this tale provides roughly the correct explanation of what would happen if our vehicle had become drenched in asphalt. Or how the erstwhile inner surface of an ocean wave manages to vanish once the wave crests and subsides into the sea.

Working the same descriptive problem in reverse (i.e. we consider *splitting* rather than *rejoining*), a continuous blob **B** may divide into two portions B_1 and B_2, each with their own newly formed

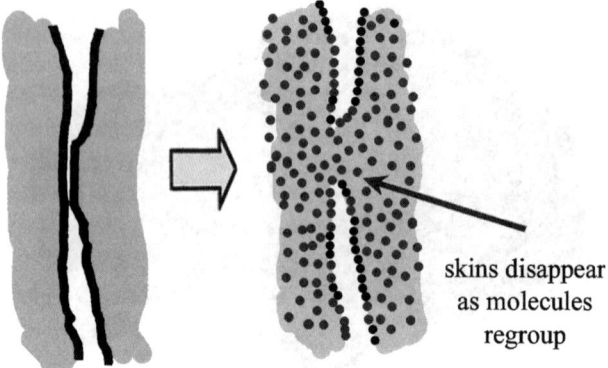

Fig. 12.4

boundary skins. But where do these new skins come from—they weren't present in the blob before? Looking into a lower scale length resolves our dilemma: the newly created surfaces of both **B₁** and **B₂** represent regions where previously interior molecules have pulled more tightly together through surface tension, each gaining a "skin" in the process. Once again, our initial quandary is resolved by exchanging a large scale modeling with a few large blobs for a smaller scale setting comprised of many smaller, detached "molecules". Indeed, this fission process roughly captures what occurs when a raindrop divides in two.

In both cases, although we begin with blobs possessing two-dimensional "skins", we readily *replace* such two-dimensional regions by fatter three-dimensional volumes of "molecular" blobs in our lower scale modelings. Through such dimensional shifts we readily accommodate processes where bounding surfaces appear or vanish. Plainly, most of our real life talk of blobs follows this scale-dependent recipe: we happily adjust the implicit scale of our modelings to suit the explanatory needs of the moment (none of this should suggest anti-realism: such adjustments are simply the natural side effect of adopting the basic policies of *variable reduction* that will be outlined in next section). However, blob language that evidences such blatant context sensitivity hardly serves our metaphysicians' purposes, for they want to know how classical blobs might behave within a *fixed* "possible world", where "spatial part" does not continually shift its significance as modeling scale is readjusted. But is it really clear that "possible worlds" meeting such stern requirements are genuinely viable? The answer may be "yes", but there are a number of surprises wrapped up in that "yes".

Approached in an absolutist way, the unexceptional everyday fission and fusion of blobs generates a deep puzzle for those who wonder whether self-consistent classical blob worlds are genuinely "metaphysically viable". For look what happens to our innocuous fission problem if we are not allowed to shift modeling. One sometimes encounters variants upon the following puzzle in the recent metaphysical literature (it is far older than that, however). "Let **C** represent a surface cutting through the interior of blob **B** along which smaller blobs B_1 and B_2 emerge on splitting. After this fission, where does **C** go? Suppose it favors B_1; where does that leave B_2's own stretch of boundary? Poor B_2's segment, it would seem, has been left nakedly *open* in a topological sense. In contrast, B_1's new boundary is *closed* (= it contains all of its limit points), which supplies it with a dandy "skin". To gain a comparable epidermis, won't B_2 need to obtain a fresh set of limit points right away, either by rapidly rescrambling some of its own parts (how?) or pulling them from the blue sky. But surely the latter would represent a creation of fresh skin matter *ex nihilo*?" In other words, a fission phenomenon that can be readily explained in readjusted scale terms becomes a significant paradox if we are forced to keep our blob modeling constant.

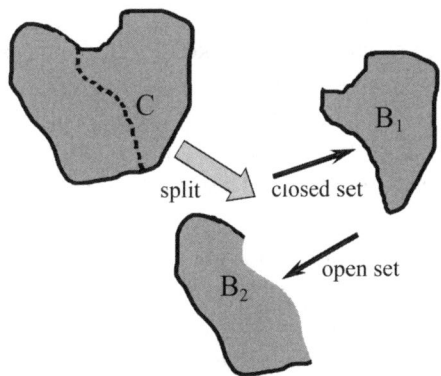

Fig. 12.5

Sometimes topological conundrums such as this prompt hasty metaphysicians to declare that genuine classical blobs can't be truly viable: the only workable "classical universes" are those comprised solely of non-contiguous mass points, exactly in the manner Boscovich advocated long ago.[16] Sometimes the argument to this end proceeds by *reductio*: "Assume that we finally arrive at a lowest scale size of blob modelings. If the blobs we now see have any size at all, isn't it possible that sufficient applied stresses should make them split or fuse? If so, we will need to find yet smaller blobs to explain these processes, contradicting our assumption that we are presently looking at the smallest blobs. One might object that such blobs can neither fuse nor split, but utterly unbreakable volumes pose many difficulties of their own. So blobs composed of mass point atoms remain the only viable classical option."

In point of historical fact, partisans of mass points often argued in exactly these ways, whereas anti-atomist advocates of continuum physics often resisted their regress arguments through appeal to anti-realism about science's purposes ("Yes, we must continually revise our blob stories along lower length scales, but science is not in the business of constructing fully viable 'possible worlds'; it merely wishes to facilitate accurate predication"[17]). But, once again, that was then and this is now and it is unfortunate that philosophers of the present day continue to retrace these venerable paths of a priorism, in light of the fact that modern continuum mechanics has developed the means to address these traditional worries about blobs in a more satisfactory manner.

Some metaphysicians[18] have looked to simple measure theoretic considerations to provide a better resolution of the fission problem. "Perhaps the exterior boundary of a blob shouldn't be reckoned amongst its true parts, simply because such a surface will be lower dimensional and its localized quantities accordingly will not

---

[16] For some examples, see the Smith article cited earlier.

[17] For a brief history of such anti-realist tropisms, see my "Duhem: Impossible Things before Breakfast," *Phil Sci Arch*, 2007.

[18] For some historical background on this venerable line of thought, see Dean W. Zimmerman, "Indivisible Parts and Extended Objects", *The Monist* 79 (1996). We shall later examine the critical importance of treating boundaries in continuum mechanics as important (albeit not "material") entities in their own right.

contribute to vital integral qualities that attach to volumes such as *mass* or *momentum*. If we approach blob 'parts' in this exclusionary way, the usual topological distinction between open and closed point sets becomes no longer pertinent and the mystery of how its boundary points rearrange themselves vanishes."

In truth, such measure theoretic "cures" (although more sensible than the arguments that establish point masses a priori) are far too tepid to suit the requirements of any plausible real life blob: they genuinely need their skins of boundary points! Worse yet, an unaugmented story based only on measure misunderstands the critical role that boundary regions play within successful macroscopic description, for the physics active within these lower dimensional regions often serves as the central determinant of blob behavior that extends over substantial volumes. Such "singular surfaces" often carry substantial (and often rather strange) quantities of their own, attributes that sometimes contribute vitally to volume integrals such as *energy* despite the fact that these quantities only live on a "measure zero" region (if standard integrals refuse to notice these regions of vanishing measure, we must utilize non-standard Stieltjes-style integrals that will pay attention). Later we'll also learn of the subtle role that certain "singular surfaces" play in redistributing quantities of *mass* and *momentum* throughout the interior of a blob. We'll find that there is no evident way to engineer these dependencies except to evoke mathematical machinery considerably more complex than simple measure theory. But the qualities of those instrumentalities commonly "live" on "measure zero" platforms.

Let me enter an obvious remark whose salience will emerge later. Let p be a point on the mathematical boundary of a blob considered at a large scale length and assume that $\mathbf{V}$ is a very small volume around p. "Is p 'part' of $\mathbf{V}$?"—if asked this question, we might well demur. "What exactly are you asking? Viewed close up, the erstwhile 'point' p actually corresponds to a physical region rather larger than $\mathbf{V}$. So I don't know how to interpret your question." This simple phenomenon will later return in a surprising guise.[19]

---

[19] The sensitivity of "part of" to scale shifts further underwrites the standard criticisms of "mereological transitivity" offered by Nicholas Rescher and others (see Varsi's encyclopedia report for details).

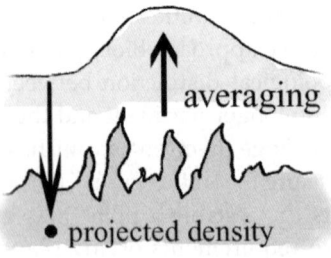

Fig. 12.6

4.

Before we consider the constructions needed, let us first survey the brisk rationale that modern primers generally offer in introducing basic continuum models to their students. "Sure, real matter is composed of more or less detached molecules that interact according to intrinsically quantum principles," these books explain, "but it is frequently advantageous to *average* over these microscopic complexities in order to produce a simpler and more manageable descriptive frame on the macroscopic level. When we attribute a ***density, pressure*** or ***temperature*** to a continuous blob, we are really speaking of complex averages over the smaller scale regional features manifested within its molecular array (as revealed under scanning tunneling microscopy). That is, the complex hills and dales found within a volume of a short scale length are first smeared together into a smoother *mass* distribution and the latter is then projected back point-wise into the blob as its continuum level description." That is, in its "classical blob" description, the target object will be assigned an exact *mass density* at any of its component points p, but this localized "density" actually reflects the *mass* scattered over a larger volume around p. Often, no mass may reside near p at all on a short scale length, but p will obtain a finite "mass density" through its "averaged" large scale description. Such "averaged and relocalized" traits might be profitably compared to the features of a human face conveyed within a coarsely digitalized photograph. The fact that our photograph is locally pink at location point p provides genuine information about the true color of our subject's nose, but only in a smeared-out (but nonetheless valuable) fashion.

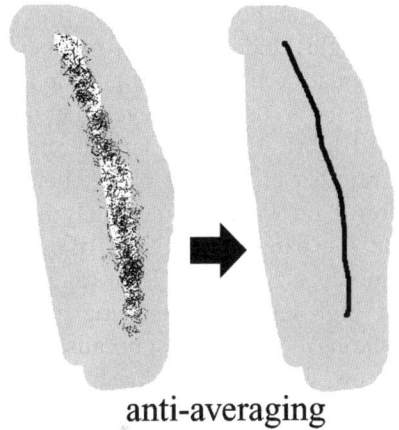

anti-averaging

Fig. 12.7

Such "averaging" represents but one recipe for generating "reduced variables" suitable to a macroscopic blob. We usually need to combine such smeared-out quantities with distinct qualities that are instead constructed through *anti-averaging*. In these applications, we concentrate the qualities found in a largish patch entirely onto a narrow surface, line, or similar variety of lower dimensional support (we no longer "smear"; we sublimate). Such anti-averaging deposits a range of special characteristics onto boundary edges, interior cracks, and movable membranes (like the shock fronts we shall investigate later[20]). In orthodox physics instruction, the importance of such "boundary conditions" is sometimes minimized, but, in a very real sense, that emphasis doesn't assign the anti-averaged regions their proper credit. The outer molecular layers of an iron bar (which are anti-averaged into the usual two-dimensional boundary conditions of elasticity theory) actually comprise an extremely complex region when viewed up close. By any rational measure, the physics active within our iron's outer layers involves a much richer array of substantial processes than remain active within its

---

[20] Much recent work in continuum mechanics explores the use of fractals and generalized functions to model dendrite boundary formation or the mushy regions of an ice/water interface. The shock wave and "Young's measure" cases we shall study should be regarded as prototypical of these wider classes of proposal.

simpler interior regions (although these can prove plenty complicated in their own right). Indeed, a large number of physical and chemical changes must occur within the "skin" of an iron ingot before it can behave in its customary, everyday manner (e.g. without the unexpected lubrication of a fair amount of atmospheric crud and a large number of "surface only" chemical adjustments, two contacting iron bars would immediately fuse robustly). Nor are conditions on the exterior similar to those inside, for gentle rubbing commonly elevates the local temperature of surface asperities to very high levels (the ensuing melting is also critical to everyday sliding). Nonetheless, because the affected region remains fairly narrow, we can often squash (= anti-average) a surface's complexities into a crude "boundary condition" and devote the lion's share of our exertions thereafter to calculating the milder changes that affect the "regular matter" inside our slab. If surface regions could talk, they might justly complain, "Why are you paying so much attention to those comparatively uninteresting interior events? Surely I represent the loci where all the serious physical activity that affects my iron occurs." To which, we can mildly reply, "Granted, but we can usually ignore most of your hidden complexities nonetheless, simply because you're not very wide. A crude anti-averaged boundary condition can characterize your condition enough that we can attend to the rest of the iron without fussing further with your persnickety details."

When we approach the "skin" of a complex system in this "reduced variable" manner, we implicitly practice what might be dubbed *physics avoidance*: we sweep the iron's most complex physical regions into lower dimensional regions patched over with a relatively unrefined rule. Indeed, it is one of the curious ironies of effective descriptive practice that the regions that *matter most* to the behavior of a physical object often represent precisely the locales that we seek to *minimize* within our linguistic policies, usually through some recipe for anti-averaging.

Such descriptive efficiency typically comes at a price, for our anti-averaging commonly erases most traces of the lower scale processes ultimately responsible for many varieties of familiar blob behaviors. Indeed, that is exactly the reason why we normally shift scale length when we consider the processes involved in fission and fusion. We thereby undo the anti-averaging policies that work so well when blobs don't alter their topologies. When we probe finer details in this way, it becomes eventually impossible to avoid scale lengths at which inherently quantum considerations begin to dominate. However, we observed that our metaphysicians are mainly interested in determining whether coherent "classical blob worlds" can be constructed in their own right, where we stick to a constant story about what kind of blobs live there (of course, we will want these "possible blobs" to thrive in normal blob-like ways, which should include capacities to fuse and fission). We do *not* obtain an account of such "worlds" from treatments that reconfigure their ontologies every time that a shift in scale length is required. Now it so happens that applied mathematicians have many reasons of their own for avoiding such forms of scale shift whenever possible—not because they inherently love self-coherent "possible worlds" for metaphysics' sake, but because they hope to provide their computers with crisp procedures for recognizing novel structural formations and for steering past potential sources of numerical infirmity. Indeed, although our earlier puzzles about blob boundaries undoubtedly sounded purely "philosophical" in my presentation, such problems also represent substantial technical obstacles that must be overcome if mathematicians are to treat behaviors like fusing and splitting without engaging in an unwelcome scale shift. But consider the mathematical difficulties that confront "Let's stay on a constant scale length" modelers in treating our blob fusion problem, say, in its "What happens to its inner boundaries when a wave crest breaks?" variant. When the upper part of the wave collapses onto the surface below, orthodox differential equation approaches to the problem leave both original surfaces intact as a doubled boundary interface between the two sandwiched masses of water, an interposed structure that can be expected to corrugate rapidly due to unequal pressures (such interfaces, if they last long enough, commonly distort into fractal-like complexity). For a certain interval, this predicted interfacial arrangement retains some descriptive validity, for a submerged boundary structure will remain empirically detectable for a short time. However, after a suitable relaxation time, we anticipate that pressures will equalize and our submerged boundary surface will disappear. Yes, but tell that to the governing equations—they simply lack any means for making the unwanted inner boundary disappear, no matter how long we wait (for essentially the same reasons that we discussed in connection with the topologies of dividing blobs: such equations can't make a closed set flow into an open set). Allied problems attend the formation of bubbles and cracks: we can stir mathematical fluids with partial differential equations all we want but they will never alter their topologies. But surely bubbles and cracks are familiar behaviors within any remotely realistic blob. So what should our "stay on the same level" modelers do?

The most commonly employed expedient simply draws or erases the salient surfaces by hand appealing to stability considerations. That is, our modeler simply watches her collapsed wave solution until its predicted pressures equilibrate sufficiently. She then declares, "Okay, it's time to erase that interfacial line." If she's interested in cases where new internal boundaries appear (e.g. cracks or bubbles), she monitors the stresses developing within the "regular matter" and decides, "Okay, it's time to insert a new boundary to relieve those stresses." Such expedients do not exactly shift modeling *scale* in our earlier manner, but they still effectively trade in an old modeling for a new one when the former waxes unrealistic. Such abrupt shifts scarcely satisfy the "blob possible world" ambitions of our metaphysicians and they are often unsatisfactory for strict predictive purposes as well, especially if we hope to pinpoint the exact locale of the emerging interface.

Fig. 12.8

However, workers in materials science have discovered a great variety of subtler techniques that can create and destroy internal boundary surfaces without requiring any evident shift in modeling. Plainly, tools more sophisticated than old-fashioned differential equations are required for the task. A basic prototype of these techniques can be found in the standard approach to shock wave creation, whose rudiments were pioneered by Riemann.[21] Let's consider what occurs on a microscopic scale first. Suppose we give a group of gas molecules a brisk shove with a plunger. At first, these fast molecules will move along the tube in a fairly normal fashion but after a certain period of time they will overtake the slower population of molecules that lie ahead, in the manner of a traffic pileup. The two populations will intermingle violently within a small area called a "shock front" and this arena of mixing turmoil will begin to move along the tube at its own anointed speed, as the front begins to interfere with the slower gas ahead.

Yes, but what happens to the shocked region when we try to describe the gas in standard "reduced variable" fashion as a continuous, compressible blob? In the as at hand, regular averaging supplies a simple differential equation that captures the gas flow beautifully up to the time that distinct populations begin to pile up within the collision region. At that moment, our "averaged" gas equation turns *inconsistent*: it assigns two distinct velocities and two distinct densities to exactly the same location in the gas tube at exactly the same time! This poor descriptive behavior on our equation's part represents a prototypical exemplar of the flavors of "blow-up" woes that were mentioned in connection with Lulu and Tubby: the blow-up represents a point where our equation stops making coherent sense for our gas (it demands that the shocked region displays incompatible conditions at the same time). However, Riemann advised, let us not succumb to our usual propensities for reconsidering these problematic events within a lower scale of blob modeling, but remain resolutely macroscopic. Let us instead view the blow-up in *velocity* as a *signal* that some new arrangement has formed within that locale, a gizmo able to

[21] Cf. J. N. Johnson and R. Chéret, *Classic Papers in Shock Compression Science* (New York: Springer-Verlag, 1998). For a history of the "weak solutions" now employed within this setting, see Jesper Lützen, *A Prehistory of Distributions* (New York: Springer-Verlag, 1982).

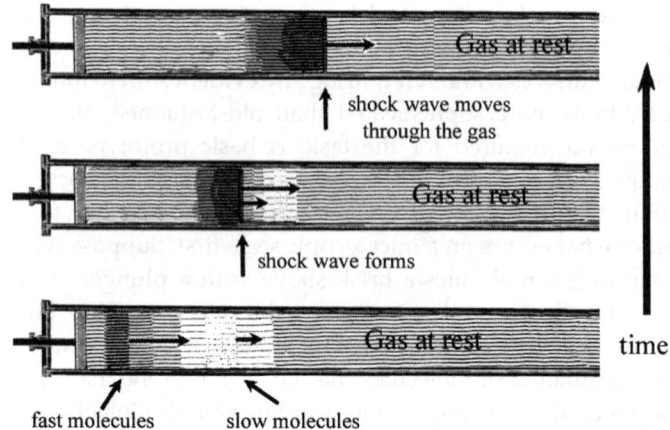

Fig. 12.9

relieve the tensions indicated by our equation's blow-up, just as a *crack* will appear in an iron steel bar to tame the local stresses whenever they become excessive. This macroscopic close cousin to a crack or bubble is called a *shock front*: it represents a two-dimensional sheet of points upon which our original gas equation manifests its descriptive inconsistencies. Mathematically, the value of inserting such a "singular surface" into the gas is that we thereby shift its special dominion of points *out* of the "governed by a differential equation" group and into the "governed by a boundary condition" class. But this adjustment in governance is exactly what we should anticipate: significantly different physical processes become active within the shocked region than elsewhere and so it is not surprising that the front's behavior will be governed by a different form of rule than the rest of the gas. This new rule appears as a (two-sided) "boundary condition" because the shocked region has been anti-averaged into a lower dimensional "singular surface". Once this new internal interface emerges, it immediately begins to exert substantial changes upon the neighboring faster portion of gas, which will pile up behind the front as a complicated wake. The entire front will begin to drift down the tube with its own characteristic velocity, fueled by the momentum channeled into the gas pileup. To be sure, we haven't yet supplied a concrete "boundary condition" rule that will move our new shock front in the right way; we'll soon see that the relevant issues are rather complex.[22]

This basic story is important for "coherent blob world" purposes because it frames the kinds of mathematical adjustments we'll require if we hope to allow a blob to alter its topology on its own terms. Indeed, introducing the shock front essentially divides our original gas blob into two pieces while remaining *within the confines of a single, unified modeling*: we needn't introduce our shock surface by hand or by shifting modeling scale (the mathematics itself "turns on" the emergence of the shock front). Specifically, the locale (or "support") for our shock wave can be identified as the collection of points where a graph of the local *velocity* evinces a sharp jump (indicating that *velocity* itself loses its meaning on the shock). We must now equip this special location with new physical capacities that can properly govern how the shock front will interact with the regular gas around it. In the usual jargon, we find ourselves modeling our shocked gas with what mathematicians call a "weak solution": a distribution of quantities that obeys our old gas equation at all of its regular points, but obeys some variant rule in the loci where gas *velocity* shows a sharp jump (= blows up). We'll worry about the required interfacial conditions[23] later, but once these are provided, we will have developed a unified mathematics for blobs with a rich potential for modeling the emergence of bubbles, cracks, and fissions, i.e. many of the everyday topology-altering behaviors that lie beyond the reach of old-fashioned differential equation models. If we work the basic technique in reverse, an interface or boundary can be made to disappear, allowing a suitable modeling to erase the unwanted interface within our collapsed ocean wave and to fuse two contacting bars of steel under sufficient pressures. More generally, it is quite difficult to delineate precisely specified "blob worlds" that will not require, at some time or other in their histories, the appearance of novel gizmos like shock fronts to relieve the descriptive inconsistences that would otherwise ruin the modeling. Blow-up difficulties do not represent an especial

---

[22] Joel Smoller, *Shock Waves and Reaction-Diffusion Equations* (New York: Springer-Verlag, 1983).

[23] More exactly, restoring uniqueness usually requires the combination of a "jump condition" along the shock front divide and a further Lax-like entropy restriction to winnow down the "weak solutions".

eccentricity of the particular gas equation we have considered, for allied woes arise whenever strong non-linearities are present in a problem (which is virtually always, unless they are removed by approximations that introduce oddities of their own). Without such expedients, the self-contained "classical blob worlds" considered by our new metaphysicians will prove unsustainable, for "worlds" that do not accommodate familiar processes such as fission and fusion seem too impoverished to merit the honorific "blob possible world". Or so I shall assume throughout the rest of our discussion. Like them or not, singular surfaces are the coherent blob modeler's unavoidable helpmates.

In many of the modern models for singular surface creation and destruction, the "signals" utilized are far more sophisticated than the appearance of a simple velocity jump, but the general strategy remains the same. From a philosophical point of view, it is important to appreciate the special physical qualities needed in a shock front in some detail, for such considerations amply demonstrate why conceptualizing blobs in naive topological terms represents a fundamental mistake (it leads us to ignore some of the chief determinants of a blob's overall behavior). A shock front, after all, represents a kind of "skin" that forms within its gas and its parochial special qualities should neither be underestimated nor neglected. We value our own skins highly; we should accord the same consideration to the lower dimensional substructures of a classical blob.

However, the properties exemplified within a shock front, considered on a strictly macroscopic scale, are stranger than seem immediately evident. For example, when we scrutinize the details of a standard treatment closely, we find that moving shock fronts temporarily overpower the local matter they run across. For example, what should happen to our gas when two shock fronts collide? The results are, in fact, quite complex but we won't be able to determine a correct answer by simply considering *the matter's local traits* in a conventional way. Normally, its salient qualities will be *density, momentum density, pressure,* and *velocity,* yet the incipient shock waves will temporarily rob our matter of precisely these qualities. Indeed, invading shock fronts typically gobble up these quantities and redistribute them over the surrounding regions in a quite significant manner. In dealing with multiple shocks, therefore, one must treat them as novel objects enjoying their own special set of rules that can also settle how they interact with one another, as well as with the "regular matter" they invade. In short, the price of restoring descriptive consistency to our flow by invoking singular shock surfaces demands that we now tolerate novel events where local packets of matter mysteriously lose their erstwhile causal capacities. Fortunately, this material prestidigitation occurs in such a manner that *collective* quantities of *mass* and *momentum* are left everywhere undisturbed, in the sense that if we take "before and after" integrals over appropriate volumes, we will discover no losses (how the mathematics achieves this surprising conservation will be discussed below). Despite the fact that our shock front only lives (= "supported") upon a narrow two-dimensional surface, it greatly affects the redistribution of *mass* and *momentum* over a large area of wake. In other cases (such as the ice/water case discussed below), a singular front can even store substantial amounts of quantities like *energy* in its own right. Yet rarely can such "fronts" be identified with any material underpinnings, for they typically move through a host material like an immaterial membrane at a velocity distinct from the flow of its regular matter. In sum, we can evade descriptive ruination within a typical "possible blob world" only by tolerating singular surfaces of a rather exotic capacity within our ontology. From a strictly empirical point of view, the utilization of "fronts" of this ilk has proved enormously successful, for the gas behind a real life shock front displays a distribution of pressures and densities quite similar to that predicted within our shock front account. And allied successes with strange singular interfaces have been replicated widely within many branches of modern materials science.

Considered in review, we see that the question, "What happens to boundary points when a blob fuses or fissions?" is not simply the "purely philosophical" conundrum it first appears, for the resolution of concrete problems in physical modeling hinges on how the issue is resolved. The blow-up in our gas equation was recognized as a puzzling formal inconsistency fairly early in the nineteenth century (by G. G. Stokes), comprising just one of a long list of continuum anomalies that were thoroughly familiar to practitioners in that period (today's metaphysicians often fail to recognize that they have merely rediscovered old conundrums).

Historically, the road to the modern treatments began when Riemann and others began to exploit special surfaces in the present manner (rendering such schemes mathematically rigorous took a very long time). Encouraged by such developments, applied mathematicians gradually learned that a toleration of singular surfaces with unusual capacities represents a very effective strategy for prolonging a macroscopic model beyond the breakdowns that otherwise render it useless. However distasteful philosophers may find the weird qualities embodied within these special surfaces, parties who value self-consistent "classical blob worlds" must clasp such devices devotedly to their bosoms. Not only do emergent singular surfaces allow "blob universes" to last much longer, they also provide agencies that can deck out a blob with its customary blobish skills.

Although a shock front's mandated features will seem peculiar when viewed upon a strictly macroscopic length scale, these same capacities generally appear unexceptional if they are considered as the natural resultants of "anti-averaging" over complex lower scale events. When a population of fast molecules catches up with a slower group within a region of shocked gas, we expect that the two groups will intermingle and interact strongly, eventually scattering their localized *mass* and *momentum* backward into the wake behind (we noted that the affair resembles a traffic pileup). Viewed on a longer length scale, the details of this microscopic flurry become invisible and the oddities of our shock front simply represent the macroscopic traces under anti-averaging of the hidden mechanisms that redistribute the qualities of colliding molecules into the wake behind. By sweeping these subterranean mechanisms into a singular surface and setting up a few appropriate rules of thumb in classic "physics avoidance" fashion, we can still determine with great accuracy how the shocked region advances through the gas and how its regularly averaged quantities of *mass* and *momentum* will redistribute themselves in the shock's vicinity. It is not surprising that the front's *capacities* will look queer when scrutinized in its large scale, anti-averaged manifestation, for any collection of skills can appear supernatural if they are credited to an excessively concentrated source (Abraham Lincoln's genuine sagacity will seem preternaturally inexplicable if every wise decision made during the Civil War is directly laid upon his shoulders).

Such considerations also explain why an adequate mathematical framework for self-contained classical blobs must rely upon functional analysis and allied stratagems. We have observed that volume-based characteristics such as *mass* and *momentum balance* must remain conserved throughout our gas's full history. When the gas flows in its normal, unshocked condition, the material flow maintains these conservation requirements through the manner in which its component points carry such quantities along: if we trace how the material points within an initial patch of blob V_1 move into a new region V_2, we will find that the total mass now found in V_2 is exactly the same as it formerly was in V_2. This is hardly a surprise, despite that fact that regions V_1 and V_2 differ greatly, for the regular gas flow carries its *mass* forward on its backs of its matter. As we saw, physics generally employs smoothly acting differential equations to govern *material transport* of this ilk. Such equations operate by telling a smallish portion of gas located at p how to move through rules that connect p's current state to its immediate past and to its infinitesimally near neighbors. But situations that demand a shock front represent circumstances where the applicability of such rules must be *cancelled* at p. Why? Our differential equation gas law formulates its rules on the basis of the rate with which the gas *velocity* changes at p. But p's "blow-up" problems stem precisely from the fact that our equation has managed to install *incompatible values* for the *velocity* at p: looked at from the left, the equation orders p to move with the "fast molecule" gas velocity V_L; looked at from the right, it orders p to move with the "slow gas" velocity V_R (the difference $V_L - V_R$ is called the "velocity jump" at p). In that sense, our differential equation "turns itself off" at p, which we regard as a signal that a shock front has formed there, with all the advantages we obtain from its fortuitous intervention.

In effect, the emergence of a singular surface *rips a tear* in the dominions of our old gas equation rules. We now require replacement "interfacial condition" rules to monitor the gas adjacent to our interface, for the cancellation of the gas equation leaves the nearby material with no instructions for its behavior.[24] This localized

---

[24] This magnitude of the disruption becomes easy to understand by considering how a finite difference scheme for the equation computes its values. The insertion of the shock obstacle prevents the scheme from filling in the grid points located within a triangle carved out by the equation's characteristic lines.

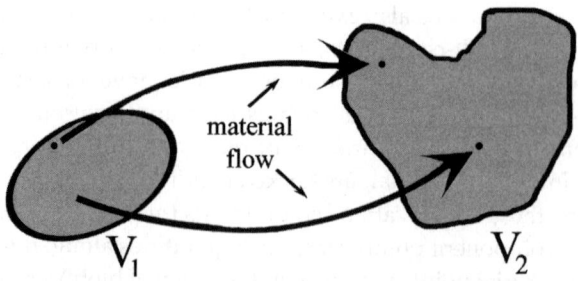

Fig. 12.10

indeciseveness quickly spreads, given how regular differential equations work, because the indeterminacy eventually affects how the entire wake behind the advancing front behaves. Worse yet, shock waves themselves can bump into walls or each other, creating even more dramatic and complex changes. Some suitable rules must complete this descriptive gap in a manner that insures that quantities like *mass* remain conserved throughout the flow. But the latter task is not readily engineered, because, in canceling the old gas law, we have *ipso facto* turned off the very mechanisms of material transport that formerly ferried such quantities throughout the flow. Somehow our shock front must be credited with an ability to insure that basic conservation requirements are still maintained. But what sort of "boundary condition" can fulfill that chore? It is as if we have murdered the postman but still expect our letters to get to their destinations properly.

It is here that the typical tools of functional analysis come to the rescue, for they recommend that we employ so-called "test functions" to situate our shock wave circumstances within larger "function spaces" where tamer "pseudo-flows" still exist that can maintain *mass* conservation through regular differential equation procedures. The essential trick is to persuade our shock wave circumstances to imitate these pseudo-flows sufficiently to insure that necessary quantities are properly conserved, while still allowing the gas to behave quite differently behind a shock front. Often very careful "top down" jury-rigging is needed to work out these arrangements properly. The recent philosophical literature displays little awareness of the tricky accommodation issues involved. But the fact that such requirements must be met explains why simple topological thinking falls far short of the mathematical setting required for a self-coherent blob world.

The quantity redistribution problems just surveyed are rather complex, but it should be recognized that even quite simple geometrical situations involving immobile objects can force the applied mathematician to treat basic physical quantities with allied varieties of *ad hoc* expedient. Quantity allocation problems can arise simply because a blob's extended shape forces us to juggle several different ranges of *dimensional concern* at the same time. An unfortunate geometrical shape can easily drive these allocations into conflict with one another. Here's a classic illustration. Cut a sharp conical notch into a steel rod and tug on its inner faces with constant tensions. A little thought reveals that some anomalous state must arise along the apex line L of the cleavage: in fact, the shearing stresses will become infinite there. If the material located along L were to respond to this stress as it does elsewhere in the metal, the iron would be forced to twist off to infinity under our tugs, no matter how feeble they were. This problem arises simply because four different ranges of dimensional concern appear in our problem: as a whole, it is *three-dimensional*, yet we can tug upon its *two-dimensional* surfaces, with results that can affect *one-dimensional* lines such as L (or even *zero-dimensional* points). In the current circumstances, we can force a fit only by excluding a singular surface or two from the requirements we demand elsewhere.

Such woes accompany the most humdrum forms of classical boundary value problem and explain why the anomalies of maintaining different dimensionalities in coherent order have bedeviled

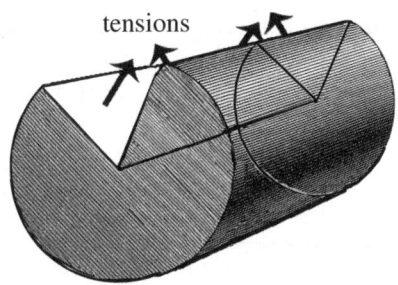

Fig. 12.11

partisans of continuously distributed matter since Zeno.[25] During the nineteenth century our notch problem was commonly brushed aside with an airy "Oh, it's just a boundary, after all" or (better) "Fortunately, its oddities remain confined to a single line and don't affect integral values like *strain energy*, so the local infinities can be ignored." Heightened requirements of rigor have forced modern mathematicians to provide better rationales than these old-fashioned forms of handwaving. Today rigorous practice demands that the interior behavior of our rod must match its bounding surfaces in the manner of a so-called *trace deposit*, which once again represents a delicate functional analysis construction involving the careful manipulation of associated spaces.[26] Truly, maintaining a brace of ill-matched dimensional animals in harmonious harness is not an easy job! Yet that is the unavoidable task of all who seek internally coherent "blob worlds".

Finally, let me conclude this section by mentioning one last illustration of the strange varieties of front-like entities that can potentially emerge when shorter length scale activities become "anti-averaged" in a manner suitable to macro-level description (I find this case especially beautiful and informative). Suppose we wish to model the advancing boundary C of frozen ground X that is advancing into soil Y that currently contains liquid water. The shape of the advancing front will be primarily determined by two factors: the pressures exerted by Y against X and C's own inclination to minimize its internal surface energy through curling (its surface tension becomes less). In real life, the bounding region between the ice and water stretches over a narrow but extended slushy region, but a sensible policy of "anti-averaging" recommends that this region should be collapsed into a one-dimensional front of some kind. But what sort of critter will then emerge? Sometimes an excellent answer is provided by a so-called "Young's measure". This odd object is nicely explained by its creator (L. C. Young[27])

---

[25] But note that the problems of "physical infinitesimals" extend far beyond the standard "cures" used to tame Zeno's difficulties. I am currently working on a historical survey of such problems.

[26] R. E. Showalter, *Hilbert Space Methods for Partial Differential Equations* (Marshfield: Pitman, 1977).

[27] L. C. Young, *Lectures on the Calculus of Variations and Optimal Control Theory* (New York: Chelsea Publications, 1980), chapter VI.

Beware of the Blob | 309

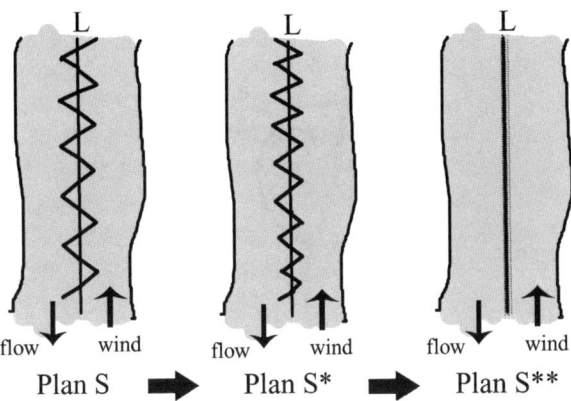

Fig. 12.12

as follows. The factors that shape our evolving interface turn out to be mathematically equivalent to the task of devising the best scheme for sailing a skiff down river against a headwind. Insofar as the river's current is concerned, it is best to keep our craft in the middle of the stream L, where the current runs the strongest. However, to take advantage of the headwind, we should wish to tack to its onslaught with an angle Iθ. What is the best overall plan for steering our craft effectively? Plainly, we need to zigzag back and forth across L somehow, maintaining the angle Iθ as much as we can. But for every zigzagging scheme **S** we propose, we find that it can be improved to **S*** by making the length of our zigs shorter. So our optimal path of sailing seems as if it must be framed by the limit of these **S**, viz., a strange "trajectory" where we crisscross L infinitesimally far infinitely often: one might think of this movement as a very fast jitter. Adjusting this conclusion back to the ice/water situation, the conditions we have imposed upon its "bounding surface" look as if they demand the same odd features as characterize our optimal sailing plan: the water/ice interface will lie upon a C curve, but only in a jittery way where it can wiggle back and forth across C infinitely rapidly.

Operationally, C looks rather like a regular curve in terms of its "location", but we will be able to tell a Young's measure boundary from a non-jittery surface by measuring the internal energy stored in the *finite regions* that overlap parts of X. That is, the energy stored

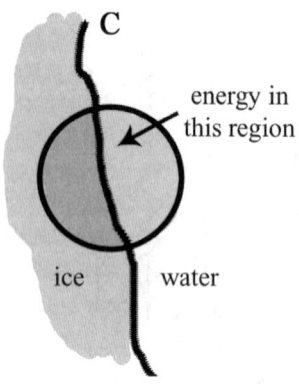

Fig. 12.13

in our oddball "curve" is less (courtesy of its infinitesimal curling) than the same region would manifest if its boundary was forced to stay tightly glued to the geometrical line lying underneath C. But to render this form of modeling precise, we must formulate rather fancy rules for how we should work with our new X + C combination (indeed, the "Young's measure" $d\mu$ that corresponds to C supplies a novel "differential" that allows us to compute the desired value for $\int_V E d\mu$). Again the entire trick is to make quantities defined by integrals behave in unexpected patterns. Modern work on moving material fronts continues to reveal an ever-expanding zoo of exotic creatures like this.[28]

In these respects, L. C. Young suggests an amusing analogy that underscores the methodological moral outlined in section (ii). Pondering the familiar qualities of everyday blobs, we initially expect that the task of extending our rough and context-sensitive everyday intuitions about blobs into a coherent and self-contained theory will prove easy and straightforward. Yet a large horde of unruly surprises emerge when the attempt is made in earnest. About this phenomenon Young observes:

A case in point occurs in R.L. Stevenson's *Essays*. He tells us of the heroine of a novel, who is stated to be a princess; however, as Stevenson says, the

---

[28] For other recent approaches, see Ball, Kinderlehrer, Podio-Guidugli, Slemrod (eds.), *Evolving Phase Interfaces in Solids* (Berlin: Springer, 1999), especially the articles by Elliot Fried and Morton Gurtin.

moment she speaks we know her to be a fishwife. On this basis, it is not only a right but a duty to reexamine our definitions [of boundary curve] in the light of their usage, and to revise them, even quite radically, if they do not fit.[29]

In other words, the blobs of the real world may first appear as elegant point set princesses in their prim behaviors, but closer inspection reveals them as function space fishwives of a rather gnarly disposition. We are not likely to frame truly coherent resolutions to the puzzling features of continua unless we confront their "fishwife" behaviors with appropriate tools.

Moral: if metaphysicians hope to eke well-behaved "possible worlds" from the familiar comings and goings of macroscopic blobs, they should expect that far stranger blob "parts" will emerge as their accounts become rigorously specified.

5.

Our survey warns that gambits of a "sets of measure zero don't matter" ilk do not approach the oddities of our singular fronts in an entirely appropriate spirit.

Beyond the technical considerations just sketched, we must appreciate that the "skin" of a blob comprises one of its most vital organs from a physical point of view: despite their puny dimensions, "skin conditions" control what happens elsewhere in the blob in significant ways (recall how dramatically the shock front affects the regular matter flow in the wake behind). We can normally "reduce variables" effectively on a macroscopic level only if we have discovered a suitable scheme for sweeping physical complexities into cramped, lower dimensional quarters. As such, the resulting "boundary conditions" should be recognized as just as important physically as what happens inside the regular interior of a blob (they differ only in whether their complexities have been "averaged" or "anti-averaged" away). For such reasons, metaphysicians should avoid dismissing edges, membranes, and their kin as non-entities or unacceptable "parts".

For all that, such "singular surfaces" act in stranger ways than we a priori anticipate. Assume we have a Young's measure $d\mu$ lying

---

[29] *Lectures*, 160.

along a regular geometrical curve **C** (in the jargon, the "support" of dμ is **C**; that's where dμ "lives", as it were). But is **C** also where the measure *acts*? Not obviously, because dμ represents the anti-averaged *trace* of an ice/water interface that rapidly crisscrosses **C**. If that interface was really glued to the placid curve **C**, it would store more energy than it does and move forward in a quite different manner. But such distinctions are not local to **C**; we can only discover the lowered energy within dμ by integrating over a *finite volume* that includes **C**. Our measure dμ may be "supported" on **C**, but it reveals its special weird characteristics by acting in regions *larger* than **C**. Asked by a metaphysician, "Should the smidgen of Young's measure 'supported' at the point p be considered 'part' of a smallish volume **V** that contains the point p?", we might reasonably reply, "Not straightforwardly, for our Young's measure gizmo works its effects over a region that may be larger than **V**. Don't crudely identify a Young's measure with its 'support'; one must consider the region in which it *acts* as well."

Considered in terms of its "anti-averaged" molecular rationale, this reluctance to firmly localize a Young's measure modeling to its "support" is entirely explicable. Recall that when we were willing to shift our modeling scale, erstwhile two-dimensional surfaces often opened out into three-dimensional regions. As we discussed at the close of section (iii), such scaling shifts render questions like "Is a point p *part* of a little volume **V** around p?" inherently ambiguous. If we now artificially remain at a macroscopic scale by appealing to a Young's measure interface rather than modeling the slushy ice/water interface with a newly evoked subpopulation of "molecules", we should anticipate that our basic reluctance to answer questions like "Is p part of V?" crisply will persist. After all, the "support"/"region of activity" distinction of the last paragraph merely reflects an anti-averaged record of the ways in which erstwhile "points" and "surfaces" open out into wider volumes when a modeling scale length is readjusted.

One commonly finds warnings that the activities of gizmos like Young's measures should not be confused with their "supports" in treatises on "distributions", which represent close functional analysis cousins to the "fronts" we have surveyed here. Of these, the most famous is the celebrated Dirac δ "function" which we might invoke to model the fact that a one kilogram portion of a blob's mass appears sharply localized around the point p. I write "around the point p," because in the rigorous theory the δ "function" doesn't take any values at any points whatsoever (it is properly a functional, not a function). Mathematicians accordingly only allow that the δ "function" 's *support* lies at p. Its "one kilogram" value is revealed by its activities within nearby volumes: if we move a small observation volume **V** through our blob, its accumulated mass value will suddenly spike up by a kilogram every time that **V** includes p.[30] Indeed, one quickly falls into deep confusions if one fancies that the δ "function" possesses a coherent "value" at p (a mistake the primers seek to discourage). Like our fronts, δ "functions" support locally, but act globally.

Many metaphysicians of the new school presume that certain a priori principles (dubbed "mereological axioms") perforce govern relationships like "spatial part of". In particular, it is assumed that "If A is wholly part of B and B is wholly part of C, then A will be wholly part of C as well." Yet our survey indicates that we should be wary of such claims when we consider the lower dimensional parts of a coherent classical blob: a shock front or Young's measure interface can't be happily steamrollered by mereological axiom.

The faulty presumptions of which we should be especially leery are frequently illustrated in the large literature on the possibilities of "atomless gunk". A blob **X** is said to contain "atoms" if **X** contains "parts" which contain no further "parts" themselves. Some writers fiercely maintain that all coherent bodies must contain such "atoms" while others contend that a contrary "atomless gunk" is possible, if unlikely. Typically they consider the situation from a simple point set point of view and consider a family of telescoping finite regions $V_1, V_2, V_3, \ldots$ that cover the point p. Advocates of "gunk" argue that if we remove all of the points from **X** following A. N. Whitehead's "method of extensive abstraction",[31] we will obtain a "gunk" that should be able to satisfy all of the physical tasks of the original "pointy" **X**. Hence an insistence upon mereological

---

[30] To explain the non-standard "volume integration" evoked here, the theory relies upon an associated set of test functions, as sketched above for shock front circumstances. Cf., J. I. Richards and H. K. Youn, *Theory of Distributions* (Cambridge: Cambridge University Press, 1990).

[31] *An Enquiry Concerning the Principles of Natural Knowledge* (Cambridge: Cambridge University Press, 1919).

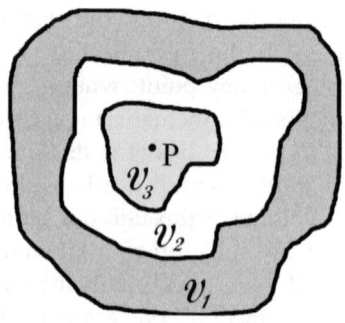

Fig. 12.14

atoms is metaphysically unreasonable. Contrary parties argue that suitable points can always be restored to such a "gunk", rendering the challenge to mereological atomism toothless. In the latter vein, Rosen and Dorr write:

> Given a gunk-postulating theory consistent with the axioms of mereology, it is not hard to come up with a new, gunk-free theory modeled after it, by adding some extra things ("points") not posited by the original theory. The gunk-free theory will of course not entail the gunk-positing one, but if we do the construction correctly, it will entail that the gunk-positing theory comes out as true when all quantifiers are restricted to things other than the points.[32]

However, this dialectic is rather irrelevant to coherent classical blobs, of the sorts considered in this chapter. When we squeeze in on points with a nested set of volumes, we encounter two quite different cases: where p is regular (e.g., subject to the usual gas equation) and where p instead lies within the "support" of some fancy boundary entity like $d\mu$. In the first case, natural qualities that belong to the nesting volumes $V_1, V_2, V_3, \ldots$ (viz., *mass* and *momentum*) will induce correspondent densities (i.e. *mass density* and *momentum density*) upon the point p, in conjunction with other wholly local traits such as *velocity* and *stress*. Typically, these qualities will seem quite familiar.[33] In the second circumstances, few of the

---

[32] Gideon Rosen and Cian Dorr, "Composition as Fiction" in Richard Gale (ed.), *The Blackwell Guide to Metaphysics* (Oxford: Blackwell, 2002), 165.

[33] In truth, a stress tensor is a rather strange gizmo from a conceptual point of view, although we've become used to them by now!

familiar local qualities will be induced upon p and their localized replacements will often seem peculiar, comprehensible only in terms of the "jobs" they perform with respect to the allocation of *mass, momentum*, and *force* over larger volumes. As we observed, the special qualities of a singular surface are usually engineered in a "top down" way precisely to insure that the surface possesses the skills to fulfill its anointed tasks satisfactorily. Persuading this rich menagerie of dimensionally inhomogeneous entities to work together harmoniously is not easy (the foundational requirements of modern continuum mechanics are quite subtle and still in flux for this reason). I don't understand what a "mereological atom" might represent within a structure as complex as this (attending only to the relationships of spatial "support" seems clearly wrong) nor do I understand why the question is important (if pressed, I would join with the "gunk" lovers in declaring, "I see no a priori reason to demand 'atoms'—even if I knew what they were"). In short, although coherent classical blob worlds do not display quite the same strange localization problems as quantum systems, they do not behave simply in these respects either.[34]

To summarize: many present day philosophers articulate their favored "metaphysical" questions about classical matter in terms of a simple trichotomy of relevant entities: (1) the *spatial points* that comprise the inertial background against which their blobs move; (2) the finite *volumes* that transport mass as the blobs move about;

---

[34] Consider this passage from a recent essay by Hawthorne and Artzenius: "Average values [= integral values assigned to extended volumes] cannot serve to determine the value of a corresponding function at any specific point. [But] this should hardly serve as an objection to an approach in which one takes average value assignments to gunky regions as primitive... Indeed, it seems plausible that the fundamental quantities of physics allow for an average value treatment" (from John Hawthorne and Frank Arntzenius, "Gunk and Continuous Variation", in Hawthorne, *Metaphysical Essays* (Oxford: Oxford University Press, 2005), 159–60). Considered literally, this passage runs counter to accepted procedure in modern continuum mechanics as I have outlined it here (however, I am not completely clear on the exact morals that the authors intend to extract from their discussion). More generally, the restricted worries about the consistency of "gunk" or "pointy spaces" that appear in the allied metaphysical literature strike me as too impoverished to properly qualify as answers to the question "What kinds of classical matter should be regarded as conceptually viable?" The substantive roles that "nested set" and "test function" techniques play in getting my "type 4" entities to behave properly *when needed* should not be confused with the "Ockham's razor" motives of a Russell or Whitehead.

(3) the co-moving "material points" that carry the corresponding local *mass densities*. A workable continuum physics requires all of these ingredients: material volumes to serve as carriers of integrated quantities such as *mass* and *momentum* and material points to support localized measures like *stress* and *strain*. But it also employs shock waves and other categories of "singular surface" to preserve blob worlds from falling into the forms of internal incoherence that would otherwise seal their doom. Let us dub these new entities "type 4": they have been mistakenly omitted from our metaphysician's inventory. Each of these *sui generis* contraptions carry their own bevy of points and areas, yet generally prove immaterial (= carry no *mass*) and move quite independently of the material flow. When described simply as "shock fronts" or "ice/water interfaces", type (4) gizmos will seem innocuous supplements to the expected ontology of a blob world, yet these weird-entities-in-sheep's-clothing embody many strange capacities which they have gained through anti-averaging, including an ability to overpower type (3) points and redistribute their erstwhile qualities over wider volumes. As peculiar as these capacities may seem, they can prevent a humdrum "possible blob world" equipped with only (1–3) ingredients from collapsing into inconsistency. To prove suitable students of genuine blob possibilities, philosophers should beware of lingering too long in the soothing realms of point set topology where such unexpected constructions never appear. Without the assistance of type (4) supplements, the pseudo-blobs of topology simply can't act as proper blobs should (devour railway cars, slither and slide, etc.).

6.

I warned earlier of "the irrelevant possibility unwisely emphasized". If we wish to build a levitated train, fond recollections of how Tom Swift, Jr. turned the trick within some favorite juvenile novel are unlikely to advance our ambitions. To the contrary, excessive musing on fictive triumphs is likely to distract us from the arduous task of learning about suitable superconducting magnets.

In this light, compare two tales that we might philosophically weave with respect to "possible blob behavior". The first is some account offered by a modern metaphysician, whose parochial "blobs" can neither creep nor leap, let alone fuse or divide. In contrast, consider the rich narrative developed within the researches of modern materials science, where we first learn that our everyday talk of classical blobs sustains its substantial macroscopic successes through a willingness to shift blob modeling substantially over lower length scales (leading eventually into quantum mechanics). We learn how the introduction of unexpected functional analysis supplements within a large scale blob setting can skillfully resolve descriptive tensions that would otherwise force a technically awkward retreat to lower length scales, although the expedients required will seem strange unless their "anti-averaged" reduced variable character is recognized. The same scientific research also explains (although I've not developed these topics here) the ways in which careful attention to experimental mini-possibilities (e.g. how Lulu might distort upon the work bench) helps steer engineers effectively to the very successful forms of macroscopic modeling they have developed.[35] From this modern story, we gain a deeper appreciation of the conceptual difficulties that confronted great philosophers and physicists in the past, as they struggled to quell the recalcitrant paradoxes inherent in the simplest forms of everyday blob behavior. We can now sharply appreciate why our forebears enjoyed no real hope of resolving these tensions adequately, given the limited palette of mathematical and conceptual tools available at the time. And we further recognize that, even if such tools had been forged, those sages would have been unable to anticipate that the tensions inherent in natural blob models must be resolved, at sufficiently small length scales, by the completely different mechanisms found in quantum mechanics.

In fine, the striking story provided by modern materials science casts a revelatory light upon many of our most effective linguistic strategies for describing the macroscopic world about us efficiently (viz., "speak of classical blobs"). In comparison, the new metaphysicians' accounts seem less illuminating, for they largely push the chessmen of days gone by about on the same old game board, seeking a nebulous checkmate that never occurs. And rarely do

[35] Observe: *localized* "modal" principles such as "virtual work" derive their utilities from close links to workbench experimentation, without thereby supporting the *globalized* "possible world" vocabulary criticized in section 2.

these philosophical narratives suggest that the materials scientists may have a richer story to offer with respect to everyday blob talk. Accordingly, I find it hard to regard such endeavors as anything other than "irrelevant possibilities unwisely emphasized". If we wish to properly understand the great utility of classical blob talk within our everyday lives, the localized/'lousy encyclopedia" structuring suggested by modern engineering research explains far more than do the ruminations of a more devoutly "metaphysical" nature.

Returning briefly to the themes of section (ii), several substantive veins of "modal" or "counterfactual" consideration weave through the fabric of our everyday thinking about blobs, but exclusively in a "mini-world" fashion linked either directly to experimental manipulation or to the question of the mathematical structures that emerge under averaging or anti-averaging. Only rarely do these "mini-possibilities" straightforwardly extend into the global "possible worlds" favored in Kripkean thinking.

Be this as it may, most new metaphysicians swear sturdy allegiance to Saul Kripke's vision, which carves out a wider arena for philosophy through the claim that scientific investigation reveals the hidden "metaphysical necessity" of facts such as "temperature = mean kinetic energy". Kripke's novel proposals offer traditional philosophical speculation a fresh opportunity to expand its historically narrowed dominions, as it teases out the unanticipated consequences of installing "temperature = mean kinetic energy" amongst the necessary architecture of the universe. Plainly, the "new metaphysics" would have never blossomed without this injection of Kripkean vigor. But "temperature = mean kinetic energy" does not represent a wholly accurate physical claim and any adequate primer in statistical mechanics informs its readers that a proper analysis of "temperature" must evoke a more abstract consideration of the ways in which a system's microscopic degrees of freedom prove uncontrollable by normal macroscopic manipulations.[36] In truth, a more accurate account of "temperature"'s underpinnings proves more hospitable to Kripke's original vision, for it should otherwise seem mysterious that Elizabethans, with

---

[36] For a survey, see my "What is this Thing Called 'Pain'?", *Pacific Philosophical Quarterly* 66 (1985).

slim microscopic resources, could have "baptized" an inherently molecular quantity such as *mean kinetic energy* successfully with the term "temperature" (the task seems the equivalent of pointing into a locust swarm and dubbing a single insect as "Ralph"). In contrast, the more abstract treatment of *temperature* provided in the better textbooks provides a quantity whose salience to the baptizers of 1600 is quite evident due to the manner in which the improved account yokes macro- and microscopic behaviors together. This finer grain within this revised story allows us to fill in the details of "temperature"'s baptismal history in a more satisfying way.

I imagine that every modern metaphysician will stand happily corrected with respect to "temperature = mean kinetic energy" when the better modern account is learned. By parallel reasoning, the deeper understanding of continuum-based description that has been slowly assembled within modern materials science offers comparable opportunities for appreciating the real life underpinnings of "spatial part" and the other major components of everyday blob talk. Following Kripke's lead, shouldn't these same philosophers conclude that "spatial part", "boundary point", et al. actually designate considerably different material properties[37] than we have heretofore fancied? A collection of properties that display a deeply ingrained sensitivity to scale size? Properties for which extensive ruminations upon point set topology should seem as irrelevant as continued musings on caloric would now seem with respect to *temperature*?

To date, contemporary metaphysics has proved unresponsive to any Kripkean reorientation of this flavor, probably due to unfamiliarity with the relevant scientific work. Yet I predict, perhaps incorrectly, that few practitioners will be swayed by our survey and will continue to presume that they know a priori how "spatial part" behaves in all possible situations, regardless of any contrarian suggestions from engineering research. If so, such an unyielding a priorism suggests that metaphysicians of this inclination are not genuinely loyal to Kripkean percept at all, but merely evidence an enthusiasm for "conceptual analysis"

---

[37] More exactly, the scale size dependence of notions like "mass" in continuum mechanics indicate that they behave like the "quasi-quantities" discussed in my *Wandering Significance*, 383–90.

of an old-fashioned stripe. But rather than affirming this uneasy suspicion further, let me conclude by requesting a fuller recounting of the methodological presumptions that our metaphysicians adopt when they ponder the "possibilities" of classically continuous matter.

INDEX

Aristotle 177
Armstrong, D. M. 107 n., 110, 125 nn., 175, 177 n., 183, 191
Arntzenius, F. 249, 250–1, 255 n. 13, 256, 258, 259–63, 267, 272–3, 315 n.

Baker, A. 119–123
Banach, S. 229–30
Benacceraf, P. 52, 66
Bennett, J. 151 n. 10
Beth, E. W. 22–3, 44–50
Bigelow, J. 173
Black, M. 40
Bohm, D. 277
Bolzano, B. 275
Braddon-Mitchell, D. 215 n.
Bradley, F. H. 178 n., 199–200
Bricker, P. 151 n. 10
Brouwer, J. 28
Brown, J. 94 n.
Burgess, J. 51, 83–8, 96 n. 11

Cantor, G. 28–9, 44, 104
Carnap, R. 9, 22–3, 28–9, 32–9, 46, 49, 52, 64–6
Chalmers, D. 146–8, 162–6, 209 n. 25
Church, A. 40
Chwistek, L. 35, 48
Clarke, B. 253

Cohintz 41
Colyvan, M. 112 n., 118–19, 123–4
Courant, R. 280 n. 5
Curry, H. B. 69

Decock, L. 41
Dorr, C. 314

Eddington, A. S. 7, 19, 39, 59
Einstein, A. 71 n.

Ferman, S. 82 n.
Field, H. 52, 96 n. 12, 116 n., 118, 121 n., 141
Fine, K. 266 n.
Fitch, F. B. 70
Forrest, P. 190, 250–1, 256, 259, 265–7, 272–3
Frege, G. 44
Friedrichs, K. 280 n. 5

Gödel, K. 16, 47–8, 67, 84 nn., 94 n., 104
Goodman, N. 16–17, 18, 21, 23, 36–7, 39–43, 46, 47, 51, 56–7, 59, 62–3, 70–73, 138, 140–42
Grelling, K. 28

Hahn, H. 9
Hawthorne, J. 147 n. 4, 150 n. 7, 155–6, 158, 160 n. 23, 255 n. 13, 258, 315 n.
Hebb, D. 94 n

Hempel, C. 36
Hilbert, D. 47, 59, 62
Hudson, H. 215 n.
Hume, D. 273

Jackson, F. 26, 159, 160 n. 23
Johnston, M. 168 n. 38
Joseph, G. 147 n. 5
Jubien, M. 209 n. 26

Kant, I. 275
Kelvin, Lord W. T. 15, 67 n., 80, 89–90
Kemeny, J. 65, 67
Kripke, S. 161, 275, 283–4, 318–20
Kuratowski, K. 180

Leibniz, G. 275
Leonard, H. 24–5
Lesniewski, S. 23–5, 48, 70
Lewis, D. 107, 150 n. 7, 158–9, 175–7, 180 n., 190–91, 248 n. 1, 275

Maddy, P. 94 n.
McDaniel, K. 215 n.
McLaughlin, B. 151 n. 10
Mancosu, P. 56–7, 59–60, 62, 70
Markosian, N. 209 n. 25, 27
Miller, K. 215 n.

Nagel, E. 263 n.
Navier, C.-L. 280

Parsons, C. 66, 69–70, 75
Parsons, J. 208 n. 23, 212 n. 30, 215 n.

Pitcher, G. 94 n.
Plato 177, 178 n. 7, 189
Poincare, H. 24, 28
Popper, K. 36
Putnam, H. 115, 118, 125, 282 n. 7

Quine, D. B. 3–4
Quine, W.V.O. 3–4, 22–44, 46–7, 51–2, 56–77, 79–97, 99–101, 105, 107–109, 115, 117, 125–129, 132 n., 135, 138, 139 n., 140–42

Reimann, A. 299, 304
Rescher, N. 293 n.
Roeper, P. 237, 241, 253
Rosen, G. 51, 96 n. 11, 314
Rossberg 41
Russell, B. 10, 13, 18, 24, 33, 38, 43, 44–5, 50, 151 n. 10, 315 n.

Saarno, U. 18
Schönfinkel, M. 69
Schaffer, J. 207 n., 208 n. 23, 211 n. 29
Sider, T. 206 n. 21, 211 n. 29, 215 n.
Sikorski, R. 259
Skyrms, B. 259
Smith, B. 281 n.
Smith, S. 283
Soames, S. 284
Stokes, G. G. 303

Tarski, A. 22–3, 31–9, 44–52, 62, 229–230, 250, 253 n. 9, 254, 260, 263, 267, 269

Urban, W. M. 9

Van Fraassen, B. 111
Varsi, A. 281 n.
von Neumann, J. 31, 179

Weiner, N. 26, 180
Weyl. H. 24, 28
Whitehead, A. N. 24–25, 70, 248, 253–4, 263, 272–3, 275, 313, 315 n.
William of Occam 61–2

Williams, J. R. G. 214 n. 34, 276, 278–9
Woodger, J. H. 33, 35, 43–4

Yablo, S. 163 n. 29
Young, C. L. 308–11

Zeno 226–228, 308
Zermelo, E. 44–5, 50